Religion and the English People, 1500–1640

Habent sua fata libelli

Volume XLV
of
Sixteenth Century Essays & Studies

Raymond A. Mentzer, General Editor

RELIGION
and the
ENGLISH
PEOPLE
1500–1640

NEW VOICES
NEW PERSPECTIVES

Edited by
Eric Josef Carlson

Sixteenth Century Essays & Studies
volume 45

Copy © 1998 by Thomas Jefferson University Press
at Truman State University
100 East Normal Street, Kirksville, Missouri 63501-4221 USA
http://tjup.truman.edu

*This book has been brought to publication with the generous support
of Truman State University, Kirksville, Missouri
and of Elizabeth R. Baer, dean of the faculty,
Gustavus Adolphus College, Saint Peter, Minnesota*

Library of Congress Cataloging-in-Publication Data

Religion and the English people, 1500–1640 : new voices, new perspectives / edited by Eric Josef Carlson

    p.   cm. – (Sixteenth century essays & studies : v. 45)
Includes bibliographical references and index.
ISBN 0-943549-62-0 (alk. paper). ISBN 0-943549-63-9 (pbk. : alk.
paper)
    1. Reformation—England. 2. Reformation—England—Historiog-
raphy. 3. England—Religious life and customs. 4. England—Church
history—16th century. 5. England—church history—17th century. I.
Carlson, Eric Josef. II. Series.
BR377.R45   1998   98—3778
274.2'06—dc21   CIP

∞The paper in this publication meets or exceeds the minimum requirements of the American National Standard for Permanence of Paper for Printed Library Materials Z39.48
(1984).

Dedicated to our mentors:
Patrick Collinson, Seymour House, Brian Levack,
Wallace MacCaffrey, Susan Karant Nunn, Steven Ozment,
Paul Seaver, Margaret Spufford, and Ann Weikel

CONTENTS

INTRODUCTION

PART 1
WORDS *and* WORSHIP

PART 2
URBAN REFORMATIONS

Contents

PART 3
PARISH CLERGY *and* PARISH REFORMATIONS

PART 4
WILLS *and* PIETY

CRITICAL AFTERWORDS

Acknowledgments

IT WAS A CONVERSATION with Susan Wabuda and Norman Jones which first provoked me to put this volume together and I am grateful to them. Since that conversation, many people have helped me to move this project along. I would especially like to thank my former research assistant, Neal Enssle; my secretaries, Janine Genelin and Connie Baum; and Sarah Daniels, director of administrative computing at Gustavus Adolphus College. All of the contributors have been indulgent and patient. I am thankful for that, as well as for the friendships that have formed and grown during the course of compiling this book. I am also very grateful to the senior scholars who agreed to write critical afterwords, thereby lending their substantial credibility to our efforts.

Major financial support towards publishing this book was provided by Elizabeth R. Baer, dean of the faculty of Gustavus Adolphus College. I am extremely grateful to her, and I am pleased to be able to acknowledge publicly her constant and generous support of my scholarly activities. I am also grateful for a sabbatical in 1995–96 which allowed me to complete work on the book. The History Department at Gustavus cheerfully absorbed most of the photocopying and postage expenses. For additional financial support, the contributors also thank the UCLA History Department and the Eberly College of Arts and Sciences of West Virginia University. Joseph P. Ward's contribution is adapted in part from chapter 5 of his book, *Metropolitan Communities: Trade Guilds, Identity, and Change in Early Modern London*, and appears with the permission of Stanford University Press.

The dedication of this book acknowledges our academic mentors. We hope that these essays will stand as a public token of our gratitude, affection and respect.

INTRODUCTION

CASSANDRA BANISHED?

NEW RESEARCH ON RELIGION IN TUDOR AND EARLY STUART ENGLAND

Eric Josef Carlson

HAS CASSANDRA REPLACED CLIO as the muse of history—at least, as the muse of Tudor and early Stuart historians? At a recent conference, Dr. Paul Hammer delivered a paper with the revealing title "The 'Thin' State of Elizabethan Historiography"[1] in which he voiced from the podium a version of the sentiments which many historians had been muttering more privately for some time: that the field seemed virtually moribund, that nothing new and interesting was being done. With the death of Professor Sir Geoffrey Elton and the retirements of a number of leading Tudor scholars such as Professor Wallace MacCaffrey and Professor Patrick Collinson, it seemed that many were anxious about the future and what new directions research would take.

During the first half of the 1990s, scholarship on religion in early modern England has, indeed, been dominated historiographically by what are now some rather old arguments. The two books which have garnered the most attention and dominated debate during those years are those of Eamon Duffy and Christopher Haigh.[2] Both books essentially develop a revisionist argument which has been well known for more than a decade: that the Reformation in England was basically unwanted and unpopular,

---

[1] Paper delivered at the North American Conference of British Studies meeting, Washington, D.C., October 1995.

[2] Eamon Duffy, *The Stripping of the Altars: Traditional Religion in England 1400–1580* (New Haven: Yale University Press, 1992); Christopher Haigh, *English Reformations: Religion, Politics and Society under the Tudors* (Oxford: Clarendon Press, 1993). Duffy's book is the most often-cited book in the footnotes of the essays in this volume.

and it assaulted a vibrant and popular piety.[3] Though both are masterpieces, neither breaks new ground.

There has also been a lively and occasionally nasty debate over the core theology of the English church. In 1990, G. W. Bernard published an article in which he posited a very conservative English church which was never truly Calvinist (the reign of Edward VI is seen as a hiccup if noticed at all) and in which Charles I and Archbishop Laud were little more than Henricians a century on.[4] Diarmaid MacCulloch's important 1991 article, "The Myth of the English Reformation,"[5] showed that Bernard's picture fits into a tradition of writing that could be traced back to the late seventeenth century in which conservative Anglicans embarrassed about the real radicalism of their church's founders wrote a more comfortable if less accurate history—a sort of Orwellian Ministry of Truth *avant la lettre*. In a recent article, Nicholas Tyacke dismissed Bernard's article as a "classic, if rather exaggerated, example of old-style Anglican apologetic" which takes a fling at "abolishing protestantism from the historical record."[6] Tyacke and MacCulloch make a very strong case for the unambiguously protestant and predestinarian character of the English church and the burden of scholarship does seem to be establishing a consensus that the English church's founders were theologically radical, and that the Elizabethan church had more in common with its Edwardian than with its Henrician heritage. Though a minority will no doubt resist, there appears to be little new material that can be contributed to this particular debate and no place for it to go.

As this introduction was being written, two massive new books appeared which are sure to become enormously influential, perhaps being to the latter half of this decade what Duffy's and Haigh's books were to the first half: Ian Green's study of catechisms and Dr. MacCulloch's biography of Thomas Cranmer.[7] Both of these marvelous books, however, are the

[3]This argument is at the heart of J. J. Scarisbrick, *The Reformation and the English People* (Oxford: Blackwell, 1984). While perhaps not the first published statement of this argument, Scarisbrick's book is generally seen as its *fons et origo*.

[4]G. W. Bernard, "The Church of England, c. 1529–c.1642," *History* 75 (1990): 183–206.

[5]Diarmaid MacCulloch, "The Myth of the English Reformation," *Journal of British Studies* 30 (1991): 1–19.

[6]Nicholas Tyacke, "Anglican Attitudes: Some Recent Writings on English Reformation History, from the Reformation to the Civil War," *Journal of British Studies* 35 (1996): 139–167; quotations from 140, 141.

[7]Ian Green, *The Christian's ABC: Catechisms and Catechizing in England c.1530–1740* (Oxford: Clarendon Press, 1996); Diarmaid MacCulloch, *Thomas Cranmer: A Life* (New Haven: Yale University Press, 1996).

culmination of many years of research by their authors and many of their central discoveries have appeared in articles and papers during the past few years.

Should we all then join the *dévotes* of Cassandra and lament the current state of affairs, our days of new frontiers behind us and our time now spent only in tilling the same fields over and over again? It was in order to offer a more optimistic vision of one major aspect of sixteenth-century English history that I undertook the task of putting together this volume of essays. Each of the eight essays is written by either an advanced graduate student or a relatively recent Ph.D. In many cases, the essays are based on dissertations that are being revised for publication. As such, these pieces all give us a sense of the new questions being asked and the new frontiers being explored. None of us would deny that we stand on the shoulders of the giants who have come before us, but we are pushing some new topics to the fore and, we hope, keeping our field moving forward. Following the essays, three distinguished senior scholars in different fields of sixteenth-century history—Norman Jones (parliamentary history), Robert Tittler (urban history), and Diane Willen (gender history)—offer their candid assessments of the contributions and suggest ways in which we and other scholars can go even further. There is no comfort here for those who want to weep over future prospects for Tudor history.[8]

⟶

In a historiographical review essay originally published fifteen years ago, Christopher Haigh observed that "the production of a revised synthesis [of the English Reformation] will be difficult."[9] To his credit, Dr. Haigh made the attempt: his *English Reformations.* Even those who disagree with Haigh's interpretations find things to praise in the effort,[10] but it is difficult, on

---

[8]It is true that not every essay in this volume strictly limits itself to the period before 1603. Issues in society have a way of inconveniently refusing to resolve themselves tidily upon the death of monarchs (or even dynasties). In order to tell their story coherently, some authors have continued into the seventeenth century, but in no case do we offer an essay which is not primarily about the sixteenth century.

[9]Christopher Haigh, "The Recent Historiography of the English Reformation," in Haigh, ed., *The English Reformation Revised* (Cambridge: Cambridge University Press, 1987): 19–33; quote from 33. (Haigh's essay was originally published in *Historical Journal* in 1982.)

[10]See reviews by Patrick Collinson in *Times Literary Supplement* (22 October 1993): 14–15; Ronald Hutton in *Times Education Supplement* (4 June 1993): A10; Robert Tittler in *American Historical Review* 100 (1995): 515; and especially Diarmaid MacCulloch in *Journal of Ecclesiastical History* 45 (1994): 319–321.

closing the book, to explain the "failure of Laud and his sacramentally minded colleagues to inspire popular enthusiasm for a more Catholic version of the Church of England."[11] Indeed, as Professor Jones notes in this volume, in the 1640s the English fought a civil war "over what kind of Protestant to be" not (as a credulous reading of Haigh might lead one to predict) "over whether to be Catholic again." The essays in this volume, from many different perspectives, suggest how this came about.

Recent revisionist studies—those which present a picture of a vital late medieval church and largely unwelcome religious change—have a disturbing tendency to end in 1580 (if not an earlier date).[12] From the vantage point of 1580 it is indeed difficult to understand the 1620s and beyond. The process by which the overwhelming majority of the English people adapted to the new church was a slow, untidy one. It involved propaganda and polemic, exposure to skilled pastors and preachers, and a host of reconstructions of familiar institutions such as guilds to accommodate the new realities. Many of these essays suggest that what in fact happened over time was a blending of old and new, so that the religion which ultimately received the loyalty of the laity might have been something less than Cranmer, Cromwell, et al. intended. When "the Reformation" is presented and seen as an event (or series of events) only, it is understood to be something imposed by the government on a resistant populace which ultimately and grudgingly accepted it because the sheer muscle of the state made resistance futile. But if the English Reformation is seen as a sort of dialectic process in which a synthesis was shaped over time, things start to make a great deal more sense. Many of these essays, taken together, do imply that the way in which the entire topic of religion in Tudor England has been approached is misguided and that a new approach is necessary to bring the picture into focus.

The German and Swiss Reformations have, naturally enough, been studied primarily from the vantage point of cities; only recently have studies with a more rural focus emerged.[13] For England, the reverse has

---

[11]MacCulloch review in *Journal of Ecclesiastical History*, 321.

[12]In addition to Duffy, *Stripping of the Altars*, and Haigh, *English Reformations*, see especially Peter Marshall, *The Catholic Priesthood and the English Reformation* (Oxford: Clarendon Press, 1994), and Martha C. Skeeters, *Community and Clergy: Bristol and the Reformation c.1530–c.1570* (Oxford: Clarendon Press, 1993).

[13]For the urban perspective, see Steven E. Ozment, *The Reformation in the Cities: The Appeal of Protestantism to Sixteenth-Century Germany and Switzerland* (New Haven: Yale University Press, 1975). For a recent study of a rural area, see C. Scott Dixon, *The Reformation and Rural Society: The Parishes of Brandenburg-Ansbach-Kulmbach 1528–1603* (Cambridge: Cambridge University Press, 1996).

been the case. England was far less urbanized than either Germany or Switzerland; only London was a city by continental standards. Although there were at least a dozen fairly substantial towns—most notably Bristol, Norwich, and York—England was an overwhelmingly rural country in every conceivable sense.

It is still surprising how slow historians have been to explore the ways in which urban England responded to the Reformation. London is, of course, a notable exception, but Susan Brigden's fine study concludes with the accession of Elizabeth I, and even for the earlier years of the Reformation, much remains to be explored.[14] York and Bristol have received some attention, but both David Palliser's pamphlet on York and Martha Skeeter's monograph on Bristol are very limited in their focus.[15] Work in progress, well represented in this volume, is filling this gap.[16] What is emerging is a clear sense that we cannot speak of an English urban Reformation as if there were one pattern which can be traced, with trivial variations, in each place. Rather, each urban area accommodated itself to religious changes in a unique way which grew organically out of the particular and peculiar past experiences and internal structures of the place.

Norwich, second only to London in wealth and population, as Muriel McClendon shows, is a case in point. In the hundred years before the Reformation, Norwich magistrates twice had their privileges reduced as a result of internal conflicts which they failed to resolve. Religious changes provided them with new and potentially disastrous sources of conflict. At the same time, however, they also provided an opportunity to rise above divisions and prove that they could govern, that they could maintain order on their own. The essay in this volume—part of Dr. McClendon's larger study of the Reformation in Norwich[17]—focuses on the way in which Norwich magistrates dealt with discord and dissent caused by its clergy.

The mayor and aldermen had jurisdiction over what in the Middle Ages were called "criminous clerks" and they exercised it to good effect during the later years of Henry VIII's and throughout Edward VI's reign.

---

[14]Susan Brigden, *London and the Reformation* (Oxford: Clarendon Press, 1989).

[15]D. M. Palliser, *The Reformation in York 1534–1553*, Borthwick Papers 40 (York: St. Anthony's Press, 1971); Skeeters, *Community and Clergy.*

[16]In addition to the research of authors in this volume, note should be made of work now underway on the Reformation in Hereford by John Dwyer, a graduate student at the University of Colorado. I am very grateful to Mr. Dwyer for discussing his preliminary findings with me.

[17]See also Muriel C. McClendon, "'Against God's Word': Government, Religion and the Crisis of Authority in Early Reformation Norwich," *Sixteenth Century Journal* 25 (1994): 353–369.

Although themselves divided religiously, as McClendon shows, the magistrates agreed that Norwich must be kept from attracting attention from the central government yet again. To this end, and in order to avoid public protests, official religious policies were not enforced rigorously. Clergy who spoke or acted in a "public and provocative" manner, regardless of their positions on the doctrinal spectrum, were hauled in for correction. At the same time, the magistrates doled out only minor punishments in order to avoid creating martyrs and escalating discord.

In Norwich, at least, magistrates found it relatively easy to work together in spite of religious differences, which suggests that we need to rethink the history of religious toleration. Moreover, their efforts make clear that the Reformation was not simply a matter of replacing Catholic doctrines and practices with those of the new official church. Rather, it was a dialectic process of blending and accommodating, not so much laying down a via media—with its implication of one path between two extremes—but erecting a "big tent" within which differences could be contained and civic peace maintained. Urban religious divisions did not have to lead, à la mode parisienne, to bloodshed in the streets. What happened in Norwich was clearly driven by its past history, its governmental structure, and the accident of a bishop who was an incompetent nonentity and provided no challenge to the secular authorities' pursuit of their goals and, because of this, its experience might well be unique. However, McClendon clearly raises issues which every future student of religious change in England's towns will need to consider.

Luke Shepherd, the London satirist whose work Janice Devereux examines, would not have been welcomed by Norwich's mayor and aldermen! At the very same time as they were working to silence provocative voices, Shepherd was writing and publishing some of the most vitriolic religious doggerel of the time, the likes of which were probably not seen again until the 1590s.[18] Shepherd is not an unknown figure, having received attention from John N. King,[19] but Devereux provides us with a critical edition of one of his major poems, *Doctour doubble ale*, which

---

[18]See Patrick Collinson, "Ecclesiastical Vitriol: Religious Satire in the 1590s and the Invention of Puritanism," in *The Reign of Elizabeth I: Court and Culture in the Last Decade*, ed. John Guy (Cambridge: Cambridge University Press, 1995): 150–170.

[19]John N. King, *English Reformation Literature: The Tudor Origins of the Protestant Tradition* (Princeton: Princeton University Press, 1982), 252–270.

allows to see particularly clearly the way in which cheap print and Protestant propaganda could operate in Edwardian London.

When censorship was relaxed during Edward's reign, there was a dramatic increase in the printing of religious polemic. Most of this, including Shepherd's various works, postdated the official religious changes associated with Somerset's regime. It was not the government to whom these works were addressed. Rather, writers such as Shepherd used satire to undermine resistance to religious change among the laity by showing that the old ways were undeserving of loyalty. In this respect, they were carrying out a campaign of negative advertising similar to that in Germany which R. W. Scribner described in *For the Sake of Simple Folk*,[20] and are the ancestors of modern American political advertisers who learned from the disastrous 1988 presidential campaign of Michael Dukakis that defining the opposition negatively in the public's mind, especially in the face of little effort by the opposition to define itself, is a virtual guarantee of victory.

Devereux describes briefly all of Shepherd's known works. From these descriptions it is clear that he identified two subjects for ridicule, suggesting that they were seen as being at the core of Catholic loyalism: the mass and the doctrine of transubstantiation, and the Catholic clergy. *Doctour doubble ale* is an example of his attacks on the latter. Its subject is a particular priest, Henry George of Saint-Sepulchre-without-Newgate, but it can easily be read as an attack on the Catholic clergy as a whole. It was certainly true in Elizabethan England that many clergy saw criticism of one of their number—even when it was patently ad hominem—as a threat to the entire order, a "defacing of the ministry."[21] This was more than just professional paranoia. Reputation was central to the credibility and thus the success of any ministry, and anything which suggested that some ministers were immoral drunken fools might lead to suspicions about others. The beleaguered conservative clergy in the late 1540s felt the same way and Shepherd counted on precisely that reaction among his audience.

The future did not belong to Shepherd's poetic vitriol. It was ballads that quickly came to dominate the market for cheap print works with

---

[20]Robert W. Scribner, *For the Sake of Simple Folk: Popular Propaganda for the German Reformation* (Cambridge: Cambridge University Press, 1981).

[21]Eric Josef Carlson, "Anticlericalism and the English Reformation," paper delivered at the North American Conference of British Studies meeting, Washington, D.C., October 1995. An expanded version of this paper will appear shortly as an article.

religious topics.[22] As a consequence, works such as *Doctour doubble ale* have not received the attention that they deserve. If we are to understand the process by which people came to accept, at whatever level of enthusiasm, the religious changes of Edward's reign, we must know something of the propaganda to which they were subjected. While not enough to account on its own for whatever popular success the Edwardian reforms enjoyed—and there were few if any places where that success was greater than in Shepherd's London—religious satire such as *Doctour doubble ale* must have played a part in the process of accommodation to religious change.

Even within Shepherd's London there were those who, like Norwich's civic leaders, worked actively to minimize the disruptive effects of religious change. Joseph Ward offers us a study of one such group, the Grocers' Company, taken from his monograph on London trade guilds.[23] Ward's contribution, together with McClendon's, should put an end to the assumption that urban community and civic unity could not survive the shock of religious change and that civic division and strife was unavoidable when the "world of shared faith was broken."[24]

Ward's study of the clerical patronage exercised by the Grocers, for example, shows how they worked to accommodate the diverse religious views of their members. While giving livings to important evangelicals, guild wardens also administered chantries and obits. The same year that Thomas Becon was given the parish of Saint Stephen Walbrook, for example, the wardens spent more than £37 on fourteen obits and distributed more than £63 to seven chantry priests!

When chantries and obits became illegal, the Grocers again found ways to accommodate themselves to change by developing "new ritual forms that encouraged members to continue to see themselves as part of a spiritual community." The Grocers were not alone. In Norwich, for example, the guild of Saint George redesigned its feast day celebration after 1547. The guild of Saint George failed miserably to accommodate the religious sensibilities of its members. The result was a complaint to the Privy Council and the embarrassment of intervention by Protector Somerset in

---

[22]Tessa Watt, *Cheap Print and Popular Piety, 1550–1640* (Cambridge: Cambridge University Press, 1991).

[23]Joseph P. Ward, *Metropolitan Communities: Trade Guilds, Identity, and Change in Early Modern London* (Stanford: Stanford University Press, 1997).

[24]Brigden, *London and the Reformation*, 639.

the guild's affairs.[25] The Grocers, however, successfully revamped the celebration of Saint Antonin's day.

They also found acceptable ways to commemorate deceased members. In this, they were like Lutherans who did not eliminate funerals but forged a new ceremony based on Lutheran soteriology and the legitimate pastoral needs of the living. The Lutheran funeral stressed that resurrection was based on salvation by faith; the funeral itself offered consolation to the living and a forum for the display of family honor, as well as an occasion to teach Lutheran doctrine on salvation.[26] Ward shows how the Grocers were able to do something similar, preserving one of the functions for which they were founded within a new religious framework. Religious change, even that which seemed to strike at the heart of guild identity, was not allowed to strip the company of its religious character. Again we see not a simple choice of old church or new, but a syncretic process designed to preserve unity while making room for differences.

Fostering unity and downplaying "potentially divisive doctrine" was not merely an urban, lay agenda. It was also, according to Sharon Arnoult, the primary goal of those who compiled the *Book of Common Prayer* and those who defended it against its critics. Astoundingly, the *Book of Common Prayer* has been almost unstudied by Tudor scholars. We are now aware, thanks to Dr. Judith Maltby, of the enormous loyalty which the Prayer Book had engendered by the time of the reign of Charles I. Those whom Maltby calls "Prayer Book protestants" both obstructed Laudian reforms, which they saw as an attack on their parochial religion, and were responsible for more than two dozen petitions in defense of liturgy and episcopacy between 1640 and 1642.[27] But *why* was the Prayer Book so successful at building loyalty? According to Arnoult, it was because of some very sensitive and shrewd designing by its authors.

Every Sunday and holy day, the laity were required by law to attend public worship. The most common service which they would have attended was a combination of Morning Prayer with the Litany and Ante-Communion. Arnoult identifies three crucial features of that service which

[25]See McClendon, "Against God's Word."

[26]Craig Koslofsky, "Honour and Violence in German Lutheran Funerals in the Confessional Age," *Social History* 20 (1995): 315–337.

[27]Judith Maltby, "'By this Book': Parishioners, the Prayer Book and the Established Church," in *The Early Stuart Church, 1603–1642,* ed. Kenneth Fincham (Stanford: Stanford University Press, 1993): 115–137. This theme is developed in Judith Maltby's monograph, *Prayer Book and People: Religious Conformity before the Civil War* (Cambridge: Cambridge University Press, 1998).

distinguish it both from other reformed services and from the Catholic mass. The first is the sheer volume of Bible reading in the service: several psalms and readings from both the Old and New Testaments. Although Protestants generally shared the view that faith alone saved, and faith came through hearing the Word, the English approach stressed the sufficiency of hearing the Word itself *without preaching*. Defenders of the Prayer Book were not antisermon, but they argued that faith came from hearing the pure, unfiltered message of the Bible, not from human interpretation of it; to demand preaching as a mark of true worship was to elevate the inventions of the preacher to a higher level than the Word of God.

Sermons also, according to the Prayer Book's defenders, tended to distract worshipers with exposition of potentially problematic doctrine when the primary goal of worship ought to be an "outpouring of Christ-centered devotion," which was the "key to sanctification," not an intellectual mastery of doctrine. All that was necessary to achieve that "outpouring" was to stress Christian fundamentals through biblical passages, recitation of the Creed, prayers, and confession. This, according to Arnoult, is the second distinctive feature of Prayer Book worship. Readings from the Bible "awakened faith through knowledge of God's saving work in Christ, creeds rehearsed the details of the Incarnation and Passion," and so on. This was what was necessary to turn the worshiper to the proper end of worship, which was Christ.

Finally, there was more congregational participation in the English service than in any other reformed service or the mass. Most of this came in the form of set prayers. Critics complained about these set prayers, arguing that the minister should be free to devise his own prayers because set prayers lacked sincerity. They would also have preferred the vast amount of time the congregation spent participating in the service through these prayers to be spent hearing a sermon. However, as Arnoult shows, the set prayers and congregational participation were deliberate and important choices. Prayer was to be *common* prayer, not the prayer of the clergy alone. The minister was a leader in prayer, but no more; the authors of the Prayer Book intended to convey the essential equality of clergy and laity in a very fundamental way. Set prayers were also important for a largely illiterate society. Familiarity made it possible for everyone to participate, even those who could not read the prayers from the book, and to affirm sincerely the prayers of the entire congregation. Arnoult's description of the Prayer

Book's design makes clear how misguided is Christopher Haigh's argument that the Reformation was "a disaster in the countryside" because it was a religion of words, especially sermons, which was unsuited for areas of relatively low literacy.[28]

The *Book of Common Prayer* was both undeniably Protestant and distinctively English. Understanding it makes very comprehensible the reactions of the English laity in the 1630s and 1640s. It offered the laity a flattering image of their spiritual potential. As they came to embrace it, it is not surprising that they found the clericalism of both ends of the ecclesiological spectrum, but especially the Laudians, distasteful. What seems especially clear from Arnoult's essay is that if one has a firm understanding of the Prayer Book, it is very difficult to sustain arguments such as Bernard's which minimize the scope and scale of Laudian reforms. Her essay also has major implications for those who try to define the English church by continental theological terms. The Prayer Book appears to be something of a square peg, unfit for jamming into a round Calvinist or Lutheran pigeonhole, but neither is it a blending of Catholic and Reformed. Instead of via media we simply have *via Anglicana.*

But in the 1530s, there was little serious thought of revising the worship service, for then the battle was being fought for the hearts and minds of the English people in a very different environment. Official actions on religion in the late 1530s were nothing so grand and consistent as a "policy"; rather, Henry lurched idiosyncratically from one line to another, driven largely by financial needs and foreign anxieties.[29] Susan Wabuda, in an excerpt from her forthcoming monograph, shows how important preaching and preachers were on both sides during these unsettled years, and how legitimate were the anxieties of the Norwich magistrates described by Muriel McClendon. In the diocese of Worcester generally and in Bristol in particular, religious change zealously advocated by Bishop Hugh Latimer (1535–1539) produced bitter divisions.[30] Latimer "disturbed the balance of local interests by allying himself with gentlemen and prominent merchants who shared his interest in promoting reforming preachers." Attention from central government—precisely what Norwich

[28]Haigh, "Recent Historiography," 24.

[29]Haigh, *English Reformations*, 121–167; Diarmaid MacCulloch, "Henry VIII and the Reform of the Church," in MacCulloch, ed., *The Reign of Henry VIII: Politics, Policy and Piety* (New York: St. Martin's Press, 1995): 159–180.

[30]For conflict in Bristol, see Skeeters, *Community and Clergy*, 34–56.

governors feared and avoided—was constant; Latimer and his allies constantly sought (and received) support and protection from Thomas Cromwell. When Cromwell could no longer afford to protect Latimer, the bishop resigned and the diocese was put through a period of reaction which included heresy hunts. This is a striking example which, when compared to McClendon's Norwich, suggests that the bishop might be the most important factor in determining whether local forces promoting harmony over dissonance would prevail.

Both Norwich's bishop Rugge and Worcester's Latimer received promotion because of their support for Henry's divorce, but unlike the ineffectual Rugge, Latimer was a determined and aggressive reformer. During his brief episcopacy he silenced conservative preachers—even those who were well educated and discreet—and used episcopal patronage to appoint preachers who would advocate reform. Latimer's policy was similar to Cranmer's, as Wabuda has shown elsewhere,[31] and it terrified conservatives. Although Latimer had only four years in which to promote reform through his preachers, conservatives felt the damage had been great. Certainly on the evidence of Foxe, preaching was extremely effective at this stage in creating a committed minority of lay adherents of reform.[32] Historians have typically focused on puritan campaigns to increase preaching to such an extent that it has often seemed as if the Elizabethans discovered preaching. The cumulative effect of Susan Wabuda's work, however, is to make abundantly clear that the late medieval church well knew the importance of preaching and it was, in many ways, a thriving enterprise decades before the puritans appeared.

The long-range impact of Latimer's work is easy to see. As Lamar Hill has shown, Sir John Bourne began in the reign of Henry VIII to build a local power base through grants and purchases. He made himself a leading member of the Worcestershire gentry and also served as a Marian privy councilor. In Elizabeth's reign, he constantly harassed bishop Sandys, defied his authority and that of the church courts, and tried to raise resistance locally. But Bourne failed. His own authority was no match for that

---

[31]Susan Wabuda, "Setting Forth the Word of God: Archbishop Cranmer's Early Patronage of Preachers," in Paul Ayris and David Selwyn, eds., *Thomas Cranmer: Churchman and Scholar* (Woodbridge: Boydell Press, 1993): 75–88.

[32]Haigh, *English Reformations*, 188–192.

of the bishop and he had no positive vision to attract people to his side.[33] Hugh Latimer and his preachers might have been little more than a faint memory in the diocese of Worcester by then, but it was they who first set in motion the process which would lead to Bourne's "experience of defeat."

In most parishes in England, it was not itinerant preachers or cheap printed satires which had the greatest effect in building loyalty to the reformed church, however. Rather, it was the hard labor of resident ministers. Although many scholars have published on the subject of the English clergy, those works have been focused on such topics as the education or social and economic position of the clergy while, astonishingly, the pastoral efforts of English clergymen have been almost unstudied.[34] My contribution to this volume is part of a forthcoming book on pastoral ministry in the Elizabethan and early Stuart church.

Richard Greenham was one of the most important figures of the Elizabethan church and yet remains one of the least well known—a good example of the amnesia about inconvenient central figures which Diarmaid MacCulloch has described.[35] In 1570, he left his comfortable and secure fellowship at Cambridge for a country parish—the first nonconformist divine to leave a university post for the practical work of pastoral ministry. In doing so, he became a role model for generations of students. He also established, by accident or design, the first "rectory seminary," a new model for training godly ministers in which students learned by observing and questioning a recognized authority in pastoral ministry *in situ*.[36] As a result of this, Greenham trained many of the most important nonconformists of the period. Due to his two decades of parish work, contemporaries held that "for practicall divinity...he was inferiour to few or none in his time." In 1591, he moved from his Cambridgeshire parish to London, where he preached until his death in 1594.

---

[33]L. M. Hill, "The Marian 'Experience of Defeat': The Case of Sir John Bourne," *Sixteenth Century Journal* 25 (1994): 531–549.

[34]See, for example, Rosemary O'Day, *The English Clergy: The Emergence and Consolidation of a Profession 1558–1642* (Leicester: Leicester University Press, 1979). Marshall, *Catholic Priesthood*, is the notable exception to the pattern of silence on pastoral roles, but is concerned with the pre-Elizabethan and Catholic clergy only.

[35]MacCulloch, "Myth of the English Reformation," 5, 11.

[36]See John Morgan, *Godly Learning: Puritan Attitudes towards Reason, Learning, and Education, 1560–1640* (Cambridge: Cambridge University Press, 1986), 293–300; T. Webster, "The Godly of Goshen Scattered: An Essex Clerical Conference in the 1620s and Its Diaspora" (Ph.D. dissertation, Cambridge University, 1993), 45–67.

Greenham had a number of difficulties with the *Book of Common Prayer*, and he did not conform to all of its provisions. But he did agree with much of its spirit as described by Sharon Arnoult. In the 1570s, he preached publicly against Thomas Cartwright and others who, in his view, wasted their time arguing over relatively unimportant matters instead of training themselves in and teaching others Christian fundamentals. When convoked before Bishop Cox for not wearing the surplice, he avoided suspension by arguing that he did not engage in debates over ceremonies or surplices, but spent his time "in preaching Christ crucified unto myselfe and Country people." Greenham, in fact, became one of Cox's most effective allies in his struggle against popery and the Family of Love sect.

Every conscientious minister faced a potentially disastrous dilemma that was at the core of his ministry. God, they all knew, would hold them accountable for every soul entrusted to them. In order for their neighbors to be saved, ministers had first to make them aware of their sinfulness and their need to repent. How precisely to create this awareness was an extremely tricky matter. There were, in fact, two schools of thought on the subject. Some godly ministers thundered away in the pulpit, even pointing fingers and naming names. Their parishes ended up riven with strife and, while a godly minority might find their approach satisfying, it was largely counterproductive. Greenham was one of the most well-known opponents of this method. He denounced ministers for destroying their potential effectiveness by antagonizing their parishioners and dividing their parishes. The residents of Dry Drayton were no different from Norwich's magistrates or London's grocers in their desire to maintain unity and harmony and in Greenham they had a minister who shared this ideal.

Christopher Haigh has used Greenham's case to argue that the Reformation was "a disaster in the countryside": When Greenham left Dry Drayton for the relative ease of London, he did so frustrated with his lack of success; if such a skilled and conscientious minister as Greenham could not succeed, the job of making godly Protestants out of English villagers could not be done.[37] I argue, however, that by most measures, Greenham *was* a success and that his removal to London was, in fact, to what he knew would be a more difficult situation. By 1591, London lectureships were no longer the comfortable refuges for nonconformists that they had been in the 1580s because, thanks to Archbishop Whitgift and Bishop Aylmer,

---

[37]Haigh, "Recent Historiography," 24.

puritans felt under siege. Greenham was recruited by desperate lay puritans trying to save the puritan cause. He did not leave his parish defeated.

Greenham's biography thus illustrates microcosmically a number of the themes in this volume, especially the importance of reconciling religious change with communal harmony and the search for appropriate ways to promote the reformed church to the laity. A detailed study of his ministry also offers a window on the work of parish ministry with all of its various duties and challenges through the actual experience of one admittedly exceptional minister. We now have a foundation from which to build a more complete understanding of the vitally important topic of parish ministry in the reformed church.

∽

The final two essays differ from the rest in that they are about a *source* for the study of religion: wills. For more than thirty years, historians have used wills in the search for understanding of local religious values and practices, both through the statements of faith with which wills begin and through the bequests for pious purposes within the wills themselves.[38] Almost every contributor to this volume does so. But the utility of wills has been hotly contested of late. With revised and expanded versions of pieces which they have previously published, Christopher Marsh and Caroline Litzenberger offer their own views on wills as sources for studying local religion.

Will-making was, above all else, about the disposition of earthly goods, but this does not mean that it was not deeply endued with religious meaning, as Marsh shows, because testators had been taught throughout their lives that whatever possessions they had were merely held in trust from God and that they would be judged on the way in which they had carried out that trust. A will was a final exercise of guardianship, and nothing should have been more important for a will-maker than to dispose of his or her goods in a godly way.

Until the eighteenth century, most wills began with pious preambles in which testators commended their souls to God. These range from the perfunctory to the modestly substantive. The former, which are very common,

---

[38]For a wide-ranging review of wills as sources, see Eric Josef Carlson, "The Historical Value of the Ely Consistory Probate Records," in *Index of the Probate Records of the Consistory Court of Ely 1449–1858*, ed. Elisabeth Leedham-Green and Rosemary Rodd, 3 vols. (London: British Record Society, 1994–96), 1:xvii–lix.

state that the soul is bequeathed, for example, "to Almighty God, my maker and redeemer."[39] Before the Reformation, and again during Mary's reign, this basic clause typically included a reference to Mary and the saints. Later, a brief doctrinal profession sometimes appeared as well: Robert Tofts of Linton offered his soul "into the hands of Almighty God my maker and to Jesus Christ my saviour and redeemer hoping steadfastly through his merits, death and passion that after this transitory life is ended I shall rest with the elect in his everlasting life."[40]

Statements such as Tofts' seem to provide an extraordinary insight into private religious beliefs. In 1971, Margaret Spufford first argued, however, that these clauses were routinely supplied by scribes, and may be suspect as unambiguous indicators of the religious views of testators themselves.[41] As Marsh shows in his exceptionally thorough description of the will-making process, after recording a testator's wishes, the scribe typically returned home to draw up the will in its final form and inserted the religious preamble. Some scribes devised a personal formula, used whenever drawing up a will: Robert Wigglesworth wrote five wills in Leverington (Cambs.) and in every case the testator's soul was bequeathed into "the hands of God the Father my maker, Jesus Christ his son my redeemer, and the Holy Ghost my sanctifier, by whose merits only I hope to be saved."[42] Some scribes used will formularies, which were accessible in costly legal works but also in cheap almanacs.[43]

Recent scholarship is forcing us to rethink the issue of scribal formulae. Litzenberger, along with John Craig, recently published a remarkable piece of detective work concerning the will of the Gloucestershire gentleman William Tracy, who vented what were then heterodox religious beliefs in the preamble to his will. The will was denied probate and condemned in convocation, but by 1535 it was in print with commentary by Tyndale and Frith. More than a dozen wills (from that of a Mendlesham testator in 1537 to one from Hull in 1640) with preambles clearly based on Tracy's have

[39]Will of Stephen Smith of Leverington, E[ly] P[robate] R[ecords,] C[onsistory] W[ill] 1571. While the wording is not always exactly the same, this is a very typical example.

[40]EPR, CW 1637.

[41]Margaret Spufford, "'The Scribes of Villagers': Wills in the Sixteenth and Seventeenth Centuries and Their Influence," *Local Population Studies* 7 (1971): 28–43.

[42]Wills of Thomas and Anne Jessop (both EPR, CW 1610), Elizabeth Denison (CW 1613), Thomas Mayhew (CW 1613), and Thomas Jones (CW 1615).

[43]See, for example, Bernard Capp, "Will Formularies," *Local Population Studies* 14 (1975): 49, for *Fly: An Almanacke*.

been identified.[44] Using Tracy's preamble, published though it was, clearly tells us a great deal about the testator, for anyone who would use it was making a deliberate and powerful statement of religious conviction. Marsh makes a similar case for the use which he uncovered of the preamble to Epaphroditus' will in Thomas Becon's popular devotional work, *The Sick Mans Salve*. For those who used the words of Becon or Tracy, the value of a preamble was measured in its expressiveness and not in its originality.

Some historians argue that scribal preambles are not without some meaning because it is unlikely that dying people chose scribes who would use formulae antipathetic to their own beliefs. This assumes, of course, that testators had an adequate supply of scribes from whom to choose. My own research on Leverington wills confirms Professor Spufford's findings that scribes were in good supply. It is also noteworthy that before the Reformation, when there was little variation in preambles, the clergy monopolized will-writing; after the Reformation, the clerical monopoly was broken. While ministers continued to write wills, they were joined by a wide range of literate lay people, including women. Thus, at precisely the point at which a more distinctive statement became both possible and theologically comprehensible, a range of choices became available through an expanded pool of scribes.[45] Moreover, some scribes used more than one preamble. John Bulward, a yeoman in Leverington and regular will-writer in the 1570s and 1580s, is associated with at least three different preambles. They range from the simple bequest into the hands of "Almighty God, my maker and redeemer" to the more elaborate bequest "into the hands of Almighty God, my savior and redeemer, only trusting in his merits and passion to have full remission of my sins, and after this frail life, to be an inheritor of his everlasting kingdom."[46] Litzenberger finds that the same is true in Gloucestershire. The choice of which of a scribe's preambles was used could also be a sign of the testator's sentiments.

But J. D. Alsop argues that while "a minority took the initial bequest of the soul very seriously...to express heartfelt convictions...the religious

---

[44]John Craig and Caroline Litzenberger, "Wills as Religious Propaganda: The Testament of William Tracy," *Journal of Ecclesiastical History* 44 (1993): 415–431.

[45]See Margaret Spufford, *Contrasting Communities: English Villagers in the Sixteenth and Seventeenth Centuries* (Cambridge: Cambridge University Press, 1974), 322–327, 333; John Craig, "Margaret Spittlehouse, Female Scrivener," *Local Population Studies* (1992): 54–57.

[46]EPR, CW 1571 (Stephen Smith); CW 1585 (John Plombe). See also CW 1572 (Nicholas Gogney), CW 1577 (Robert Adam), CW 1577 (Walter Smith), CW 1586 (William Jonson, Robert Smith).

preamble is an untrustworthy guide to the religion of the testator—or at least a guide for which the trustworthiness is suspect and, in most instances, impossible to establish." To the argument that testators would only trust the writing of their wills to someone in whom they had confidence, and who thus would be likely to approximate their religious views, Alsop responds that this "assumes that confidence would necessarily be based upon religious affiliation" while scribes were, in fact, chosen on the basis of the confidence testators had in their abilities to manage the temporal details in will-making.[47] A number of details support Alsop's argument, most especially that some preambles seem inconsistent with bequests made within the will, suggesting that testators did not pay much attention to them, and deeply religious testators might use only the most basic, inexpressive preambles. In 1586, William Rushbrigg began his will with a bland dedicatory clause; he owned a copy of *Sick Mans Salve*, but felt no need to follow its model of a long expressive preface. He made extensive gifts to the poor, provided money for erecting an almshouse and repairing the church way, and requested a total of five sermons. This case confirms the need to search a will for its bequests such as requests for chantry priests or legacies for a preacher as true indicators of personal beliefs.[48]

For Marsh, then, the will preamble *may* say something about an individual testator's views, but that is not reliably the case. Religiously expressive preambles were simply not a special Christian duty, and it is within the body of the will that the more useful indicators will be found. Marsh concludes that "statistical analysis of categorized preambles is beginning to look like a somewhat limited exercise" because changes in wording which are observed over time are more likely to reflect official policy and not changes in personal piety.

Caroline Litzenberger agrees with Marsh on most points. However, she is more sanguine about the usefulness of preambles. The range of choice available to testators in Tewkesbury and Cirencester suggests, she argues, that choice was important for at least a substantial share of the will-making populace. For Litzenberger, the most comfortable with computer analysis

---

[47]J. D. Alsop, "Religious Preambles in Early Modern English Wills as Formulae," *Journal of Ecclesiastical History* 40 (1989): 19–27.

[48]Michael L. Zell, "Fifteenth- and Sixteenth-Century Wills as Historical Sources," *Archives* 14 (1979), 69; idem, "The Use of Religious Preambles as a Measure of Religious Belief in the Sixteenth Century," *Bulletin of the Institute of Historical Research* 50 (1977), 246–249. Rushbrigg will: EPR, CW 1586.

of all of us, the problem with statistical surveys of preambles is with the methods used. She offers a more sophisticated analysis based on a larger sample and finds that changes over time do not merely reflect changes in official policy but hint at opinions contrary to official policy. For example, during Edward's reign bequests to Mary and the saints would be inconsistent with official theology and references to assurance of salvation would be more in conformity. What Litzenberger finds, however, is that while preambles mentioning Mary and the saints did become quite rare, more protestant statements did not appear in their place. Rather, people—in her view—hid conservative theological views behind a "safe" minimal formula such as a bequest "to Almighty God, my maker and redeemer." As Marsh encourages, Litzenberger also analyzes internal evidence from the wills, particularly bequests to parishes, to the poor, and for prayers for the dead. Her will sample is also analyzed by gender of testator and region of the county. The result is precisely the sort of context-sensitive study for which Marsh argued.

In addition, Litzenberger unveils in this essay a significant reconceptualization of the vocabulary which scholars use to discuss will preambles. Until now, it has been customary to refer to dedicatory clauses which betrayed no explicit confessional position as "neutral." This has never been a very satisfactory term, since it implies a kind of partisan positioning on the part of the testator. In place of that term, Litzenberger offers the far more descriptive "ambiguous." This certainly deserves to become common usage, since it is a far more accurate term for these preambles.

By way of conclusion, I offer this example: After commending his soul to "the Almighty Godhead, when it shall please the same to take me from the miseries of this wretched world," the Leverington yeoman William Acres went on:

> And because the breach of God's law is eternal death which, with all flesh I acknowledge to have justly deserved by means of my disobedience thereof, even so with the elect I firmly believe that through the most precious death of Jesus Christ my only redeemer, mediator and saviour, the second person in Trinity, I shall with this self same body and soul conjoined be saved and numbered amongst his father's children and inherit his blessed kingdom which he hath ordained for us world without end. And therefore according to my bounden duty, I right humbly beseech his fatherly

goodness to pardon me all my past faults and offences, to blot out all my imperfections, to cloth me with the garment of Christ his righteousness, and to grant me his grace and Holy Spirit to persevere in faith, hope and charity unto my life's end.[49]

This extraordinary preamble makes abundantly clear that for some this was an opportunity to make what could be an ostentatious display of faith. If it was not so for all testators, these two essays show us nonetheless how testamentary evidence, if not used crudely, may continue to serve as a major source for studying religion in early modern England.

∾

There is no comfort in this volume for those who want to feel gloomy about the future of our field. As we look forward we can see a number of new areas of study opening up. The pastoral work of the clergy and their relations with the laity are beginning to receive long-overdue attention. The examination question "English Reformation, success or failure. Discuss" is clearly on the way out, as that crude view is abandoned for a study of the ways in which the English people accommodated themselves to religious change and, in the process, reshaped that change more in their own image. The impact of early preaching, religious satire, and the *Book of Common Prayer* itself on this process is now being addressed. All of this will be helped along by a more sophisticated and reliable use of sources such as wills. There is every reason to think that we are about to take enormous leaps ahead in our understanding of religion in early modern England.

[49]EPR, CW 1590.

PART 1

WORDS
and
WORSHIP

"SPIRITUAL *and* SACRED PUBLIQUE ACTIONS"

THE *BOOK OF COMMON PRAYER* AND THE UNDERSTANDING OF WORSHIP IN THE ELIZABETHAN AND JACOBEAN CHURCH OF ENGLAND

Sharon L. Arnoult

THE *BOOK OF COMMON PRAYER* and its public worship services both embodied and promoted religious attitudes which made up a distinctly English Protestantism. Not only were contemporaries conscious of this, but for the defenders of England's religious establishment, it was precisely the combination of basic reformed doctrine with these attitudes expressed in worship which set English reformed Christianity apart from all other forms, and made it uniquely suited to the English people.[1] Worship services in the English church were seen as expressing views on the relationship between clergy and laity, the role of Scripture, the unity of the Christian community, and the proper focus and response of the worshiper. Moreover, the Prayer Book provided the context in which such doctrinal issues as justification and predestination were presented to English Christians, and so conditioned a "theological response" to doctrine—a point certainly well acknowledged by the Prayer Book's critics. Thus, any understanding of the development of English religious identity in this era must include an examination such as this one. It tells us what a commitment to the Prayer Book meant in religious terms. It helps illuminate the religious differences of those who were in doctrinal accord. Moreover, it is only when we know how the Prayer Book and worship were understood that we

---

[1] I will concentrate on the most commonly performed and experienced public worship services in the Elizabethan and Jacobean church. Therefore, I will not deal with occasional services such as marriage or confirmation, or clerical services such as ordination and consecration. My source for the understanding of worship is primarily the literature defending the Prayer Book, most but not all of which was written by the higher clergy.

can grasp what the later changes in worship under Archbishop Laud meant and why they were so widely detested.

During this period, what an English churchgoer usually encountered on a Sunday morning was Morning Prayer, the Litany, and the first part of the communion service, or Ante-Communion,[2] but neither communion itself nor a sermon. This was not because either preaching or communion was not valued. The Prayer Book reflected its author Thomas Cranmer's intention for there to be both a sermon and communion every Sunday,[3] and all the Prayer Book's later supporters expressed their high regard for both, a position completely in accord with most continental reformed theology. The problem, rather, was a practical one: a lack of clergy both willing and able to preach, on the one hand, and on the other, the sheer logistics and expense of communicating to the entire parish.

Although the Royal Injunctions of 1559 had instructed parish clergy to preach or provide a sermon monthly, the bishops' privately circulated Interpretations of 1560–61 agreed, "for want of able preachers and parsons, to tolerate [parish clergy] without penalty, so they preach in their own persons, or by a learned substitute, once in every iii months of the year."[4] The Canons of 1571 focused on ensuring that every parish have at least this quarterly sermon, pressing deans and prebends into preaching service for their dioceses, as well as bishops.[5] A survey of the ministry compiled by reformers in 1586 showed that of approximately 2,537 parishes,

---

[2]The *Book of Common Prayer* directed Morning and Evening Prayer to be said daily, and the Litany on Sundays, Wednesdays, and Fridays. It explained how the communion service was to be concluded if there were no communicants: *The Book of Common Prayer, 1559*, ed. John E. Booty (Charlottesville, Va.: Folger Shakespeare Library, 1976), 17, 68, 267 [hereafter *BCP*]. There was no explicit directive to perform all three of these continuously until 1571, when Archbishop Grindal directed that they should be said "without any intermission, to the intent the people... not depart out of the church during all the time of the whole Divine Service": *Visitation Articles and Injunctions of the Period of the Reformation*, ed. Walter Howard Frere, 3 vols. (London: Longmans, Green & Co., 1910), 3:286. Grindal's directive suggests less that he was initiating the performance of all three together than that he was ensuring the congregation had no occasion to leave before all three parts were completed. Performing the three together might have arisen naturally from the Royal Injunctions of 1559, which directed that the Litany be said immediately before communion, and in conjunction with public prayers on Wednesdays and Fridays: *Visitation Articles*, 3:14, 22. Performing the three together seems to have become standard in Elizabethan and Jacobean England. See William Harrison, *The Description of England*, ed. Georges Edelen (Ithaca, N.Y.: Folger Documents of Tudor and Stuart Civilization, 1968), 33, for a description of such a service.

[3]John Booty, "History of the 1559 Book of Common Prayer," in *BCP*, 373.

[4]*Visitation Articles*, 3:69.

[5]*A Booke of certaine Canons, concernyng some parte of the discipline of the Churche of England* (London, 1571) [hereafter *1571 Canons*], 7.

only 472—about one fifth—had clergy characterized as being "preachers." Those who did preach by no means did so often. A more detailed survey of Oxfordshire revealed that, out of the thirty-five clergymen who were listed as preachers, only eight preached once a week or more, nine preached "often" or "some," fifteen preached quarterly, and six preached "seldom" or "little."[6]

Parish ministers were directed to urge frequent communion, and the church's goal was to have a communion in every parish once a month for those who wished to communicate.[7] But the Canons of 1571 required only the presentment of those who did not take communion at Easter, although the Prayer Book required communion three times a year, and so the old tradition of annual Easter communion persisted for most people.[8] Jeremy Boulton's study of communion in two London parishes in this period demonstrates the difficulty parishes had in accommodating large numbers of communicants, as well as the expense.[9] Thus religiously dedicated or "godly" people, if they were lucky enough to live in a place which had both the motivation and resources, could enjoy frequent sermons and take communion several times a year. The majority, however, only had the opportunity of a sermon about four times a year, and only made an annual communion. The service combining Morning Prayer, the Litany, and the Ante-Communion was more common.

[6]*The Seconde Parte of a Register*, ed. Albert Peel, 2 vols. (Cambridge: Cambridge University Press, 1915), 2:88, 130–142.

[7]The Prayer Book contained exhortations to frequent communion (*BCP*, 255–256) and the *1571 Canons* directed the parish ministers to "admonish the people to come oftener to the holy Communion" (15). Bishop Bentham ordered monthly communion in all the parishes of Coventry and Lichfield in 1565 (*Visitation Articles*, 3:167) and Archbishop Grindal ordered the practice throughout the province of York in 1571 (ibid., 275). Although the *Book of Common Prayer* specified a communion every Sunday "at the least" in cathedral and collegiate churches (267), Archbishop Parker's *Advertisements* required monthly communion (*Visitation Articles*, 3:175), which individual bishops seem to have already instituted in their own articles for their cathedrals and colleges (ibid., 37, 79, 94, 116, 135, 139, 152).

[8]*1571 Canons*, 14; *BCP*, 268; also see Patrick Collinson, *The Religion of Protestants: The Church in English Society 1559–1625* (Oxford: Clarendon Press, 1981), 210–214.

[9]J. P. Boulton, "The Limits of Formal Religion: The Administration of Holy Communion in Late Elizabethan and Early Stuart London," *London Journal* 10 (1984), 135–154. The monthly communions were charged to the parish, but a fee was charged to householders for the annual Easter communion, to offset the cost. This meant, however, that there was no financial incentive to encourage too many parishioners to communicate at other times. In a large parish like St. Botolph's Aldgate, one of the two Boulton studied, "Easter Communion" was spread out over the Sundays of about two and a half months, in order to accommodate everyone. At a "non-Easter" monthly communion, the number of communicants averaged about fifty. St. Botolph's was a "godly" parish, which had a paid lecturer to augment the number of sermons.

All clergy were required to say Morning and Evening Prayer every day. Colleges and cathedrals required daily attendance of their members. While parish laity were not required to attend, parochial clergy were encouraged to make it possible for them to do so. The service itself presumed a congregation, and anecdotal evidence suggests lay attendance.[10] By law, the laity were only required to attend Divine Service (Morning Prayer with the Litany and Ante-Communion or full communion, and Evening Prayer) every Sunday and holy day. If parishioners came on a day when there was a communion, but did not communicate, they were usually allowed to leave after the Ante-Communion.[11] While a sermon was an incentive to attend for some, for others the length it added to the service was a deterrent.[12] However, parish churchwardens were conscientious about their duty to ensure regular attendance at services, although they made exceptions (accepted by ecclesiastical authorities) for such exigencies as child care, weather, and distance.[13] While all English men and women were not in the pews every time the law specified, the vast majority kept the spirit if not the letter of the law and attended more often than not.

Three things are most striking about the English worship service: the tremendous amount of Bible reading that took place; the active part the congregation played; and the overwhelming focus on what might be called "Christian fundamentals"—Scripture, creeds, confession, and prayers. The minister began Morning Prayer by reading sentences of Scripture from a selection in the Prayer Book. The general confession followed, "to be said of the whole congregation after the minister, kneeling"; in other words, the congregation repeated each phrase or sentence after the minister.[14] When the minister pronounced absolution, the people answered, "Amen." The minister then said the Lord's Prayer and began the Versicles, four sentences

[10]Thomas Hutton referred to ministers' "using [the Prayer Book] in the congregation before many, and that daily." *Reasons for Refusal of Subscription to the booke of Common praier... With an Answere at several times returned* (London, 1605), 71.

[11]Hooper's 1551–52 articles for Gloucester and Worcester dioceses explicitly ordered noncommunicants to leave "in the time of the administration": *Visitation Articles*, 2:274.

[12]In 1606, although they knew he was coming to preach, no one came to a church in the East Riding to hear Archbishop Matthew's sermon: Collinson, *Religion of Protestants*, 209.

[13]Eric Josef Carlson, "The Origins, Function, and Status of the Office of Churchwarden, with Particular Reference to the Diocese of Ely," in Margaret Spufford, ed., *The World of Rural Dissenters, 1520–1715* (Cambridge: Cambridge University Press, 1995), 171–175; F. G. Emmison, *Elizabethan Life: Morals & the Church Courts* (Chelmsford: Essex County Council, 1973), 75–80.

[14]*BCP*, 50; Francis Proctor and Walter Howard Frere, *A New History of the Book of Common Prayer* (London: Macmillan & Co., 1901), 370.

spoken alternately by minister and congregation. After the minister recited a *Gloria Patri* (in English), a solid block of Bible reading occurred: Psalm 95 (said or sung), the Psalms appointed for that day, a chapter of the Old Testament (followed by a canticle), and a chapter of the New Testament (followed by the canticle *Benedicte* or Psalm 100). Next, standing, minister and people together repeated the Apostle's Creed and, kneeling, the Lord's Prayer, followed by a series of suffrages spoken alternately by the minister and the people. The minister then read three collects, or prayers, which ended Morning Prayer proper.[15]

On Sundays, Wednesdays, and Fridays, the service immediately continued the recitation of the Litany, a long series of petitions and prayers, with the congregation making occasional responses.[16] On Sunday, the minister would follow the last invariable Collect of the Litany with the Lord's Prayer and first invariable Collect of the Ante-Communion. Then the minister pronounced the Ten Commandments, the people responding, "Lord have mercy upon us, and incline our hearts to keep this law," after each one. After two more collects came more Bible reading: the Epistle and Gospel texts appointed for that Sunday. The recitation of the Nicene Creed followed. At this point either a sermon was given or, more usually, a homily was read either whole or in part from the Book of Homilies.[17] Finally, after the collection of alms for the poor, the minister ended the service with the prayer for the church militant and one or more collects.[18] The entire service, excluding sermon or homily, lasted about an hour. The service stretched to at least two hours if there was a sermon, communion, or baptism, even longer with more than one of these.[19]

---

[15]*BCP,* 49–60.

[16]Ibid., 68–76.

[17]Ibid., 248–251. The government authorized the first volume of twelve homilies in 1547 and it was reauthorized after Elizabeth's accession; in 1563 a second book of twenty-one homilies joined it, with a homily against rebellion added in 1571. Each homily was divided into parts, so it could be read in its entirety or over successive Sundays. The first twelve focused especially on the errors of Roman Catholicism; the later ones added exhortations on decent behavior (especially obedience), explanations of the significance of the church's calendar, and warnings against religious radicalism. See *Certaine Sermons or Homilies Appointed to be Read in Churches in the Time of Queen Elizabeth I* (Gainesville, Fla.: Scholars' Facsimiles & Reprints, 1968), especially the introduction by Mary Ellen Rickey and Thomas B. Stroup.

[18]*BCP,* 251–254, 267.

[19]John Whitgift claimed the amount of service time spent "in praying and reading" to be "not more than an hour." Thomas Cartwright replied that a sermon added another hour, and a communion another: John Whitgift, *Works,* ed. John Ayre, 3 vols. (Cambridge: Parker Society, 1851), 2:455 & n. 3. Richard Hooker stated that the service, with a sermon, lasted two hours. Richard Hooker, *The Laws of*

The amount of Bible reading was, of course, due to Protestantism's emphasis on *sola scriptura*. Faith alone saved, and "faith commeth by hearing of the word," Robert Some reminded his readers in justifying the magistrate's right to compel church attendance. "Therefore refusal to hear, hinders both the beginning and growth of faith,"[20] especially, we must recall, in a society with a generally high rate of illiteracy. Richard Hooker could see no other way "how the scripture could be possibly made familiar unto all," noting "in a manner the whole book of God is by reading every year published." Moreover, because of the church's authority and the solemnity with which it presented the Bible in worship, Hooker maintained that an individual would listen seriously and with respect, until Scripture's authority on its own became clear.[21] Henry Howard considered the reading of Scripture in church "as an article too plain to be called in question."[22]

Yet the use of Scripture by the Prayer Book was called into question, and especially by those who have been characterized as the "hotter sort" of Protestant, who wanted to see the English church brought more into line with continental reformed churches. Critics of the Prayer Book objected to the use of Bible selections which included the Apocrypha but excluded parts of the canonical Scriptures, and argued that the word was not really being preached, because it was set forth without exegesis in the form of a sermon.[23]

In answering these charges, defenders of the established church revealed how they believed Scripture should be understood and used. The Apocrypha could be used "for manners if not for faith" where its "excellent

---

Ecclesiastical Polity, Folger Library Edition, ed. W. Speed Hill, 4 vols. (Cambridge: The Belknap Press of Harvard University Press, 1977), 2:139 [hereafter *LEP*]. The *Book of Common Prayer* directed baptism to be done after the second lesson in Morning Prayer (*BCP*, 270) but William Harrison recalled that baptisms were performed in his parish after the homily or sermon: *The Description*, 34.

[20]Robert Some, *A Godly Treatise containing and deciding certaine questions...touching the Ministrie, Sacraments, and Church* (London, 1588), 2.

[21]Hooker, *LEP*, 2:88–89.

[22]Henry Howard, *A Defense of the Ecclesiasticall Regiment in Englande...* (London, 1574), 25.

[23]Although controversy over the Prayer Book is as old as the book itself, the Elizabethan and Jacobean debate took form and substance with the publication of *The Admonition to Parliament* by the presbyterians John Field and Thomas Wilcox in 1571, and their subsequent defense by Thomas Cartwright, a more important adversary because he was one of the leading, and most learned, proponents of presbyterianism. John Whitgift, Henry Howard (a layman), and Richard Hooker wrote specifically in response to the Admonitioners. However, criticism of the Prayer Book became so associated with the

precepts" agreed with the overall sense of the canonical Scriptures.[24] Indeed, it was more edifying to read such passages of the Apocrypha than the parts of the canonical Scriptures which were unclear (as in Revelation) or were for knowledge only (such as the genealogies) or bred deplorable attitudes (such as the Song of Solomon, which caused some "in such corrupt manner to speak of Christ his holy marriage with his Church, as if they would read some wanton, idle, amorous pamphlet").[25] The consensus was that any one part of Scripture could and should only be understood in the context of the whole.[26]

This approach to the Bible put emphasis on the entire sense of the Scriptures than on any specific passage. Therefore, it was also used to justify the Church's position that not everything done in worship had to have an explicit Scriptural warrant. Overall, the Bible clearly commanded *what* to do: preach the word and rightly administer the sacraments, which were the Protestants' two marks of a true church. Yet, the church's supporters

---

presbyterian movement that later defenders saw the agenda of the presbyterian Admonitioners in all criticisms of English worship, even after the presbyterian movement was dead among English reformers and the objections against the Prayer Book had become much less substantial, such as those contained in the Millenary Petition of 1603. Robert Some was a Cambridge divine who had leaned toward presbyterianism in his youth, but in the tract cited here he rejected it. He also wrote against the separatist John Penry. Thomas Hutton, an Oxford divine, wrote on behalf of the Bishop of Exeter, William Cotton, in response to the reasons some ministers in Devon and Cornwall gave for refusing to subscribe, that nothing in the Prayer Book was against the word of God. Bibliographical guides to religious controversy in this period are Peter Milward, *Religious Controversies of the Elizabethan Age* (London: Scolar Press, 1977), and idem, *Religious Controversies of the Jacobean Age* (Lincoln: University of Nebraska Press, 1978).

[24]*The Answere of the Vicechancelour, the Doctors, both the Proctors, and other the Heads of Houses in the Universitie of Oxford: (Agreeable, undoubtedly, to the joint and Uniforme opinion, of all the Deanes and Chapters, and all other the learned and obedient Cleargy, in the Church of England.) To the humble Petition of the Ministers of the Church of England, desiring Reformation of certaine Ceremonies and Abuses of the Church* (Oxford, 1603), 14. An edition of 1604 adds "And confirmed by the expresse consent of the Universitie of Cambridge." I have used a collation of the two editions. This tract responded to the Millenary Petition, which had been signed by over seven hundred ministers. William Covell, *A Modest and reasonable examination, of some things in use in the Church of England, sundrie times heretofore misliked...*(London, 1604), 191. Covell was refuting Josias Nichols, *The Plea of the Innocent: Wherein is averred: That the Ministers & people falslie termed Puritanes, are injuriouslie slaundered...*(London, 1602). See also Hutton, *Reasons for the Refusal*, 96–97, 125.

[25]Hutton, *Reasons for the Refusal*, 125–128.

[26]It was on the basis of this understanding of Scripture that Thomas Hutton also argued that discrepancies in translation between the Great Bible and the Geneva Bible, given as one reason for refusing subscription, could not be used to discredit either Bible, since "variety of translation proveth not contrairity in God's word," as long as the overall sense of Scripture was maintained: *Reasons for the Refusal*, 44, 79–125.

maintained, the Bible did not specify *how* to do these, save that all be done "decently and in order."[27] Henry Howard used argument from the sense of Scripture when he cited examples from the Gospels to show that "things were devised by those godly persons to glorify our saviour's body without commandment and these ceremonies are devised to none other end, but to garnish and adorn his ministry, wherefore…it doth by this appear, that Christ sometimes accepteth somethings which himself gave not in charge." Howard specifically rejected the narrower, more literal approach, for even "the godliest orders" could be refuted "if every text unfitly applied may be allowed…."[28]

The charge that the word was not truly preached in English churches, because of the lack of sermons, was a more serious charge since it attacked the Church of England's claim to be a true church. The establishment's defense of reading Scripture without exegesis was a defense of the very power of the word of God itself. To equate preaching or edification with sermons only was to denigrate Scripture, which alone contained all things necessary to salvation. Rather than to a minister's exegesis, John Whitgift averred, "To the Scriptures I give the pre-eminence."[29]

This was by no means to be antisermon, but rather, as Richard Hooker stated: "That which offendeth us is…the great disgrace which they offer unto our custom of bare reading the word of God, and to his gracious Spirit, the principal virtue whereof thereby manifesting itself for the endless good of mens' souls, even the virtue which it hath to convert, to edify, to save souls, this they mightily strive to obscure."[30] For the Prayer Book's supporters, reading *was* preaching: "the only reading of Scripture…is properly to be termed a Preaching."[31] Faith came by the word, not any man's particular interpretation of it, and to say otherwise was to set man's efforts above God's word: "rather that the people should hear us, than God himself."[32] A minister who preached no sermons was nonetheless a valid minister since those "which being not so fully furnished to perform that which in common speech we call preaching, do teach according to the

---

[27]*An answere for the tyme, to the examination put in print…* (London, 1566), 66–67, 72–73. This work lists the bishops' answers to some London ministers' objections to wearing vestments and replies to those answers.

[28]Howard, *A Defense*, 180, 185.

[29]Whitgift, *Works*, 3:342; also 1:182, 206; 3:15, 29–39.

[30]Hooker, *LEP,* 2:88.

[31]Covell, *A Modest and reasonable examination*, 136.

[32]Ibid., 188.

ability given unto them of God, and publish forth his will out of the word, though it be only by reading."[33] Indeed, "how much better hath our Church devised" to make up any deficiencies in the clergy "as namely by the frequent reading of the Scriptures: a matter more available unto faith and godliness....By a most religious and excellent form of Common Prayer....By Sermons and Homilies printed and appointed to be read, both for the confirmation of the faith, and for reformation of manners. All which in a Church not new to be planted...are ordinary effectual means, to continue and increase [the people], in the true faith and fear of God."[34] Moreover, reading was to be preferred to bad preaching.[35]

Even worse, according to John Whitgift, was the "most untrue, and...foul error that 'the life of the sacraments dependeth on the preaching of the word of God'...for the life of the sacraments depend upon God's promises expressed in his word, and neither upon preaching nor upon reading."[36] Robert Some also stressed that the unpreaching ministers' sacraments were valid, for the "word is added to the Element, and it becomes a Sacrament" solely by the Trinitarian formula in baptism and Christ's words of institution in communion.[37] While it might be best if a sacrament such as communion was ministered with a sermon, "that it should not be ministered without a sermon, is absurd...as if, not the word of Christ's Institution, but rather the word of a Minister's exposition, were a necessary and an essential part of the Communion."[38]

Indeed, since it was the essential form of word and element that comprised the substance of a sacrament, it not only did not require a sermon; it did not even require an ordained minister, as some reformers claimed. For "as the word of God is the word of God, by whomsoever it be preached, minister or other," John Whitgift wrote, "so is the sacrament of baptism true baptism, by whomsoever it be celebrated: the usurper of the office hath to answer for his intrusion; but the sacrament is not thereby defiled."[39] Although defenders of the English church denied that the Prayer

---

[33]Richard Cosin, *An Answer To the first principall Treatises of a certeine factious libell...*(London, 1584), 29. Cosin, the dean of Arches, was answering an anonymous work that purported to list laws and canons requiring a learned ministry which the Church of England violated.

[34]*The Answere of...the Universitie*, 16.

[35]Ibid., 15; Covell, *A Modest and reasonable examination*, 132.

[36]Whitgift, *Works*, 3:22.

[37]Some, *A Godly Treatise*, 22–24.

[38]*The Answere of...the Universitie*, 11.

[39]Whitgift, *Works*, 2:531.

Book allowed baptism by women, or any layperson, they also held that such a sacrament, if so done, was valid if the essential form of the sacrament was correct.[40] Like a woman preaching, it was excusable only in times of great necessity and, as Whitgift noted, "there is no such necessity in this church (God be thanked)."[41] Still, while Whitgift and other churchmen in no way condoned the usurpation of clerical offices by the laity or denigrated the high calling of the ministry, they emphasized that there was nothing in the nature of a clergyman which rendered the sacrament—or the preaching of the word—valid at his hands and not at another's. Ordination was a matter of external order; it was neither sacramental in character nor did it convey or confirm a spiritual status: "That God hath committed the ministery of baptism unto special men, it is for orders sake in his Church, and not to the end that their authority might give being or add force to the sacrament itself."[42]

Although not necessary to word or sacrament, still only a minister could legally preach or administer the sacraments in England, and a minister both led and spoke most of the liturgy in worship. Nonetheless, lay participation was higher in the Prayer Book services than in either Catholic or other reformed services. The latter did include set forms of prayer (only the most radical were against *any* prescript forms of prayer), but allowed much more latitude for the minister to frame his own prayers and to adapt the sense of the set prayer to the needs of the congregation. However, whether set or spontaneous prayer, it was always *clergy* prayer, with the minister alone speaking all the prayers and the confession, and the congregation remaining silent except for occasional psalm-singing.[43] By contrast, in the Prayer Book services described above, the clergy were tied to the

[40]Ibid., 2:500–519; *The Answere of…the Universitie*, 11; Covell, *A Modest and reasonable examination*, 190.

[41]Whitgift, *Works*, 2:501. Thomas Hutton noted that preaching was "not utterly forbidden" to women in case of necessity, although, quoting John Calvin, "not ordinarily": *The Second and last part of the answere to the Reasons for refusall of Subscription*, bound with *Reasons for the Refusal* (London, 1605), 99.

[42]Hooker, *LEP*, 2:286.

[43]*Liturgies of the Western Church*, ed. Bard Thompson (Philadelphia: Fortress Press, 1961), includes Calvin's *The Form of Church Prayer* (197–224), which was the basis for John Knox's *The Forme of Prayers* (295–305), drawn up in Geneva in 1556, which was what most English reformers meant by the "Geneva form," and the *Middleburg Liturgy* (322–340), drawn up by reformers in 1586. Bills for adopting a version of the Geneva form as the legal form of worship in England were introduced in the Parliaments of 1584 and 1587. Patrick Collinson, *The Elizabethan Puritan Movement* (Berkeley: University of California Press, 1967), 356–371, still contains the best discussion of the reformers' conception of worship.

prayers of the liturgy, and the congregation made responses and recited such things as the creed and confession. Critics of the English liturgy attacked this congregational participation because it took up too much time, leaving less opportunity for a sermon, and on the grounds that only the minister should speak in church. They argued that the minister ought to have more liberty to frame his own prayers either because spontaneous prayer was more sincere or because such prayer would be more timely to the need of the congregation.

To the Prayer Book's supporters, these criticisms were part and parcel of a clericalism which also lay behind the critics' position of "no sermon, no service" and "no minister, no baptism." They also saw this same clericalism in the reformers' advocacy of presbyterianism, which accompanied demands for changes in worship prior to the 1590s. Defenders of the Elizabethan settlement believed that presbyterianism, like Catholicism, gave the clergy too much independence from the secular magistrate and too much power over the spiritual lives of individuals. Henry Howard warned that if men like Thomas Cartwright were "tolerated and borne withall a little longer, their consistorie would creep from corners to carpets, and their Segniorie ascend from several parishes, to Westminster palace."[44] Richard Cosin called presbyterianism "the popedome which they gape after"[45] and Richard Bancroft claimed the presbyterian reformers sought a "papal jurisdiction [and] they shoot at greater superiority and preeminence, than ever your Bishops did use or challenge unto them: and would no doubt tyrannize…over both prince and people…."[46]

The defenders of the establishment believed this clericalism was both antithetical to English religious sensibility, and dangerous to the basic Protestant doctrine of the priesthood of all believers. They saw the structure of English worship as being deliberately contrived to avoid such a clericalism in which "the people should wholly depend upon the minister's words, and as it were hang upon his lips…."[47]

By no means the least important of the minister's functions in worship was "the public offering up of the prayers of the whole Congregation."[48]

---

[44]Howard, *A defense*, 32.

[45]Cosin, *An Answer To…a certaine factious libell*, iii.

[46]Richard Bancroft, *A Sermon preached at Paules Crosse the 9 of Februarie, being the first Sunday in the Parleament* (London, 1589), 74–77, 93–94.

[47]Whitgift, *Works*, 2:493.

[48]Covell, *A Modest and reasonable examination*, 133.

The minister was, according to Richard Hooker, "to stand and speak in the presence of God" for the congregation.[49] In this the minister had to be viewed as being a leader, and yet a part, of the congregation. "True also it is, Every godly man and woman is a Priest…the people offer up the calves of their lips, and their bodies a living reasonable sacrifice," wrote Thomas Hutton, echoing the words of the Prayer Book's communion service. What set the minister apart from the congregation was only that "they offer up for themselves…but he in public by virtue of his office both for himself, and for them in the name of the congregation…."[50]

It was therefore important that the prayers be those of the people, the *common* prayer, prayers that were known and consented to as being the will of the community. This was seen as exactly what the set prayers of the liturgy were. To Richard Bancroft, a set form of prayers ensured that "poor men by often hearing of them might the better know and understand them, and peradventure have them by heart, or at the least be so cunning in them…that when the minister shall begin with any prayer, understanding before the drift thereof, their hearts might fully concur with him in every particular sentence, and with a better resolution in the end say, Amen." Bancroft charged that the reformers would rather have the minister pray

> as the spirit of God shall move his heart, to that effect, framing himself according to the time and occasion….If he conceiving a prayer upon the sudden, shall after say it was to the same purpose that is prescribed in the book, you may not control him. And how by such kind of prayers you are like to be edified, and in what danger you are thereby left, he is of simple judgement that cannot discern it….For sometimes they will so wander either by error or malice, in framing their prayers…that no true Christian, if he had time to consider of their meaning, ought in charity when they have done, to say, Amen….[51]

Thomas Hutton maintained that "prayers advisedly, deliberately, reverently aforehand thought upon are accordingly to be received." He asked,

[49]Hooker, *LEP,* 2:114.
[50]Hutton, *The Second and last part of the answere,* 41.
[51]Bancroft, *A Sermon,* 64–67. William Covell agreed that "it bringeth much advantage to have the people familiar with those prayers, which concern all; and that they may not say Amen, to any thing that is unsound…the voluntary, sudden, and extemporal supplications of one man…may easily fail in asking what is behooveful for the whole Church": *A Modest and reasonable examination,* 178–179.

"Is more attention due to the wiser, and of more experience the Church of England, or some one of a private, fantastic, broken wit, many or one, the aged discreet mother, or one of her wantons...?"[52] A liturgy set forth by authority embodied consent, since as Richard Cosin stated, when a reformer referred to the canon law as churchmen's own law, "he might have said as well his and every Englishman's laws, for all be parties to an act of Parliament."[53] And it was an act of Parliament which had established religion in England, including the liturgy. So Thomas Hutton defended the minor changes in the 1604 Prayer Book as "small additions," agreeable to the Articles of Religion, and not a real alteration in the Prayer Book, which, like an alteration in religion, only the monarch and Parliament could effect.[54]

So too, in view of a congregation's particular needs, "small additions, and explanations" could be made to the liturgy; such were allowable "upon occasion of the plague, and pestilence...or other some like cause," or in the case of port towns which had set prayers "for our Merchants and merchandise." But the condition in all such cases was that the additions be "all consonant to the truth of God's word, and the book of common prayer" and not "so many alterations, augmentations, diminutions, differences, that the book in a little while would not be like itself."[55] That would destroy the very unity the *Book of Common Prayer* embodied and promoted, "the unity of the spirit in the bond of peace," in which uniformity was "a gracious outward good means to knit us all in one...."[56]

Since the English liturgy contained above all the people's prayers, and since the minister was always speaking *for* them when not speaking the word of God *to* them, there was no reason why the people could not speak. "For, although it be true that the minister is the mouth of the people to God, yet doth it not follow that he is the 'only mouth of the people unto the Lord,'" John Whitgift wrote. Although in the Bible the people gave their

---

[52]Hutton, *Reasons for the Refusal,* 46–47, 72.

[53]Cosin, *An answer To...a certaine factious libell,* 34.

[54]Hutton, *Reasons for the Refusal,* 77. The reformers also acknowledged this point in their attempts to use Parliament to further reformation. The exact division of authority in religious matters between the Church, Parliament, and the monarchy was not completely clear; the reforming party was frustrated both in Convocation and in Parliament, and what changes and additions the monarchy made in the liturgy from time to time were too minor to constitute an alteration in religion—until the ascendency of Archbishop Laud under Charles I.

[55]Ibid., 138–39.

[56]Ibid., 47.

consent to prayers pronounced by their priests with "Amen," yet that in no way meant "that they ought only to say 'Amen,' and at no time join as well in voice as in heart with the minister."[57]

In fact, unlike preaching or providing the sacraments, there was no part of the usual English worship service which could not be conducted by a lay person. Laymen had been licensed to lead services in the early years of Elizabeth's reign, in order to fill the vacancies left by the deprived Marian clergy. Although forbidden to preach or provide the sacraments (except emergency baptism), these readers were allowed to conduct daily and weekly services, bury the dead, and church women. They seem to have been replaced by ordained ministers by 1564—most of the readers themselves were eventually ordained—and lay readers were forbidden by the 1571 Canons.[58] Yet their existence dramatized the spiritual equality between clergy and laity which lay at the heart of Protestantism and the Prayer Book, an equality which made the ministerial role—however exalted and important the ministerial calling—a matter of order and a form of ecclesiastical magistracy. It does appear that ministers, on occasion, continued to have laymen read Scripture or a part of the service. Richard Baxter's childhood minister, because of failing eyesight, "said Common Prayer without book: but for the reading of the psalms and Chapters, he got a common thresher and day laborer one year, and a tailor another year."[59] Thomas Hutton recalled a minister who, performing his daughter's marriage, simply handed her the book to read her vows, instead of repeating them after him. At least one woman was so determined to have her churching, despite her reformist minister's objections, that "she did take the Book of Common Prayer and read the thanksgiving herself openly in church."[60] Such lay presumptions were not approved of—the nonmarrying minister and the self-churching woman were both disciplined—but only as a matter of order, not blasphemy or spiritual presumption, for no part of the Common Prayer was exclusively the minister's.

---

[57]Whitgift, *Works*, 2:492.

[58]*Visitation Articles*, 3:67. (Injunctions to be subscribed by the readers, included in the bishops' Interpretations.) Also see John Strype, *Annals of the Reformation*, 4 vols. (Oxford, 1824), 1(part 1): 203–226; *1571 Canons*, 6.

[59]From Baxter's autobiography, printed in T. M. Parker, *The English Reformation to 1558*, 2d ed. (New York: Oxford University Press, 1966), 153–154.

[60]Hutton, *The Second and last part of the answere*, 97; David Cressy, "Purification, Thanksgiving and the Churching of Women in Post-Reformation England," *Past and Present* 141 (1993): 130.

The Prayer Book's advocates believed the congregation's participation not only expressed this essential spiritual equality, but also unity. Therefore the practice was not only allowable, but commendable: "custom and example tell us that this…is to the people an advantage, whose universal consent exprest by their voices, is like the roaring of the waves against the sea bank."[61] Richard Hooker also stressed the importance of the laity's giving voice in worship, to "openly declare ourselves united as brethren in one."[62] Thomas Hutton felt the congregation's participation not only emphasized the communal and consensual nature of the service, the unity it expressed, but also each individual's application of the service to himself or herself. So important was the need for the people to participate, that Saint Paul's prohibition against women's speaking in church did not, in this context, apply.[63]

The belief that religion should be, above all, unifying and personal can also be seen in the understanding of the sacraments by the Prayer Book's defenders. All of them maintained the orthodox Reformed understanding of the relationship between sacraments and salvation. Salvation, or justification, was determined by God's eternal decrees of election. Therefore, the sacraments did not convey justifying grace, nor was "the necessity of salvation so tied to the sacraments, that whosoever hath the external signs shall therefore be saved."[64] So baptism was, according to Hooker, "a seal perhaps to the grace of election before received."[65] But the Prayer Book's supporters were adamant that issues of justification—who were the elect, who comprised the mystical body of the invisible church—were known only to God, and "God's secrets are not to be searched, but adored."[66] Since it could only be known who was in the visible church here on earth, not of the invisible church of the elect, church services, including the sacraments, should express the charity and inclusion to all who made any external profession of Christianity. So too, the church was to pray that all men be saved, because "it is the revealed will of God; and although we know that all are not, yet because we know not exactly who are…charity commandeth for to pray for all."[67] Neither the church nor anyone else should be concerned

---

[61]Covell, *A Modest and reasonable examination*, 190.
[62]Hooker, *LEP*, 2:148.
[63]Hutton, *The Second and last part of the answere*, 98.
[64]Whitgift, *Works*, 2:537.
[65]Hooker, *LEP*, 2:256.
[66]Some, *A Godly Treatise*, 3.
[67]Covell, *A Modest and reasonable examination*, 193.

with sorting out the elect since "in this world it cannot certainly be by any man determined who among Christians is faithful, who be unfaithful."[68]

Moreover, the doctrine of predestination was not to denigrate the role of sacraments. The Prayer Book's defenders emphasized the efficacy of sacraments, that "a sacrament can never be without promise of salvation."[69] Indeed, that promise, really and truly affixed to the sacrament, was what made the sacrament and set it apart from mere ceremonies. A sacrament did not convey or guarantee salvation, but nonetheless it was a manifestation and an assurance of a share in the promise of salvation annexed to it. As Richard Hooker explained: "we take not baptism nor the Eucharist for bare resemblances or memorials of things absent, neither for naked signs and testimonies assuring us of grace received before, but (as they are in deed and in verity) for means effectual whereby God...delivereth into our hands that grace available unto eternal life, which grace the sacraments represent or signify."[70] John Whitgift referred to communion as "the sacrament of unity" and baptism as the "sacrament of faith" and insisted that there was such a similarity between sacrament and thing signified that in this world everyone must count the baptized as having faith and those communing to be one with Christ.[71] So too Thomas Hutton: "It is an effectual sign;...therefore we may affirm God will give the child baptised eternal life...."[72] Therefore, both Whitgift and Bancroft agreed on the urgency of baptizing a child near death: "what Christian would willingly suffer his child to die without the sacrament of regeneration, the lack whereof (though it be not a necessity) yet may it seem to be a probable token and sign of reprobation."[73]

In short, their position seemed to be that while salvation came from justification alone, and justification was predestined, yet the sacraments were signs which were so truly the things they signified that a providential God most probably, although not absolutely, would not allow them to be bestowed on a person He had not elected. Thus lack of baptism was no sure

[68]Whitgift, *Works*, 3:138.

[69]Some, *A Godly Treatise*, 28–29.

[70]Hooker, *LEP*, 2:247. See also Howard, *A Defense*, 136.

[71]Whitgift, *Works*, 3:112, 130, 356–357. The remark on communion was made in a discussion about its propriety at marriage services. On baptism, Whitgift quotes Saint Augustine.

[72]Hutton, *Reasons for the Refusal*, 170–171.

[73]The words are Whitgift's (*Works*, 2:537–538) but Bancroft uses virtually the same words: see Nicholas Tyacke, *Anti-Calvinists: The Rise of English Arminianism* (Oxford: Clarendon Press, 1982), 15–16.

sign a dead child was not elect, but being baptized was an assurance of the child's election. With adults the church insisted questions of salvation should be private, not public: "hypocrites and dissemblers who would seem to profess the gospel...we must count professors because we see not their hearts," nor can one person, even a minister, judge another's perception of his spiritual state.[74] "Let a man examine himself....The Apostle doth not say, Let every man examine the rest of the communicants."[75] Both at baptism and burial, a person could be referred to as saved "for anything the church of God knoweth to the contrary."[76] Thus the Prayer Book advocates held the inclusivity of the English church was based in a right understanding of the doctrine of predestination and was spiritually warranted, as well as being congenial to the practical needs of a national church that wished to have coterminous religious and civic memberships. The effect, in terms of practical spirituality and public worship, was to eliminate predestination as an issue.[77]

This was certainly true of the Prayer Book, which stressed the unity of the congregation and the individual application of spiritual benefits, as well as limiting the role of the minister, who had neither sacerdotal powers (since the ultimate effect of the sacraments lay in a predetermined faith) nor the ability to judge the state of another's salvation. Two examples of this personal focus were in the communion service itself, in contrast to Genevan practice: the exhortation to communion, which urged self-examination and private preparation beforehand (as opposed to examination by the minister) and the use of the singular "thou" instead of the plural "ye" in the words of administration, which John Whitgift defended not only on the grounds that the singular included the plural, but that everyone had to apply the sacrament to himself individually.[78] In his study of lay religious

---

[74]Whitgift, *Works*, 1:380. "I will not enter into your hearts to judge what you think of your inward purity": ibid., 1:174.

[75]Some, *A Godly Treatise*, 18.

[76]Hutton, *Reasons for the Refusal*, 167; *The Second and last part of the answere*, 1–10.

[77]Diarmaid MacCulloch refers to this as a "credal" predestination, "merely accepting predestination as one aspect of the whole range of Christian doctrine" and not giving it a central position in spiritual life: *The Later Reformation in England 1547–1603* (New York: St. Martin's Press, 1990), 89.

[78]*BCP*, 258–259, 264; Whitgift, 3:97. Peter Lake has noted that Whitgift had a focus on individual and inward preparation that stressed a concern for one's own spirituality, not others': *Anglicans and Puritans? Presbyterianism and English Conformist Thought from Whitgift to Hooker* (London: Unwin Hyman, 1988), 40. Lutherans and the Catholic mass also used the plural second person, but all other reformed churches used the singular. See William Seth Adams, "Given and Shed for Whom? A Study of the Words of Administration," *Anglican Theological Review* 67 (1985): 31–45.

thought in England between 1590 and 1640, Marc Schwarz found that such an emphasis on personal religion and resistance to clerical control transcended any religious differences among the Protestant laity.[79]

The Prayer Book's defenders staunchly maintained it was rooted in the solidly reformed doctrine of the Thirty-Nine Articles,[80] but the Prayer Book's references to the doctrine of election were oblique, not the didactic expositions those more in tune with continental reformed religion wanted. Alister McGrath has noted that doctrine plays a role in religious identity by marking off one group from another: we believe this, they believe that. Doctrinal formulation is thus most pronounced when a group feels a need to elaborate fully its reasons for separate social existence on the basis of belief. Thus there was an ever-increasing elaboration of doctrine in continental Europe in the later sixteenth century, especially in Germany, as Catholic, Lutheran, and Reformed found themselves in close proximity and competition. Doctrinal formulation is also, by its very nature, divisive, adding new criteria for membership into the faith community by its further definitions of faith. In contrast, a religious group which has its identity rooted in a social and/or political basis—such as a national church—eschews such elaborations of doctrine in favor of unity, by focusing on such aspects of belief as are beyond dispute and the outward show of the individual's unity with the community. This attitude toward doctrine encourages keeping theological speculation and formulation inward, individual, and limited. It tolerates a good deal of private religious opinion, as long as the holders of such opinion keep it to themselves and do not seek to impose it on the whole community. This is, of course, what Elizabeth I meant by "not opening windows into men's souls."[81]

---

[79]Marc L. Schwarz, "The Religious Thought of the Protestant Laity in England, 1590–1640" (Ph.D. dissertation, University of California, Los Angeles, 1965). Schwarz found that while "Anglican" laymen might embrace Arminianism, they rejected the sacerdotalism of the Arminian high clergy, which made the laity dependent upon the sacraments—and the clergy—for salvation. "Puritan" laymen used the doctrine of predestination to affirm their soteriological independence of the clergy.

[80]For example, Thomas Rogers, *The English Creede, consenting with the true auncient catholique and apostolique Church in al the points, and articles of Religion which everie Christian is to knowe and beleeve that would be saved* (London, 1585 & 1587). Rogers called the Thirty-Nine Articles "the badge of English Christians" (*2) and held that the Prayer Book was so grounded on them that no one refused to subscribe the Prayer Book because of its doctrine, but only because of questions about "directions and rubrics."

[81]Alister E. McGrath, *The Genesis of Doctrine: A Study in the Foundations of Doctrinal Criticism* (Oxford: Basil Blackwell, 1990), 37–52. Diarmaid MacCulloch has said "the English lack of capacity for abstract theological invention is so marked through national history as to constitute a dangerously

Instead of doctrinal issues, whose medium was the sermon, the services of the English church stressed Christian fundamentals: Scripture, creeds, confession, prayers. Scripture awakened faith through knowledge of God's saving work in Christ, creeds rehearsed the details of the Incarnation and Passion, confession presented the sinner for Christ's mercy to those He had redeemed, and prayers gave thanksgiving for benefits received and supplications for mercies yet to come. The Prayer Book's advocates argued that these things all directed the worshiper to the proper focus of worship, which was Christ, the cause and source of both justification and sanctification, the "we in him and he in us" of the Prayer Book, the origin of both word and sacrament in whom was the unity and life of the church. Richard Hooker began his entire exposition on the sacraments with the Incarnation: "for as our natural life consisteth in the union of the body with the soul; so our life supernatural in the union of the soul with God. And...there is no union of God with man without that mean between both which is both...."[82] Too much discoursing on God's eternal decrees of election obscured the centrality of Christ and the Cross. Richard Bancroft maintained "that when you have attained the true grounds of Christian religion, and are constantly built by a lively faith upon that notable foundation...which is Jesus Christ, being incorporated into his mystical body in your baptism by the holy Ghost: and afterwards nourished with the heavenly food...in the Lord's supper: you then content yourselves and seek no farther...."[83]

The Prayer Book's supporters argued that the ceremonies of the English church, indifferent in themselves, reinforced this Christocentricity. Therefore they were not only appropriate, but even a "secondary" means of edification because ceremonies in worship kept the worshiper properly directed, and in the proper state of mind. A ceremony stirred

---

plausible argument for persistent national characteristics": *Later Reformation*, 66. In *The Religion of Protestants*, Patrick Collinson has shown that, within the fairly broad boundaries of the 39 Articles, the Elizabethan and Jacobean church tolerated a wide range of theological opinion and doctrinal interpretation among its bishops, from committed Calvinists to proto-Arminians, *de jure divino* advocates to determined "low-churchers." It worked because all were seen as being in the bounds of accepted belief, and the English church—most of it—was not particularly interested in issues of doctrinal refinement and also because the bishops balanced each other out and no one group of opinion was able to impose its views on the whole church, a situation that changed, with disastrous results, under Charles I.

[82] Hooker, *LEP*, 2:208.
[83] Bancroft, *A Sermon*, 41.

those gathered "with greater holiness to become outwardly religious" while it prevented them "from wavering in that they do, and others from contempt of that which is done." So ceremonies were "the hedge of devotion, and though not the principal points, yet…intermediate means not to be despised of a better and more religious service."[84]

Because of its Christocentric meaning, kneeling at communion was not idolatry, for "no man is so foolish as to adore the sign, but the thing itself represented by the sign"[85] and "the whole action of this supper is a thanksgiving" for the benefits of Christ's death and passion.[86] So worshipers "declare the thankfulness of our hearts, with the reverence and curtsey of our knees," and at what more appropriate time than at the reception of the tokens of redemption?[87] Bowing at the name of Jesus was likewise "no superstition, but an outward sign of our inward subjection to his divine Majesty, and an apparant token of our devotion";[88] surely "neither can it be against Christianity to shew bodily reverence, when he is named."[89] Due to their Christological content, the Benedictus, Nunc Dimittis and Magnificat were "especially profitable" because they contained "the mystery of our salvation [by Christ] and the praise of God for the same."[90]

The liturgical calendar of the English church also reinforced this Christocentricity, and it was the holy days associated with Christ that were most warmly defended. John Whitgift extolled the observance of Good Friday and Easter because "they draw us to a more near consideration of the benefits that we have received by the death, passion and resurrection of Christ." The universities were appalled that reformers would have men work on holy days, "on the very feast of Christ's Nativity," and William Covell singled out the Transfiguration and Annunciation for praise.[91]

For the Prayer Book's advocates, devotion was the key to sanctification and an end in itself of worship; doctrine was not. For a committed Calvinist ideologue, of course, the exact opposite was true. The worship provided by

[84]Covell, *A Modest and reasonable examination*, 55.
[85]Howard, *A Defense*, 140.
[86]Whitgift, *Works*, 3:91–92.
[87]Howard, *A Defense*, 139.
[88]*The Answere of…the Universitie*, 14.
[89]Whitgift, *Works*, 3:390–391.
[90]Ibid., 2:477–482. See also Covell, *A Modest and reasonable examination*, 189.
[91]Whitgift, *Works*, 2:568–569 (Easter); 1:232–233 (Good Friday); *The Answere of…the Universitie*, 13; Covell, *A Modest and reasonable examination*, 191.

the Prayer Book, and envisioned by its supporters, did not expound on the intellectual comprehension of doctrinal points. Rather it stirred up a dynamic outpouring of Christ-centered devotion by a people unified as one in Him. This was the process of sanctification, as understood by the English religious establishment, and the proper purpose and benefit of worship, whose ordinary means were "diligent reading and hearing of the word of God, joined with earnest and hearty prayer."[92] Scripture and prayer interacted in the person of the worshiper; prayer made the worshiper fitter to hear the word, and kindled a desire to know God. The mind receiving God's word was made fitter to pray and stirred up to more fervent prayer. So a unity, a knitting of heart and mind, body, and soul, occurred within the worshiper as he or she experienced and expressed unity with the congregation and Christ.[93] Thus, public prayer had more virtue, force, and efficacy than private prayers, because corporate worship wrapped each person in this unity, making up for individual deficiencies. By the end of Elizabeth's reign, corporate prayer was so valued and esteemed by some that it was implicitly held to be a third sign of a true church and more edifying than sermons.[94]

Also by the early 1600s, England's years of relative religious peace compared to the continent were seen as a sign of God's pleasure with England's worship of Him.[95] Since the time of the Marian exile, the Prayer Book's supporters had held that the English church, consonant in essentials with other reformed churches, had no need to conform its services to continental models.[96] Its advocates held that English worship embodied a distinctly *English* reformed Christianity. The Prayer Book had been blessed

[92]Whitgift, *Works*, 2:443.

[93]Hooker, *LEP*, 2:140; Covell, *A Modest and reasonable examination*, 186–187. Covell was directly influenced by Hooker.

[94]Hooker, *LEP*, 110–114. Hooker puts corporate prayer on the same level with doctrine in his image of doctrine descending from heaven and prayer ascending as part of a continuing interchange between God and mankind. In book 3 (1:205), Hooker names corporate prayer as one of the church's three "apostolical duties," the other two of which, instruction (the word preached) and the breaking of bread (sacrament), are recognized marks of a true church. See also Covell, *A Modest and reasonable examination*, 177, 188. Hooker, Covell, and Bancroft elevated the Prayer Book to a near necessity for the English church.

[95]For example, William Covell: "the miraculous blessings bestowed and continued upon this land could not otherwise be rightly understood, than the true effects of that church which was planted in it": *A Modest and reasonable examination*, preface. The universities argued that to conform to continental churches would be to conform to "the calamities of other places": *The Answere of…the Universities*, 30.

[96]Whitgift, *Works*, 2:452.

and sanctified by the blood of English martyrs under Queen Mary I.[97] After more than forty years of use, the Prayer Book had become a bond in the timeless communion of English saints, linking past and present, "between our forefathers, and our generations after us to execute the service of the Lord before him, in our Liturgy."[98] Moreover, by the reign of James I, the Prayer Book had risen in the estimation of its supporters: from simply "a godly book" it had become "not the like this day extant in Christendom," "a most holy and chaste form of Church service," whose "irreprovable collects" mirrored the true Christian heart.[99] It was no longer merely an acceptable but the best form of worship, contempt of which was worse than contempt of prayer itself, and despising it was the source of "all atheism and hypocracy."[100]

This increasing estimation of the Prayer Book's central role in English religious identity caused some of its advocates to elevate it ever closer to the same level of importance as doctrine. No English churchman, or layman, explicitly made the Prayer Book an essential part of the English church, as was true doctrine, i.e., that without it, the English church was not a true church. But they came as close as they dared. The turning point was Richard Bancroft's sermon at Saint Paul's Cross in 1589. Taking the old (by then) theme of the Prayer Book being sealed by the blood of English martyrs, Bancroft added a crucial innovation. He argued that the authority of "our learned English fathers," such as Thomas Cranmer, was as competent to judge in matters of "ceremonies, forms of prayer" as in matters of faith and doctrine. Then Bancroft explicitly equated quarreling with the Prayer Book to quarreling with the Thirty-Nine Articles.[101] So too, as noted above, Richard Hooker and William Covell also elevated the Prayer Book

---

[97]For example, Howard, *A Defense*, 190; Whitgift, *Works*, 2:494–495; Covell, *A Modest and reasonable examination*, 182–184; Hutton, *Reasons for the Refusal*, 50.

[98]Covell, *A Modest and reasonable examination*, preface. Hutton also comments on the length of the liturgy's use as a bond: *Reasons for the Refusal*, 199.

[99]Whitgift, *Works*, 1:173. Whitgift explicitly denied that he thought the Prayer Book "perfect," since that applied only to Scripture; Bancroft, *A Sermon*, 53; Covell, *A Modest and reasonable examination*, 183; Hutton, *The Second and last part of the answere*, 21–25, 42–45.

[100]Covell, *A Modest and reasonable examination*, 177–179.

[101]Bancroft, *A Sermon*, 43–44: "is it likely that that Church which was able to discern betwixt truth and falsehood in so great points of doctrine being wrapped through continuance of time in so deep an obscurity; should be unable to judge of ceremonies, forms of prayer, decency, order, edification, and such like circumstances of no greater weight? You would not, I think, take it in good part, that men should now begin to sift and quarrel at the articles of religion…yet I see no reason why they may not as well do it, as to carp and control at such orders, as were then likewise established for order and government."

to a level near doctrine by implicitly making corporate prayer a mark of a true church.

By the time of the Jacobean church, therefore, the *Book of Common Prayer* had become an integral part of an English religious identity that it had played no little part in shaping. Rooted in the Bible, the Prayer Book's services stressed the spiritual equality of all, especially clergy and laity. It filtered doctrine, especially potentially divisive doctrine, through the unity of corporate worship and sacraments and emphasized Christ, Christian fundamentals, and a personal, devotional spirituality. This, then, was English reformed Christianity, as embodied, promoted, and understood in the *Book of Common Prayer.*

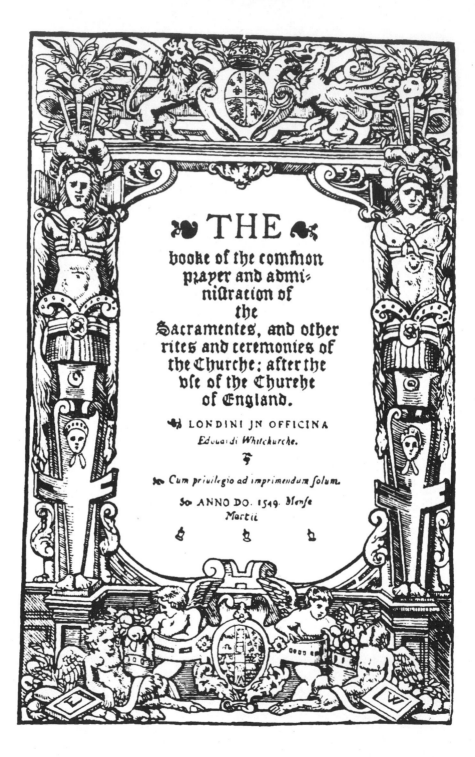

THE
booke of the common
prayer and admi-
nistration of
the
Sacramentes, and other
rites and ceremonies of
the Churche; after the
vse of the Churche
of England.

LONDINI JN OFFICINA
Edouardi Whitchurche.

Cum priuilegio ad imprimendum solum.

ANNO DO. 1549. Mense
Martii

"FRUITFUL PREACHING"
in the DIOCESE *of* WORCESTER

Bishop Hugh Latimer and His Influence, 1535–1539[1]

Susan Wabuda

During his morning sermon before the Convocation of the Clergy on 9 June 1536, Bishop Hugh Latimer of Worcester expressed some of his most cherished views on the role of the clergy as Christ's stewards. He admonished the bishops and other prelates because they did not preach. Latimer declared: "'What is this I hear of you?' God would ask. 'You preach very seldom.'" Latimer also observed that the high clergy persecuted good preachers and he warned his audience that God would castigate them for their efforts to bring preachers into shame, contempt, and even worse: "'Yea, more than this, ye pull them into perils, into prisons, and, as much as in you lieth, to cruel deaths.'"[2]

Latimer's criticism of the clergy in his convocation sermon was based upon three main premises. First, the English clergy as a whole was not performing one of the major responsibilities entrusted to it by God. Jesus himself had commanded his followers to "Feed my sheep," which had been interpreted by the church to mean that priests were supposed to preach to the people. Second, Latimer argued that God had not commanded priests to "teach your own traditions, and seek your own glory and profit." Therefore, when they had preached on purgatory or the honor paid to images of the saints, they had promoted themselves and "counterfeit doctrine." Third, when there were preachers who were "faithful dispensers of God's

---

[1]Versions of this paper were delivered before Professor Patrick Collinson's seminar at Trinity College, Cambridge, and the Tudor and Stuart Seminar at the Institute of Historical Research, led by Professor Conrad Russell. I wish to thank all of those in attendance for their helpful comments, and most especially I am grateful to Professor A. G. Dickens for his encouragement.

[2]*Sermons by Hugh Latimer, Sometime Bishop of Worcester, Martyr, 1555*, ed. George Elwes Corrie (Cambridge, 1844), 38.

mysteries," who did advance God's commandments, they found that their work was "trodden underfoot."[3] Latimer denounced the persecution that many of those sitting in convocation had inflicted upon reforming preachers.

Of all the leaders of the effort to reform the English church in the sixteenth century, undoubtedly Hugh Latimer was the greatest preacher. Many historians have written about his sermons and his preaching skills, and his role in promoting reformed doctrine in England. His execution for heresy on 16 October 1555 has also received much attention from scholars.[4] However, other aspects of his career, especially his tenure as bishop of Worcester, and his patronage of preachers there and elsewhere, have not been adequately explored.[5]

Although Latimer's criticism of some traditional practices, including pilgrimages and purgatory, was an unwelcome innovation to many of his listeners during his convocation sermon, he was hardly advocating anything new when he advised the episcopal bench to preach. The standard for preaching had been set by Saint Paul himself, who charged bishops Timothy and Titus to "Preach the word."[6] And even if bishops had so many pressing duties that they could not fulfill their responsibilities themselves, they were supposed to introduce good preachers into their dioceses.

During the Middle Ages, the bishops' duty to send itinerant preachers to the areas under their jurisdiction was recognized by the Fourth Lateran Council, and was based upon Paul's determination in his Epistle to the Romans that patrons who would send preachers out to the multitude were necessary to encourage faith: "And how shall they preach, except they be

---

[3]"Feed my sheep": John 21:15–17, cited by Latimer, *Sermons*, 33–40, esp. 38.

[4]Latimer as a preacher has been most recently discussed by Rosemary O'Day, "Hugh Latimer: Prophet of the Kingdom," *Historical Research* 65 (1992): 258–276; and Martha C. Skeeters, *Community and Clergy: Bristol and the Reformation c. 1530–c.1570* (Oxford: Clarendon Press, 1993), 38–46. Allan G. Chester, *Hugh Latimer: Apostle to the English* (Philadelphia: University of Pennsylvania Press, 1954), is the fullest treatment but is no longer adequate in light of recent studies of the English Reformation. See also Harold S. Darby, *Hugh Latimer* (London: Epworth Press, 1953). For Latimer's execution, see Patrick Collinson, "Truth and Legend: The Veracity of John Foxe's Book of Martyrs," *Elizabethan Essays* (London: Hambledon Press, 1994), 177.

[5]Professor G. R. Elton briefly considered the imposition of the royal supremacy and reforms in Worcester diocese from the standpoint of policies that were created by Henry VIII and Thomas Cromwell in *Policy and Police: The Enforcement of the Reformation in the Age of Thomas Cromwell* (Cambridge: Cambridge University Press, 1972), 30–32, 35–37, 88, 117, 121–123, 132, 298–299, 317–318, 375–380. See also Joseph Block, "Thomas Cromwell's Patronage of Preaching," *Sixteenth Century Journal* 8 (1977), 37.

[6]2 Tim. 4:2. Also 1 Tim. 2:7–15, 3:1–16, 4:6–16; 2 Tim. 2:23–26; Tit. 1:9–16, 2:1, 9–15, 3:1–11.

---

sent?...So then faith cometh by hearing, and hearing by the word of God."[7] All English bishops, or their deputies, had the right and responsibility to license clergymen to preach throughout their dioceses.

Latimer's awareness of his duty to sponsor preachers is the subject of this essay. I have shown elsewhere how Archbishop Thomas Cranmer used his powers for licensing itinerant preachers to promote reformers and religious change. Latimer and Cranmer worked hand-in-hand to advance reforming preachers.[8] We can use Latimer's patronage of preachers when he was bishop of Worcester from 1535 to 1539 to trace his efforts to encourage religious change in his diocese. I wish to demonstrate that Latimer disturbed the balance of local interests by allying himself with gentlemen and prominent merchants who shared his interest in promoting reforming preachers. While Latimer was not ultimately successful in establishing long-lasting reforms in his diocese, his efforts caused great concern among conservative officials during and after his brief tenure as bishop.

Much of our information about Latimer's promotion of preachers comes from material preserved in episcopal records at the Hereford and Worcester Record Office,[9] and the State Papers collection at the Public Record Office. Unfortunately, the sources we would most like to have, sermons by Latimer's licensees, are almost completely lacking. The early reformers as a group printed few sermons during Henry VIII's reign, perhaps because it was too dangerous for them to do so, and many manuscript versions of sermons have not survived. Nevertheless, even without the reformers' sermons, we can begin to determine what they believed and

---

[7]See the decree in "X. De praedicatoribus instituendis," in *Sacrorum Conciliorum nova, et amplissima collectio*, ed. J. Mansi (Venice, 1778), 22: cols. 998–999; Rom. 10:14–17. Latimer often made reference to this verse in *Sermons*, e.g. 123, 178, 200–201, 290–291.

[8]Susan Wabuda, "Setting Forth the Word of God: Archbishop Cranmer's Early Patronage of Preachers," in *Thomas Cranmer: Churchman and Scholar*, ed. Paul Ayris and David Selwyn (Woodbridge: Boydell Press, 1993): 75–88. For Bishop John Longland of Lincoln's control of itinerant preachers, see Margaret Bowker, *The Henrician Reformation: The Diocese of Lincoln under John Longland 1521–1547* (Cambridge: Cambridge University Press, 1981), 144–146, 163–168.

[9]Chester was unable to see Latimer's Register. The registers have been described in David M. Smith's *Guide to Bishops' Registers of England and Wales: A Survey from the Middle Ages to the Abolition of Episcopacy in 1646* (London: Royal Historical Society, 1981), 226–228. Since the shelf numbers for the sources at the H[ereford and] W[orcester] R[ecord] O[ffice] are rather long, they will be referred to as follows: b716.093 BA.2648/7(ii) = Morton's Register; b716.093 BA.2648/8(ii) = Ghinucci's Register I; b716.093 BA.2648/9(i) = Ghinucci's Register II; b716.093 BA.2648/9(ii) = Latimer's Register; b716.093 BA.2648/9(iii) = Bell's Register; b716.093 BA.2648/9(iv) = Heath's Register; 802/BA.2764 = Bell's Visitation Book.

preached, as other sources have been preserved, including letters and accusations raised against them.

What were the reforms that Latimer wanted to encourage in Worcester diocese and in England as a whole? And why were the views of Latimer and his preachers so contentious that many of their hearers wished to suppress them? In the 1530s, Latimer and his friends questioned many traditional tenets concerning the nature of salvation and how it was achieved. Following in the footsteps of the continental reformers, Latimer challenged the existence of purgatory, and with it the elaborate beliefs, ceremonies, and practices employed in English society to help expedite souls to heaven through good works. He raised questions concerning the efficacy of masses that were celebrated for the dead, the role of the saints as mediators, the power of relics, and the usefulness of pilgrimages.

It would be incorrect, however, to argue that Latimer simply wanted to sweep away many traditional usages in the church in the 1530s. His position was much more complicated and subtle. Having been endangered several times during his early career, Latimer learned that "preachers must be wary and circumspect, that they give not any just occasion to be slandered and ill spoken of by the hearers." Latimer maintained that he opposed the "abuses" of many tenets, rather than the underlying doctrines themselves. One example can illustrate the complexity of his views. Preaching during Edward VI's reign, Latimer remembered that he had been criticized years earlier for his opinions concerning the Virgin Mary. He maintained that he had argued in his sermons that "our blessed lady, which conceived and bare Christ in her womb, did ever after resemble the manners and virtues of that precious babe that she bare." Misunderstanding him, his audience spread the rumor that Latimer had disseminated an old Lollard heresy, that Mary was no better than any other woman, any more than a bag of spice resembled the spice. Latimer denied that he had ever "used that similitude." He would maintain that his views of the Virgin were completely honorable and orthodox. Nevertheless, even if Latimer had never said the words imputed to him by his listeners, it cannot be denied that his implication undermined the idea that Mary could intercede for sinners. Latimer would perceive Mary's role as mediator as an abuse, even if he shrank from articulating this dangerous opinion clearly. Through the skillful use of ambivalence, Latimer could impress controversial opinions upon his audiences, and yet protect himself from charges of heresy.[10]

In his early sermons, Latimer made no plain statement concerning his ideas on justification by faith, and the role of works. But his sermons were notable for what they did not say, as much as for what they did. Latimer emphasized "the merits of the bitter passion of Christ," and the necessity for Christians to believe in them and keep Christ's commandments. Although keeping Christ's commandments would not preclude the possibility of the role of good works in salvation, Latimer recommended relieving the poor rather than the "building of churches, giving of ornaments, going on pilgrimages," and other works.[11]

By the time he was bishop, Latimer may have embraced the Protestant view that the Christian was justified by faith alone, and not good works, but his habitual ambivalence does not permit us to say so with total certainty. As the government was only gradually beginning to determine what constituted orthodoxy for the English church, it was far too dangerous for many preachers to define their beliefs precisely in public. But Latimer's comment in a letter to Cromwell in 1537, when he wrote to recommend the preaching of Robert Barnes, strongly implies that Latimer supported Protestant opinions. "Surely he is alone in handling a piece of scripture, and in setting forth of Christ he hath no fellow." Latimer's implication here was that Barnes could preach Christ, that salvation came through Christ and belief in him, and not through any other form.[12] As we will see, Latimer supported other preachers who believed in the doctrine of justification by faith alone, including Thomas Garrard, and Edward Large.

The fact that Latimer could encourage religious change, or that he was a bishop at all, was due to the protection he enjoyed at court. Even excluding his unorthodox views, Latimer was an unusual choice for

---

[10]*Sermons*, 41–58 (abuses), 60–61 (Virgin Mary; wariness of preachers).

[11]See the Sermons on the Card, *Sermons*, 3–24.

[12]*Sermons and Remains*, ed. George Elwes Corrie (Cambridge, 1845), 389. Also, *Miscellaneous Writings and Letters of Thomas Cranmer, Archbishop of Canterbury, Martyr, 1556*, ed. John Edmund Cox (Cambridge, 1846) 339; W. D. J. Cargill Thompson, "The Sixteenth-Century Editions of *A Supplication unto King Henry the Eighth* by Robert Barnes, D.D.: A Footnote to the History of the Royal Supremacy," *Transactions of the Cambridge Bibliographical Society* 3 (1960), 133–42; James P. Lusardi, "The Career of Robert Barnes" in *The Complete Works of Saint Thomas More*, ed. Louis A. Shuster et al. (New Haven: Yale University Press, 1973), 8:1367–1415. Dr. John Craig has recently discovered important new evidence of a previously unknown sermon by Barnes among documents in the Warwickshire County Record Office.

bishop. He had never held an appointment higher than rector of the parish of West Kington in Wiltshire.[13] He had been examined and excommunicated by convocation in March 1532 for his sermons concerning purgatory, pilgrimages, and the intercession of saints, and if he had not been willing to retract some of his opinions, he would have been burnt then.[14]

Latimer's rise to ecclesiastical preferment must be explained by his eagerness to support King Henry VIII's marriage to Anne Boleyn, his desire for reform (which well suited the government's plans, at least temporarily), and his usefulness in denouncing the papal supremacy. By the mid-1530s, Henry had removed England from communion with the Roman Catholic Church, and the regime demanded that preachers speak in support of the king's headship over the Church in England. All Henrician bishops, from the time of the breach from Rome until the end of the reign, who wanted to keep their sees and even their lives, had to manage a precarious balancing act. The bishops learned from the example of John Fisher of Rochester, who was imprisoned and then executed in 1535 for maintaining the authority of the pope. Bishops saw that they had to endorse the royal supremacy, and whatever other policies, political and doctrinal, the king and Thomas Cromwell wanted to promote. But the government's standard of what constituted orthodoxy kept shifting, first permitting a period of limited reform in the 1530s, and then swinging back to more conservative positions starting in 1539. Latimer became bishop because Henry VIII needed his considerable powers as a preacher and patron. But bishops could be unmade as well as made, and ultimately Latimer's episcopate was a casualty of changes in policy which proceeded from the king himself.

Before Latimer was elevated to the bishopric in 1535, he developed powerful friends and enemies in and around Worcester diocese through his preaching. While Latimer was rector of West Kington, Cranmer licensed him to preach throughout Canterbury province in 1533,[15] and he made frequent preaching tours in the west country, including Exeter, where he spoke against "Idolatrie supersticion and popery," and converted John

[13]Wiltshire County Record Office, Campeggio's Register (no class reference), fol. 24v.

[14]B[ritish] L[ibrary], MS Harley 425, fols. 13r–14v; *Remains*, 218–219. For his equivocal stance, see Susan Wabuda, "Equivocation and Recantation during the English Reformation: The 'Subtle Shadows' of Dr. Edward Crome," *Journal of Ecclesiastical History* 44 (1993), 231.

[15]BL, Harley MS 6148, fols. 42r–42v; Cranmer, *Writings*, 308–309.

Cardmaker, then warden of the Franciscans, to his views.[16] He developed a following among some of the local clergy. Friar John Erley, who was punished by the bishop of Bath for his heretical sermons in 1533, was known as one of Latimer's "disciples."[17]

Latimer's most famous preaching tour during this period occurred in Bristol during Lent 1533, when he spoke at the invitation of the clergy and merchants there, including the mayor, Clement Bays. Latimer became the ally of a committed network of reformers in Bristol, whose activities have been most recently explored by Martha Skeeters.[18] She has written about the intense controversy which resulted from Latimer's sermons, when he seemed to criticize pilgrimages, the veneration of saints, images, and purgatory, and how he was opposed by several conservative clergymen, including William Hubberdine and Edward Powell. Powell was an opponent of the Boleyn marriage, and the controversy highlighted the nature of papal authority in England and the bitterness surrounding alterations to religion.[19]

When Latimer was denounced to Thomas Bagard, the chancellor of Worcester diocese and effective ordinary for the permanently absent Italian bishop Geronimo de' Ghinnucci, Bagard acted to stop the uproar. As chancellor, he had the right to license and oversee preachers for Worcester diocese, and he attempted to stem disruptions by inhibiting all those clergymen from preaching who did not have his own permission to preach. This move, in effect, overruled Archbishop Cranmer's authorization for Latimer to speak, a fact which eventually threatened to cost Bagard dearly. Bagard could not prevent Latimer's supporters from marshaling strong allies to come to his aid. Mayor Bays sent a petition to Thomas Cromwell which defended Latimer's sermons. It denounced "the synystrall prechinge" of Powell and Hubberdine, who, the petition said, had denigrated the king's marriage to Anne Boleyn and upheld the papal supremacy. The

---

[16]*Gleanings from the Common Place Book of John Hooker, relating to the City of Exeter*, ed. Walter J. Harte (Exeter, n.d.), 7–8, 13–14; Robert Whiting, *The Blind Devotion of the People: Popular Religion and the English Reformation* (Cambridge: Cambridge University Press, 1989), 245, 254–255, 257.

[17]P[ublic] R[ecord] O[ffice], S[tate] P[apers] 1/79, fols. 124v–125r; *Letters and Papers, Foreign and Domestic, of the Reign of Henry VIII*, ed. J. S. Brewer et al., 21 vols. in 33 parts (London, 1862–1910), 6: no. 1192 [hereafter *LP*].

[18]Skeeters, *Community and Clergy*, 38–46; Wabuda, "Cranmer's Early Patronage," 79–80.

[19]Latimer owned a copy of Edward Powell's *Propvgnacvlvm Svmmi Sacerdotij euangelici, ad Septenarij sacramentorum…aduersus Martinum Lutherum fratrem famousum et VViclefistam insignem* [1523], now at Cambridge University Library. I owe this knowledge to Dr. Richard Rex.

signers of the petition included several men who would continue to be Latimer's friends once he was elevated to the bishopric, including William Shipman, William Cary, and David Hutton, and the clergymen Henry Marshall and William Benet.[20]

His supporters were successful in their efforts to protect Latimer in Bristol. Hutton may have been a key figure in the episode. He was both a client of the queen's and a "lovyng ffrend" to the archbishop. He also had close connections with accused heretics. Hutton had been the overseer of the will of Thomas Browne of Bristol, which, like that of the Gloucestershire gentleman William Tracy, was condemned by convocation in 1531 because of its heretical contents. Only Cranmer's direct intervention ensured that Browne's will was proved in the Prerogative Court of Canterbury.[21] Very likely, Hutton was one of the financial backers of Richard Webbe, a seller of heretical books in Bristol, London, and elsewhere, who had once been accused before Sir Thomas More.[22] Cranmer or Anne may have encouraged Hutton to act on Latimer's behalf in 1533. When Cromwell sent a commission to investigate the preaching controversy, Mayor Bays and Bristol's corporation successfully influenced it in favor of Latimer. His opponents were arrested, and Bagard's inhibition against his preaching was lifted.[23]

In the months before his elevation to the bishopric, Latimer and Cranmer tried to consolidate their control over the area's pulpits, and the archbishop licensed preachers at Latimer's request.[24] Dr. Roger Edgeworth,

---

[20]The petition: PRO, SP 1/76, fol. 183r; *LP* 6: no. 596. See also SP 1/77, fol. 208r; SP 6/3, fols. 59r–61r; *LP* 6: nos. 572[iv], 796; Skeeters, *Community and Clergy*, 38–46.

[21]For Hutton's connections with the queen and Cranmer, see BL, Harley MS 6148, fols. 41d, 76v; Cranmer, *Writings*, 275–276. The proved version of Browne's will does not contain any erroneous or controversial material, leading me to suspect that Cranmer edited it to make it possible to prove. It was made on 31 March 1531, and proved 1533/4. Shipman was a witness. PRO, PCC, PROB 11/25, fols. 65v–66v. See David Wilkins, ed., *Concilia Magnae Britanniae et Hiberniae*, 4 vols. (London, 1737), 3:746–747; Skeeters, *Community and Clergy*, 38, 41–42; Thomas S. Freeman, "Research, Rumour and Propaganda: Anne Boleyn in Foxe's 'Book of Martyrs,'" *Historical Journal* 38 (1995): 797–819.

[22]In his own will, Hutton remitted to Webbe the twenty pounds that Webbe owed to him. Shipman and Cary were among the overseers, and Marshall and Benet were among his witnesses. It was made 27 October 1535, and proved 13 March 1535/6, PRO, PCC, PROB 11/25, fol. 225. See K. G. Powell, "The Social Background to the Reformation in Gloucestershire," *Transactions of the Bristol and Gloucestershire Archaeological Society* 92 (1973): 96–120; Thomas More, *The Confutation of Tyndale's Answer*, in *Works of Saint Thomas More*, 8:17–21, 813–817; Skeeters, *Community and Clergy*, 37–38.

[23]Skeeters, *Community and Clergy*, 38–46.

[24]Wabuda, "Cranmer's Early Patronage," 80–81.

an outstanding conservative preacher, found that he was no longer permitted to deliver sermons.[25]

Latimer's defense of the Boleyn marriage, and his opposition to the papal supremacy, made him an asset to the regime. Since the breach from Rome made the Italian bishops (including Ghinucci) redundant, Latimer was rewarded by Queen Anne and Cromwell with the bishopric of Worcester in 1535.[26] As we will see, those local friends whom he made had already stood him in good stead after he became bishop. Richard Webbe became Latimer's servant for six years.[27]

With Latimer's elevation, Chancellor Bagard was in an uncomfortable position. Ghinucci had been Worcester diocese's fourth absentee Italian bishop since 1497. The diocese (until 1541) comprised Gloucestershire east of the river Severn (including part of Bristol), Worcestershire, and southern Warwickshire. The administration of this area had been delegated to deputies, like Bagard, who were used to running matters themselves without much interference from the bishop.[28] The fact that Latimer was resident in his diocese for at least one-third of the forty-five months of his tenure meant that he could place his own mark upon administration, thus causing resentment among some of the long-term diocesan officials, many of whom were opponents of reform. And in addition, the singular circumstances surrounding Latimer's rise probably exacerbated the tensions he had already felt with some of the diocesan staff. For how many bishops were once taken to task for contentious preaching by their future chancellors?

Latimer did not initially move to replace Bagard. Cromwell had raised Bagard to the office of chancellor in 1532,[29] and Latimer may not have wanted to challenge his choice. The surviving diocesan documents also

---

[25]*Sermons Very Fruitfull, Godly and Learned by Roger Edgeworth: Preaching in the Reformation c. 1535–c. 1553*, ed. Janet Brewer (Cambridge: D. S. Brewer, 1993), 96; Skeeters, *Community and Clergy*, 166–167.

[26]"William Latymer's Cronickille of Anne Bolleyne," ed. Maria Dowling, *Camden Miscellany XXX*, Camden Society, 4th series, 39 (London, 1990), 59. (William Latymer was not related to Hugh Latimer.) *LP* 8: no. 48; 9: no. 236(12); 10: no. 1257(9); 11: no. 117(7); *The Acts and Monuments of John Foxe*, ed. George Townsend, 8 vols. (London, 1843–49), 7:461 [hereafter Foxe]; Diarmaid MacCulloch, *Thomas Cranmer: A Life* (New Haven: Yale University Press, 1996), 49–51, 115–116, 139.

[27]Foxe, 4:127–129.

[28]Smith, *Guide to Bishops' Registers*, 215, 225–226; F. Douglas Price, "Gloucester Diocese under Bishop Hooper 1551–53," *Transactions of the Bristol and Gloucestershire Archaeological Society* 60 (1938), 51; Chester, *Hugh Latimer*, 105; Roy M. Haines, "Aspects of the Episcopate of John Carpenter, Bishop of Worcester, 1444–1476," *Journal of Ecclesiastical History* 19 (1968), 37.

[29]PRO, SP 2/P, no. 18; *LP* 7: no. 722.

show that Bagard was a hardworking and able administrator. His services were valuable to the new bishop, and Bagard struggled to make amends to Latimer for having inhibited him from preaching in 1533. Latimer and Bagard initially got along surprisingly well together, and Latimer rewarded him with a benefice in 1536.[30]

A much greater threat to Latimer's security as bishop was the implacable opposition he faced from another veteran administrator, Dr. John Bell, who had been chancellor and vicar-general under three previous bishops. He was archdeacon of Gloucester throughout Latimer's tenure, and his other positions included warden of the collegiate church of Stratford-upon-Avon. Although Bell was willing to work tirelessly for Henry's divorce, he was conservative in his religious views, and was always a keen suppressor of ecclesiastical irregularities and heresy. In 1526, he and Edmund Bonner, future bishop of London, had investigated heresy cases in Worcester diocese, and Bell would continue to wish to eliminate unorthodoxy during Latimer's tenure.[31]

Archdeacon Bell was probably related to the Gloucestershire gentry family of Bell, two of whose members shared his distaste of Latimer and his policies. They were half-brothers, both named Thomas, and they enjoyed important positions of authority. Thomas Bell senior was mayor of Gloucester from 1536 to 1537, and his half-brother Thomas Bell junior was sheriff of Gloucestershire from 1535 to 1536.[32] In Archdeacon Bell and his relatives, Latimer had dangerous adversaries whose machinations eventually helped to deprive him of his see.

[30]Bagard's licensing and inhibitions: PRO, SP 1/75, fol. 288r; *LP* 6: no. 411; HWRO, Ghinucci's Register I, fols. 71, 92; Ghinucci's Register II, fol. 131; Latimer's Register, fol. 6. The living Latimer bestowed on him may have been Dutisbourne Abbots, Gloucestershire. *Remains*, 375–377; *LP* 11: no. 1374; HWRO, Ghinucci's Register I, fol. 101; *The Victoria History of the County of Worcester*, ed. J. W. Willis-Bund, et al., 4 vols. (Westminster: A. Constable and Co., 1910–24), 2:43; *Valor Ecclesiasticus*, 6 vols. (London, 1810–34), 2:217. MacCulloch, *Thomas Cranmer*, 49, 139.

[31]Archdeacon Bell was from Worcestershire. Chester, *Hugh Latimer*, 103; *LP* 2: no. 2698; 4: no. 932; 14(2): no. 400; *Victoria History of the County of Worcester*, 2:39–45, esp. 43; *Dictionary of National Biography*, s.v. Bell; Price, "Gloucester Diocese," 51; A. B. Emden, *A Biographical Register of the University of Oxford A. D. 1501 to 1540* (Oxford: Clarendon Press, 1974). Bell contributed to the Bishops' Book: *The Institvtion of a Christen Man* (London, 1537), preface. He was a royal chaplain, and held a prebend in the collegiate church of Saint Stephen in Westminster Palace: *LP* 5: no. 1366; 14(2): no. 264(29). For heresy cases, see HWRO, Bell's Visitation Book, esp. fol. 25.

[32]Henry Chitty and John Phillipot, *The Visitation of the County of Gloucester Taken in the Year 1623*, ed. Sir John Maclean and W. C. Heare (London: Harleian Society, 1885), 21:17–18; S. T. Bindoff, ed., *The House of Commons 1509–1558*, 3 vols. (London: HMSO, 1982), 1:413–414; *List of Sheriffs for England and Wales, From the Earliest Times to A.D. 1831* (reprint, New York, 1963), 184. (I owe this last reference to Miss Joan Henderson.)

As bishop, Latimer preached frequently,[33] and promoted preaching throughout the diocese. His visitation injunctions of late 1537 ordered that time should be devoted to sermons in each parish: "That preaching be not set aside for any manner of observance in the church, as procession, and other ceremonies." His emphasis was placed squarely upon the importance of preaching, to encourage faith, rather than upon other traditions in the church. He ordered that long bidding prayers should not prevent the "fruitful preaching of God's word."[34] Instead of closing all religious houses, he was a proponent of turning them into centers of teaching, preaching, and study.[35]

Latimer must have begun to license preachers immediately following his consecration. We know that he licensed more than a dozen men, but most of their names were not written into his register, and it is possible that they were kept in another record, now lost. We can reconstruct a list of Latimer's early licensees from a 1536 letter written by Sheriff Bell to denounce them,[36] but we will probably never know all of their names, particularly those active late in his tenure.

In order to understand the extent of Latimer's intervention by imposing preachers in many areas of his diocese, and to show that he employed reformers, including some of the most notable figures of the English Reformation, we should look in some detail at the men he sponsored. Many of the preachers Latimer licensed were reformers who already had strong connections with the area. Latimer obtained his former benefice of West Kington for Henry Marshall, who had defended him in Bristol. He licensed Marshall to preach in Worcester diocese by June 1536.[37] Latimer also licensed William Benet, and made him one of his chaplains. At the end of April 1536, Benet preached in Gloucester, speaking on purgatory and the efficacy of masses for the dead. In late August of the next

---

[33]For the sermons and the mention Latimer made of preaching while he was bishop, see *Sermons*, 25–58, 208; *Remains*, 388–389.

[34]Latimer's injunctions have been reproduced in *Remains*, 240–244; Wilkins, *Concilia*, 3:832 (for the convent of Saint Mary's Worcester); Walter Howard Frere, ed., *Visitation Articles and Injunctions of the Period of the Reformation*, 3 vols. (London: Alcuin Club, 1910), 2:12–18; *LP* 12(2): nos. 841–842.

[35]Latymer, "Cronickille," 57; *Remains*, 410–411; E. W. Ives, "Anne Boleyn and the Early Reformation in England: The Contemporary Evidence," *Historical Journal* 37 (1994): 389–400.

[36]PRO, SP 1/104, fols. 157r–157v; *LP* 10: no. 1099.

[37]West Kington was in the gift of the bishop of Salisbury, and Bishop Nicholas Shaxton collated Marshall at Latimer's request. PRO, SP 1/104, fols. 157r–157v; *LP* 10: no. 1099; Emden, *Biographical Register*, 380; *Valor Ecclesiasticus*, 2:134; Wiltshire County Record Office, Salcot's Register, fol. 2v.

year, Latimer collated him to the vicarage of Saint Nicholas parish church, Warwick, and instituted him there himself.[38]

Several other licensees were also local men who had had careers in the diocese before Latimer's elevation, and Latimer must have sought them out because of their interest in promoting reform. They included James Ash, who was admitted to the church of Staunton in Gloucestershire in the late 1520s.[39] John Joseph was probably warden of the Grey Friars at Worcester. Bagard had licensed him to preach in 1533, and renewed his license a year later. Latimer granted him a license by June 1536. After Joseph received a dispensation to hold a benefice and change his habit, Latimer presided over his institution to Saint Martin's parish church, Worcester, in 1538.[40] Another licensee was Anthony Sawnders, whom Cromwell had appointed to be pastor at the parish church of Winchcombe in Gloucestershire before November 1534, in order to preach the royal supremacy, and to read the Bible to monks at Winchcombe's Benedictine abbey. Sawnders was praised by one of the monks as being among the "syncere and pure prechers of the word of god."[41]

For preachers who had the responsibilities of a parish to bear, time to prepare and deliver sermons might be limited. Sawnders wrote of his difficulties to Cromwell in 1535. The parish of Winchcombe was "wide and

---

[38]Benet had been priest at Spycers Chantry in Bristol's Saint Nicholas parish church since 1533. See HWRO, Bell's Visitation Book, fol. 99; Ghinucci's Register I, fol. 76; Ghinucci's Register II, fol. 139; Bell's Register, fol. 9; Latimer's Register, fol. 21. For Latimer's license and promotions of Benet: PRO, SP 1/104, fols. 157r–157v; *LP* 10: no. 1099; HWRO, Latimer's Register, fol. 21; Bell's Visitation Book, fol. 159. See also Skeeters, *Community and Clergy*, 72, 76–77, 156.

[39]HWRO, Ghinucci's Register II, fol. 84; *Valor Ecclesiasticus*, 3:245; K. G. Powell, "The Beginnings of Protestantism in Gloucestershire," *Transactions of the Bristol and Gloucestershire Archaeological Society* 90 (1971): 141–57; idem, "Social Background," 104–105, 119.

[40]HWRO, Ghinucci's Register I, fols. 71, 83; Ghinucci's Register II, fols. 130, 149. Emden identifies Joseph as warden of the Franciscans, Worcester; however, there may be some confusion on the point, as Friar Robert Knowles was termed "guardiano" in a 1535 preaching license: HWRO, Ghinucci's Register I, fol. 91; Ghinucci's Register II, fol. 160. Joseph and Knowles were dispensed to hold a benefice and change their habits in July 1536: D. S. Chambers, ed., *Faculty Office Registers 1534–1549* (Oxford: Clarendon Press, 1966), 63. See also PRO, SP 1/104, fols. 157r–157v; *LP* 10: no. 1099; HWRO, Latimer's Register, fol. 34.

[41]PRO, SP 1/86, fols. 161r–162v; SP 1/89, fols. 145r–145v; SP 1/104, fols. 157r–157v; *LP* 7: no. 1376; 8: no. 171; 9: no. 747; 10: no. 1099; BL, Cotton MS Cleopatra E. iv, fols. 60r–60v; Powell, "Beginnings of Protestantism in Gloucestershire," 149. For the abbey, see David Knowles and R. Neville Hadcock, *Medieval Religious Houses: England and Wales* (New York: St. Martin's, 1971), 60; *The Victoria County History of the County of Gloucester*, ed. William Page et al., 11 vols. to date (London: A. Constable and Co., 1907–), 2:66–72. There are no institutions for the parish of Winchcombe in the bishops' registers. Sawnders was granted letters dismissory on 3 February 1532/3, and was made subdeacon on 20 September 1534: HWRO, Morton's Register, fols. 173–174; Ghinucci's Register I, fol. 67.

broad," and there were at least two thousand persons there. He declared that he was so busy with parish and liturgical work that he had little time to study, preach, and read God's word. Local gentlemen, including Richard Tracy, often invited him to preach, but sometimes he could not go to them, as he had no assistance. Sawnders begged Cromwell to appoint a coadjutor to help him, so that he would have more opportunity to preach the royal supremacy. Despite his difficulties, Sawnders traveled to Blockley in Worcestershire to preach, having heard that a clergyman there did not accept Henry as supreme head.[42]

Perhaps the greatest reformer Latimer invited to preach was Robert Barnes, in 1537. Barnes was one of the most important, and among the most controversial, of the early reformers. By 1537, he had already been in trouble many times with authorities, and Latimer's cautious support of him shows not only his desire to advance reform in Worcester diocese, but his wariness that he might not offend Cromwell and the king. Latimer was well aware of the limits to their favor. Barnes had recently been released after having been imprisoned for a sermon delivered in the capital, and in July, Latimer wrote to Cromwell with a report of Barnes' resumption of preaching: "Dr Barnes, I hear say, preached in London this day, a very good sermon, with great moderation and temperance of himself." Latimer may have been trying to evaluate Barnes' behavior and doctrine, and was willing to bring him to Cromwell's favor if he proved himself: "I pray God continue with him, for I know no man shall do more good."[43]

The following December, Latimer asked Barnes to preach with him at Hartlebury, where he had a residence. This is the only example I found of Latimer's having preached with another clergyman while he was a bishop. He may have continued to scrutinize Barnes as they prepared to preach. Only after Barnes had proved himself to Latimer's satisfaction did Latimer send him to preach in Worcester and Evesham. Only then did Latimer write to Cromwell that surely Barnes was preeminent in expounding Scripture and setting forth Christ. To all who saw them together, the bishop's presence must have demonstrated that Barnes enjoyed his approval, and even

---

[42]PRO, SP 1/89, fol. 145r; SP 1/86, fols. 161r–162v; BL, Cotton MS Cleopatra E. iv, fol. 60r; *LP* 7: no. 1367; 8: no. 171; 9: no. 747; Powell, "Beginnings of Protestantism in Gloucestershire," 149. The disobedient clerk's name was Martin Cave, and he was still in his position in 1540: *LP* 13(1): no. 34; 13(2): no. 1232; *Valor Ecclesiasticus*, 3:256; HWRO, Bell's Visitation Book, fols. 49, 311.

[43]*Remains*, 378.

that his Protestant views were orthodox. Latimer would even write Cromwell: "I would wish that the king's grace might once hear him...."[44]

Perhaps the preachers Latimer employed most in his see were his chaplains. Bishops were allowed to employ four chaplains at any one time,[45] and we know the names of six men who served Latimer as chaplain over the years of his tenure: William Benet, Rodolph Bradford,[46] Thomas Garrard, Rowland Taylor, William Turpin,[47] and Hugh Rawlyns (alias Williams). All of these men were capable preachers, and records survive to show that at least three of them preached in the diocese. Several had been at Cambridge with Latimer. Thomas Garrard and Rodolph Bradford had been involved with Latimer in illegally distributing English New Testaments at the universities and in London in the late 1520s.[48] Latimer had converted Rowland Taylor at Cambridge, and he probably brought him straight from the university to be his commissary general. In 1538, Latimer collated him to the benefice of Hanbury. Latimer could trust Taylor's loyalty, and he began to introduce his own men into the diocesan administration, which, as we will see, deeply offended the old-time officials. Through the good offices of Cromwell or Cranmer, Taylor was issued with a royal license to preach throughout the realm. This type of license permitted Taylor to preach anywhere, even in dioceses where he would not ordinarily be permitted to speak by a hostile bishop. Taylor delivered sermons in London when he accompanied Latimer to the capital. It is a mark of the suspicion in which

[44] *Remains*, 378, 388–389; Chester, *Hugh Latimer*, 105.

[45] 21 Henry VIII, c. 13, in *Statutes of the Realm*, 11 vols. in 12 (facsim., London: Dawsons, 1963), 3:292–296.

[46] According to John Strype, Bradford preached on holy days at Cambridge, but there is no evidence for his preaching in Worcester diocese: Strype, *Ecclesiastical Memorials, Relating Chiefly to Religion, and the Reformation of It and the Emergencies of the Church of England under King Henry VIII., King Edward VI., and Queen Mary I.* (Oxford, 1822), 1(1): 486–487; *Institvtion of a Christen Man*, preface; *Remains*, 376–377.

[47] We know little of Turpin. He was rector of Little Bowden, Northamptonshire, and was recorded in Lincoln diocesan documents as being one of Latimer's chaplains in 1538. Two sermons were preached in his living in that year, and he preached one sermon at Lutterworth. L[incolnshire] A[rchives] O[ffice], Vj 10, fols. 18r, 56v. It is not certain if he preached in Worcester diocese.

[48] Chester, *Hugh Latimer*, 36–37; Mary Bateson, ed., *Grace Book B Part II: Containing the Accounts of the Proctors of the University of Cambridge, 1511–1544* (Cambridge: Cambridge University Press, 1905), 145, 163, 189; *LP* 4(2): nos. 3962, 3968, 3999, 4017, 4030, 4073–4075, 4125, 4175, 4150; Powell, "Social Background," 109; Bowker, *Henrician Reformation*, 61–62. In addition to being a leader in the illicit book trade, Garrard had been forced to recant his belief in justification by faith alone in the late 1520s: Guildhall Library, Tunstall's Register, MS 9531/10, fols. 122r–123r, printed in Foxe, 5: app. VI (no. 10).

the conservative Bishop John Stokesley of London held him that Taylor's royal license was carefully copied into Stokesley's own register, so that his authority to preach was on record. Stokesley could not prevent Taylor from preaching, but he could ensure that Taylor was monitored.[49]

How often did Latimer's chaplains preach? They often waited on Latimer, and since Taylor's administrative duties were also fairly heavy, it is doubtful that he was resident at his cure. However, to judge from the career of Garrard, even a pluralist could exercise his preaching duties as he traveled from one position or cure to another, even from one diocese to another. Garrard's preaching itineraries are some of the most extensive known for any Henrician preacher. Even accounting for the fact that many tours by preachers cannot now be reconstructed, Garrard must have been unusually well traveled. In the mid-1530s, he had been chaplain to Latimer's friend Sir Francis Bigod. Bigod had obtained Cranmer's license for Garrard to preach anywhere in the realm in 1535, and took him on preaching tours through Yorkshire.[50] Garrard was preaching in Worcester diocese by June 1536, and he also delivered sermons in Lincolnshire that year, to the annoyance of conservative bishop John Longland.[51]

Garrard also had ecclesiastical positions in Sussex, and in 1537, he preached in and around Rye, probably in the company of three men, including Cranmer's licensee Thomas Swynnerton, and Thomas Lawney, the archbishop's chaplain. Protests against their sermons have survived. They were indicted for infecting more than twenty men of Rye and Winchelsea with erroneous opinions. Garrard was accused of speaking against purgatory, masses for the dead, offering to saints, and pilgrimages, but it is

---

[49] *The Works of Nicholas Ridley, D.D. Sometime Lord Bishop of London, Martyr, 1555*, ed. Henry Christmas (Cambridge, 1841), Appendix III, 487–494 (Turner to Foxe); HWRO, Latimer's Register, fol. 25, 31–32; Bell's Visitation Book, fol. 363; Chambers, *Faculty Office Registers*, 191. Taylor's license is in Guildhall Library, MS 9531/12, pt. 1, fol. 43v. Bishop Stokesley recorded very few of the licenses that were issued to itinerant preachers by other authorities or jurisdictions in his register. The fact that Taylor's appears here is a mark of the suspicion and caution with which Stokesley held him. See also Chester, *Hugh Latimer*, 107; William James Brown, *The Life of Rowland Taylor LL.D.: Rector of Hadleigh in the Deanery of Bocking* (London: Epworth Press, 1959), esp. 4, 10, 15–16; J. S. Craig, "The Marginalia of Dr. Rowland Taylor," *Historical Research* 64 (1991): 411–420.

[50] PRO, SP 1/93, fols. 50r–50v; SP 1/104, fols. 157r–157v; *LP* 8: nos. 854, 1025(1–2), 1033, 1069; 9: no. 37; 10: nos. 981, 1099; 13(1): no. 1179; Foxe, 5: App. VI (no. 12); A. G. Dickens, *Lollards and Protestants in the Diocese of York 1509–1558* (London: Hambledon Press, 1982), 58–59, 76, 79–83, 103–106. Bigod was executed for his role in the Pilgrimage of Grace, and Latimer spoke to Henry in favor of his widow: *LP* 12(2): no. 194; 13(1): no. 1.

[51] PRO, SP 1/103, fols. 106v–109r; *LP* 10, nos. 804, 850, 891; Foxe, 5: App. VI (no. 11).

not clear whether he criticized only the abuses of these practices, or denounced these tenets outright. He was not punished,[52] and in 1538, Latimer collated Garrard to the parish church of Hartlebury. At some time before mid-1539, Garrard also became a chaplain to Archbishop Cranmer.[53] We can only assume that Garrard was an energetic, as well as a regular and frequent, preacher in Worcester diocese. Without a doubt, he preached in the same manner in Latimer's see as he did elsewhere. In late July 1538, Latimer sent Taylor and Garrard to preach in and around Kidderminster. Garrard preached at Kidderminster parish church "on the righteousness that cometh by Christ and of the righteousness of works."[54] Under more conservative bishops, like Longland, or even according to the views of conservative administrators in Worcester diocese, as we will see, Garrard's sermons were anathema, but as long as Latimer enjoyed the support of the regime, Garrard could not be stopped.

Bishops were responsible not only for licensing preachers, but for inhibiting those who preached heresy. Under a conservative bishop like Longland of Lincoln, reformers posed a threat that he tried to inhibit, but for a diocese like Worcester, where the reformers held power under Latimer's leadership, the conservative, or Catholic clergy had the most to fear. Latimer refused to license conservative preachers, even if they had degrees in theology, were highly experienced, and were known as discreet. He probably suppressed conservative preachers in addition to Roger Edgeworth, who was still not permitted to deliver even a single sermon during the whole of Latimer's tenure.[55]

On occasion, Latimer had to turn to Cromwell for assistance to protect his licensees. Anthony Sawnders was particularly vulnerable. The abbot of Winchcombe would not alleviate the burdens of Sawnders' cure by sending him an assistant, and indeed tried to drive away his only help, a chantry priest who favored the gospel.[56] Sawnders was also opposed by the

---

[52]PRO, SP 1/113, fols. 106v–109r; *LP* 11: no. 1424. Garrard was master, warden, and chaplain of Saint James's Hospital in Seaford (*LP* 14(1): no. 906), vicar of Sutton cum Seaford, and chantry priest at Sullyngton (*Valor Ecclesiasticus*,1:339, 318). See also Graham Mayhew, "Religion, Faction, and Politics in Reformation Rye: 1530–59," *Sussex Archaeological Collections* 120 (1982): 139–160. Powell assumed that the Rye sermons were delivered in Worcester diocese: "Beginnings of Protestantism in Gloucestershire," 149–150. See Elton, *Policy and Police*, 85–90.

[53]HWRO, Latimer's Register, fol. 31, and passim. MacCulloch, *Thomas Cranmer*, 139n, 142, 262.

[54]PRO, SP 1/134, fols. 298r–300r; *LP* 13(1): no. 1509.

[55]PRO, SP 1/104, fols. 157r–157v; *LP* 10: no. 1099.

[56]The incumbent of the perpetual chantry of the Blessed Virgin Mary in the parish church of Winchcombe from 9 March 1532/3 to 26 September 1541 was Christopher Glanfylde. He was also the

preacher George Cotes, who may have been licensed by Cromwell and was certainly supported by the abbot of Hailes. The abbey was most famous for its relic, the renowned Blood of Hailes, which was supposed to be a vial of the blood of Christ. The abbot had no reason to be well disposed towards anyone who was allied with such a critic of the miraculous as was Bishop Latimer.[57] So fierce an opponent of Sawnders was Cotes that a "tumulte" due to his sermons broke out among the gentlemen and other people of the area. Sawnders wrote that he was actually in fear for his life. Latimer acted to protect Sawnders by examining Cotes's sermons, and he sent him to Cromwell with the request that, if Cromwell could not "reform him," then he should inhibit him from the diocese.[58]

Latimer also required Cromwell's assistance when he wanted to suppress two monks preaching in Evesham in 1537. Evesham was exempt from episcopal authority, and Latimer sent Barnes to report to Cromwell about them.[59] Latimer also relayed information to Cromwell about seditious preachers who spoke in other dioceses.[60]

In addition to Cromwell, Latimer needed the assistance of the local gentry to support his policies. He relied upon several Worcestershire and Gloucestershire gentlemen to promote his reforms and preachers. Three gentlemen in particular—Richard Tracy, William Lucy, and Robert Acton—were among his greatest allies.

Richard Tracy was the son of William Tracy, whose unconventional will caused members of convocation in 1531 to order the exhumation and burning of his bones as those of a heretic. Latimer castigated this decision in his convocation sermon of 1536, and defended the elder Tracy's memory as "a very good man; reported to be of an honest life while he lived, full of

---

schoolmaster. HWRO, Bell's Visitation Book, fols. 52, 93; Ghinucci's Register I, fol. 68; Ghinucci's Register II, fol. 126; Bell's Register, fol. 54; *Valor Ecclesiasticus*, 2:440 (where name is given incorrectly as Clanfield).

[57]In contrast to Latimer, Longland acted against a man who said that the Blood of Hailes consisted merely of duck's blood. LAO, Vj 10, fols. 75r–85v, 93r. See also Eamon Duffy, *The Stripping of the Altars: Traditional Religion in England c. 1400–c. 1580* (New Haven: Yale University Press, 1992), 104.

[58]BL, Cotton MS Cleopatra, E. iv, fol. 60r; *LP* 9: no. 747; *Remains*, 373–374.

[59]*Remains*, 389. In 1539, the abbot and convent of Evesham wrote to Cromwell, asking that their monastery be turned into a college for preaching the word of God, teaching, and hospitality, but it was not. *LP* 14(1): no. 1191.

[60]Friar Alexander Barklay preached in Suffolk, Cornwall, and Devonshire, often without mentioning the royal supremacy, and probably in favor of images and the mediation of saints. *LP* 13(2): nos. 571, 596, 709.

good works, good both to the clergy, and also to the laity." Richard Tracy helped Latimer to dismantle and examine the Blood of Hailes in 1538. As we have already seen, Tracy requested sermons from Sawnders, and corroborated accounts of Sawnders' troubles to Cromwell. He was the author of a work printed in 1544, *A supplycacion to our moste souerainge lorde Kynge Henry the eyght...*, which ascribed England's former allegiance to the papal supremacy as the result of unprofitable preaching. Tracy advocated a proper preaching clergy who would base their sermons upon "true knowlege of Gods worde."[61]

Tracy's brother-in-law, William Lucy, was a defender of the preacher Edward Large, who had been accused of heresy as expressed in his sermons at Bishops Hampton. Lucy interested Latimer in Large's case, and one of Large's sermons, written to defend himself, survives in manuscript in the State Papers Collection. It provides a striking example of the type of sermon which Latimer wished to protect and promote. Preaching on Matthew 22:21, in addition to speaking on loyalty to the king, Large argued that all of those would be saved who believed that Christ was the only mediator, redeemer, savior, and atonement-maker between them and God. Large spoke in favor of the Protestant tenet of justification by faith alone. Every true Christian man, he argued, believed without doubting that through faith in Jesus Christ's merits he was freely justified and made righteous before the sight of God, without his own merit and without works. Still, good works had their place, since God had commanded them to be performed, and they certified that the true Christian was indeed among the chosen. Latimer asked for Cromwell's help in solving Large's troubles, arguing that if his accusers were to be suffered to succeed against him, "it will be but folly for any true preachers to come to that part of my diocese." And indeed, Cromwell did come to Large's aid.[62]

---

[61]*Sermons*, 45; Richard Tracy, *A supplycacion to our moste soueraigne lorde Kynge Henry the eyght* ...([Antwerp], 1544), sig. A3v; John Craig and Caroline Litzenberger, "Wills as Religious Propaganda: The Testament of William Tracy," *Journal of Ecclesiastical History* 44 (1993): 415–31; Duffy, *Stripping of the Altars*, 412; Latymer, "Cronickille," 61–62; Diarmaid MacCulloch, "Worcester," in Patrick Collinson and John Craig, eds., *The Reformation in the English Towns* (Basingstoke: Macmillan, forthcoming); Peter Marshall, "The Rood of Boxley, the Blood of Hailes and the Defence of the Henrician Church," *Journal of Ecclesiastical History* 46 (1995): 689–696.

[62]Large's sermon is PRO, SP 1/141, fols. 196r–207v; *LP* 13(2): no. 1279. For Lucy's letters: PRO, SP 1/123, fols. 42r–45v, 46r–56v; E 36/120, fols. 1r–3v; *LP* 12(2), nos. 215, 302–303, 496. See also *Remains*, 381–384, 399; Elton, *Policy and Police*, 375–380; *Faculty Office Registers*, 108. Lucy presented Large to the parish church of Charington in November 1537: HWRO, Latimer's Register, fols. 24–25.

Latimer not only encouraged religious reform, but his patronage was heavily weighted toward rewarding those gentlemen in his diocese who supported his views. He acted as a new channel of patronage between them and Cromwell and the Court. While he was rector of West Kington, his intervention with Anne Boleyn on behalf of a gentleman, "an earneste and zealous embracer of Godes worde," who had suffered a financial loss, resulted in the queen's giving the gentleman and his wife a substantial cash gift.[63] His letters to Cromwell were filled with requests for Tracy and Lucy. Indeed, Lucy and "master Acton, my godsip and friend," carried Latimer's messages, and in 1538, he thanked Cromwell "for your singular goodness shewed, as I understand, to master Lucy, a very good gentleman; and also towards Master Acton, another of the same sort...."[64]

Bishop Latimer's patronage of preachers and gentlemen threatened to upset not only the religious beliefs in his diocese, but the local political balance as well. We know that his licensees offended the conservative clergy and gentlemen of the diocese, as in the tumult created by Sawnders' controversy with George Cotes, or Large's sermons at Bishop Hampton. Before Latimer became bishop, one of the priests at Marshfield, which lay between West Kington and Bristol, felt that Latimer and his "disciples" had "doon more hurt yn this contrey then luther & all his disciples hath doon by yondsee."[65]

Only a year after Latimer became bishop, alarmed conservative clergy and laymen united to stop his preachers and undermine his position. In mid-1536, Archdeacon Bell made a visitation at Great Malvern. The gentleman William Horton and several other Staunton parishioners had complained against James Ash. They reported that Ash had said in a sermon that he would call Henry "Antecryste" if the king did not continue to make laws that favored reform. Ash was bound to appear at the king's council.[66]

Mid-1536 was a dangerous time for reformers. Queen Anne, who had been a great sponsor of religious change, had recently been executed. It was a propitious time to strike against Latimer, who had been so frequently associated with her. Sheriff Bell sent a list of the charges against Ash to

[63]Latymer, "Cronickille," 57.

[64]*Remains*, pp. 381–384, 387–389, 399–401, 405–406, 410–411, 413–415.

[65]PRO, SP 1/79, fols. 124v–125r; *LP* 6: no. 1192.

[66]Emden, *Biographical Register*, 15; PRO, SP 1/104, fols. 93r–94r, 157r–157v; *LP* 10: nos. 1027, 1099. Latimer presided over Ash's institution to the parish church of Alderton in July 1538: HWRO, Latimer's Register, fol. 34. Ash preferred to spell his name "Aissh": HWRO, Bell's Visitation Book, fol. 156. See also Elton, *Policy and Police*, 35–36, 298–299.

Bishop John Stokesley of London. Stokesley was no friend to Latimer, as we have already seen. It was at his request that Latimer was tried before Convocation in 1532, and he had inhibited Latimer from preaching in London diocese in 1533.[67]

Sheriff Bell denounced Latimer's choice of preachers, and his letter to Stokesley is our most important source to identify those whom Latimer licensed. In addition to Ash, Sheriff Bell complained against the warden of the Grey Friars in Worcester, Sawnders, Benet, Garrard, Marshall, and others, who followed Sawnders' example in their preaching. He lamented that Latimer did not allow any discreet or learned clergymen to preach, though they had a degree in theology. The sheriff accused Benet of preaching in Gloucester that if purgatory priests prayed with their tongues until they were worn to the stumps, their prayers would not help the dead, nor would masses help departed souls. Bell told Stokesley that Latimer had admitted a Dominican friar called Two-Year-Old (possibly John Erley) to preach, whom Archdeacon Bell (when chancellor under a previous bishop) had banished for his bad living and drunkenness. Sheriff Bell felt that Marshall was similarly evil. The sheriff asked Stokesley to forward his letter to the duke of Norfolk in the hope that they would be able to redress some of these wrongs in Parliament.[68]

Sheriff Bell's antagonism was so great, that Latimer's chaplains probably did not venture to preach in Gloucester for six months or more. In addition, the Bells were involved in the complicated troubles of Hugh Rawlyns, alias Williams, curate of Holy Trinity parish church in Gloucester. Rawlyns, who was suffering from a cold, wore a cap while censing the high altar. For this and other infractions in demeanor, Archdeacon Bell reported Rawlyns to Cromwell and banished him from the diocese. Rawlyns' punishment infuriated several parishioners, including John Huggyns, John Restell, and Arthur Porter. They wrote in his defense to Latimer and Cromwell. Cromwell restored Rawlyns, against the will of the Bells and the vicar, who then may have had him removed a second time.

In response, Rawlyns' defenders shifted their attention to the Bells and their hatred of Bishop Latimer. Huggyns and Restell submitted lengthy reports of the Bells' behavior to Garrard, whom Latimer sent to investigate.

---

[67] *Remains*, 474–478; Wabuda, "Crome," 231 n. 27.
[68] PRO, SP 1/104, fols. 157r–157; SP 1/115, fols. 166r–167r; *LP* 10: no. 1099; 12(1): no. 308; Elton, *Policy and Police*, 121–123.

From mid-1536, Sheriff Bell had called Latimer a heretic in various places before several witnesses. His brother the mayor said before forty people at the high cross in Gloucester (perhaps during a sermon by one of Latimer's chaplains) that it was not likely that Latimer was an honest man, because he kept none but heretic knaves about him. Porter heard Sheriff Bell call Garrard a heretic in front of the abbot of Gloucester. The sheriff "setteth not a point" by Latimer or Cromwell, because the Bell brothers enjoyed so much favor, locally and in the capital, with Archdeacon Bell, Bishop Stokesley, and others, including Sir William Kingston.[69] By Easter 1537, Cromwell was acting on Latimer and Rawlyns' behalf, and summoned Sheriff Bell to appear in London. Nicholas Arnold, a Gloucestershire gentleman, wrote his kinsman Thomas Wriothesley that he trusted Cromwell would defend the true preachers of God's word from violent suppression by all such ungodly people, of whom this Bell was a ring leader.[70]

Presumably Cromwell gave the sheriff a warning, and Bell had to submit himself to Latimer. Cromwell's support gave the bishop a temporary triumph. Ash was probably not punished, and Rawlyns became one of Latimer's chaplains, perhaps replacing Bradford, who had died in Worcester in 1537.[71]

Bagard's role in the Bells' attack is not clear, but even if he had not been involved, he dissatisfied Latimer in other ways. The one preaching license he probably issued in mid-1537 was to a conservative Franciscan friar, Brian Sandey of Oxford.[72] At the same time, William Lucy asked Latimer to send Rowland Taylor to investigate Edward Large's case, writing "for I doo mystrust" chancellor Bagard and his interference in the matter.[73] Clearly, Bagard now had to go, and Latimer replaced him with Garrard, who had performed well in investigating the bishop's enemies.[74]

For much of the rest of Latimer's tenure, Cromwell protected him with several royal commissions, often composed of Latimer's friends, sometimes

[69]PRO, SP 1/115, fols. 166r–167r; SP 1/117, fols. 265r–265v; *LP* 12(1): nos. 308, 701, 831; 12(2), App. 13; 14(2): no. 255; Elton, *Policy and Police*, 121–123.

[70]PRO, SP 1/117, fols. 265r–265v; *LP* 12(1): no. 831. Arnold was one of Cromwell's servants. See also PRO, SP 1/115, fols. 166r–167r; *LP* 12(1): no. 308; 14(2), no. 167; Bindoff, *House of Commons*, 1:413–414.

[71]Elton, *Policy and Police*, 36; *LP* 14(2): no. 255.

[72]Sandey had also been licensed in 1533: HWRO, Ghinucci's Register I, fol. 71; Ghinucci's Register II, fol. 130; Latimer's Register, fol. 6.

[73]PRO, SP 1/123, fols. 42r–45v; *LP* 12(2): no. 302.

[74]On Lucy: PRO, SP 1/123, fol. 45r; *LP* 12(2): no. 302. On Garrard: HWRO, Latimer's Register, fols. 14, 17, 31; *LP* 12(2): no. 303.

at the bishop's recommendation. In addition to enforcing the royal injunctions, the commissioners protected Latimer, to the detriment of conservatives. In Bristol in 1537, a commission not only investigated the sermons of Franciscan and Dominican friars, but sent several people to prison for calling the bishop a heretic worthy of burning.[75] During their attack upon the Bells, John Huggyns and John Restell expressed their desire for a commission like Bristol's, hoping that Nicholas Arnold and Arthur Porter could be among its members.[76] A royal commission was sent to Kidderminster in 1538 to examine Miles Denyson, a drunkard, a very seditious person, and a "despiser of the preachers and doctrine of Christ," who made a disturbance at Taylor's and Garrard's sermons when he criticized Garrard as "a foolish knave priest come to preach of the new learning which I set nought by," and charged that Latimer, in employing these men, "hath sent a foolish puppy and a boy to make a sermon of the new law." The commissioners were at pains to tell Cromwell that Denyson's criticisms were not shared widely, and that on the contrary, Garrard's listeners "were much stirred to Christ."[77]

Probably due to Cromwell's pressure, Archdeacon Bell resigned the wardenship of the college of Stratford-upon-Avon. When Cromwell wanted to present Anthony Barker there, Latimer stipulated that Barker should reside to "preach at it and about it, to the reformation of that blind end of the diocese."[78] To the end of his tenure, Latimer kept a close watch upon Stratford's clergy. In January 1539, one of Barker's parish priests made a recantation (to a charge that remains unknown to us) before William Lucy, who was a commissioner in Stratford-upon-Avon. Latimer sent one of his chaplains to preach at the recantation.[79]

Despite their apparent setback, Latimer's opponents did not surrender. In 1537, Richard Tracy, acting with Walter Walsh, sheriff, reported to Cromwell that Dr. Richard Smith of Oxford had preached in Evesham. Taking advantage of the fact that Evesham was exempt from Latimer's

[75]PRO, SP 1/116, fols. 119r–124v; SP 1/119, fols. 184r–197v; *LP* 12 (1): nos. 508 (i–ii), 1147; 12(2): no. 530.

[76]PRO, SP 1/115, fols. 166r–167r; SP 1/117, fols. 265r–265v; *LP* 12(1): nos. 308, 831.

[77]PRO, SP 1/134, fols. 298r–300r; *LP* 13(1): no. 1509.

[78]*LP* 12(2): no. 909; 14(1): no. 79; *Remains*, 383–384, 413–414. Bell left a five-pound legacy to the poor of Stratford-upon-Avon in his will, made 10 August 1556, proved 24 October 1556: PRO, PCC, PROB 1/38, fols. 118r–119r. That Stratford-upon-Avon remained essentially conservative well into the late sixteenth century is indicated by Patrick Collinson, "William Shakespeare's Religious Inheritance and Environment," in *Elizabethan Essays*, 218–252.

[79]*Remains*, 413–414; *LP* 14(1): no. 542.

jurisdiction, Smith concluded his sermon with ostentatious prayers for the leading clerical defenders of conservative opinion, including the abbots of Evesham and Winchcombe, and Bishop Stokesley, whom Smith especially recommended as a founder of the faith of Christ. Smith's act was nothing less than a calculated affront to Latimer's policies and authority. Once again, London's bishop had his influence felt in the diocese of Worcester, as he was held up as an example as the leader of the true faith. Smith returned to Oxford unscathed, leaving to Latimer's friends a protest to Cromwell as their only recourse.[80]

Due to the renewed conservatism of Henry VIII, Latimer's success over the Bells was only short-lived. The presentation before Parliament in 1539 of the bill of the Six Articles by the duke of Norfolk, with the king's approval, represented the end of the period of toleration for limited doctrinal experimentation. The Six Articles stipulated that all must believe in the doctrine of transubstantiation, and that masses for the dead were efficacious. Those who refused to accept the Six Articles' tenets were to be considered heretics, and were liable to be burnt.

Cromwell's vulnerability was increasing during this period. Latimer was expensive to protect, and his failure to work compliantly for the passage of the bill made him a liability. Cromwell forced Latimer to resign in July 1539, and he was confined.[81]

Latimer was immediately replaced as bishop by Archdeacon Bell, who moved to return diocesan administration to the state it had been in before Latimer's intrusion. Bell made Bagard his vicar-general.[82] Bishop Bell also acted swiftly to suppress heresy, using the new Act of the Six Articles to attack the men Latimer had promoted. On 3 June 1539, Cromwell permitted a royal commission to act against heresy in Bristol, and Bishop Bell soon had another commission to enforce the Six Articles throughout the

---

[80]Alan Kreider, *English Chantries: The Road to Dissolution* (Cambridge, Mass.: Harvard University Press, 1979), 141; *LP* 12(2): no. 534 (1–2).

[81]G. R. Elton, "Thomas Cromwell's Decline and Fall," *The Cambridge Historical Journal* 10 (1959), 167–168; Glyn Redworth, "A Study in the Formulation of Policy: The Genesis and Evolution of the Act of the Six Articles," *Journal of Ecclesiastical History* 37 (1986), 66–67; Chester, *Hugh Latimer*, ch. 20; Brendan Bradshaw, "George Browne, First Reformation Archbishop of Dublin, 1536–1554," *Journal of Ecclesiastical History* 21 (1970), 315.

[82]*LP* 14(2): no. 113 (2) (6) (13). For Bagard, HWRO, Bell's Visitation Book, fols. 155–156. He remained administrator until 1544: Heath's Register, fols. 8–11.

diocese. In 1540, Bell conducted a visitation of his see.[83] He discovered evidence of sacramentarian heresy dating from the late 1530s in Garrard's benefice of Hartlebury, and in Ash's parish of Staunton.[84] He also examined Latimer's servant Richard Webbe.[85]

Many of Latimer's preachers were scrutinized. Among Bishop Bell's visitation papers, we find that Large, Ash, Joseph, and Benet were ordered to deliver three special sermons each. Bell carefully chose where each sermon was to be delivered. The men had to speak in their own churches and two others. Ash had to preach at Winchcombe, and Large had to preach at Stratford-upon-Avon. Each man was given instructions on what to say and the manner in which the sermons were to be delivered. Large and Benet were told what verses from Scripture they should take as their texts. All of them were to preach on the Six Articles. Ash was ordered to praise the Virgin Mary, and Benet to condone masses for the dead, exactly those tenets they had previously called into question. These sermons were submissions, and were deliberately devised to contradict the preachers' previously expressed opinions in places where Latimer had encouraged reform. For anyone who had been familiar with these men before Bell's episcopate, they would have recognized that these sermons were akin to recantations. These sermons also signaled the reversal of Latimer's policies. Ash sent Bagard a letter to certify that he had concluded his sermons to the satisfaction of the congregations, "to the which I doubt not but they will bere recorde."[86] Conservative clergymen promised to teach the Six Articles in their parish churches, and those, including Edgeworth, who had not been permitted to speak during Latimer's tenure, could preach again.[87]

Some of Latimer's protégés were expelled from the diocese. When Rawlyns and Erley preached against the Six Articles at Gloucester before February 1540, they caused great disagreements, and were forbidden the

[83]Lambeth Palace Library, Cranmer's Register, fols. 68r–68v; HWRO, Bell's Register, fol. 13; Bishop Bell's Visitation Book, fols. 111–113; PRO, SP 1/157, fol. 155v; *LP* 15: no. 183. Among the victims was the Scottish preacher George Wishart, who had expected support from Latimer. Skeeters, *Community and Clergy*, 51–56, 120–121, 131, 141.

[84]HWRO, Bell's Visitation Book, fols. 107, 109–110, 115, 171–173.

[85]HWRO, Bell's Visitation Book, fol. 170; Foxe, 4:127–129.

[86]HWRO, Bell's Visitation Book, fols. 151–161. Ash's letter was carefully stitched into the book at fols. 155–156. See also Powell, "Beginnings of Protestantism in Gloucestershire," 150. In 1551, Bishop John Hooper, a reformer, found in his visitation that Ash (then incumbent of Alderton) was one of the few clergymen in the diocese who were able to preach: James Gairdner, "Bishop Hooper's Visitation of Gloucester," *English Historical Review* 19 (1904), 108.

[87]HWRO, Bell's Visitation Book, esp. fols. 267–268; Edgeworth, *Sermons*, 24, 96.

diocese by Cromwell's agent.[88] Some of Latimer's preachers were rescued through promotions. Cranmer extended his patronage to at least three of Latimer's licensees, including Joseph, who became his chaplain and later preached in favor of justification by faith in London soon after Henry's death.[89] Taylor became one of the archbishop's chaplains. He was collated rector of Hadleigh in Suffolk (an ecclesiastical peculiar in Cranmer's gift), and became a Six Preacher at Canterbury in 1551.[90]

Three of Latimer's preachers ended their lives at the stake. Taylor was burned during Mary's reign. Garrard was accused in Oxfordshire by Bishop Longland in August 1539 of breaking a holy fast by eating buttered chicken on the eve of Assumption. Garrard was already a chaplain to Cranmer, who increased the number of miles Garrard traveled on preaching tours when he sent him to preach in Calais,[91] and Garrard and Barnes had also found favor with Cromwell. They were inextricably linked with him, were caught up in his fall, and were burnt two days after Cromwell's beheading in 1540. Bishop Bell's register noted carefully that Garrard had been executed for heresy.[92] Reformers mourned these deaths. John Bale praised Garrard's ability to preach Christ and to question the efficacy of good works. Garrard, he wrote, "taught Christ here for an onlye sauer without the mangye merytes of menne."[93] There can be no question that conservative clergy waged a strong campaign to overturn Bishop Latimer's attempt to encourage Protestant reforms in the diocese of Worcester.

---

[88]PRO, SP 1/157, fol. 155r; *LP* 15: no. 183.

[89]Susan Wabuda, "Bishops and the Provision of Homilies, 1520–1547," *Sixteenth Century Journal* 25 (1994), 565.

[90]HWRO, Bell's Register, fol. 6; Heath's Register, fol. 14; *Faculty Office Registers*, 194; Brown, *Rowland Taylor*, 11, 17–25, 42–44; Foxe, 6:676–703; Diarmaid MacCulloch, *Suffolk and the Tudors: Politics and Religion in an English County 1500–1600* (Oxford: Clarendon Press, 1986), 163, 170–172. "Six Preacher" refers to the establishment of six itinerant preacherships at the refounding of Canterbury Cathedral. Each of the men holding one of these positions was known as a Six Preacher and was expected to preach in the cathedral, the town of Canterbury, and in villages and towns in the countryside where the cathedral had its lands. See *The Statutes of the Cathedral and Metropolitical Church of Christ, Canterbury* (Bungay, 1925), 42–45; Derek Ingram Hill, *The Six Preachers of Canterbury Cathedral, 1541–1982: Clerical Lives from Tudor Times to the Present Day* (Canterbury: K. M. McIntosh, 1982); Craig, "Marginalia of Rowland Taylor," 411–420.

[91]Wabuda, "Cranmer's Early Patronage," 85–87; Foxe, 5:501; MacCulloch, *Thomas Cranmer*, 369–370, 435, 442n.

[92]*LP* 13(1): no. 1170; 14(2): no. 71; 15: no. 1024 (46); HWRO, Bell's Register, fol. 26; Susan Brigden, *London and the Reformation* (Oxford: Clarendon Press, 1989), 307–325; MacCulloch, *Thomas Cranmer*, 307, 353, 369, 387, 456–459, 562, 568.

[93]John Bale, *A mysterye of inyquyte contayned within the heretycall Genealogye of Ponce Pantolabus* (Geneva [Antwerp: A. Goinus], 1545), sigs. 66r–66v.

At the same time that his friends suffered in 1540, Latimer was still being held in ward, expecting every day also to be put to death.[94] Eventually, he was released, but he was never permitted to preach again while Henry VIII lived. Those in Worcester diocese who had called for Latimer's burning eventually had their wish, but they had to wait another fifteen years. The same Dr. Richard Smith, Regius Professor of Divinity of Oxford, who had prayed for Stokesley in Evesham in 1537, preached at Latimer's execution in 1555.[95]

The final question to be addressed is whether Latimer's preachers were successful in their missions. Some historians have concluded that Latimer's episcopate was ineffective in spreading reform because his tenure was so short.[96] But that is not what conservative clergymen thought at the time. Edgeworth claimed that Latimer infected the whole diocese during his ascendancy.[97] Bishop Bell's visitation and commissions were dedicated to extirpating heresies that had flourished in the late 1530s, which Latimer had either encouraged or ignored. Sheriff Bell and Bishop Bell recognized the potential of Latimer's preachers to create change, especially where there was already a desire for reform, including among the influential gentlemen of the region. The advancement of reform, like the suppression of heresy, was highly dependent upon the policies instituted by the bishops. A reiteration of Latimer's convocation sermon can be heard in his friend Tracy's *Supplycacion* of 1544. Tracy's work was the product of disappointment with recent events. He denounced the Six Articles, and called for more preaching. Echoing Latimer's convocation sermon, he denounced conservative bishops who had burned books and attacked those who studied God's word: "Suche they call heretyques and persecute with puttynge them to open shame/ with enprysonmente/ and in conclusyon with deathe most fearefull and paynefull." Tracy maintained that as long as the bishops "doo persecute the worde and suche as syncerely preache the same, so longe shall synne increase."[98]

[94]*Sermons*, 164.
[95]Chester, *Hugh Latimer*, 215; Kreider, *English Chantries*, 141.
[96]Price, "Gloucester Diocese," 51; Powell, "Social Background," 96.
[97]Edgeworth, *Sermons*, 96.
[98]Tracy, *Supplycacion*, sigs. A5v, B5r–B6v, C1r, C8v, D3v.

PART 2

URBAN REFORMATION

RELIGIOUS DIVERSITY *and* GUILD UNITY *in* EARLY MODERN LONDON

Joseph P. Ward

THE 16TH OF JULY 1574 WAS A TYPICAL FIRST-QUARTER DAY for the Grocers' Company, one of the wealthiest and most influential trade guilds in London. During its morning meeting, the company's Court of Assistants reappointed its clerk and beadle for another year, arranged for the auditing of the wardens' accounts, and sold several leases on company property. After lunch, Warden Richard Thornhill delivered, in the words of the court's minutes, an "excellent exhortation" to a general assembly of the company. He began by reminding his audience that the company's founders had been moved "by the word of God" to devise "very godly and wise ordinances" designed to keep them in "brotherly love and verity." Thornhill then warned the company that the neglect of that inheritance would produce "contention and disagreement" of the kind that would lead to the "dissolution and overthrow" of all governments from companies to commonwealths. He concluded his address by declaring his desire to maintain the company's "good government and continuance in worship." Following Thornhill's remarks, the clerk read the company's ordinances to the assembly, and the meeting ended.[1]

At its heart, Thornhill's speech addressed the problem of disunity within the company. There were many reasons why the officers of the Grocers' Company, like urban elites elsewhere in Europe, could have desired to maintain the appearance of unity.[2] The power of trade guilds—which were

---

[1]G[uildhall] L[ibrary], MS 11588/1, fols. 255r–255v.

[2]On the problem of civic unity see R. W. Scribner, "Civic Unity and the Reformation in Erfurt," *Past and Present* 66 (1975): 29–60; Mark Konnert, "Urban Values versus Religious Passion: Châlons-sur-Marne during the Wars of Religion," *Sixteenth Century Journal* 20 (1989): 387–405; Ian Archer, *The Pursuit of Stability: Social Relations in Elizabethan London* (Cambridge: Cambridge University Press, 1991); Muriel C. McClendon, "'Against God's Word': Government, Religion and the Crisis of Authority in Early Reformation Norwich," *Sixteenth Century Journal* 25 (1994): 353–370.

known as "livery companies"—in London's economy rested on the City's charter of 1319, which required all citizens to occupy a trade, and which stipulated that anyone who was not a member of a guild would need to acquire the assent of the commonalty of the City before gaining the freedom of London.[3] Although the medieval Grocers' Company dealt primarily in spices, by the early seventeenth century the expansion and diversification of trade led the company's officers to claim jurisdiction over a variety of goods stretching from sugar to rhubarb, and from perfume to gunpowder.[4] Such variety of economic interests among the members was a constant challenge to the company's officers. Evidence of mixed loyalties among the grocers emerged in the later sixteenth and early seventeenth centuries, when a determined group of members defied the company's authority over the drugs trade and eventually convinced King James I to create an Apothecaries' Company which soon absorbed one-fifth of the Grocers' Company's membership.[5]

Recent research has shown that in addition to dealing with the diversity of economic interests among members, company officers had to cope with the consequences of religious change. According to Susan Brigden, their common beliefs and practices enhanced the sense of community among early-sixteenth-century Londoners. After the Reformation, however, division was "inevitable, because everyone agreed that anyone not of their Church was against it, heretic and schismatic"; as a result, their "world of shared faith was broken...and the Christian community divided."[6] Reflecting their origins as medieval fraternities, the religious life of livery companies prior to the Reformation included chantries, obits, and funeral processions, all of which maintained the spiritual links among members both living and dead. Nevertheless, Brigden found that behind the façade of guild unity developed cells of evangelicals—that is, proselytizing Protestants—whose personal beliefs surfaced during the Reformation.[7] Similarly, in his recent study of secularization in early modern England, C. John Sommerville proposed that the Reformation overturned

---

[3]Steve Rappaport, *Worlds within Worlds: Structures of Life in Sixteenth-Century London* (Cambridge: Cambridge University Press, 1989), 31, quoting the charter of 1319 in W. de G. Birch, ed., *The Historical Charters and Constitutional Documents of the City of London* (1884), 45–50.

[4]GL, MS 11588/3, p. 97.

[5]For more on the apothecaries see Joseph P. Ward, *Metropolitan Communities: Trade Guilds, Identity, and Change in Early Modern London* (Stanford: Stanford University Press, 1997), chap. 5.

[6]Susan Brigden, *London and the Reformation* (Oxford: Clarendon Press, 1989), 378, 639.

[7]Brigden, *London*, 411–413.

"the religious character" of trade guilds because the government seized corporate property which had been devoted to the support of religious observances. In particular, Sommerville argued that the Chantries Act of 1547 ensured that there would no longer be any "spiritual benefits" given to those who made gifts to their guilds.[8]

The Grocers' Company provides an important example of the ways in which companies responded to such religious changes during the sixteenth and early seventeenth centuries. The records of the company's Court of Assistants are not extant for the period before 1556, but the wardens' account books and other records allow the company's religious life to be surveyed after 1511. As expected, the theological component of the company's ceremonial practices evolved in response to the Reformation. However, this essay will argue that in other important ways the company's spiritual life deviated from the pattern which Brigden and Sommerville observed because the Grocers' officers took steps to minimize the disruption associated with the Crown's reformist policies, thereby allowing some members to express rather traditional views well into the seventeenth century.[9] The distribution of the company's clerical patronage throughout the period suggested that its officers kept their ranks open to members of differing religious opinions, and that such individuals found ways to work with one another even on issues that were theologically controversial. Furthermore, while the national government's policies led the company to abolish or reform its chantries, obits, and funeral processions, the company's officers developed new ritual forms that encouraged members to continue to see themselves as part of a spiritual community. While the various reforms that the government mandated forced the company to alter the forms of its ceremonies, their spirit remained much the same, suggesting that religious change may not have been as disruptive as historians have often suggested.

∽

[8]C. John Sommerville, *The Secularization of Early Modern England* (New York: Oxford University Press, 1992), 78.

[9]On the persistence of traditional beliefs and practices after the Reformation see J. J. Scarisbrick, *The Reformation and the English People* (Oxford: Basil Blackwell, 1984); Tessa Watt, *Cheap Print and Popular Piety, 1550–1640* (Cambridge: Cambridge University Press, 1991); Eamon Duffy, *The Stripping of the Altars: Traditional Religion in England c. 1400–c. 1580* (New Haven: Yale University Press, 1992).

Religion had always been an essential feature of the corporate life of the Grocers' Company. The company's roots stretched back to 9 May 1345, when a group of spice and soap merchants formed a fraternity dedicated to the honor of God, the virgin Mary, Saint Antonin, and all the saints. Their corporate status was elevated in 1428, when Henry VI issued a charter to the members of the "mystery of grocery" in London. Henry placed the company under the direction of three wardens and empowered the freemen grocers to choose the wardens' successors. The company, in turn, soon created a court of assistants to work with the wardens in the management of the Grocers' affairs. As a corporation, the company could acquire property in its own name, which allowed it to administer the estates of deceased members.[10] The surviving records indicate that grocers often entrusted the company to manage their chantries, obits, and other spiritual bequests. By the early sixteenth century, the company's religious portfolio included two chantry priests, six obits, and the advowsons of two London parishes: Saint Stephen Walbrook and All Hallows Honey Lane.[11]

The allocation of the company's religious patronage may have indicated the theological disposition of its membership. According to Susan Brigden, the company's clerical appointments may have displayed the support for reform among company members. In 1525, the Grocers nominated Robert Forman to the bishop of London to be rector of All Hallows, an office which he held until his death in 1528.[12] Forman was a committed evangelical whose sermons attracted the attention of reformers across London. He also stood at the center of an illicit book trade that circulated the works of Luther, Wycliffe, Hus, and Zwingli throughout London. Forman's involvement in that operation led to his arrest and imprisonment in 1528, but the intercession of Anne Boleyn ensured that his life ran its natural course.[13]

Although Forman was a leading reformer, his appointment sheds only a dim light on the spiritual disposition of the Grocers' Company on the eve of the Reformation. In the absence of Court of Assistants records, there is

---

[10]GL, MSS 11654, pp. 6–7; 11570, fol. 59v. For the early history of the company, see Pamela Nightingale, *A Medieval Mercantile Community: The Grocers' Company and the Politics and Trade of London 1000–1485* (New Haven: Yale University Press, 1995).

[11]GL, MS 11616, fols. 30r, 74r–82r; GL, MS 11571/3, fols. 91r–93r.

[12]George Hennessey, *Novum Repertorium Ecclesiasticum Parochiale Londinense* (1898), 77.

[13]Brigden, *London*, 113–114, 128, 161. Brigden suggested that Forman's "known reforming sympathies" may explain why he was "chosen for the City cure by its patrons, the Grocers, because there were in that company already some who favoured the new doctrines..." (113).

no evidence of how his nomination was approved. The surviving records indicate only that the wardens presented Forman to the bishop of London on the company's behalf.[14] The wills of two of the wardens have survived, but even if they are accurate representations of the wardens' religious views, they do little to clarify the politics behind Forman's selection.[15] William Campion, the upper warden, set out his will in 1530, and it indicates that, in typical Catholic fashion, he bequeathed his soul to God, Saint Mary, and "to all the holy company of saints in heaven." He also left 10 shillings to the Society of Jesus in Saint Paul's, £4 to the wardens of the Grocers' Company for a dinner among the livery after his death, and a gift for his son-in-law Edward Murrell, another of the wardens who presented Forman to the bishop.[16] Murrell's will, which was composed in 1537, contained a more reformist preamble in which he bequeathed his soul to Jesus "in whom and by the merits of whose blessed passion" he placed his "whole trust of clear remission and forgiveness" of his sins, but in the absence of further evidence of provisions of a religious sort, his will is an unreliable indicator of his theological disposition.[17] The selection of Forman for the All Hallows post could therefore suggest either that conservatives, whose ranks may have included Warden Campion, were outvoted by their reform-minded colleagues, or that there were a few evangelicals among the assistants who were more aware of Forman's views than their colleagues were, and that it was they who pushed for his selection. For example, John Petit, an influential reformer with close ties to Forman, had been a company warden in 1519, and he may have served as Forman's patron among the assistants.[18]

However, even if reformers were in control of the company by the early 1520s, they continued to maintain chantries, conduct obit masses for

---

[14]GL, MS 9531/10, fol. 10v. The presentment was in the name of "Thomas" Forman.

[15]On the difficulty of using wills to determine the religious views of testators see J. D. Alsop, "Religious Preambles in Early Modern English Wills as Formulae," *Journal of Ecclesiastical History* 40 (1989): 19–27; Christopher Marsh, *infra*, 201–244. In what follows the emphasis will be on the bequests for spiritual uses in the wills rather than their preambles, which were their most problematic features. For an example of this approach to the interpretation of wills, see Barbara J. Harris, "A New Look at the Reformation: Aristocratic Women and Nunneries, 1450–1540," *Journal of British Studies* 32 (1993), 103–105.

[16]P[ublic] R[ecord] O[ffice], P[rerogative] C[ourt of] C[anterbury], PROB 11/24, fol. 84v.

[17]PRO, PCC, PROB 11/27, fol. 97v.

[18]Brigden, *London*, 113,178; idem, "Thomas Cromwell and the 'brethren'" in C. Cross, D. Loades, and J. J. Scarisbrick, eds., *Law and Government under the Tudors* (Cambridge: Cambridge University Press, 1988), 44. Brigden incorrectly identifies Petit as a warden in 1525. The wardens for 1519–1520

deceased members, and accept new spiritual bequests on the company's behalf. The will of John Billesdon, which was completed in 1522, left a variety of properties in central London to the Grocers' Company on condition that it would maintain two chantry priests in the church of the priory at Halliwell in suburban London. Billesden had served as a warden of the company in 1517 and 1518, and the witnesses to his will included two of the wardens of 1522, as well as future upper wardens William Campion and Nicholas Lambert.[19] In 1523, John Drayton's will bequeathed properties to the company in order for it to keep a chantry priest at a London church. The will named Campion and Lambert as the executors of Drayton's estate, and it implored the company's wardens to carry out his intentions as they "would have their own will[s] performed."[20] At the close of the decade, Catholic William Butler left the company lands with which to fund a chantry priest in a Bedfordshire parish church. Butler served as upper warden nine times during the period 1511 to 1533, and his long career in the company's government may have given him a sense of the extent to which reformist opinions had been circulating among the assistants. Although he had been warden before, during, and after the evangelical Robert Forman's tenure at All Hallows, Butler's will demonstrates that he believed that the company would carry out his traditional spiritual wishes.[21] The subsequent wardens' accounts indicate that Butler's trust was well placed.[22]

After Forman's death, the company's ecclesiastical nominations displayed a confusing pattern. The Catholic Dr. John Coke followed Forman at All Hallows in 1528, and his seven-year career there was studded with

---

are identified in the Wardens' Accounts (GL, MS 11571/3, fol. 272r) as John Rest, Nicholas Lambert, and John Petit; for 1524–1525 as William Campion, Thomas Stevens, and Edward Murrell (GL, MS 11571/4, fol. 118r). Wardens typically rejoined the ranks of the assistants at the completion of their terms in office. Brigden (*London*, 113) also suggested that Geoffrey Lome had been a company member at the time of Fenton's appointment in 1525. However, he was bound as an apprentice—along with Ralph Clervis, who was indicted under the Act of Six Articles in 1540 (Brigden, *London*, 412)—in the year following Fenton's appointment: GL, MS 11571/4, fol. 356r.

[19]C[orporation of] L[ondon] R[ecords] O[ffice], Husting Roll 240/54. The unnamed witnesses included William Butler and the chantry was to benefit the souls of Sir Thomas Lovell and his wife, Isabell.

[20]CLRO, Husting Roll 240/55. The chantry was to benefit the souls of the family of Henry Adye and all Christians.

[21]CLRO, Husting Roll 241/35.

[22]GL, MS 11571/5, fol. 332r.

scandals, most notably in 1532, when he became embroiled in a citywide tithes dispute and also preached against the royal divorce. His subsequent arrest and imprisonment in the Tower did little to dissuade him from his conservative views, which he often shared with his parishioners.[23] After Coke's resignation, the company appointed Thomas Garret, Forman's cleric and assistant in the evangelical book trade, to the rectorship. During his tenure at All Hallows, Garrett continued to pronounce his evangelical views until they cost him his post as well as his life in 1540.[24]

The years which followed the Act of Six Articles in 1539 brought confusion to most English people, leaving the church on the defensive and traditional forms of worship in decline. Across London, the number of wills that included bequests for chantries and obits plummeted, and at All Hallows, the parishioners left an income that had provided for a chantry priest unutilized after 1540.[25] Despite such trends, the Grocers' Company continued to fulfill its spiritual obligations to its deceased members until Edward VI seized their chantry assets. During 1547, the company spent over £37 on fourteen obits and it distributed over £63 to seven chantry priests; such totals compare favorably with those of the other years for which records are available.[26]

There is circumstantial evidence that the company may have acquired a reputation for being hospitable to evangelicals. John Foxe suggested that the Protestant martyr John Lambert had considered joining the Grocers in 1533, but he provides no evidence for how Lambert developed his interest in the company.[27] Although several influential evangelicals were members of the company, the surviving records do not indicate that they played leading roles in the company's affairs. In 1540, four grocers were indicted under the Six Articles, but in 1536, the year closest to 1540 for which company records have survived, only one of the indicted members was listed among the junior liverymen of the company, a rank just below that of the assistants.[28] Perhaps the strongest evidence for the company's openness to

[23]Brigden, *London*, 201, 209.

[24]Brigden, *London*, 114–115, 235, 265–266, 311–322.

[25]Brigden, *London*, 387.

[26]GL, MS 11571/5, fols. 310r–v.

[27]Brigden, *London*, 411; John Foxe, *Acts and Monuments*, ed. S. R. Cattley and G. Townsend, 8 vols. (London, 1837–41), 5:225–226.

[28]Brigden names the influential evangelicals as John Petit, Geoffrey Lome, and John Blage, but see GL, MS 11571/5, fols. 114v and 118v. Both Blage and his former apprentice Richard Grafton were importers and distributors of translated Bibles during the midcentury; Brigden, *London*, 411, n. 155,

evangelicals came in 1547, when it nominated Thomas Becon for the Saint Stephen's rectorship, a post which he held until he was deprived because of marriage in 1554.[29] Becon had been an outspoken reformer who fled from London during Henry's final years, and his appointment only weeks after Edward's accession indicated that people in position to influence the assistants' decision were well connected among evangelicals.[30]

The surviving records of the Grocers' Court of Assistants from the middle of Mary's reign shed further light on the company's religious policies. Despite the progress of reform under Edward, Mary's accession allowed those who were not convinced by the new faith to express their views once more. In May 1556, a man identified as "Parson Jennings" offered to bequeath his house to the company if it would use the property's annual rents to maintain an obit for him, and the assistants formed a committee, which included Protestant Richard Grafton, to consider the offer. Although no record of the committee's report survives, Jennings returned to the court six months later and offered the grocers £40 with which to carry out his will. The assistants decided that his offer could not "be profitable" to the company, and so they politely rejected it.[31]

However, that decision did not mean that the grocers were not receptive to bequests with spiritual dimensions. If a clear theological consensus had emerged among the company's officers during that period, Sir William Laxton, former lord mayor and warden of the Grocers' Company seven times between 1534 and 1553, was well placed to have understood its implications. In 1556, he bequeathed his estate to the assistants after they agreed to use its proceeds to establish a free school and an almshouse in his native town of Oundle, Northamptonshire. Among Laxton's instructions to the assistants was the insistence that the almsmen be beadsmen and, although Laxton did not specify what the beadsmen were to do, the term traditionally referred to people who were set the task of praying for the souls of the dead.[32] Thus, under Mary the Grocers' officers continued to

---

412, 419. The four who were indicted in 1540 were Ralph Clervis, Richard Grafton, John Mayler, and John Blage, but only Blage wore the livery of the company in 1536: GL MS 11571/5, fols. 114v–115r.

[29]E. L. C. Mullins, "The Effects of the Marian and Elizabethan Religious Settlements upon the Clergy of London 1553–1564" (M.A. thesis, University of London, 1948).

[30]Derrick S. Bailey, *Thomas Becon and the Reformation of the Church of England* (Edinburgh: Oliver and Boyd, 1952), 54–57; Brigden, *London*, 458.

[31]GL, MS 11588/1, fols. 6r, 10v.

[32]CLRO, Husting Roll 249/18. The will was proved in November 1557. The Court of Assistants

maintain the trust of influential company members who subscribed to theological principles that would have been out of fashion in Edward's reign.

After Mary's death, the company's policies appeared to shift with the political winds. The assistants took steps to encourage a preaching ministry, one of the centerpieces of the puritan reform program, by sponsoring two divinity students at Cambridge.[33] The company required their scholars to preach in London at least once during the tenure of their fellowship, at which time they were to acknowledge the company's patronage.[34] Of course, that policy may have been no more than a test of a scholar's ability. For example, in August 1589, the company required Bernard Robinson to "make a sermon before the company that they may judge his worthiness of their exhibition conferred upon him."[35] Robinson therefore traveled to London to deliver a sermon on the company's election day in 1590. After leading the lord mayor, several aldermen, and the leading members of the company from the Grocers' Hall to Saint Stephen Walbrook, he delivered a sermon that pleased the assistants so much that they gave him more than £3 for his travel expenses.[36]

Nevertheless, the case of Edmund Campion suggested that the sermon was a test of orthodoxy as well as of talent. In July 1568, the company informed Campion that his sermon was long overdue, and warned him that he would lose his fellowship if he did not publicly endorse the "religion now authorized at Paul's Cross." Campion replied that to preach at Paul's Cross was something that he was "loathe to presume unto," and so the

---

discussed Laxton's estate "sundry times" before agreeing to accept it "with thanksgiving." Richard Grafton was among those appointed to oversee its undertaking: GL, MS 11588/1, fol. 6v. Brigden makes no mention of Laxton, but by her reckoning, he must have been among the last Londoners to provide for beadsmen in his will: Brigden, *London*, 581. Although there is no way to attribute definitively the authorship of the will to Laxton, the preamble was ambiguously Catholic, leaving his soul to "almighty God and to my maker and redeemer Jesus Christ his only son and to all the holy company of heaven."

[33]On the importance of preaching for puritans: Christopher Hill, *Society and Puritanism in Pre-Revolutionary England* (Harmondsworth: Penguin, 1964), 31–77; Paul S. Seaver, *The Puritan Lectureships: The Politics of Religious Dissent 1560–1662* (Stanford: Stanford University Press, 1970), 15–54; Patrick Collinson, "Lectures by Combination: Structures and Characteristics of Church Life in 17th-Century England," in his *Godly People: Essays on English Protestantism and Puritanism* (London: Hambledon Press, 1983): 467–498.

[34]GL, MS 11588/1, fols. 115v, 116v; Hill, *Society and Puritanism*, chap. 2.

[35]GL, MS 11588/1, fols. 376v, 378v, 411v.

[36]GL, MS 11588/1, fols. 421v, 423r. The lord mayor was Grocer John Hart.

company offered to have him deliver a sermon instead at Saint Stephen's.[37] By October, Campion informed the company that because "he dare not, he cannot, neither was it expedient he should preach as yet," he would resign his fellowship.[38] Unfortunately, the company's records do not provide sufficient evidence of the process by which Campion, who later became one of Elizabethan England's great Jesuits, was awarded his fellowship, so there is no way to determine whether he had received the support of any like-minded members of the company. Perhaps in an effort to avoid such embarrassment in the future, the company loosened its preaching requirements for scholars and, after 1566, relied upon the recommendations of mainstream Protestant divines such as John Whitgift when granting awards.[39]

While the assistants' support of divinity students required them to seek the advice of outside experts, the exercise of their clerical patronage involved input from overlapping groups of parishioners and company members. In 1563, the assistants considered the request of a minister named Sheriff for the rectory at Saint Stephen's. Sheriff's principal referee was Miles Coverdale, who had been a leading translator of the Bible into English during the 1530s, an activity which probably brought him into contact with assistant Richard Grafton.[40] However, Sheriff's appointment was delayed because of the absence of Alderman Jackman, one of the company's assistants and a parishioner of Saint Stephen's. Jackman attended the next court meeting, at which Sheriff was passed over for the benefice in favor of Richard Leyfield.[41] The court record mentioned no reason for Sheriff's failure, but it seems unlikely that Coverdale's influence impeded his candidacy because in 1564 and 1565 the assistants appointed Coverdale to be among four "famous and learned men" whom the company nominated to judge the qualifications of candidates for the rectory at All Hallows.[42]

---

[37]GL, MS 11588/1, fol. 185v.

[38]L, MS 11588/1, fol. 187v. For more on Campion's career, see J. H. Pollen, *The English Catholics in the Reign of Queen Elizabeth* (London: Longmans, Green, 1920).

[39]For examples of Whitgift's recommendations: GL, MS 11588/1, fols. 151r, 205r, 261r.

[40]Brigden, *London*, 286–287.

[41]GL, MS 11588/1, fols. 100v–101r.

[42]Hennessey, *Novum Repertorium*, 386; GL, MS 11588/1, fols. 109v, 141v. That court record suggests that the recommendations of four divines was a requirement of the estate that gave the advowson to the company. In that year Coverdale also advanced the nominations of Thomas Cartwright and William Power to be the first two recipients of the company's fellowships for divinity students at Cambridge and Oxford; their fortune proved to be better than Sheriff's: GL, MS 11588/1, fols. 117r–v.

A case that involved the broader membership of the parish came in December 1562, when Thomas Becon, who had returned to his former benefice at some point after Elizabeth's accession, asked the company for permission to turn his position over to his curate, Philip Pettit. Becon described Pettit as "well learned and of good behavior" and "one that well pleases the parish and they are well contented with him." Three months later, the assistants received a petition from some of the parishioners of Saint Stephen's that asked them to appoint Pettit upon Becon's retirement. The assistants complied with that request in May, citing both his skill in preaching and the recommendation of the parishioners. Pettit's cause may also have been advanced by the willingness of two assistants—one of whom was a City alderman—to guarantee that Pettit would fulfill the company's expectations.[43]

At the turn of the century, the parishioners of Saint Stephen's again cooperated with the company in managing the replacement of their rector. In July 1601, the parishioners requested that the company present Roger Fenton to the bishop upon the resignation of Henry Tripp, who had lost the support of several influential parishioners. The assistants—who had heard a sermon by Fenton at the election of the company's wardens two weeks earlier—encouraged the parishioners to proceed "in the said cause" according to ecclesiastical law, after which their request would again be considered "with all love and favor."[44] Although the nature of that cause remains obscure, the parish vestry minute book indicates that one Lawrence Greene was authorized to join with the churchwardens to finance their attempts to remove Tripp from his post. Greene may have served as a liaison between the company and the parish in this regard, for he was a company member and had served as an overseer of the poor of the parish in 1600.[45] In any event, the negotiations between the parishioners and Tripp produced an amicable separation. In August, after Tripp vacated the rectory, the company assistants named Fenton to the benefice after they were convinced of his aptitude for the post by their own proceedings as well as the "great commendation" of the parishioners.[46]

---

[43]Hennessey, *Novum Repertorium*, 386. GL, MS 11588/1, fols. 76v, 83v, 87v. In 1573, the successful candidacy of Thomas Cooke for the pastorship of All Hallows was advanced by the testimony of two assistants that he was "an honest man": GL, MS 11588/1, fols. 246r–v.

[44]GL, MS 11588/2, pp. 253, 255.

[45]GL, MSS 594, pp. 46, 48; 11588/2, p. 245.

[46]GL, MS 11588/2, p. 258. The popularity of Fenton's preaching among company members continued through his tenure at Saint Stephen's. In 1615, the company paid to publish a sermon that

The company's clerical appointments did not always meet with such broad approval. In 1625, the assistants nominated Aaron Wilson for the benefice of Saint Stephen's.[47] Nine years later, King Charles I elevated Wilson to a vicarage in Plymouth, and requested that the company not appoint a successor to the Saint Stephen's rectory until they had consulted with him. The assistants expressed their willingness to comply with Charles' request, but they also received a petition from several parishioners that nominated three candidates to be Wilson's successor.[48] Two months later, Charles again wrote to the assistants asking them to nominate a royal chaplain, Thomas Howell, to the vacant rectory, but the assistants also considered the petition of Thomas Saxby, who was the son-in-law of the company clerk and one of the parishioners' nominees. The assistants then interviewed Howell, who informed them that although he intended to continue as rector of a parish near Guilford in Surrey which was more valuable than Saint Stephen's, he would reside in London during the winter and ensure that an able preacher replaced him during his absences. The assistants then offered Howell time to reconsider his position, but he pressed them to an immediate vote which Saxby won with a "plurality of hands."[49] Two weeks later, the assistants received a letter from Charles indicating his displeasure with Saxby's election. When they informed Saxby of Charles' stance, the rector asserted that he had no doubt of his legal right to occupy Saint Stephen's, "but now seeing his majesty is displeased with the said choice, he therefore did freely and willingly surrender up his presentation," after which the assistants gave him £20 and named Howell to the rectory "by the free and unanimous consent of the whole Court."[50]

Howell's triumph was not long-lasting. In February 1635, the assistants chose not to reimburse Howell the £80 that he spent on repairs to his rectory, and in April 1638, Howell refused to preach before the company at its annual liturgy.[51] On 18 March 1640, a petition from "the most part" of the parishioners notified the Grocers' Court of Assistants that they anticipated

---

Fenton delivered to them "for the public good that may grow in others who were not hearers thereof and are desirous to learn godly and divine instructions by reading the same." GL, MS 11588/2, p. 862.

[47]GL, MS 11588/3, p. 307.

[48]GL, MS 11588/3, p. 541. The three nominees were "Mr Lechford, Mr. Molines, and Mr Saxby."

[49]GL, MS 11588/3, pp. 546–547.

[50]GL, MS 11588/3, p. 547. In 1636, the assistants appointed Saxby to the rectory at Norhill in Bedfordshire, an advowson which they administered through Lady Slany's estate: GL, MS 11588/3, p. 568.

[51]GL, MS 11588/3, pp. 559, 596.

the vacancy of their parish's rectory in the near future. They therefore requested that the assistants make sure to appoint "an able learned and conformable divine" who would be nominated by "the greater part of the voices of the parish." After the assistants debated the parishioners' proposition, they remained concerned that it would involve their yielding their influence in such appointments, but they pledged to give "a special care and respect" to the parishioners' candidate when the post became vacant.[52]

When the assistants met to consider the vacancy two months later, the Saint Stephen's parishioners presented them with a list of five candidates for their rectory. The assistants agreed to consider the nominees, so long as they could do so "lawfully…without prejudice to this company's ancient and undoubted rights of the presentation." The assistants then added five nominees of their own to the list, and they held an election that narrowed the field to two finalists: Michael Thomas, a nominee of the assistants, and William Strong, a nominee of the parishioners. After further debate, the assistants decided to resolve the contest with a ballot, in which Thomas was victorious by the margin of fifteen votes to thirteen. After the assistants installed Thomas as their appointee, they read a letter on his behalf from a member of Parliament denying allegations that Thomas was "a time server and a bower to our late devised altars" and certified that "both in opinion and practice he is and hath been utterly averse from all those late innovations of our church."[53]

The election of Thomas did not end the controversy. In October, three members of the company requested that the assistants show them the documents that would confirm the company's right to nominate the rector of Saint Stephen Walbrook. Upon questioning, the three members refused to tell the court of their intentions, and so the assistants denied their request, suggesting instead that they might sue them at law if they questioned their rights to the advowson.[54] Three weeks later, the assistants received a petition from "the greater part" of the parishioners of Saint Stephen's which praised their rector, a man who from "anything we know or ever could hear by diligent enquiry is a man without taint in his doctrine, life, and conversation." The petitioners concluded by suggesting that "though there be some few in the parish that aim at the bringing in of some other in his place

---

[52] GL, MS 11588/3/19. See also Tai Liu, *Puritan London: A Study of Religion and Society in the City Parishes* (Newark: University of Delaware Press, 1986), 60.

[53] GL, MS 11588/4, pp. 26–27.

[54] GL, MS 11588/4, p. 35.

if possible they could, yet our humble requests are that he may be continued."[55] The assistants thereupon confirmed their appointment of Thomas, but the controversy surrounding their action lingered into the next year. The assistants paid his first fruits out of the company's stock because some of his parishioners refused to pay their tithes until the suit concerning the company's control of the advowson was resolved. Thomas ended the stalemate by accepting another, more valuable, benefice and the assistants named Thomas Warren—whose sponsors remained unidentified—to replace him in March 1642.[56]

The assistants also moved to suspend Samuel Warner, one of the Grocers who protested against the appointment of Thomas. They alleged that Warner had complained about Thomas to one of the bishop's officials, though Warner subsequently claimed that "his memory was weak and he did not well remember the very words he had then spoken, some time being since past, but his opinion is still that the said Mr. Thomas was a very unworthy minister." Although the assistants found Warner's behavior to have been "rash," they decided to forbear punishing him "according to his desert" until some "worshipful persons" had spoken with him. Five weeks later, the assistants asked him to submit to their judgment, but when Warner refused to conform they suspended him.[57] Warner's position in the company again became an issue in 1644, when he was elected an alderman of the City. After the assistants allowed him to explain his misbehavior privately to a committee of aldermen and company wardens, they elevated Warner to their ranks.[58]

The foregoing has demonstrated the difficulties of assuming that the officers of the company shared a common view of religious change. Throughout the period being considered, assistants were concerned both to uphold orthodoxy and to maintain working relationships with the national government and with members of parishes in which the company had influence. The surviving records for the late sixteenth and early seventeenth centuries indicate that parishioners played an important role in the company's clerical appointments. Although there is no way to determine that the same had been true during the early phases of the Reformation, it suggests that historians should not assume that the company was evangelical

---

[55]GL, MS 11588/4, p. 36.
[56]GL, MS 11588/4, pp. 41, 46–47.
[57]GL, MS 11588/4, pp. 36–39.
[58]GL, MS 11588/4, p. 103.

simply because it appointed prominent Protestants or because a few of its members were evangelicals. Some assistants may have been more concerned with the company's religious policies than others, and so long as the company remained in the mainstream, it seems quite possible that a moderately interested majority could have allowed a committed minority to direct the company's course on a particular issue.

ॐ

Religious patronage was not the only theological topic that manifested diverse attitudes among company members. The disputes that swirled around religious ceremonies during the sixteenth century transformed the company's social customs because forms which were intended to enhance feelings of shared values could, in the unsettled atmosphere of the Reformation, have excited further controversies.[59] In particular, although the company's late medieval rituals often served to foster a sense of commonality among members and to encourage prayers for the souls of the company's benefactors, the official abolition of belief in purgatory during the Reformation challenged such ties between the company and its past and may, thereby, have loosened the bonds of loyalty among members in the present.

The semipublic state of the religious, social, and political events surrounding the selection of the company's wardens presented the assistants with a set of particularly thorny issues. The typical practice early in Elizabeth's reign required the company's aldermen, wardens, assistants, and livery to assemble at Grocers' Hall "in their best livery gowns" and then to proceed to Saint Stephen Walbrook to hear a "service sung by solemn note." Afterwards, they returned to the hall, "where they drank according to the old custom," and nominated the wardens for the following year. At nine in the morning on the next day, they would again meet at the Hall in their livery and return to Saint Stephen's to hear a sermon "and other divine service done" by the rector and to receive communion. They would then return to the Hall for dinner and the selection of the warden.[60] Although the court minute book often used the phrase "divine service" to describe the ceremony on Sunday, it was not clear that this meant that all of the liverymen were expected to receive the sacrament on that occasion.

[59]Brigden, *London*, 565.
[60]GL, MS 11588/1, fols. 64r–65r.

In any case, the assistants probably hoped that the nomination of the wardens would not provoke contentions among the assembly.[61] Because the grocers often marked their wardens' election with a feast for the company and invited dignitaries, it was crucial that the assistants had worked out their differences during the previous two days.[62] However, things did not always go according to plan. In 1557, Upper Warden Thomas Bowyer was appointed to "sit at the high table" and to select his replacement from among two nominees whom the assistants had appointed. Rather than accept the honor and authority of that position, Bowyer complained about his share of the costs of the upcoming feast, and so he avoided his office altogether. As a result, the court fined Bowyer more than £6 for having "moved and stirred sundry inconveniences amongst the whole company."[63] In that context, the company's officers may have hoped that their ceremonies would display their unity, but they must have realized that unity was not a thing that they could take for granted.

The reinvention of the feast of Saint Antonin also indicated their concern for the company's ceremonial traditions. The ordinances of the medieval fraternity which lay at the company's roots required every member to attend high mass on the saint's feast day in May.[64] In the early sixteenth century, the wardens' accounts contain sporadic references to dinners and processions on that day, but they also suggest that the form and content could vary from year to year. In 1519, the company spent more than £3 donated by a deceased member on the dinner, and although it was not common for an individual to fund the dinner, the range of expenditure usually did fall between £3 and £4.[65] Although the church under Henry and Edward had discouraged the celebration of feast days, the grocers continued their tradition with worship and dinner throughout the Reformation, and each year the assistants appointed two liverymen to provide the meal.[66] In 1563 the Court of Assistants agreed that the feast day would "be kept on the Tuesday in rogation week being the 18th day of May," at which

[61]Sometimes the company would hear a sermon on each day: GL, MS 11588/1, fol. 334v.

[62]For examples, GL, MS 11588/1, fols. 322r, 333v, 345v.

[63]GL, MS 11588/1, fols. 10v–12r.

[64]GL, MS 11570, fol. 59r. The saint's name is spelled in a variety of ways in the company's early modern records; Nightingale argues that "Antonin" is the "correct" spelling and that the feast day was May 18: *Medieval Mercantile Community*, 35–41.

[65]GL, MS 11571/3, fol. 286v.

[66]David Cressy, *Bonfires and Bells: National Memory and the Protestant Calendar in Elizabethan and Stuart England* (London: Weidenfeld and Nicolson, 1989), 5–7.

time the "whole livery" was to meet at Grocers' Hall at eight in the morning and then go "in order in their best livery gowns to the church of Saint Stephen in Walbrook there to hear divine service and from there return to the Grocers' Hall to dinner according to the old custom." In the event, William Ormeshaw, one of the stewards for the dinner that year, refused to pay his share of the expenses, claiming that "he would rather spend £20 and lie in prison than to be one of the stewards for it was but a slavery"; the assistants therefore fined him 40 shillings for his "unfitting words."[67]

If the nature of Ormeshaw's complaint had been theological, he may have received comfort in 1576 when the company decided that the custom of having the livery worship and dine together in May should be continued not in regard of the saint's feast but "in commemoration of the beginning of the company" in May 1345.[68] Of course, since the company's origins lay in a fraternity, it seems likely that its first meeting occurred around the feast day of its patron saint. In any case, the assistants' practice of referring to the reformed custom as "the feast of Saint Antonin alias the commemoration dinner by an anniversary solemnity in commemoration of the beginning of this worshipful company," reflected the limited appeal of any attempt to shift the focus of the ceremony away from the company and its founders.[69]

Commemoration was an individual as well as a collective act. After the Reformation, the company could no longer maintain chantries and obits, but it could still offer members a means for perpetuating their memories. Sir William Laxton's will not only endowed a free school and an almshouse, but it required the company to see that the school would be "perpetually...called the free grammar school of Sir William Laxton knight Alderman of the City of London," and that the schoolmasters, ushers, and beadsmen would be similarly named.[70] Subsequent records

---

[67]GL, MS 11588/1, fols. 86v, 87v.

[68]GL, MS 11588/1, fol. 274v.

[69]GL, MS 11588/2, pp. 807, 912. According to the standard interpretation of late medieval and early modern urban ceremony, the year had two halves, one ritualistic and the other secular; the grocers' decision to leave their commemoration dinner in the ritualistic half of the year, which stretched from Christmas to Midsummer, suggests their unwillingness to push change too far; Charles Phythian-Adams, "Ceremony and the Citizen: The Communal year at Coventry 1450–1550," in Peter Clark and Paul Slack, eds., *Crisis and Order in English Towns 1500–1700* (London: Routledge, 1972), 73; Michael Berlin, "Civic Ceremony in Early Modern London," *Urban History Yearbook* (1986), 24. On the changing meaning of ritual in community more generally see David H. Sacks, "The Demise of the Martyrs: The Feasts of Saint Clement and Saint Katherine in Bristol, 1400–1600," *Social History* 11 (1986): 141–169.

[70]CLRO, Husting Roll 249/18.

indicate that his desire was met. In 1593, the schoolmaster was ordered to "set up Sir William Laxton's arms" on the school, and although beadsmen were archaic, in 1638, the company reminded the residents of the almshouse "of the foundation of the memorable benefactor Sir William Laxton," and ordered them to perform "their duties towards God and praying for their benefactors."[71] In 1650, the company's inspectors told the master and scholars of the "pious and worthy act of the founder in his care and provision for the propagation of learning and civil education of posterity, and their great obligements to the company for perpetuating the memory of such a benefactor by their liberality, care, and oversight of the due performance of his good intentions."[72]

The company's ability to commemorate deceased members extended beyond those whose gifts were as large—or whose wishes were as explicit—as Laxton's. In 1570, Edward Jackman left the company £40 to be spent on a plate that would have his arms engraved "upon it whereby it might be known to be [his] gift."[73] In 1574, Henry Cloker arranged to bequeath a house to the company in return for its agreement to spend the proceeds on gilded ale pots with "the name Henry Cloker...graven and set upon them."[74] In 1614, Grocer Philip Rogers left a bequest to fund a dinner for those liverymen who attended his burial. However, since he was buried in Surrey, none of the livery attended him, and so the company applied his donation to the purchase of plate "to remain forever...in remembrance of the testator's love" to the company.[75]

Similarly, after 1568, anyone who bequeathed to the company "lands, money, plate, or other ornaments" would have their names read "once in a year at the least as time shall seem at the discretion of the wardens."[76] Although the form of the ceremony bore a loose resemblance to that of a collective obit, a grocer would not have to be dead to be counted a benefactor. In October 1622, Sir Stephen Soame was present when the wardens registered him "among the worthy benefactors of the house" because he had contributed £500 towards a new ceiling for the company hall.[77] While

---

[71]GL, MSS 11588/2, p. 39; 11588/3, p. 601. Similarly, in 1642, the company's inspectors visited the almspeople and "exhorted them to pray for their benefactors": GL, MS 11588/4, p. 53.

[72]GL, MS 11588/4, p. 242.

[73]GL, MS 11616, fol. 250r.

[74]GL, MS 11616, fol. 205v.

[75]GL, MS 11588/2, p. 807.

[76]GL, MS 11588/1, fol. 179r.

[77]GL, MS 11588/3, p. 57.

adding to the company's ornaments, some benefactors became ornaments themselves; in 1612, the assistants arranged for "pictures of famous and worthy magistrates and benefactors of this company to be made and placed in most fit and convenient places in this hall (as in the Haberdashers' Hall) for continuance of memory of them to future posterity."[78]

Funerals could also demonstrate diversity and change as well as unity and stability among the Grocers during the Reformation.[79] The company's ancient ordinances required all liverymen to attend the burials of their deceased colleagues, but the practice may not have lived up to the policy. A survey of the wardens' accounts for the third, sixth, and ninth years of each decade from 1510 to 1600 produced no evidence that a liveryman was ever fined for being absent at a funeral, although the accounts usually did include the fines of those who were absent from other company meetings. The wills of Grocers' wardens also suggest that the company's attendance at funerals was optional rather than mandatory. In 1537, Edward Murrell left money for a dinner for "such of them as shall come and bring my body to burial" in their livery, an indication that he may not have expected all of them to attend.[80] In 1547, the will of Andrew Woodcock made no reference to the company, although it gave his executors the ambiguous instructions to bury him "without pomp" but with "four or five priests and clerks" to receive his "body at the church door with psalms."[81] A clearer expression of the testator's wishes came in 1558, when Thomas Bowyer instructed his executor "not to trouble" his "master nor company of the grocers" to his burial.[82]

However, they probably would have attended if they had been invited. In 1556, the diarist Henry Machyn reported that the funeral procession of Grocer Sir William Laxton included the lord mayor and aldermen, all of whom found refreshment at the Grocers' Hall after the burial. On the next day, three masses were said for Laxton, and they were followed by, in Machyn's estimation, "a[s] great [a] dinner as I have seen at any burying."[83]

---

[78]GL, MS 11588/2, p. 733.

[79]For the changing organization of death rituals after the Reformation see Dan Beaver, "'Sown in Dishonour, Raised in Glory': Death, Ritual and Social Organization in Northern Gloucestershire, 1590–1690," *Social History* 17 (1992): 389–419.

[80]GL, MS 11571/3–8; PRO, PCC, PROB 11/27, fol. 97v.

[81]PRO, PCC, PROB 11/39, fol. 280r.

[82]PRO, PCC, PROB 11/41, fol. 90r.

[83]*The Diary of Henry Machyn, Citizen and Merchant Taylor of London, 1550–1563*, ed. J. G. Nichols, Camden Society, 42 (1848), 111–112.

In 1560, the diarist noted that the company's officers and several "priests and clerks singing" accompanied the body of a grocer named Hansley. Despite such a traditional ceremony, Bishop John Jewel, an outspoken critic of the belief in purgatory, preached over Hansley's corpse.[84] The Court of Assistants' decision in 1616 to allow liverymen to request the attendance of the company's officers at the burials of their wives was further evidence of their flexible attitudes; their only requirement for the execution of that "commendable work of charity" was a gift to the company of more than £6.[85]

Controversy surrounding the use of the company's hearse cloth suggested that the assistants considered funerals to have been opportunities to focus the spiritual interests of grocers on the company. Traditionally, the assistants allowed the hearse cloth to be used only for the burial of former wardens, but in 1564 they allowed the widow of liveryman William Bridger to "have the best cloth," although they noted that they complied with her request only by their "special license."[86] While the exclusivity of the best cloth may have made it an attractive feature for some grocers, others were upset by its symbolic content. In October 1573, the court of assistants considered a report that "some of the company had heard that diverse men were offended at certain things" about the hearse cloth, and so they authorized the wardens to "take away such things as are unlawful and to set good things in their place."[87] In May 1575, the court instructed the wardens either to "sell the old best hearse cloth and make a new of velvet or else make the side and ends of new velvet fair embroidered with the company's arms and other good things as they shall think good."[88] In October, they sent the hearse cloth to an embroiderer to be bordered, and although the records do not indicate what the "bad things" were, they suggest that the wardens adopted the design which included the company's arms.[89]

And so, while the national government's religious policies transformed the religious practices of the company, they did not divide members into discrete, opposing camps of conformists and heretics. As a community, the company remained open to individuals with a variety of attitudes towards

[84]Ibid., 232.
[85]GL, MS 11588/3, p. 10.
[86]GL, MS 11588/1, fol. 129r.
[87]GL, MS 11588/1, fol. 243v.
[88]GL, MS 11588/1, fol. 264r.
[89]GL, MS 11588/1, fol. 270r.

theology and religious practice. The one thing that the company's officers did not tolerate was a member who challenged their authority and created a public row over a ceremonial issue. Those who were troubled by aspects of the company's ceremonies—such as the hearse cloth, funeral processions, or Saint Antonin's feast day—could either seek reform or avoid participation. The relationship between the living and the dead grocers changed noticeably, but the company found a variety of ways to maintain the memories of its deceased benefactors long after the abolition of chantries and obits.

∽

The Reformation generated a number of controversies which tested the ability of company officers to urge members, in the words of Richard Thornhill cited at the outset of this essay, to avoid "contention and disagreement." During the early phases of the Reformation, it is clear that the ranks of the company's officers contained both Catholics and evangelical Protestants and that, despite their different opinions, they cooperated in a variety of areas including the maintenance of chantries and obits for deceased members. As time went on, the officers continued to deal with religious controversy within the company because the company held the advowsons of two London parishes and established scholarships for divinity students. On occasion—such as in the case of Samuel Warner— contentions reached a dangerous intensity, but when dealing with conflict the officers were guided by a desire to maintain company unity as well as religious orthodoxy. The ability of the company's officers to reform company ritual helped them to maintain unity among their members. While the forms of the rituals changed, much of their substance remained the same. Chantries and obits were abolished, but the company remained an institution which members trusted with the preservation of their memories. Rituals of commemoration not only offered spiritual benefits to individuals who donated money to the company, but also provided company officers such as Thornhill with a way to remind members of the common heritage they received from the company's founders. Thornhill's message was clear: members had to be sure not to allow their differences to undermine the "good government and continuance in worship" that maintained the unity of the guild.

DISCIPLINE *and* PUNISH?

MAGISTRATES AND CLERGY IN EARLY REFORMATION NORWICH

Muriel C. McClendon

IN THE HISTORY OF THE EUROPEAN REFORMATION, towns have received considerable scholarly attention. Urban areas had high concentrations of population that were usually more literate than the populations of their surrounding countrysides. Towns were also significant centers of communication, and many were important ecclesiastical centers where a variety of religious institutions were located. These features made them, generally speaking, more receptive to the Protestant message and also allowed them to serve as bases for evangelization.[1] In England towns have also been credited with a special role in the reception of the Reformation, but their position was somewhat different from continental cities.[2]

None of the cities in England, except London, could compare in size and complexity to their continental counterparts. Moreover, English towns did not have political independence similar to that enjoyed by the German Imperial cities. English towns, even the capital city of London, were reliant on the Crown for the continued exercise of their political privileges. Many provincial communities also found it advantageous to seek the patronage of a local gentleman or aristocrat who they hoped would look after their interests when at court or in Parliament. This enmeshment in a larger political,

[1]For a recent discussion of these issues, see Bob Scribner, "A Comparative Overview," in *The Reformation in National Context*, ed. Bob Scribner, Roy Porter, and Mikulas Teich (Cambridge: Cambridge University Press, 1994), esp. 219–223. An example of a European town that was not particularly receptive to the Reformation may be found in R.W. Scribner, "Why was there no Reformation in Cologne?" in idem, *Popular Culture and Popular Movements in Reformation Germany* (London and Ronceverte, W.Va.: Hambledon Press, 1987).

[2]On the role of towns in the English Reformation see for example, Patrick Collinson, *The Birthpangs of Protestant England: Religious and Cultural Change in the Sixteenth and Seventeenth Centuries* (London: Macmillan, 1988), 32–36, and Christopher Haigh, *English Reformations: Religion, Politics and Society under the Tudors* (Oxford: Clarendon Press, 1993), 197–198, 272–274.

social, economic, and cultural world had a decisive impact on how urban elites coped with the religious change and its accompanying disturbances within their jurisdictions. Ever conscious of the several masters that they might have had to serve, urban governors felt increasingly squeezed between the expanding power of the Tudor state, their local ecclesiastical hierarchy, and the threat of emerging religious conflict.

The predicament that civic leaders faced can be seen in the case of Norwich and the ways in which its corporate elite handled religious conflict that erupted among local clergy during the early Tudor Reformation. Examining their response to religious discord highlights some of the pressures that all English communities faced, to varying degrees, during these difficult years. The attacks against the English church and its disintegration posed difficult problems for local leaders. But the example of Norwich and its magistrates and clergy also reveals how different the impact of the Reformation could be on members of even a single community. When conflict over religious change erupted among some of the local clergy, the magistrates upon whom the task fell of contending with this friction worked to defuse dissension. They were lenient in their treatment of dissidents and loathe to bring expressions of religious nonconformity to the attention of the ecclesiastical hierarchy or the central government. The magistrates studiously avoided becoming entangled in religious controversy themselves so that their ability to govern the city would not be impeded. Their practice of suppressing discord helped to prevent the city from becoming engulfed by the religious controversies of the Reformation.

∾

Although its population of about 8,500 in the 1520s would not have placed it at the top of the urban hierarchy on the continent, Norwich was nevertheless the second city in sixteenth-century England and the regional center of East Anglia.[3] In wealth, as measured by its inhabitants' contribution to the 1524–25 lay subsidy, Norwich was also surpassed only by

---

[3]For population estimates, see work of John F. Pound: "Government and Society in Tudor and Stuart Norwich, 1525–1675" (Ph.D. dissertation, University of Leicester, 1974), ch. 1; "The Social and Trade Structure of Norwich 1525–1575," *Past and Present* 34 (1966): 49–69; and *Tudor and Stuart Norwich* (Chichester: Phillimore, 1988), 28. Pound's earliest estimates for the population of sixteenth-century Norwich were as high as 13,000 ("Social and Trade Structure," 50) but in his most recent research he argues for the lower figure of 8,500. He still holds that Norwich was England's largest provincial city, estimating populations of 6,500 for Bristol, 4,600 for Exeter, and 5,250 for York. See also James Campbell, *Norwich*, Historic Towns, ed. Mary D. Lobel (London: Scolar Press, 1975), 18, n. 47.

London.[4] The city enjoyed a great degree of self-government as one of the nation's largest and most prosperous urban communities. Political authority had been placed chiefly in the hands of an annually elected mayor and twenty-three aldermen, a privilege that citizens enjoyed only at the pleasure of the crown.[5]

Norwich's status as a provincial capital was augmented by its role as the cathedral seat for the diocese of the same name, one of the largest dioceses in England. The church had strong and highly visible representation in the city. In addition to the cathedral and its priory, Norwich was home to over forty parish churches, four friaries, and two colleges of secular priests. A Benedictine nunnery, two cells of the cathedral monastery, and five hospitals, all on the outskirts of town, completed the array of religious establishments from which the inhabitants of the city and the surrounding area could draw spiritual comfort.[6] For many residents, however, particularly members of the Norwich corporation, the cathedral priory loomed largest in their lives, even more so than any bishop who occupied the see in the early Tudor period. The history of relations between the city and cathedral provides an important context for understanding the course of the Reformation in the city.

Like other communities where secular government existed alongside significant ecclesiastical institutions, there was almost constant friction between the Norwich corporation and the cathedral priory in the centuries before the Reformation.[7] Tensions between the two, which most often revolved around problems of competing jurisdiction over the areas in and around the priory, extended back over several centuries. In 1272 Norwich

---

[4]Pound, "Social and Trade Structure," and Alan Dyer, *Decline and Growth in English Towns 1400–1640* (London: Macmillan, 1991), Apps. 2, 4. For a comparison of Norwich's tax burden to that of other towns, see also W. G. Hoskins, "English Provincial Towns in the Early Sixteenth Century," *Transactions of the Royal Historical Society,* 5th ser., 6 (1956): 1–19; reprinted in Peter Clark, ed., *The Early Modern Town: A Reader* (London: Longman, 1976), of which see page 92 for a table of taxes paid by London and the twenty-five leading provincial towns in the subsidies of 1523–27.

[5]On the constitutional history of Norwich see William Hudson and John C. Tingey, eds., *The Records of the City of Norwich,* 2 vols. (Norwich: Jarrold & Sons, 1906–10), 1:lviii–lxxviii. In 1404, Henry IV granted the city a charter of incorporation that separated it from the county of Norfolk, making it a county in its own right. An abstract of the charter appears in ibid., 31–36. Only four other cities in England had county status at that time: London, Bristol, York, and Newcastle.

[6]See Norman P. Tanner, *The Church in Late Medieval Norwich 1370–1532* (Toronto: Pontifical Institute of Medieval Studies, 1984), ch. 1.

[7]The most famous example of ongoing friction between town and church is probably Bury Saint Edmunds; see Robert S. Gottfried, *Bury St. Edmunds and the Urban Crisis: 1290–1539* (Princeton, N.J.: Princeton University Press, 1982).

was the site of one of the most notorious incidents between the secular and ecclesiastical arms during the Middle Ages. A group of citizens attacked the monastery, burning some of its buildings, which left thirteen people dead, none of them monks. Whatever satisfaction the citizens may have gained from the offensive was short-lived, as the church responded to the incursion swiftly and dramatically. The bishop of Norwich, Roger Skerning, excommunicated the participants in the attack and placed the entire city under interdict. Henry III also responded to the outrage by seizing the city's liberties, exacting a £2,000 fine for damage to the monastery from the city government, and calling for the execution of about thirty citizens.[8]

These penalties did not establish or increase harmony between the municipality and the monastery, but set the tone for continuing hostilities. Thus in the mid-fifteenth century, the priory was again the site of a siege by Norwich citizens, with results that were comparable to the 1272 incident. This time the archbishop of Canterbury took the step of excommunicating the assailants, but the bishop of Norwich refused to lay the entire city under interdict. The government of Henry VI confiscated Norwich's charter, imposed a fine of £2,000 on the corporation and levied fines on a number of individuals, and imprisoned the city's mayor in the Fleet.[9] Once more, harsh penalties did not end the strife between the two parties.

By the turn of the sixteenth century, the long-standing issues of contested jurisdiction that continued to inflame controversy between the corporation and the cathedral began to find expression in tangled lawsuits rather than in physical violence. Even so, the corporation continued to find itself on the losing end of these new battles. In 1517, Cardinal Wolsey came to the city, uninvited, after the enduring disputes between town and cathedral had come to his attention by way of a lawsuit that had been languishing in Star Chamber for some years.[10] The cardinal, who announced his intention to settle the quarrel once and for all upon his arrival in Norwich, found that his diplomatic skills were sorely tested as the parties refused to reach an agreement. Seven years later, in 1524, an exasperated Wolsey simply imposed his own solution to the problem. He declared that

---

[8]Hudson and Tingey, *Records of Norwich*, 1: xii, xxx; Walter Rye, "The Riot between the Monks and Citizens of Norwich in 1272," *Norfolk Antiquarian Miscellany* 2 (1883): 17–89.

[9]Hudson and Tingey, *Records of Norwich*, 1: lxxxviii–xciii; R. L. Storey, *The End of the House of Lancaster*, 2d ed. (Gloucester: Alan Sutton, 1986), App. III.

[10]J. A. Guy, *The Cardinal's Court: The Impact of Thomas Wolsey in Star Chamber* (Hassocks, Eng.: Harvester Press, 1977), 68–69.

from that time forward, the cathedral and priory would no longer be deemed a part of the city of Norwich, but rather a part of the county of Norfolk, an administratively separate unit. The magistrates fiercely opposed a settlement that placed an area within city walls under an alien jurisdiction. Wolsey did not heed their objections, and royal charters granted in 1524 and 1525 ratified the new agreement.[11]

The loss of control over the cathedral priory was a serious defeat for Norwich magistrates who, like other urban authorities across Europe, prized their authority highly and had no wish to see it diminished. On at least one occasion, the city governors attempted to provoke a rivalry between the monks and local friars, or perhaps to exploit a preexisting one, in order to compel the former to reinstate civic jurisdiction over the priory. In January 1534 members of the corporation stopped attending Sunday sermons at the cathedral, as had apparently been their custom. They informed the prior, William Castleton, that if he wished them to resume their attendance there regularly in the future, he would have to agree that "the monastery aforesaid shall be within the county of the said city [of Norwich]." Furthermore, the magistrates declared that while the prior was considering their proposal, they would be spending their Sundays attending services at the church of the White Friars instead. Not surprisingly, the prior rejected the offer almost immediately, and the magistrates reiterated their intention to stay away from sermons at the cathedral.[12] It is not known how long they may have boycotted cathedral services, but the magistrates eventually won their battle with the monks in large part because of the Dissolution. In 1538, Norwich became the first monastic cathedral to be converted to a secular foundation.[13] In the following year, Henry VIII granted letters patent which separated the new dean and chapter of Norwich cathedral from the county of Norfolk and replaced it under the jurisdiction of Norwich city. All the area within the city walls was once again united under a single authority, the corporation of Norwich.[14]

---

[11]Hudson and Tingey, *Records of Norwich*, 1:cix–cx, 43–44; 2:cxxxvii–cxxxix; Tanner, *Late Medieval Norwich*, 153. The agreement is printed in *Evidences related to the Town Close Estate* (Norwich, 1887), 27–36, and the charters on ibid., 62–64.

[12]N[orfolk] R[ecord] O[ffice], Norwich Assembly Book 1510–1550, fols. 152r, 153v; Proceedings of the Municipal Assembly 1510–1550, fols. 174v–175r.

[13]Stanford E. Lehmberg, *The Reformation of Cathedrals: Cathedrals in English Society, 1485–1603* (Princeton, N.J.: Princeton University Press, 1988), 81–82.

[14]Hudson and Tingey, *Records of Norwich*, 2:cxxxix; see 1:44 for an abstract of the charter confirming the letters patent.

This protracted dispute undoubtedly reinforced the magistrates' dislike for the inmates of the cathedral priory. In fact, they would continue to squabble with the dean and chapter periodically for the rest of the sixteenth century and the early decades of the seventeenth.[15] But the conflict also left the magistrates with a profound aversion for outside intervention in local matters. The religious conflict that began to erupt in the city among the clergy seemed another opportunity for additional intrusions if the magistrates once again failed to quiet internal disorder. Their response to religious strife suggests a greater concern to protect civic authority and autonomy than to uphold and enforce the religious policies of the central government.

The magistrates rarely meted out much in the way of punishment to the clergymen who appeared before them in the mayor's court, nor did they rush to hand over religious dissidents to outsiders who might then wish to scrutinize activities in the city further. They worked to mute expressions of religious conflict and to prevent them from escalating to a point where someone else might take interest in them.

The threat of outside interference was first raised in 1535 when Edward Harcocke, the prior of the Blackfriars, preached a sermon which came perilously close to denouncing royal supremacy. Word of the sermon reached London, and Cromwell ordered a Norfolk gentleman, Sir Roger Townsend, to arrest the prior. But Harcocke was not arrested; instead the mayor of Norwich assured Sir Roger that the prior would remain in the city and accessible for dispatch to London indefinitely. Harcocke returned to the Blackfriars and remained there undisturbed until the house was dissolved three years later. Harcocke disappeared from local records at that time, but resurfaced in Norwich in Mary's reign as the rector of Saint Michael Coslany and died peacefully in that post early in Elizabeth's reign.[16] Although he had preached a sermon that could have been construed as treasonous and the mayor had "marvelled what moved him to meddle with such matters," Harcocke remained a free man. The rulers of Norwich had

---

[15]On relations between the city and cathedral in the seventeenth century, see John T. Evans, *Seventeenth-Century Norwich: Politics, Religion, and Government, 1620–1690* (Oxford: Clarendon Press, 1979), 84–104.

[16]G. R. Elton, *Policy and Police: The Enforcement of the Reformation in the Age of Thomas Cromwell* (Cambridge: Cambridge University Press, 1972), 16–18. A copy of Harcocke's offending sermon may now be found at the P[ublic] R[ecord] O[ffice], E36/153, fols. 23–25. On Harcocke's later career in Norwich, see NRO, REG/30, Tanner's Index. Harcocke was presented to the Norwich parish of St.

not been eager to deliver him into the hands of outsiders and arranged for the prior to remain under their watchful eyes instead.

Most of the magistrates' efforts to contain religious controversy among the clergy can be traced through the records of the mayor's court. Although the mayor and aldermen operated in the shadow of diocesan power in Norwich, religious controversies involving the clergy, as well as other disciplinary matters, were routinely handled by the mayor's court. The correction of clerical faults was theoretically the sole province of the church, but in practice it was not uncommon to find secular rulers shouldering that responsibility. Susan Brigden has found that in sixteenth-century London, for example, the wardmote enquests commonly disciplined priests who had been found to be the clients of local prostitutes.[17] Much the same was true in Norwich: the mayor and aldermen disciplined clergy for a range of offenses including sexual misconduct, debt, and other "misbehaviors."[18]

The cases in the Norwich mayor's court that stemmed from religious conflict involving the clergy were not numerous in the early years of the Reformation under Henry VIII. Nevertheless they do highlight the local authorities' efforts to minimize the intensity and impact of religious conflict and to keep it from attracting the attention of unwelcome outsiders. In June 1538 the mayor and aldermen listened to testimony against Sir John Neell, priest of the Norwich parish of Saint Michael Coslany. At a recent sermon at Norwich cathedral, during which the preacher had spoken on the royal supremacy, the previously usurped authority of the bishop of Rome and the abrogation of certain holy days, Sir John had been heard by several witnesses to utter the words "they then liest."

At the same session of the mayor's court one of the city's aldermen, Nicholas Sywhat, recounted a rather earlier incident involving the priest. In

---

Michael Coslany by Bishop John Hopton, who had been Mary's personal chaplain before his elevation to the see. Harcocke's will was proved in the Prerogative Court of Canterbury in March 1563: PRO, PCC 13 Chayre.

[17]Susan Brigden, *London and the Reformation* (Oxford: Clarendon Press, 1989), 64–65.

[18]In 1538, for example, the mayor's court imprisoned Sir Thomas Wellys, the parson of Saint Margaret Westwick. Sir Thomas had authored "a bill containing misbehaviors and sedition," and had apparently been foolish enough to share his handiwork with one Agnes Couper. The magistrates sentenced the priest to remain in jail "until he find surety of good abearing," but the records contain nothing further about his case. In January of the following year, they took a deposition from Katherine West, the servant of Nicholas Grave, in which West charged that Sir John Page had slept with her master's daughter: NRO, M[ayor's] C[ourt] B[ook] 1534–1540, 106–107; 1534–1549 fols. 25v, 32v.

1534, Sywhat had been in London just before Parliament had passed the Act of Supremacy. The impending rejection of the pope had been, not surprisingly, a constant topic of conversation in the capital. Upon his return to Norwich, the alderman was at Saint Michael Coslany relating the news to Neell and to a Dr. Buckingham. Sir John declared "This is a new thing, it will not last long; the king will not live [for]ever."[19] Both of the priest's remarks could be considered inflammatory, which was probably what earned him an appearance before city magistrates. But it appears that the mayor and aldermen did not punish the priest at all. At first, they decided to turn Neell's case over to the next Norwich Assizes for consideration, but then decided against it. Both sets of testimony against the priest, while still part of the city court book, were stricken through and Neell never appeared before the magistrates in connection with these incidents again.

Nearly two years later, on the eve of Pentecost 1540, Sir Robert Spurgeon appeared before the court. The source of the priest's trouble was a "canon of the mass" found in his possession (by whom the record does not tell) that had not been amended along recently dictated lines. While some references to the pope had been stricken out, "the commemoration of Thomas Becket" remained unaltered. A royal proclamation of 1538 asserted that Becket had not been a saint, and really ought to be "esteemed to have been a rebel and traitor to his prince." As such, his feast day had already been abrogated and his name was also to be "erased and put out of all books...."[20] Although Sir Robert claimed that he had received the book from another Norwich cleric and that "he used it not this quarter of a year," the mayor and aldermen jailed him nevertheless. They bound him over to appear at the next session of the Norwich Assizes, with one John Pettons, a local tailor, standing surety for him. After Spurgeon's recognizance was entered into the court book, his case disappeared from the city records and he was never called before the magistrates again.[21]

During the feast of Saint Bartholomew in 1540 a third priest, Bachelor Newman, from the city's fashionable Saint Peter Mancroft church, appeared before the court in connection with recent inflammatory outbursts. John White testified that he had heard Newman declare one day in church that "it was never merry in England since the king had such knaves

---

[19]NRO, MCB 1540–1549, 124–125.

[20]*Tudor Royal Proclamations*, ed. Paul L. Hughes and James F. Larkin, 3 vols. (New Haven: Yale University Press, 1964–69), 1:270–276.

[21]NRO, MCB 1534–1540, 156.

and young boys to his counsel." Another local priest, John Kempe, told the court that he had heard Newman rail against Robert Barnes (a member of the White Horse circle at Cambridge), Martin Luther, and the recently executed Thomas Cromwell, calling them heretics and traitors. This testimony was confirmed by the cleric Nicholas Thorp. Despite the testimony of these witnesses, there is no evidence that the mayor and aldermen imprisoned Newman or bound him over to the Norwich Assizes or Quarter Sessions. Nothing further was recorded about the case and it seems probable that they warned the priest to keep his opinions to himself before releasing him.[22]

There is no way of knowing if these cases were the only occasions on which the magistrates had to confront and manage outbursts of religious discord among the clergy. The incident involving the prior of the Blackfriars suggests that not all religious friction resulted in an appearance before the mayor's court for the clergy concerned. Local records would leave no evidence of similar outbursts that might have been smoothed over by an alderman outside the formal setting of the court. But what this sparse evidence does reveal is a magisterial preference in Norwich for settling religious disputes locally by not enforcing official religious policies rigidly and by avoiding contact with extramural authorities. The cases against Neell and Newman also suggest that the magistrates were more likely to treat incidents in court in which provocative remarks had been made publicly, because they were more likely to escalate beyond their control.[23]

Another notable feature about these early manifestations of clerical religious discord in Henrician Norwich is that they all involved expressions of conservative religious sentiments. The three clergymen who appeared before the mayor's court, as well as Edmund Harcocke, had in some way voiced opposition to the Henrician innovations in religion. It is thus tempting to argue that the magistrates were indeed working to uphold the religious policies of royal government, for even if the clergymen involved received no significant punishment, they were certainly singled out by an appearance in the mayor's court. But if the magistrates' management of clerical religious conflict is seen in a larger context, there is little support for such a contention. The laymen who also appeared before the mayor's

[22]NRO, MCB 1540–1549, 21.

[23]Ralph Houlbrooke, *Church Courts and the People during the English Reformation, 1520–1570* (Oxford: Oxford University Press, 1979), 230.

court in connection with religious strife during the same period did so for a wider variety of religious opinions.

Thus the Norwich capper Thomas Myles appeared in the mayor's court in 1535 for his sometimes drunken, but nevertheless public, attacks against the saints and the Virgin ("Our Lady of Grace and Our Lady of Walsingham were strong whores and bawdy whores") and against several traditional religious rites ("God never made or commanded fasting, but knave priests").[24] In February 1538, a witness reported that one Geoffrey Rede had boasted that he would not be "shriven of none priest," whether "he had been with twenty men" or had "stolen an horse."[25] Such cases taken alongside those involving Norwich clergy suggest that city magistrates were chiefly concerned to mute any provocative and public religious expression with less concern about its ideological content. The fact that the only clergy who came before the court did so for voicing opposition to the divorce and to innovations in religion is perhaps a better barometer of clerical sentiment in Norwich during the early years of the Reformation or of the willingness of conservative clergy to speak out.

After 1540, however, when the clerics Spurgeon and Newman appeared before the court, there were no more cases of religious conflict involving either clergy or laity for the remainder of Henry VIII's reign. The disappearance of religious conflict as part of the court's normal business at that time was undoubtedly a consequence of the passage of the Six Articles the previous year.[26] In London, where enforcement of religious policy often fell to City governors as it did in Norwich, the Act occasioned a wave of persecution spearheaded by the mayor. The outcome of those efforts, Susan Brigden has noted, was that "the City's prisons filled with suspect heretics." The persecution only ceased when the king learned of the resulting mistreatment of both clergy and London citizens.[27] The situation in Norwich was quite different: faced with the prospect of having to mete

---

[24]NRO, MCB 1534–1540, 13–15. It is hard to know how to decipher Myles' remarks, especially given his intoxication at the time of making them. It would be difficult to argue that Myles was a committed Protestant from these comments alone. His case reveals that by the mid-1530s unconventional religious views had appeared in Norwich and made some type of impact. On the confusing nature of Myles' statements, see also Ralph Houlbrooke, "The Persecution of Heresy and Protestantism in the Diocese of Norwich under Henry VIII," *Norfolk Archaeology* 35 (1972), 312.

[25]NRO, MCB 1534–1540, 108.

[26]31 Henry VIII, c. 14.

[27]Brigden, *London*, 321.

out harsh penalties for religious heterodoxy, the magistrates avoided hearing any such cases.

Nevertheless, the level of clerical religious conflict in Norwich intensified after the accession of Edward VI in 1547. The new government introduced a variety of reforms in religion, some of which provoked a strong response among some clergy, leaving Norwich magistrates striving still to quell any expression of religious dissension. Some of the new reforms enacted by the Edwardian regime explicitly empowered secular rulers to monitor clergy more closely and to take on the task of enforcing religious conformity, although without the brutality of the Six Articles, which was repealed in 1547. In Norwich the magistrates used these new powers to continue their campaign to contain religious strife rather than to take punitive action against clergy or to enforce religious homogeneity strictly.

Edward's reign began quietly in Norwich despite the commotion that some of the government's earliest religious measures provoked elsewhere. Injunctions echoing the Cromwellian ones of the 1530s were issued in July 1547 and they suggested that further changes in religious doctrine and practice were to follow. In the nation's capital, for example, the injunction that sanctioned the destruction of "false images" was taken up enthusiastically by reformers in the City. By mid-September the iconoclastic impulse had become so widespread that the Privy Council had to order London's mayor and aldermen to punish responsible priests and churchwardens. In a similar vein, the City's Court of Aldermen resolved that each of its members would work to keep churches closed, as well as to keep track of the damage already done to parish images and the identities of those involved in their destruction.[28] In Norwich the mayor and aldermen decried a recent series of iconoclastic incidents in city churches in September 1547, the first indication of any religious strife in the new reign. They suspected Thomas Conyers, the parish priest of Saint Martin at Palace, and the beer brewer Richard Debney as ringleaders. The record of that discussion indicates that the magistrates merely called upon the priest and his accomplice "to surcease of such unlawful doings" without even requiring them to appear in court.[29]

---

[28]Brigden, *London*, 427–430.

[29]NRO, MCB 1534–1549, fols. 52r–53v. Although this entry bears no date, see Basil Cozens-Hardy and E. A. Kent, *The Mayors of Norwich 1403–1835* (Norwich: Jarrold & Sons, 1938), 51. The date they give is probably taken from MCB 1540–1549, 402–403, where this entry also appears.

Other than this incident, clerical appearances in the mayor's court during the first year and a half of Edward's reign were confined to routine considerations of clerical misconduct. Thus in August 1548, for example, the mayor and aldermen committed the iconoclast Conyers to prison for suspicious behavior with William Gohe's wife, but decided that "upon divers considerations" the priest should be "delivered on bail."[30] Similarly, during the same month the priest Nicholas Thirketill appeared before the court because he, Cecily West, and her daughter Joan stood accused of "misusing themselves together" but "upon certain considerations" Thirketill was dismissed upon "trust of amendment."[31]

There was only a single instance of religious conflict involving a clergyman during this period. Not long before Thirketill's appearance before the magistrates, Thomas Heberd, a Norwich butcher, told the mayor's court that he had heard the cleric Philip Curston declare "fie on preachers, arrant knaves and renegades and heretic knaves." Curston's remark was particularly explosive as it came at a time when there was considerable unrest in the city over the activities of Thomas Rose. Rose was the priest whose conversion to Protestantism and career as a preacher are chronicled in Foxe's *Book of Martyrs*. He had been an associate of the martyr Thomas Bilney in the Suffolk parish of Hadleigh.[32] In the spring and summer of 1548 Rose had been preaching in Norwich and his sermons had provoked a number of publicly hostile responses that had culminated in cases brought to the mayor's court.[33] Although Curston denied having said anything about preachers, the court committed him to ward for his outbursts until he could find surety.[34] Whatever the final outcome of Curston's case, it was not sufficient to discourage him from further provocative behavior, as he would reappear before the magistrates in a matter of months.

---

[30]NRO, MCB 1540–1549, 496. Conyers would next come to the attention of city rulers in the summer of 1549 when he preached to and conducted daily services for Kett's rebels in their camp on Mousehold Heath.

[31]NRO, MCB 1540–1549, 500.

[32]John Cumming, ed., *Fox's Book of Martyrs: The Acts and Monuments of the Church* (London, 1844), 3:1056–1063; Diarmaid MacCulloch, *Suffolk and the Tudors: Politics and Religion in an English County 1500–1600* (Oxford: Clarendon Press, 1986), 155.

[33]During May and June 1548, there were six cases in the mayor's court stemming from Rose's sermons. In May, for example, witnesses testified that Robert Barman had declared one day in the parish church of Saint Gregory that "he had rather go to a bear baiting as to Mr. Rose's sermons." Thomas Brygges allegedly told Richard Bety and Matthew Herman that "it was pity that Mr. Rose was not hangen when he was [three] days old." Barman was bound to good behavior; Thomas Brygges received no punishment: NRO, MCB 1540–1549, 432, 433.

[34]NRO, MCB 1540–1549, 493.

While religious conflict involving Norwich's clergy had been minimal during the first year or so of Edward's reign, from the end of 1548 it intensified, resulting in a marked increase of cases brought before the mayor's court. It is not clear exactly what sparked such an upsurge in clerical religious discord at that time, but at least some of it may have been ignited by the increasing number of religious directives emanating from the nation's political center. In 1548, a ban on images previously confined to London was extended to the entire country.[35] A proclamation issued in February prohibited all "private innovations in ceremonies." It explicitly empowered and charged secular rulers to enforce religious conformity, although the proclamation did not prescribe penalties for offenses. The "Order of Communion," authored by Archbishop Cranmer, introduced the novelty of English prayers into the Latin mass along with communion in both kinds, also by proclamation in March 1548.[36]

Even in the face of increased religious discord, the magistrates still sought only to contain conflict. At a single court session in December 1548 or early January 1549, the mayor and aldermen disciplined three local clergymen. Thomas Seman, the priest of Saint John Sepulchre, was jailed for using "certain ceremonies" on Christmas day contrary to the king's order. Similarly, the priest John Floraunce was imprisoned because he too had conducted "communion contrary to the book sent . . . by the king's majesty. . . ." Finally, Philip Curston was jailed for a second time. He had refused a mayoral summons to come to the Guildhall, telling the constable sent to fetch him that "he had nothing to do with Mr. Mayor." In addition to his imprisonment, the mayor and aldermen warned him "that while he is in the city that [he] shall use him[self] as other priests [do] within the same city. . . ." Like many other cases of this nature, nothing further was recorded about any of these cases. Also notable is that for each one, the exact nature of the offense in question is not indicated. The court book does not tell why Philip Curston had been summoned before the mayor, or how Thomas Seman and John Floraunce had celebrated their respective religious services.[37] This lack of attention to details underscores that Norwich magistrates were less concerned with the *content* of religious discord than with the *fact* of its existence. All three men had made a public statement—

[35]Haigh, *English Reformations*, 170.
[36]*Tudor Royal Proclamations*, 1:416–418.
[37]NRO, MCB 1540–1549, 538.

Curston by flouting a constable and the other two by violating the king's order before their congregations. The magistrates sought to dampen public controversy through their disciplinary actions rather than mete out harsh penalties.

The magistrates' lack of interest in taking punitive action against errant clergymen was made clear when William Stampe, the parish priest of Saint Augustine, appeared before the court in May 1549, just two months after the passage of the Act of Uniformity.[38] One evening at about ten o'clock Stampe and a small group of what the record calls his "adherents" broke into the church and "brake down the altar called the high altar of the said church of his own froward mind without the assent of the parishioners...." Despite this provocative action, the magistrates dismissed Stampe's case after he had confessed and apologized for it. They required him to rebuild the church's altar, although there is no evidence that they checked to see that he completed the task.

Norwich's rulers continued their pattern of suppressing discord involving clergy during the spring and early summer of 1549. Even when a dispute was not directly connected to changes in religious doctrine and worship, the mayor and aldermen were still anxious to short-circuit the matter quickly. In June, the parson of Saint Stephen became embroiled in an argument over tithes with John Garden that took place outside the latter's shop and was overheard by others who testified before the court. The parson, Stephen Prowett, was committed to ward, after which there was no more official attention given to the case.[39]

The following month, the mayor's court took up two more matters involving local priests. On July 3, the magistrates first chided Andrew Colby of Saint Michael Berstreet because "he useth not and order himself in his church according to the king's majesty's book concerning an altar...." Colby's response to the charges suggests that his parishioners had torn down the altar and he did not note that anything else stood in its place. If they were to erect another one, he assured the court, he would certainly use it. But Colby's failure to minister at the altar was not the sole cause for his appearance. For reasons that are not clear, the magistrates also questioned whether Colby was indeed a priest at all. They debated the matter for a long time, according to the court book, and reached the decision that "it is doubted by the court that he is a priest." They consigned him to prison

[38]NRO, MCB 1534–1549, fol. 59r.
[39]Ibid., fol. 62v.

until he could produce witnesses who could testify to his clerical status and entered a recognizance to that effect in the court book. Colby was never called back before the court nor were any witnesses who could verify his clerical status. On the same day, the priest of Saint Paul, John Beston, was in court. The magistrates warned him to conduct religious services in his church as prescribed by the Prayer Book, to which the priest responded that he was already doing so. Beston was apparently released after this warning.[40]

Magisterial involvement in clerical discipline in Norwich then came to an abrupt end. By the end of July 1549, Robert Kett and his rebels had overrun the city, the government had fallen, and Thomas Conyers was ministering to the rebels on Mousehold Heath.[41] But after the city was delivered from its occupation at the end of August, the magistrates saw no more clergymen in the mayor's court. At first, there was the aftermath of the rebellion with which to contend. The court filled with those who had publicly sympathized with Kett and his followers.[42] Yet even when sentiments about the rebellion had cooled, the mayor and aldermen did not focus their attention again on local clergy. It was not until Elizabeth's reign that the mayor's court would be a site for clerical discipline again.[43]

[40]Ibid., fols. 65r–66v.

[41]Two contemporary accounts of the rebellion stand out: by Norwich citizen Nicholas Sotherton which appeared in B. L. Beer, "'The commoyson in Norfolk, 1549: A Narrative of Popular Rebellion in Sixteenth-Century England," *Journal of Medieval and Renaissance Studies* 6 (1976): 73–99; and by Alexander Neville, secretary to the then-future Archbishop of Canterbury Matthew Parker, *The History of the Rebellion in the Year MDXLIX: Which was conducted by Robert Kett, a tanner by trade at Wymondham* (Norwich, c. 1750). See also Anthony Fletcher, *Tudor Rebellions*, 3d ed. (London: Longman, 1983), 54–68; Julian Cornwall, *Revolt of the Peasantry 1549* (London: Routledge and Kegan Paul, 1977); Stephen K. Land, *Kett's Rebellion: The Norfolk Rising of 1549* (Ipswich: Boydell Press, 1977).

[42]For example, in September 1549, before Kett was hanged in Norwich, Robert Burnam, the parish clerk of Saint Gregory's, remarked that "there are too many gentlemen in England by five hundred," drawing on the rebels' distaste for and distrust of the gentry. In November, John Rook was heard to predict that "except for the mercy of God, before Christmas, you shall see as great a camp upon Mousehold as ever was": NRO, MCB 1549–1555, 3. For other examples, see Walter Rye, ed., *Depositions Taken before the Mayor & Aldermen of Norwich 1549–1567* (Norwich: Norfolk and Norwich Archaeological Society, 1905), 18–21.

[43]However, while city magistrates recovered from the debacle of Kett's rebellion, the Norwich consistory court disciplined two local clergymen for exhibiting excessive Protestant enthusiasm. One, William Stampe of Saint Augustine's church, was punished for wearing his cope inside out. See Houlbrooke, *Church Courts*, 245; Elaine M. Sheppard, "The Reformation and the Citizens of Norwich," *Norfolk Archaeology* 38 (1981): 48. Only in February 1560 did the mayor's court resume its earlier practice when it jailed the priest John Norton for ten days for resorting to the house of one Barney at an unlawful time; he was released on his own bond. In April, the court disciplined Norton again for keeping illicit company with a woman named Skinner; they were sentenced to ride around the city market with papers on their heads: NRO, MCB 1555–1562, 362, 379.

∽

The rise and fall of the civic elite's discipline of local clergy in Norwich raises a number of questions. An obvious one concerns the response of the local church. Of course, during Edward VI's reign secular rulers gained more control over the church as they were explicitly appointed to undertake some aspect of clerical discipline by proclamations such as the one prohibiting innovations in ceremonies and the Act of Uniformity. The Act of Uniformity also invited bishops to work together with secular rulers to enforce the use of the Prayer Book.[44] But in Norwich there had been no such cooperation. And before that Act was in force, no member of the local ecclesiastical hierarchy had attempted to intervene at all in the magistrates' proceedings against its priests.

A primary cause for the church's failure to respond was that from the 1530s the diocese lacked effective episcopal leadership. Richard Nix, bishop from 1501 until his death in 1535, had once been an energetic man who oversaw his jurisdiction vigorously. But during his last years he had been ruined by increasing bad health and by charges of *praemunire*, the price for his stanch opposition to Henry's divorce.[45] Nix's successor was William Rugge, whose elevation to the see was a reward for his support for the divorce. He has been aptly described as a nonentity and a timeserver who provided little in the way of pastoral leadership. His episcopate is best remembered for the financial degradation of the see, and Rugge's incompetence was a cause of his forced resignation in 1550.[46] The lack of ecclesiastical leadership left Norwich city magistrates with a freer hand to control the clergy than they might otherwise have had.[47]

---

[44]2&3 Edward VI, c. 1.

[45]MacCulloch, *Suffolk and the Tudors*, 130–156.

[46]MacCulloch, *Suffolk and the Tudors*, 157; Houlbrooke, *Church Courts*, 22, 49, 197.

[47]The quality of episcopal leadership helps to explain the return of magisterial discipline of clergy in 1560. The Marian bishop of Norwich, John Hopton, was a spirited participant in the discovery and execution of Protestant heretics during his episcopate. There was little prosecutorial activity in the Norwich mayor's court during Mary's reign concerning religion, as the magistrates undoubtedly wished to avoid becoming enmeshed in the persecutions. Hopton died in August 1558. Richard Cox was nominated to the see of Norwich in June 1559, but translated to Ely in December of that year. John Parkhurst, a Marian exile, was consecrated September 1560. Parkhurst was a man of considerable pastoral zeal but proved to be a poor bishop, lacking administrative skills. On Hopton see MacCulloch, *Suffolk and the Tudors*, 180–181. On Parkhurst's life and episcopate see *The Letter Book of John Parkhurst Bishop of Norwich Compiled during the Years 1571–5*, ed. R. A. Houlbrooke, Norfolk Record Society, vol. 43 (1974–75), 17–57, and MacCulloch, *Suffolk and the Tudors*, 184–193.

Even so, the pattern of clerical discipline requires some explanation. The magistrates first saw clergy in their court in the 1530s, but all such prosecutions ceased in the wake of the Six Articles which dictated harsh penalties for infractions against them. The court began to prosecute clergymen again in Edward VI's reign, slowly at first, and with a sizeable increase in late 1548 and into 1549, all of which halted in the wake of Kett's rebellion. If there were chronological fluctuations in prosecution of the clergy, the outcome of those encounters remained consistent throughout the period under consideration. What brought a clergyman before the magistrates was usually a provocative comment—"fie on preachers"—or action, such as tearing down an altar. The court was less concerned with the ideological element of the comment or action than with its public and provocative nature. In some cases, like those concerning clergy who had conducted religious services improperly, the records do not provide enough information to reveal the religious outlook of the priests involved. If Norwich magistrates were not interested in the religious sentiments of clerical defendants before them, neither were they keen to take punitive measures against them. Jail terms tended to be brief and some defendants were bound in recognizance to reappear but were never called. And in several instances outcomes of cases were not recorded at all, suggesting that no serious action was taken. It is evident that the magistrates' chief interest was to defuse religious conflict and prevent it from escalating, with no regard for maintaining Protestant or Catholic uniformity.

Why were Norwich magistrates not concerned with rigorously upholding the religious policies of Henry VIII and Edward VI? The available evidence about their own religious sentiments—chiefly wills—indicates that they were not religiously unified themselves. The problems with using wills, particularly their preambles, as an indicator of religious belief are well known and have most recently been highlighted in the work of Eamon Duffy[48] and essays by Christopher Marsh and Caroline Litzenberger in this volume. While the wills of Norwich aldermen may not show clear divisions into traditionalist, reformist, and Protestant groups, categories which Duffy has shown to be problematic, if read carefully they do suggest that religious opinion among them was not completely uniform. Many aldermanic wills were similar to that of Robert Ferror, who penned his last

---

[48]Eamon Duffy, *The Stripping of the Altars: Traditional Religion in England c. 1400–1580* (New Haven: Yale University Press, 1992), ch. 15.

will and testament in 1542. Ferror committed his soul to God, the Virgin, the saints, and "unto Saint Michael my advow." He left money to maintain the mass at Saint Peter Mancroft and for an anniversary mass for himself as well as sums for masses for his parents and late wives.[49] Richard Grene, who died in 1541, bequeathed his soul to "our redeemer and savior Jesus Christ; by the merits of his blessed passion I trust to be saved," as well as to the Virgin and saints. His will underscores Duffy's point that sixteenth-century Catholics were hardly unfamiliar with the central role of Christ in their religion.[50] When Thomas Grewe made his will in 1548, he bequeathed his soul only to God, but made sure to leave his daughter Alice "a pair of beads of coral with Pater Nosters silver and gilt...."[51]

Alongside wills like these were the much smaller number like that made by William Rogers in 1542 and proved in 1553. It began with a lengthy preamble in which he committed his soul to Christ alone and renounced "all my good works" as well. Rogers made no provisions for obits, but left a cash bequest for a preacher to give sermons in and around Norwich for five years while receiving room and board from Rogers' widow.[52] John Trace, who died in 1544, after only a year of aldermanic service, offered his soul to Christ in a brief preamble and left no money for masses, but some to have sermons preached in and around the city over the following two years. He counted among the witnesses to his will John Barret, the ex-Carmelite who had been an early and vocal convert to Protestantism.[53] Barret was also a witness to two other aldermen's wills made between the mid-1530s and Kett's rebellion.[54]

This evidence, while not conclusive, is nevertheless suggestive. The men who ruled Norwich in the Reformation's early years were not of identical opinions in matters of religion. Yet they did not allow this divergence of opinion to complicate or destroy their conduct of city government. There is no evidence that factions formed among them along religious

[49]NRO, N[orwich] C[onsistory] C[ourt], 211 Mingay.

[50]NRO, NCC, 386 Attmere; Duffy, *Stripping of the Altars*, 507.

[51]NRO, NCC, 342 Wymer.

[52]PRO, PCC, 12 Tashe.

[53]PRO, PCC, F 16 Pynnyng. See *DNB*, sub Barret; J. Venn and J. A. Venn, eds., *Alumni Cantabrigiensis, Part I: From the earliest times to 1751.* 4 vols. (Cambridge: Cambridge University Press, 1922–27), 1:96; Leslie P. Fairfield, *John Bale: Mythmaker for the English Reformation* (West Lafayette, Ind.: Purdue University Press, 1976), 39–40.

[54]See the wills of Leonard Spencer, written and proved in 1539 (PRO, PCC, 16 Crumwell) and Edmund Wood, written and proved in 1548 (PRO, PCC, F 19 Populwell).

lines that influenced magisterial rule. All the evidence points to attempts to downplay the religious divisions that the Reformation was in the process of creating. Not only did the magistrates appear to keep the peace among themselves, but they worked hard to maintain it among clergy in the city for whom religious divisions occasioned conflict. Hence they did not punish any religious dissident severely, but intervened in conflict only to muffle religious tensions.

What can magisterial handling of religious conflict among the clergy reveal about the nature of the English Reformation? It suggests, first of all, that religious division was not always intolerable. Recent writing on the Reformation has emphasized resistance and conflict as predominant themes in the sixteenth-century religious experience, and the bitterness that the division between Protestant and Catholic generated.[55] But the example of Norwich demonstrates that religious division was not an inevitable cause of intense conflict. Events at Norwich show that religious change did not spread uniformly nor was its impact uniform across England or even within a single community. Among some of the clergy there religious change provoked conflicts that threatened the peace and stability of the city, while the magistrates endeavored to put aside their religious differences.

Magisterial willingness to disregard religious differences among themselves and to suppress conflict among others highlights an important development that emerged out of the Reformation but has received little attention from historians. The magistrates' response to religious changes shows that they had begun to forge a distinction between the religious and secular spheres, at least in part.[56] Differing religious commitments did not prevent them from working effectively in the conduct of government. They maintained this distinction as they contended with religious conflict in their jurisdiction, refusing to uphold any one religious policy. This represents a dramatic shift in late medieval culture, where religion was so deeply embedded in virtually every aspect of life. The Reformation had something of a different meaning to the magistrates of Norwich than it did to others in the city and perhaps points to some of the ways in which religious change was received in an urban environment. The history of the Norwich

---

[55]See esp. Haigh, *English Reformations*, and Brigden, *London*.

[56]The only recent discussion of this issue has been C. John Sommerville, *The Secularization of Early Modern England* (Oxford: Clarendon Press, 1992).

magistracy and clergy in the early Tudor period suggests the need to widen the focus of Reformation studies, as the Reformation was more complex than a story of shifting religious allegiance from Catholic to Protestant. The case of Norwich also indicates the necessity for continued investigation into the role of towns in the Reformation. Fundamental changes in the relationship between religion and society wrought by the Reformation may have first emerged in England's urban centers.

PART 3

PARISH CLERGY *and* PARISH REFORMATIONS

PROTESTANT PROPAGANDA
in the REIGN OF EDWARD VI

A Study of Luke Shepherd's
Doctour doubble ale

Janice C. Devereux

Luke Shepherd was a popular Protestant satirist whose works were published anonymously in London in 1548. He was a physician who lived in Coleman Street, a well-known reformist area of the City, during the 1540s. Shepherd was strongly anti-Catholic in his religious beliefs and he voiced his criticism of the Roman church in short verse satires, most of which were printed by the Protestant printer, John Day. Regrettably, apart from these general biographical details we know very little about him. His contemporary, John Bale, the Tudor bibliographer and dramatist, lists Shepherd in his bibliography under the Latinized version of his name, Lucas Opilio, names his birthplace as Colchester, in Essex, and compares him favorably with the earlier poet, John Skelton.[1]

While there is no absolute proof that Bale's Lucas Opilio and the satirist Luke Shepherd are one and the same person, it seems clear that the writer described by Bale is the same person whom another contemporary of Shepherd's, Edward Underhill (fl. 1539–1561), a Gentleman Pensioner at the courts of Henry VIII, Mary I, and Elizabeth I, refers to as: "mr. Luke, my very frende, off Colemane strete visissyone [physician]," in his autobiography.[2] Underhill states that his friend wrote many books against the Catholics and was imprisoned in the Fleet for his pains. He singles out the

---

[1]Bale describes Shepherd as: "poeta ualde facetus erat, qui in poematibus ac rhythmis Skeltono non inferior, in patrio sermone eleganter edidit, honestis iocis ac salibus plenos." John Bale, *Scriptorum Illustrium Maioris Brytanniae Catalogus*, 2 vols. (Basel: 1557, 1559; repr. facsimile Farnborough: Gregg International Publishers Limited, 1971), 2:109.

[2]Edward Underhill, "Autobiographical Anecdotes," *in Narratives of the Days of the Reformation, Chiefly from the Manuscripts of John Foxe*, ed. John Nichols, Camden Society, o.s. 77 (London, 1859), 171.

"boke called *John Boone and Mast Parsone*," comments that it was written in the time of King Edward VI, and explains that it upset various powerful papists and, in particular, the mayor of London, Sir John Gresham. Underhill then relates a dramatic anecdote explaining that Gresham sent for John Day, the printer of this tract, demanding to know the name of the anonymous writer and suggesting that the printer should accompany the author in prison. Underhill, who by chance had called on the mayor about another matter and was invited to stay for dinner, informed Gresham that Shepherd's poem was being circulated about the court and was much admired. He was also able to produce a copy of it for the mayor to read there and then. Gresham's response to the satire was positive: he pronounced the work "bothe pythe and mery" and John Day was duly released instead of being imprisoned.[3] As Bale also lists *Iohn Bon and Mast person* as Shepherd's work in his catalog of English authors it seems certain that both Underhill and Bale are referring to the same author.[4]

Unfortunately, nothing else is known about Shepherd's life, and while bibliographers other than Bale, as well as later chroniclers, mention him and his work, he does not appear on any extant university roll or on any official list of physicians. Raphael Holinshed refers to a "Lucas Shepherd of Colchester," but describes him as a poet during Mary I's reign.[5] The bibliographer and bookseller Andrew Maunsell lists several of Shepherd's works anonymously.[6] John Strype reprints Underhill's account of how Gresham was dissuaded from punishing either the author or the printer of *Iohn Bon and Mast person*, and also records Shepherd's imprisonment, inferring that it occurred at the close of Henry VIII's reign, but offers neither evidence nor details of this internment.[7] Thomas Warton later writes him off as "a petty pamphleteer in the cause of Calvinism" and both

[3]Ibid., 172.

[4]John Bale, Index Britanniae Scriptorum, ed. Reginald Poole and Mary Bateson (Oxford: Clarendon Press, 1902), 283.

[5]Raphael Holinshed, *Chronicles of England, Scotland, and Ireland*, ed. Henry Ellis et al., 6 vols. (London, 1807–8), 3:1168.

[6]Andrew Maunsell, *The First Part of the Catalogue of English Printed Bookes: Which concerneth such matters of Diuinitie, as haue bin either written in our owne Tongue, or translated out of anie other language,* (London, 1595), pt. 1, passim.

[7]John Strype, *Ecclesiastical Memorials, Relating Chiefly to Religion, and the Reformation of it, and the Emergencies of the Church of England, under King Henry VIII. King Edward VI. and Queen Mary I.,* 3 vols. (Oxford: 1822), 2/1:181–182.

Warton and Bale refer to Shepherd's now lost translation of the Psalms.[8] A later bibliographer, Joseph Ritson, adds that Shepherd "wrote, in elegant Engleish, certain jocular and witty pamphlets, against the haters of truth: versify'd certain psalms and did many other little things, none of which are now to be met with."[9] Unfortunately, Ritson does not list his sources, or give any other indication of what these "many other" works might have been. Recent inquiries and extensive research have not elicited any new information about Shepherd's life and there is no indication as to when, or where, he died.

Shepherd's verse satires position him within the literary environment of the religious debates in popular printed English verse during the years before the establishment of the first Prayer Book of 1549. As one of the main writers of the polemical verse published in London during the late 1540s, Shepherd attacks the mass, the Real Presence in the Eucharist, and the celebration of the feast of Corpus Christi. Shepherd's oeuvre includes eight verse satires and one prose work and his canon widens our appreciation of popular genres.[10] His writing is an excellent example in English Reformation literature of the Protestant perspective which criticizes the Roman church and its conservative clergy, instead of employing persuasive arguments for reform.[11]

Doctour doubble ale, which is printed at the end of this introductory essay, is a highly entertaining but ruthless portrayal of a conservative curate who lives in London. Shepherd depicts the corrupt cleric as a drunkard who neglects his parish duties in favor of ale-drinking in taverns. In it, as we shall see, Shepherd satirizes a number of aspects of the Roman Church and its clergy, which is true of much of his other work as well. The clergy's moral conduct is frequently the focus of Shepherd's polemic. In the poem, *A pore helpe*, he mocks and censures Catholic priests for their lecherous behavior instead of arguing the case for married clergy:

[8]Thomas Warton, *History of English Poetry*, 4 vols. (London, 1774–1790; repr. facsimile, ed. René Wellek, New York and London: Johnson Reprint Corporation, 1968), 3:316; Bale, *Catalogus*, 109.

[9]Joseph Ritson, *Bibliographia Poetica* (London, 1802), 330–331.

[10]Shepherd's works include: *Antipus* (STC 683), *The comparison betwene the Antipus and the Antigraphe or answere thereunto, with: An apologie or defence of the same Antipus: And reprehence of the Antigraphe* (STC 5605a), *Iohn Bon and Mast person* (STC 3258.5), *Phylogamus* (STC 19882), *Doctour doubble ale* (STC 7071), *A pore helpe* (STC 13051.7), *The vpcheringe of the messe* (STC 17630), *Pathose, or an inward passion of the pope for the losse of hys daughter the Masse* (STC 19463) and *Cauteles preseruatory concerning the preseruation of the Gods which are kept in the pixe* (STC 4877.2).

[11]Robert W. Scribner, *For the Sake of Simple Folk: Popular Propaganda for the German Reformation* (Cambridge: Cambridge University Press, 1981).

ye leade euyll lyues
With other mennes wyues
And wyll none of your owne
And so your sede is sowne
In other mennes grounde
True wedlocke to confounde (ll. 84–89)

This is a good example of Shepherd's negative approach: rather than directly espouse clerical marriage he attacks the practices of the celibate clergy.

Clerical immorality is also the main concern of *Phylogamus*. The central point of this satire is that the Roman church's insistence on clerical celibacy is impractical and foolish and encourages sinful behavior on the part of its priests. Shepherd begins his poem with an abusive, personal attack on John Mason, the author of the *Antigraphium* (an attack on Shepherd's *Antipus*). Mason's writings, together with those of his conservative colleague Richard Smith, are ridiculed and dismissed. It seems certain that Shepherd is responding to a specific work by Mason, now lost, in which he defends clerical celibacy in a classical, poetical style. Shepherd's final response to Mason's work is to reply to it in barbarous Latin. Shepherd ends his poem with an attack on Smith, which echoes strongly Luther's idea that if we come to the Eucharist expecting to taste Christ then we go away empty, and satirizes the conservative view that Christ is bodily present in the host.

A number of Shepherd's texts expand this attack on transubstantiation. *Antipus* is a very short tract written in couplets. These verses paradoxically state reversals of Biblical references as though they were correct. The narrator argues it is as nonsensical to believe that a priest can create Christ in the Eucharist as it is to believe that the poem's contrary Biblical quotations are true. The work ends with a short ad hominem attack on a Catholic priest, William Leighton, who was an outspoken contemporary defender of the mass. Note that rather than state the Protestant view on the Eucharist, he mocks those who believe "these thefes the prestes can make their maker" by changing bread and wine into Christ's body and blood (l. 22).

Antipus is reprinted in the work *The comparison betwene the Antipus and the Antigraphe or answere thereunto, with An apologie or defence of the same Antipus And reprehence of the Antigraphe*, a polemical work which contains two other tracts, the *Antigraphium*, probably written by John Mason, and the *Apologia Antipi*, which is Shepherd's reply.[12] The *Antigraphium* is an attempt to refute *Antipus* line by line. Like *Antipus*, it begins with a heading followed by eleven couplets. These are an inversion of Shepherd's pairings. Mason's rebuttal is followed by a short attack on the Gospellers and then by a brief affirmation of the Eucharist. *Apologia Antipi* is Shepherd's reply to Mason's refutation and is written mostly in rhyme royal stanzas. It contains an ad hominem attack which accuses Mason of being a conservative and satirizes his writing for being imitative rather than original. Shepherd also denounces those who are foolish enough to believe that Christ's body and blood are actually present in the Eucharist.

Iohn Bon and Mast person likewise focuses on the doctrine of transubstantiation and also attacks the celebration of the feast of Corpus Christi. Composed as a dialogue between a common sense ploughman in the tradition of Piers Ploughman and an ignorant and gullible priest, this satire ridicules the Catholic doctrine of the Real Presence through Iohn Bon's absurd questions regarding the gender of Corpus Christi:

Iohn

But tell me mast parson one thinge and you can
What saynt is copsi cursty a man or a woman?

Parson

Why Iohn knoweste not that? I tel the it was a man,
It is Christe his owne selfe and to morowe is hys daye
We beare hym in prosession and thereby knowe it ye maye

Iohn

I knowe mast parson? and na by my faye
But methinke it is a mad thinge that ye saye
That it shoulde be a man howe can it come to passe
Because ye maye hym beare with in so smal a glasse (ll. 10–18)

The ploughman emphasizes the ridiculousness of the priest's claim to be able to "make his maker" and rightly points out that the doctrine of transubstantiation is not detailed in any Creed. He tries to apply logic to the parson's arguments about the true nature of the Eucharist, remarking that the wafer is too small to contain Christ. When the curate explains that

[12]Shepherd attributes the authorship of this reply to Mason in his work *Phylogamus*, ll. 25–29, 51–54.

we cannot see Christ's manhood or His godhead in the host, Iohn Bon concludes that the host must be simply a wafer cake because that is all he can see.

A pore helpe, *The vpcheringe of the messe* and *Pathose, or an inward passion of the pope for the losse of hys daughter the Masse* are all satires against the mass, each written from the point of view of a conservative narrator. In *A pore helpe* the narrator defends the mass against scurrilous attacks by the new men of learning. Ironically, the narrator lists the reformers' seemingly logical arguments against the doctrine of transubstantiation, while lamenting their rejection of the mass. While the main argument of the poem centers on the mass and Christ's bodily presence in the Eucharist, which the narrator stoutly defends against the arguments listed by the reformers, Shepherd also satirizes the practice of Catholic rituals, images and purgatory, and constructs another biting attack on clerical celibacy. Later in the satire, he devotes several lines to scornful remarks about the bishop of Winchester.

The conservative narrator of *The vpcheringe of the messe* also mourns the demise of the mass and the current popularity of the Scriptures. Satirically, the Protestants' argument that the mass is not mentioned in the gospels and has no scriptural authority for its celebration is frequently reiterated. The mass is "made bi men" (l. 33), we are told and must be accepted as doctrine as a matter of faith. Though the mass is criticized by some people, because her ministers lead sinful lives, she can still effect many benefits and the narrator details a long list of things which she can cure or ease or provide. Throughout the poem the mass is personified as Mistress Missa and, as the narrator's voice changes to a more reformist one, she is depicted as the enemy of the Gospel, the pope's daughter, a prostitute, and finally a dweller in hell.

In *Pathose* the mass is portrayed as a sick, diseased harlot whose father, the pope, intercedes with the classical gods and goddesses to restore his daughter to health. When this strategy proves unsuccessful he performs a parody of the rite of Extreme Unction on her and sends her off to hell to live with the devil. There is a developed level of sophistication in the personification of the mass in this satire. The narrator (the pope) is also a character in the poem and it is through his eyes that we see the mass. She is described by her "father" as:

my greatist treasure
In whome I had moste pleasure

. . . .

My glory and my goste
My braggyng and my boste
Whome I haue loued moste (ll. 29–39)

Besides condemning the Catholic insistence that the mass is a daily reenactment of Christ's sacrifice for the sins of humanity, Shepherd, in this satire, again attacks the doctrine of transubstantiation. He emphasizes the idolatrous worship of the elements of the mass by having his pope/narrator offer the sacrifice of the mass not to God, but to the pagan goddess Ceres and the pagan god Bacchus.

Shepherd's sole surviving prose work, *Cauteles preseruatory concerning the preseruation of the Gods which are kept in the pixe,* is a short, blasphemous satire concerned with instructions to the Catholic clergy on how to preserve the unconsumed Communion hosts against attacks from bacteria, birds, and small animals such as mice and monkeys. The suggestions include consecrating hosts only on a fair, clear day (if possible), storing the hosts in closed boxes inside the chimney to keep them dry, breathing on them gently when consecrating them, and taking care not to wink during the mass in case the hosts are seized upon by vermin at this time. The writer also warns against allowing a priest "that hath a stinkinge breath...or hath the pokkes to blowe or breath" on the hosts as the infection may be transmitted to "them that eate them as their God" (Sigs Aiv^v–Av). Despite the comic approach throughout the work this treatise ends in a serious, Protestant way with a declaration of the Creed and a hope that all idol worshipers (conservatives) shall be confounded, while all those who believe truly in God (reformers) shall experience eternal joy.

Although Shepherd turned to writing for only a very brief time and his corpus of works is small, his clever, witty poems illustrate that he read widely and was well educated. He frequently pretends a Catholic persona in his narratives so that the irony that he creates is double-edged. His texts are full of religious, literary, and classical allusions as well as liberally sprinkled with Latin and pseudo-Latin lines. In addition to dealing with some of the general issues of the Reformation, Shepherd also engages in personal invective in his poems, and makes biting, scathing attacks on specific conservative figures.

Shepherd's works were printed during the first two years of Edward VI's reign, a time when the slackening of censorship produced an enormous upsurge of polemical writings and a phenomenal increase in the number of printed works. In 1548 there were 225 works printed in London,[13] more than double the number of the previous year, and almost all of these works were openly Protestant in their argument or point of view. What was their intention? By the middle of 1548 many of the traditional, Catholic, devotional practices which they attacked had already been ended, or at least modified, by law. For example, numerous feast days had by this time been abrogated and most sacramentals (including ashes, beads for praying, candles, palms, and the practice of creeping to the cross on Good Friday) had already been banned. Images in private homes as well as in parish churches had been officially abolished and Evensong and Matins were no longer celebrated in Latin.[14] Moreover, the doctrine of the Real Presence had been relinquished and Communion in both kinds reinstated for the laity. Most importantly, with the introduction of the Order of Communion on 8 March 1548, the way had been cleared for the mass to be said in English instead of in Latin.[15]

Officially, at least, the Reformation had already taken place by the middle of 1548, but the upsurge in printed pamphlets and tracts which were so anti-Catholic or pro-reformist—which vastly overrepresent the numerical importance of the reformers—needs explaining.[16] Why did so many Protestant writers in the first few months of Edward VI's reign continue writing these polemical works—works which concentrated on the same topics which had so occupied the reformers before all the changes to the liturgy? If Protestant reforms had already taken place what could possibly be the reason for the abundance of anti-Catholic writing which was

[13]Susan Brigden, *London and the Reformation* (Oxford: Clarendon Press, 1989), 438.

[14]Gilbert Burnet, *The History of the Reformation of the Church of England*, 4th ed., 3 vols. (London, 1715), 2, pt. II, bk. I, 56–57; Richard Watson Dixon, *History of the Church of England from the Abolition of the Roman Jurisdiction*, 6 vols. (London, 1878–1902), 2:491; Eamon Duffy, *The Stripping of the Altars: Traditional Religion in England c. 1400–c. 1580* (New Haven: Yale University Press, 1992), 457; Philip Hughes, *The Reformation in England*, 3 vols. (London: Hollis and Carter, 1953–54), 2:101.

[15]Philip Hughes and James F. Larkin, eds., *Tudor Royal Proclamations*, 3 vols. (New Haven: Yale University Press, 1964–69), 1:#300.

[16]The most important Catholic writers of this period are Miles Hogarde and Richard Smith. I am aware that this is an area in which more research and study is still to be undertaken, but even so it seems that the number of conservative works from this period is significantly fewer than those which are Protestant-inspired.

published in London at that time? Why was *any* Protestant propaganda necessary if liturgical and doctrinal changes had actually been achieved?

Luke Shepherd's satire *Doctour doubble ale* suggests some answers. Viewed from a conventional literary perspective, Shepherd's satire is an overtly traditional anticlerical tract in which a local London curate is berated by the narrator for both his appalling ignorance and his nefarious behavior. In an energetic and amusing piece of writing, Shepherd presents us with a dissolute cleric whose fondness for that beverage gains him the name of Doctor Doubble Ale. This curate's intellectual ability has been so clouded by the results of his drinking habits that he now neither cares for his parishioners to any great extent, nor even carries out his Catholic duty of saying his daily prayers, preferring to spend most of his time in the local ale house. Throughout the entire poem Shepherd brilliantly juxtaposes his Protestant narrator's scathing comments about clerical ignorance with the drunkard priest's justification of his corrupt practices. Repeatedly, this curate is exposed as a man who cannot tell the difference between God's word and the devil's, who refuses to contemplate change of any sort, and who explains and justifies his behavior in terms of his affiliation to the Roman religion, a man "ernest in the cause / Of piuish popish lawes" (ll. 9–10).

However, as readers, we are very quickly made aware that something else is going on in this text than the usual Lollard-type accusations being leveled at the Catholic clergy. Within the first forty-five lines, "Gods worde," or a synonym for this phrase, is mentioned four times. Doctour Doubble Ale, we are told, as well as not being able to differentiate between "Gods worde" and "the Deuels" (l. 14), in fact does not *understand* God's word, and of course he cannot, in the sense that, in such a reformist text, this phrase refers not just to the Scriptures, that is, to "Christes true doctrine" (l. 31), but also to the whole Protestant religious movement.

Having introduced the idea of a Protestant narrator who attacks the Catholic clergy, Shepherd now sets out the tale of this particular cleric who typifies the worst of the abuses that the reformists were determined to correct. Despite the recent official changes in church practices, Doctour Doubble Ale still adheres to the old ways. He still keeps his bede rolls, he acts as an advocate for the souls in purgatory, and he watches out for any heresy in his parish. This part of the narrative, however, centers mainly on the curate's love of the ale pot, his habit of seeking out alehouses where the drink is served in large rather than small measures, and his custom of per-suading other idle fellows to join him in his carousing. Moreover, the closest this curate comes to fulfilling his preaching duty is the drunken advice he gives to his drinking companions in the taverns. Nonetheless, Doctour Doubble Ale has a very high opinion of his own cleverness, a per-spective which is beautifully undercut by the narrator's ironic statement: "His learning is exceding / Ye may know by his reading" (ll. 169–170). In fact, he is not learned at all because what he reads (his Breviary) cannot teach him the truth (whereas the Scriptures could), and he is too lazy to read his prayer book in any event.

In addition to these remarks regarding the curate's lack of intelligence, the narrator also points out that Doctour Doubble Ale cannot interpret the Gospel correctly, something that even a young, inexperienced, and uneducated boy is able to do. At this point in the satire the focus shifts, we get the sense of an actual historical event, and we begin to hear a markedly Protestant voice. In just five short, onomatopoeic lines we are drawn into the commotion and uproar surrounding the apprehension and presentation before the authorities of a young lad on a heresy charge. The boy is dragged to the Counter, the prison which served the London Guildhall, and which at this time was located in Bread Street (close to where Shepherd himself lived in Coleman Street).[17] This account is most likely a reference to Richard Mekins, a youth of fifteen years, who was accused of being a sacra-mentarian and who went to the stake on 30 July 1541, even though the evi-dence against him was extremely conflicting. The execution of one so young horrified the populace of London, and its bishop, Edmund Bonner, acquired a reputation for cruelty on account of the case.[18] The inclusion of such a story within this satire presents us with a Protestant martyr, reminds us of some of the Catholic excesses which the reformists wished to abolish, but, most of all, provides the conservative cleric with an antagonist to rail against and thus allows the Protestant narrator a double-edged irony when we are told that the "cobblers boy" who has no training, but who can read and is sober, is more suited to be a curate than the papist who now holds that position.

The narrative perspective changes halfway through the poem and the voice, which up until this time has been simply describing the character

---

[17]John Foxe, *The Acts and Monuments*, ed. S. R. Cattley, 8 vols. (London, 1838), 5:705.
[18]Ibid., 5:440–442.

Doctour Doubble Ale, now assumes that persona, and for much of the remainder of the work continues the tale from the point of view of "I." Interestingly, it is not the curate's life story that we hear, but a hodgepodge of seemingly unconnected bits and pieces, which echoes the "hubble shubble" of the lines about the capture of the "cobblers boy," and which shows us some personal aspects of the character, Doctor Doubble Ale. He begins by detailing his enthusiasm for consuming ale. He then turns his attention to his parish affairs. He relates his contempt for those people who follow the new learning and his hope that most of them will end up at Smithfield at the stake. He then goes on to lament the changing of the old ways and explains that though certain practices have fallen victim to the newfangled ideas he draws the line at allowing the sacraments to be administered in his parish church in English. Indeed he will stick to his old ways, despite the growing number of reformists in his parish. He determines to convert them or, if that fails, to ignore them. He hopes for promotion within the church system, but he intends to continue to enjoy his drinking. Above all else he affirms his belief in the efficacy of the celebration of the mass and vows that he will never "forsake / That I of a cake / my maker may make" (ll. 328–330).

However, as readers, we are being hoodwinked about what is going on here. At this point what is important, I suggest, is not what Doctour Doubble Ale thinks at all, but the superb propaganda that Shepherd is creating. Doctour Doubble Ale states something that is true—"And let these heretikes preach / And teach what they can teach"—as though it were a nonsense, and something which is untrue—"My parish I know well / Agaynst them wyll rebell"—as though it were the truth (ll. 242–245). By drawing attention to the distance between what the character Doctour Doubble Ale says and what these words signify, and what we, as readers, are meant to understand by them, the reformist narrator contrives an image which emphasizes the very stuff of Protestantism: preaching and teaching. The effect of the satire is twofold here because the reader is being asked to interpret these words literally, and also is required to understand that Doctour Doubble Ale himself treats them as an absurdity. Furthermore, by altering the perspective in this way, the narrator is able to list all the church reforms that have already officially taken place, not as the curate does, in a litany of laments, but as a catalog of positive improvements.

Ultimately (l. 331) the original narrator replaces Doctour Doubble Ale
in the text and illustrates, by way of a story, just how skillful the curate is at
deceiving his parishioners. It is an old story, one of those traditionally used
to discredit the clergy, and one which allows the narrator to conclude that
there is no hope that Doctour Doubble Ale will ever change. He is past
being able to learn the new ways, even if he wanted to do so. All he is good
for by now is saying his rosary and mumbling his way through the prayers
in his Breviary.

The narrator further undermines the situation in the next few lines by
inventing mock Latin rhymes; a contrivance which implies that Doctour
Doubble Ale is one of those clerics who are not well educated enough to
know the correct Latin words and who can only say their prayers because
they have learned them (sometimes wrongly) by rote. The existence of
semiliterate or poorly educated clergy who were unable to read the Gospel
correctly or to interpret the Bible was one of the key issues in the Reformation and this general concern is emphasized here by the specific structure
of the following lines of this satire which parody Doctour Doubble Ale's
bad Latin. Moreover, the lines which imitate the curate's corrupt Latin are
a mocking mimicry of the act of changing bread and wine into the Eucharist in the sacrifice of the mass. "You cannot do as much as I can," the curate
tells us,[19] meaning that he can do what his audience cannot: consecrate
bread and wine into the body and blood of Christ.[20] There is a lovely irony
here if we interpret Doctour Doubble Ale's priestly duty of celebrating
mass as his drinking the communion wine. The irony is deepened if we
remember that just a few lines earlier in this poem the curate has been
praising the excellent ale he is drinking, which, he claims, is [much] better
than wine.[21] The irony is extended even further when, instead of the words
of consecration of the host, "Hoc est enim corpus meum" ("For this is my
body"), Doctour Doubble Ale misquotes, "Hoc est lifum meum" ("This is

---

[19]"Tu non potes facio / Tot quam ego," *Doctour doubble ale*, ll. 407–408.

[20]This is similar to the late medieval work, *Missa de Potatoribus* (*The Mass of the Drunkards*),
which parodies the Catholic mass by substituting the pagan god Bacchus for the priest who changes the
wine into Christ's blood: British Library, Harley MS 913, fol. 13ᵛ; Thomas Wright and James Orchard
Halliwell, eds., *Reliquiae Antiquae: Scraps from Ancient Manuscripts Illustrating Chiefly Early English
Literature and the English Language*, 2 vols. (London, 1841–43), 2:208–210. Shepherd uses comparable
parodies in *Pathose* ll. 142–143 and ll.709–711, *Phylogamus* l. 131, and *The vpcheringe of the messe* ll.
360–361.

[21]"This alum finum / Is bonus then vinum," *Doctour doubble ale*, ll. 400–401.

my life").[22] Summing up, the narrator describes the curate as a considerable source of profit for the alewives of the district and explains that even raking over hell could not yield a more dissolute curate than Doctour Doubble Ale.

So who is this Doctour Doubble Ale? He is an actual contemporary character, Harry George of St. Sepulchre-without-Newgate, in London, according to the text (ll. 83–84, 280).[23] The parish church of St. Sepulchre was situated between St. Paul's Cathedral and Smithfield.[24] Like St. Faith-under-St. Paul's or St. Martin Ludgate, St. Sepulchre's was well known in London in 1548 as a church where the mass was still said in Latin.[25] Before becoming curate of St. Sepulchre's, Henry George had been a member of the community of Augustinian canons at St. Bartholomew's Hospital, and he is listed in the records of the Court of Augmentations as receiving a pension after the dissolution of that monastery.[26] We can be fairly certain that Henry George remained a conservative cleric after his discharge from St. Bartholomew's and his appointment to St. Sepulchre's because the wills he witnessed there, even during Edward VI's reign, were predominantly Catholic.[27] Moreover, he was a friend of John Twyford (also of St. Sepulchre's parish), who had built the fires at Smithfield for the execution of the reformers Bainham, Bayfield, Frith, and Tewkesbury, and whom John Foxe described as "a furious papist." Twyford refers to Harry George as his "ghostly father" and calls him as a witness when he makes his conservative will in 1549.[28] Doubtless the most interesting connection between the two characters, Doctour Doubble Ale and John Twyford, however, is the fact that Twyford owned a tavern, possibly the King's Head in Little Old Bailey, close to St. Sepulchre's church (l. 241).

---

[22] *Doctour doubble ale*, l. 413.

[23] Brigden, *London*, 440.

[24] R. Newcourt, *An Ecclesiastical Parochial History of the Diocese of London*, 2 vols. (London, 1708), 530. Unfortunately, these records do not list the names of the curates of St. Sepulchre's and neither are all the incumbents recorded for this church; William Copland was vicar there until about 1536.

[25] *A new dialog called the endightment agaynste mother Messe* (1548), Avi, suggests that those who sought such a service would find the mass "in one of those plasys wytheoute fayle."

[26] Sir William Dugdale, *Monasticon Anglicanum: A History of the Abbeys and Other Monastries, Hospitals, Friaries, and Cathedral and Collegiate Churches*, ed. John Caley, Henry Ellis, and Rev. Bulkeley Bandinel, 6 vols. (London, 1830), 6/1:297; *Letters and Papers, Foreign and Domestic, of the Reign of Henry VIII*, ed. J. S. Brewer, J. Gairdner, and R. H. Brodie, 22 vols. (London: Her Majesty's Stationery Office, 1862–1932; repr. facs. Vaduz: Kraus Reprint Ltd., 1965), 21/2, no. 775.

[27] Brigden, *London*, 440.

[28] Foxe, *Acts*, 5:601; Brigden, *London*, 421.

Returning to the question of why so many polemical works were written during 1547–48, I suggest that Shepherd's satires, especially *Doctour doubble ale*, are a direct, personal, and Protestant response to the ordinary, day-to-day situation which he observed around him in London. Officially, legally, the old Catholic ways had been abolished, but Shepherd was surrounded by plenty of evidence to show that in practical terms this in fact was not the case. In many places very little had changed at all and adherence to Catholic practices and rites still prevailed. While many London parishes made the transition from the established, Catholic services and practices to the newer, more Protestant ones, not all clerics were willing to give up their personal, traditional beliefs and some parish clergy became well known for their stubborn, conservative adherence to the old ways. Although the banning of images was largely enforced throughout the London parishes, there were still many wills witnessed which were Catholic in their format and tone, and some vicars and curates who were not overtly Protestant retained their church offices.

While the authorities were clearly not too bothered about these small-fry who, like Doctour Doubble Ale, were reluctant to change to the new ways, those in high office who refused to conform were dealt with very promptly. Officials moved quickly against Bishop Gardiner in order to curtail his public conservatism. Gardiner had been a staunch supporter of the Henrician reforms, but he had been barred from the regency council on Henry VIII's death and on Edward VI's accession he was excluded from the council of state as well. Refusing to accept the Injunctions and the *Book of Homilies*, he was committed to the Fleet in September 1547 and, although released in January, he continued to resist doctrinal reformation. Gardiner continued to maintain the doctrine of the Real Presence and was accused of having performed the forbidden practices of bearing palms and creeping to the cross during the Easter ceremonies of 1548. After his famous sermon at St. Paul's Cross in which he publicly refused to accept the authority of the Privy Council over religious matters, Gardiner was imprisoned in the Tower of London on 30 June 1548.[29]

Gardiner being powerless in the Tower, the way was clear for Shepherd's reformist attacks, and in fact the writer pours scorn and ridicule on the bishop in his satires *A pore helpe* and *The vpcheringe of the messe,*

---

[29]On Gardiner, see Glyn Redworth, *In Defence of the Church Catholic: The Life of Stephen Gardiner* (Oxford: Basil Blackwell, 1990).

mocking him for his personal appearance, his position as victualler of the navy (which earned him the nickname of Stephen Stockfish), and his episcopal estate in Southwark (a location infamous for its brothels), as well as for the fact that his nephew had earlier denied the Royal Supremacy and had been executed for treason. Gardiner's incarceration also allows Shepherd to satirize those conservative clerics who might otherwise escape criticism because of his influence, clerics not so conspicuously in the public eye who were likely to be overlooked by the authorities unless they became the targets of propaganda such as Shepherd's poems.

As the example of Harry George alias Doctour Doubble Ale shows, Shepherd would have had firsthand experience of such conservative clergymen. Although Coleman Street, where Shepherd lived, had long been known as a Protestant locale, it was situated near several parish churches, such as those named above, which had the reputation of still being Catholic, including Doctour Doubble Ale's St. Sepulchre.[30] Shepherd openly mocks conservative clerics in many of his satires. In *Comparison* he satirizes William Bell, the rector of St. Mildred Bread Street, and in *Phylogamus* he parodies two conservatives, John Mason and Richard Smith. In *Antipus* Shepherd also links Mason and Smith with another conservative cleric, William Leighton, a prebendary of St. Paul's Cathedral. Both Leighton and Smith were strong defenders of the mass, and as such are vehemently ridiculed by Shepherd.

In the satire *Doctour doubble ale*, Shepherd intensifies his general attack on conservative clerics, fashioning a narrative which focuses fully on the main character. Despite the official changes in the practice of the liturgy, this cleric still maintains his allegiance to Rome and the pope because of his personal belief in Catholic doctrine, but also because he has no intention of abandoning what he perceives as his benefits of office. Certainly he has no desire to give up all his familiar pleasures, his privileges, and his drinking, in order to follow the new ways of the Protestants, which would involve him in the very things that he avoids most assiduously: reading and studying the Bible and preaching and teaching God's word to his flock. Adhering to the old religious ways allows Doctour Doubble Ale to continue to enjoy the life he leads. Shepherd clearly sees such clerics as hypocritical and dangerous.

[30]Brigden, *London*, 103–106.

While there are still parish curates like Doctour Doubble Ale, whose religion is not founded in the true faith, there is still a need for polemical writing because, although the authorities are prepared to move against the obvious conservatives like Gardiner, the still-far-from-stable political situation does not allow them to give their full attention to the lesser nonconformists like Henry George. These traditional conservative clerics are part of Shepherd's London landscape. Shepherd's aim, like that of many other reformist authors, is to highlight, mock, and condemn, through ridicule, those who will not change and conform to the new way. In his satire *Doctour doubble ale*, Shepherd mounts a scathing assault on the Catholic Church by means of a derisive attack on a specific London cleric. The poem reflects in a humorous way what was still the most important element in the writings of many Protestants at this time, the rectification of conservative practices and abuses. Shepherd's satire illustrates these concerns in a colorful and realistic narrative and shows us the ways in which Protestant writers at the time felt reformist propaganda and satire to be necessary even after conservative practices and rituals had already been officially reformed.

DOCTOUR DOUBBLE ALE. [Sig A 1]

Although I lacke intelligence   [Sig A i*v*]
And can not skyll of eloquence
Yet wyll I do my diligence
To say sumthing or I go hence
Wherin I may demonstrate   5
The figure gesture and estate
Of one that is a curate
That harde is and endurate
And ernest in the cause
Of piuish popish lawes   10
That are not worth two strawes
Except it be with dawes
That knoweth not good from euels
Nor Gods worde from the Deuels
Nor wyll in no wise heare   15
The worde of god so cleare
But popishnes vpreare
And make the pope Gods peare
And so them selues they lade
Wyth bables that he made   20
And styll wyll holde his trade
No man can them perswade
And yet I dare say
Ther is no day
But that they may   25
Heare sincerily
And right truly
Gods worde to be taught
If they wolde haue sought
But they set at nought   30
Christes true doctrine   [Sig A ii]
And them selues decline[1]
To mens ordinaunce
Which they enhaunce
And take in estimation   35
Aboue Christes passion
And so this folish nacion
Esteme their owne facion[2]
And all dum ceremonies
Before the sanctimonies   40
Of Christes holy writ
And thinke their owne wit[3]

To be far aboue it
That the scripture to them teachis
Or honest men preachis   45
They folowe perlowes lechis
And doctours dulpatis
That falsely to them pratis
And bring them to the gates
Of hell and vtter derkenes   50
And all by stubborne starkenes
Putting their full trust
In thinges that rot and rust
And papisticall prouisions
Which are the deuels dirisions   55
Now let vs go about
To tell the tale out
Of this good felow stout
That for no man wyll dout
But kepe his olde condicions   60
For all the newe comyssyons   [Sig A ii*v*]
And vse his supersticions
And also mens tradicyons
And syng for dead folkes soules
And reade hys beade rolles   65
And all such thinges wyll vse
As honest men refuse
But take hym for a cruse
And ye wyll tell me newes
For if he ons begyn   70
He leaueth nought therin
He careth not a pyn
How much ther be wythin
So he the pot may wyn
He wyll it make full thyn   75
And wher the drinke doth please
Ther wyll he take his ease
And drinke ther of his fyll
Tyll ruddy be his byll
And fyll both cup and can   80
Who is so glad a man
As is our curate than
I wolde ye knewe it a curate
Not far without newgate

[1]decline] de[c]line 1548.
[2]facion] [f]acion 1548.
[3]wit] wi 1548.

Of a parysh large   85
The man hath mikle charge
And none within this border
That kepeth such order
Nor one a this syde Nauerne
Louyth better the ale tauerne   90
But if the drinke be small   [Sig A iii]
He may not well withall
Tush cast it on the wall
It fretteth out his gall
Then seke an other house   95
This is not worth a louse
As dronken as a mouse
Mon syre gybet a vous
And ther wyll byb and bouse
Tyll heuy be his brouse   100
Good ale he doth so haunt
And drynke a due taunt
That alewiues make ther vaunt
Of many a peny rounde
That sum of them hath founde   105
And sometyme mikle strife is
Amonge the alewyfes
And sure I blame them not
For wrong it is God wot
When this good dronken sot   110
Helpeth not to empty the pot
For sumtime he wyl go
To one and to no mo
Then wyll the hole rout
Upon that one cry out   115
And say she doth them wronge
To kepe him all day longe
From commyng them amonge
Wherfore I geue councell
To them that good drinke sell   120
To take in of the best   [Sig A iii v]
Or els they lese their gest
For he is redy and prest
Where good ale is to rest
And drinke tyll he be drest   125
When he his boke shulde study
He sitteth there full ruddy
Tyll halfe the day be gone
Crying fyll the pot Ione
And wyll not be alone   130
But call sum other one
At wyndowe or at fenestre

That is an idell ministre
As he him selfe is
Ye know full well this   135
The kinde of carion crowes
Ye may be sure growes
The more for carion stinking
And so do these in drinking
This man to sum mens thinking   140
Doth stay hym muche vpon the kyng
As in the due demaunding
Of that he calleth an head peny
And of the paskall halpeny.
For the cloth of corpus Christy   145
Four pens he claymith swiftely
For which the sexton and he truly
Did tog by the eares earnestly
Saying he can not the king well paye
If all such driblars be take away   150
Is not this a gentill tale   [Sig A iiii]
Of our doctour doubble ale
Whose countenaunce is neuer pale
So wel good drinke he can vphale
A man of learning great   155
For if his brayne he wolde beat
He coulde within dayes fourtene
Make such a sermon as neuer was sene
I wot not whether he spake in drinke
Or drinke in him how do ye thinke?   160
I neuer herde him preach God wot
But it were in the good ale pot
Also he sayth that fayne he wolde
Come before the councell if he coulde
For to declare his learning   165
And other thinges concerning
Goodly councels that he coulde geue
Beyond all measure ye may me beleue
His learning is exceding
Ye may know by his reading   170
Yet could a cobblers boy him tell
That he red a wrong gospell,
Wherfore in dede he serued him well
He turned himselfe as round as a bell
And with loud voyce began to call   175
Is chere no constable among you all,
To take this knaue y^t doth me troble?
With that all was on a hubble shubble
There was drawing and dragging
There was lugging and lagging   180

And snitching and snatching   [Sig A iiii*v*]
And ketching and catching
And so the pore ladde
To the Counter they had
Some wolde he shuld be hanged   185
Or els he shulde be wranged
Some sayd it were a good turne
Such an heretyke to burne
Some sayde this and some sayd that
And som dyd prate they wist not what 190
Some did curse and some did ban
For chafing of oure curate than
He was worthy no lesse
For vexing with his pertnesse
A gemman going to Messe,   195
Did it become a cobblers boy
To shew a gemman such a toy?
But if it were wel wayde
Ye shuld fynde I am afrayde
That the boy were worthy   200
For his reading and sobrietie
And iudgement in the veritie
Among honest folke to be
A curate rather then he.
For this is knowen for certentie   205
The boy doth loue no papistry
And our Curate is called no doubte
A papist london thoroughout.
And truth is it they do not lye,
It may be sene wyth halfe an eye.   210
For if there come a preacher,   [Sig A v]
Or any godly teacher
To speake agaynst his trumpery
To the alehouse goth he by & by
And there he wyl so much drinke   215
Tyll of ale he doth so stinke,
That whether he go before or behynde
Ye shall him smell without the winde
For when he goeth to it he is no hafter[4]
He drinketh dronke for two dayes after 220
With fyll the cuppe Ione,
For all this is gone
Here is ale alone
I say for my drinking
Tush, let the pot be clinking   225
And let vs mery make,

No thought wyll I take
For though these fellowes crake
I trust to se them slake
And some of them to bake   230
In smithfelde at a stake
And in my Parysh be some
That if the tyme come
I feare not wyll remember
(Be it august or september   235
October or Nouember
Or moneth of December)
To fynde both wood and timber
To burne them euery member
And goth to borde and bed   240
At the signe of the kinges head.   [Sig A v*v*]
And let these heretikes preach
And teach what they can teach
My parish I know well
Agaynst them wyll rebell   245
If I but once them tell
Or geue them any warning
That they were of the new learning.
For with a worde or twayne
I can them call agayne   250
And yet by the Messe
Forgetfull I was
Or els in a slumber
There is a shrewde nomber
That curstly do comber   255
And my pacience proue
And dayly me moue
For some of them styll
Continew wyll
In this new way   260
Whatsoeuer I saye
It is not long ago
Syns it chaunsed so
That a buriall here was
Without dirige or Masse   265
But at the buriall
Chey song a christmas carall
By the Masse they wyll mar all
If they continew shall
Some sayd it was a godly hearing   270
And of their hartes a gay chering[5]

---

[4]hafter] haf[t]er 1548.

[5]a gay chering] The bottom of the page is cut away here 1548.

Some of them fell on weping   [Sig A vi]
In my church I make no leasing
They harde neuer the lyke thing
Do ye thinke that I wyll consent   275
To these heretikes intent
To haue any sacrament
Ministred in English?
By them I set not a rysh
So long as my name is hary George   280
I wyll not do it spight of theyr gorge.
Oh Dankester Dancastre
None betwene this and Lancaster.
Knoweth so much my minde.
As thou my speciall frynde   285
It wolde do the much good
To wash thy handes in the bloude
Of them that hate the messe
Thou couetest no lesse
So much they vs oppresse   290
Pore priestes doubtlesse
And yet what than
There is not a man
That soner can,
Perswade his parishons   295
From such condicions
Then I perse I
For by and by
I can chem conuert
To take my parte   300
Except a fewe
That hacke and hew   [Sig A vi v]
And agaynst me shew
What they may do
To put me to   305
Some hynderaunce
And yet may chaunce
The bisshops visitour,
Wyll shewe me fauour
And therfore I   310
Care not a fly,
For ofte haue they
Sought by some way
To bring me to blame
And open shame   315
But I wyll beare them out
In spight of their snout
And wyll not ceasse
To drinke a pot the lesse

Of ale that is bygge   320
Nor passe not a fygge
For all their malice
Away the mare quod walis
I set not a whitinge
By all their writing,   325
For yet I deny nat
The Masses priuat
Nor yet forsake
That I of a cake
My maker may make   330
But harke a lytle harke
And a few wordes marke   [Sig A vii]
Howe this caluish clarke
For his purpose coulde warke
There is an honest man: 335
That kepte an olde woman
Of almes in hyr bed
Liyng dayly beddered
Which man coulde not I say
Wyth popishnes a way   340
But fayne this woman olde
Wolde haue Messe if she coulde
The which this priest was tolde
He hearing this anone
As the goodman was gone   345
Abrode aboute his busines
Before the woman he sayd Messe
And shewed his pretty popishnes
Agaynst the goodmans wyll
Wherfore it is my skyll   350
That he shulde him endight
For doing such dispight
As by his popish wyle
His house wyth Masse defyle
Thus may ye beholde   355
This man is very bolde
And in his learning olde
Intendeth for to syt
I blame him not a whyt
For it wolde vexe his wyt   360
And cleane agaynst his earning
To folow such learning   [Sig A vii v]
As now a dayes is taught
It wolde sone bring to naught
His olde popish brayne   365
For then he must agayne
Apply him to the schole

And come away a fole:
For nothing shulde he get
His brayne hath bene to het   370
And with good ale so wet
Wherfore he may now iet
In feldes and in medes
And pray vpon his beades
For yet he hath a payre   375
Of beades that be right fayre
Of corall gete, or ambre
At home within his chambre
For in matins or Masse,
Primar and portas   380
And pottes and beades
His lyfe he leades
But this I wota
That if ye nota
How this idiota   385
Doth folow the pota
I holde you a grota
Ye wyll rede by rota
That he may were a cota
In cocke losels bota   390
Thus the durty doctour
The popes owne proctour   [Sig A viii]
Wyll bragge and boost
Wyth ale and a toost
And lyke a rutter   395
Hys latin wyll vtter
And turne and tosse him
Wyth tu non possum
Loquere latinum
This alum finum   400
Is bonus then vinum
Ego volo quare
Cum tu drinkare
Pro tuum caput

Quia apud   405
Te propiciacio
Tu non potes facio
Tot quam ego
Quam librum tu lego,
Caue de me   410
Apponere te
Iuro per deum
Hoc est lifum meum
Quia drinkum stalum
Non facere malum   415
Thus our dominus dodkin
Wyth ita vera bodkin
Doth leade his lyfe
Which to the ale wife
Is very profitable   420
It is pytie he is not able
To mayntayne a table   [Sig A viii v]
For beggers and tinkers
And all lusty drinkers
Or captayne or beddle   425
Wyth dronkardes to meddle
Ye cannot I am sure
For keping of a cure
Fynde such a one well
If ye shulde rake hell   430
And therfore nowe
No more to you
Sed perlegas ista,
Si velis Papista,
Farewell and adewe   435
With a whirlary whewe
And a tirlary typpe
Beware of the whyppe.
Finis.
Take this tyll more come.   440

NOTES TO POEM TEXT

4   *or*] Before.
8   *endurate*] Hardened, obstinate, stubborn.
12   *dawes*] Literally jackdaws, but used figuratively to mean fools. It has implications of hypocrisy but also illustrates the color of the clothing worn by priests. Also an allusion to the conservative clergy, especially the chantry priests. Proverbial. Morris Palmer Tilley, *A Dictionary of the Proverbs in England in the Sixteenth and Seventeenth Centuries* (Ann Arbor: University of Michigan Press, 1966), B 375.
19   *lade*] Load.

20   *bables*] Foolish things, but with a connotation of idolatry or popery as well. See also note to l. 333.
32   *decline*] Incline, lean.
33   *ordinaunce*] Authority.
34   *enhaunce*] Exalt, elevate spiritually.
38   *facion*] Behavior, fashion, mode of action.
39   *dum*] Meaningless.
44–48 Adapted endings pretending to be real Latin: *teachis*] Teaches; *preachis*] Preach; *lechis*] Physicians; *dulpatis*] Dullard, stupid person; *pratis*] Prate. See lines 383–390 for other examples. Shepherd also

employs this technique in *The vpcheringe of the messe* ll.230–233, 347–351, 368–372.

46 *perlowes*] Dangerous.

49–50*gates / Of hell*] Mt. 7:13. The gates of hell are wide and always open and the road to them is easy. A suggestion that those who follow the false teaching of the Roman church will be easily led away from God. Also a reference to Christ's promise to the Apostles that His church will be able to stand firm against the powers of evil: "And the gates of Hades will not prevail against it" (Mt. 16:18–20). This text was claimed by both Protestants and Catholics as proof that theirs was the true church.

50 *derkenes*] Darkness.

51 *starkenes*] Absoluteness, utterness.

52–53 *trust / In thinges that rot and rust*] Mt. 6:19–20.

54 *papisticall prouisions*] Appointments to a see or benefice not yet vacant, especially such appointments made by the pope in derogation of the right of the regular patron. In this poem the narrator is satirizing those clerics, like Doctour Doubble Ale, who look forward to the return of the pope's rule and all the old ways associated with it.

55 *dirisions*] Derision, objects of ridicule.

58 *this good felow stout*] Doctour Doubble Ale himself. A pun on stout and ale.

60–61 *olde condicions*] Adherence to the old Catholic ways.

newe comyssons] The new laws. Very likely the reference is to *The Order of the Communion*, 8 March 1548, which allowed English to be used for the first time in the sacrament of the Eucharist.

64 *syng for dead folkes soules*] Chantry priests earned their living by singing masses for the souls of the dead. Catholics believed that the prayers of others could shorten the time a person's soul stayed in purgatory and so often left money for this purpose in their wills. Another contemporary Protestant writer, William Punt, satirically remarks: "[the mass can] bring da[m]pned soles out of hel, also she saith she can purchase remission of sinnes by offering vp againe of Christes bodi and bloud"(*A new dialog called the endightment agaynste mother Messe* [1548], Av). The Protestants abhorred this practice as being similar to the abuses of indulgences. By 1545 chantries could no longer legally secure gifts and endowments and the Dissolution of the Chantries Act (which forbade chantry masses) was implemented under Edward VI in December 1547 (1 Ed. VI, c. 14).

65 *beade rolles*] Bede rolls. Lists of names of the dead, usually benefactors, kept by every church. The priest would read it in full at the annual requiem for the benefactors of the parish and read a shorter version at the bidding of the bedes at every mass on Sundays so that the congregation could pray for those whose names were on it: see Eamon Duffy, *The Stripping of the Altars: Traditional Religion in England c. 1400–c. 1580* (New Haven: Yale University Press, 1992), 334–337. See also note on l. 374.

68 *cruse*] Drunkard.

72 *careth not a pyn*] Cares not at all. Proverbial. B. J. and W. H. Whiting, *Proverbs, Sentences and Proverbial Phrases from English Writings before 1500*

(Cambridge, Mass.: The Belknap Press of Harvard University Press, 1968), 210.

78–79 *And drinke ther of his fyll / Tyll ruddy be his byll*] The Injunctions of 1536–1537 specifically forbade the clergy to frequent alehouses and taverns or to spend their time drinking or playing cards: John Foxe, *The Acts and Monuments*, ed. S. R. Cattley, 8 vols. (London: R. B. Seeley and W. Burnside, 1839), 5:167.

83 *a curate*] Henry George, curate of Saint Sepulchre's in Newgate. See also note to l. 280.

84 *without*] Outside.

newgate] Newgate Street, London.

86 *charge*] Authority to impose spiritual injunction or penance.

89 *a*] Abbreviation for "at" or "of."

Nauerne] Most likely Navarre, a northern province of Spain. Claiming that no one this side of Navarre loves taverns more than Doctour Doubble Ale himself, the narrator employs exaggeration to underline the curate's fondness for taverns and their products. Shepherd has a similar usage ("on thys syde Spayne") in *Phylogamus* l.27 where John Mason's new work is being discussed. With the reference to Catholic Spain, the author reinforces the conservative links between these two men.

94 *fretteth*] Consume, devour.

gall] Bile.

97 *As dronken as a mouse*] Proverbial. Whiting, *Proverbs*, M 731. Skelton has: "Dronken as a mouse / At the ale house" in *Collyn Clout*, ll.801–802: John Skelton, *The Complete English Poems*, ed. John Scattergood (Harmondsworth: Penguin, 1983), 266.

98 *Mon syre gybet a vous*] Monsieur gibet a vous. "Sir Gallows, to you." The exact reference is unclear.

99 *byb and bouse*] Booze and drink.

100 *heuy*] Hay; *brouse*] Fodder.

102 *drynke a due taunt*] From "ataunt," "as much" (Fr.). The curate intends to steep himself thoroughly in drink. A slightly later example has the same sense: "And there they prate and make theyr auant / Of theyr deceytes and drynk adew taunt": Robert Copland, *The hye way to the spyttel house* (circa 1550), Cii^v and Di.

103 *vaunt*] Boast, brag.

122 *lese*] Lose; *gest*] Guest.

123 *prest*] Prepared.

126 *boke*] His breviary. A book containing the Divine Office for each day, which those in orders are bound to recite. The Divine Office consists of psalms, collects (short prayers in the form of petitions), and readings from the Scriptures and the lives of the saints. This curate sits drinking rather than reciting his prayers. See also note to l. 380.

129 *Ione*] Joan. A traditional name for an alewife.

130–139 This idle curate is not the only one of his kind. He seeks out others like himself whom the narrator compares to vulturelike crows because of their black clothes and their association with death.

132 *fenestre*] Lattice, window.

141 *stay vpon*] Attend.

143–147 *head peny*] An individual ecclesiastical payment; *paskall halpeny*] Paschal half-penny. The curate's due from all his parishioners at Easter, used to pay for the bread and wine used in the mass: W. Carew Hazlitt, ed., *Remains of the Early Popular Poetry of England,* 4 vols. (London, 1864–1866), 3:311; *sexton*] The sacristan who had charge of the vestments and sacred vessels in a church. By showing the curate and his sexton quarreling over who should keep this money, Shepherd is pointing out more abuses of the Roman church. The curate even pretends that he will not have enough money left over to pay the king his dues unless the tiny amounts like half pennies from the parishioners make their way into his pocket.

146 *claymith*] Claims.

150 *driblars*] A reference to these small monetary offerings.

151 *gentill*] Noble. (Used ironically here.)

155–169 *A man of learning great...His learning is exceding*] Shepherd is satirizing Doctour Doubble Ale's intellectual ability here. The curate could write a sermon if he had to, as he is able to read, but he cannot interpret the Gospel correctly because he adheres to the old faith.

163 *fayne*] To be delighted or glad. See also l.341.

171 *a cobblers boy*] Someone young, inexperienced, and uneducated.

172 *a wrong gospell*] Either the curate interprets the Scriptures incorrectly or else at mass he reads the wrong Gospel for the day (Hazlitt, *Remains,* 312, n. 1).

174 A reference to the rector of St. Mildred's Bread Street, William Bell, who held the living from 26 October 1536 to 15 January 1557 and who is mentioned in Shepherd's satire *Comparison*: R. Newcourt, *An Ecclesiastical Parochial History of the Diocese of London,* 2 vols. (London, 1708), 499. We know that Bell was a conservative clergyman because in May 1538 three of his parishioners reported him for reading the forbidden name, "Saint Gregory Pope," at the Easter mass and because at the sessions against Bishop Gardiner before the King's Commissioners in 1550–1551, Bell was one of the conservative witnesses called for Gardiner: Susan Brigden, *London and the Reformation* (Oxford: Clarendon Press, 1989), 281; Foxe, *Acts,* 6:201.

176 *chere*] There. For similar expressions see l. 267 and l. 299. Shepherd may be suggesting a Northern background for Henry George. (See also note to l. 282.)

178 *hubble shubble*] Commotion, uproar.

182 *ketching*] Catching.

183 *the pore ladde*] On 30 July 1541, at the age of fifteen, Richard Mekins went to the stake as a sacramentarian, despite opposing evidence (Brigden, *London,* 334–335; Foxe, *Acts,* 5:440–442). The reformers held Mekins up as a martyr and John Bale was convinced that the jury which condemned him had been rigged. Although Shepherd's account of the lad's being dragged off to prison has its comic side, there is an undertone of horror that the authorities would imprison and execute someone so young.

184 *Counter*] The Counter (Compter). The prison attached to the London Guildhall. Until September

1555, it was located in Bread Street: Foxe, *Acts,* 5:705; *Chronicle of the Grey Friars of London,* ed. John Nichols, Camden Society, o.s. 53 (London, 1852), 96; Charles Wriothesley, *A Chronicle of England during the Reigns of the Tudors, from A.D. 1485 to 1559,* ed. William Douglas Hamilton, Camden Society, n.s. 11 (London, 1875), 128.

186 *wranged*] Tortured on the rack.

195 *gemman*] Gentleman. See also l. 197; *Messe*] The mass, the celebration of the Eucharist.

197 *toy*] Something of no value.

200–204 *the boy were worthy...thoroughout*] Both Doctour Doubble Ale's dissolute life and his conservative religion make him less suitable for the curate's position he now holds than an untrained youth who reads God's word.

213 *trumpery*] Nonsense, especially applied contemptuously to religious beliefs or ceremonies.

219 *hafter*] Dodger, haggler, objecter, wrangler.

228 *crake*] Boast, brag.

229 *slake*] Come to an end, be extinguished.

231 *smithfelde*] Smithfield, an open space outside the northwest walls of the city of London which was used in the sixteenth century for executions.

232–239 *in my Parysh be some...euery member*] The curate's parish is a conservative one and some of its members obviously support the burning of those Protestants whom they see as heretics.

238–239 *To fynde both wood and timber / To burne them euery member*] This is probably a reference to John Twyford of St. Sepulchre's parish who provided the wood for the executions of Bainham, Bayfield, Frith, and Tewkesbury (Foxe, *Acts,* 5:601). Twyford was also responsible for the indictment of Thomas Merial before John Stokesley, the bishop of London, for commenting unfavorably on the bishop's sermon regarding the efficacy of the mass in delivering souls out of purgatory. Merial, a bricklayer of St. Sepulchre's, was described by Foxe as "a zealous favourer of God's word" (loc. cit.). He was accused by Twyford of affirming that Christ's passion helped only those already in limbo when He died and not those who came after Him, but, although he denied the charges, and in fact appealed against them, he bore a faggot at Paul's Cross on 19 November 1535 (Brigden, *London,* 272, n. 95). See also note to l. 285.

240–241 *And goth to borde and bed*] Most likely a reference to John Twyford who was known to have owned a tavern (Foxe, *Acts,* 5:601); *At the signe of the kinges head*] A tavern called The King's Head. From the context this tavern must be within the parish of St. Sepulchre's and is very likely the public house in Little Old Bailey, in Eliot's Court, close to St. Sepulchre's and near the premises of the printers John Day and William Seres by the Holborn conduit; and the tavern owned by Twyford.

248 *the new learning*] Protestantism.

254 *shrewde*] Malicious, wicked.

255 *curstly*] With curses; *comber*] Harass, impede, trouble.

258–261 The curate now admits that despite his efforts some of his parishioners are of the new faith.

265 *dirige*] Dirge. So called for the first word of the antiphon at Matins in the Office of the Dead, which

begins: "Dirige, Domine, Deus meus, in conspectu tuo viam meam"; "Direct, O Lord, my God, my way in Thy sight" (Ps. 5:8).

266–267 The curate is shocked that the old ceremonies are disappearing. At a recent funeral, he says, there was no mass, no Office of the Dead, and only a Christmas carol was sung! This seems to be a reference to a real (though untraceable) event when, instead of the Office for the Dead, a carol was sung at a funeral. Interestingly, Robert Crowley comments on a similar and presumably topical event which actually occurred at St. Sepulchre's. In his petition to the 4 November–24 December 1547 Parliament, Crowley criticizes the parish curate of St. Sepulchre's for not carrying out his clerical duties correctly and accuses him of usury: "But when the corps was buried, wythout other crosse or holy water sticke, Dirige, or Masse, wyth prayers of as small deuocion as any pore curate could saye, yet must we nedes paye vii. d. more": *An informacion and peticion agaynst the oppressours of the pore commons of this realme, complied [for] the Parliamente* (1548), ll. 665–668. Shepherd's lines may also be an allusion to William Clinch of the parish of St. John Baptist in Walbrook (near St. Paul's) who in 1541 was presented in London for questioning regarding three offenses: "for saying, when he seeth a priest preparing to the mass, 'Ye shall see a priest now go to masking.' ...For calling the bishop of Winchester, 'False flattering knave.' ...[and] for burying his wife without dirge, and causing the Scot of St. Katherine's to preach the next day after the burial" (Foxe, *Acts*, 5:443). The Scot was John Willock, curate of St. Katherine Coleman, who preached against praying to the saints, confession, and the use of holy water, and as well argued for clerical marriage. He denied the existence of purgatory and therefore the efficacy of praying for the souls of the dead and was imprisoned for a time in the Fleet (Foxe, *Acts*, 5:448). Increasingly, people willed money to be used to pay for funeral sermons to be preached as they had once for chantry masses to be said for their souls (Brigden, *London*, 484).

267 *Chey*] They.

271 *a gay chering*] A gay cheering. Something to gladden their hearts. The bottom of the page is cut away here, but the sense is as in the above and Shepherd uses the same phrase with slightly different spelling ("gay chearynge") in *Iohn Bon and Mast person* (l. 79).

272 *fell on*] Began, commenced, fell to.

273 *leasing*] Falsehood, lying.

275–278 Another example of the curate's backward conservative thinking. He will not allow the sacraments in English in his church.

279 *set not a rysh*] Place no value on. Proverbial. Whiting has "Not worth a rysh": *Proverbs*, R 250.

280 *hary George*] Harry George.

281 *I wyll not do it*] I will not allow the sacraments to be administered in English.

282 *Dankester Dancastre*] Probably a reference to Doncaster, but the exact allusion is unknown. Although Henry George is not listed in the Order of St. Austin at Doncaster, he may have originally come from that area.

285 *my speciall frynde*] Another reference to John Twyford.

295 *parishons*] Parishioners.

297 *I perse I*] I per se, I. I by myself, I.

299 *chem*] Them.

308 *bishops visitour*] An official (usually an ecclesiastic) appointed to visit churches, either at regular intervals or on special occasions, in order to prevent or remove abuses or irregularities. This reference suggests that some of these dignitaries were not always impartial nor above being bribed. The Injunctions dated 31 July 1547 required each parish church, for the instruction of the laity, to provide a copy of the Bible in English as well, the *Paraphrases* of Erasmus, ordered all preachers to read a sermon from the *Book of Homilies* each Sunday, and charged the bishops to enforce this policy. A royal visitation was set up to ensure that these requirements were met. The country was divided up into six regions and thirty commissioners (most of them laymen) were named. The commissioners (chosen by Cranmer and the Privy Council) were all staunch Protestants apart from Sir John Mason and Sir James Hales who were only recent converts from conservatism. Bishop Gardiner opposed the Injunctions and it is interesting to note that his official refusal on 30 August was made to Mason: Philip Hughes, *The Reformation in England*, 3 vols. (London: Hollis and Carter, 1953–1954), 2:93; W. K. Jordan, *Edward VI: The Young King* (London: George Allen & Unwin Ltd., 1968), 161, n.3. Shepherd may be suggesting that Gardiner expected to receive special treatment because of Mason's conservative background.

311 *Care not a fly*] Care not at all. Probably proverbial. Whiting has "Not worth a fly": *Proverbs*, F 345.

316 *beare them out*] Overcome, withstand.

321 *passe not a fygge*] Care not at all. Proverbial. Whiting, *Proverbs*, F 137.

323 *Away the mare*] Banish melancholy. Proverbial. Whiting, *Proverbs*, M 375. *A merie geste of the frere and the boye* (1510–13) has "But sange hey howe awaye the mare." Possibly it is also a drinking cry. Skelton uses the same expression in *Magnyfycence* and *Elynour Rummynge*, and Dyce suggests that it is a portion of a song or a ballad: *The Poetical Works of John Skelton with Notes and Some Account of His Writings*, ed. Rev. Alexander Dyce, 2 vols. (London, 1843, with addenda 1844; repr. New York: AMS Press, Inc., 1965), 2:162–163. The whole line ("Away the mare quod walis") is most likely a song refrain.

324–325 *I set not a whitinge / By all their writing*] I do not put any value upon their writing. (Whiting, which is a highly prized small fish with pearly white flesh, is also sometimes used as a term of endearment.) Also proverbial. Whiting, *Proverbs*, W 317.

326–327 Private or privy masses were those which were held in the private chapels and residences even though they had been forbidden by the Privy Council's Proclamation in February 1548. These masses were still in Latin. Edmund Bonner, bishop of London, was commanded at the end of June 1549 to stop the private masses in St. Paul's parish.

From this point on the Eucharist was to be held only at the high altar. See Brigden, *London*, 447.

329–330 The curate holds to his belief in the consecration of bread into Christ's body. The Protestants' objection to the doctrine of transubstantiation was that they held it impossible and illogical to believe that a human being could "make" God. If the priest saying the words of consecration could change bread into the body of Christ, then this in effect meant that the priest, a man, had made his maker, God.

333 *caluish*] Papist. Aaron set up the golden calf for the people to worship while Moses was on Mount Sinai (Exod. 32:4–7); Jeroboam established idols at Bethel and Dan (1 Kings 12:28–33).

334 *warke*] Work.

346 *abrode*] Abroad.

347 *he sayd Messe*] This line suggests a real incident, but the specific persons referred to are not known. In *A Declaration of Edmonde Bonner's Articles* (1554), Bale suggests that such home visitations by clerics were common, and sometimes involved sexual gratification rather than the celebration of the mass. He recounts a story he heard about a Welsh priest visit to a sick parishoner "wyth hys cake God in a boxe." Leaving the sexton outside with his bell and lantern and "The doore beinge fast barred … he put downe his breche, and gotte him to bed to the wyfe" (Miii–Miii^v).

352 *dispight*] Malice.

357 *learning olde*] Catholicism.

362–363 *such learning / As now a dayes*] The new Protestant beliefs.

372 *iet*] Boast, brag.

372–382 This curate is now past learning. Even if he desired to learn the new ways his brain is so befuddled from drinking that he would not be able to understand. So his life now consists of praying his rosary or reading his prayers from his breviary. There is also a strong hint that drink is still an important part of his daily life.

373 *medes*] Meadows.

374 *beades*] Originally prayers, now small beads used for counting prayers said; often referred to as a rosary.

376 *fayre*] Fair.

377 *gete*] Black lignite, jet; *ambre*] Amber.

379 *matins*] Matins, one of the canonical hours of the breviary: properly a midnight office, occasionally recited at daybreak.

380 *primar*] Primer, a devotional manual or prayer book for the use of the laity; *portas*] A portable breviary. A book containing the Divine Office for each day which those in orders are bound to recite.

383–390 Another example of adapted endings pretending to be real Latin: *wota*] Know; *nota*] Note; *idiota*] Silly person; *pota*] Ale pot; *grota*] Groat, a thick coin officially worth 4d. in England until circa 1600, though as a result of debasements to offset war expenses, silver coins were often worth (in real terms) only about half their face value; *rota*] Rote; *cota*] Coat; *bota*] Boat. See also note below.

390 *cocke losels bota*] Presumably a misprint for lorels. Reference to a rogue or a reprobate after a character in *Cocke Lorelles Bote*, a popular satire in

verse printed by Wynkyn de Worde circa 1515. In it types of various tradesfolk take ship and sail through England. The captain of the boat, Cocke Lorell, is a tinker.

391–392 *the durty doctour / The popes owne proctour*] A proctor is the person responsible for the collection of tithes and other church dues, but the term is also used to describe an agent appointed to beg or to collect alms for the leprous. This image of a diseased pope reinforces Protestant references to the Roman church as the whore of Babylon (Rev. 17–18).

393 *boost*] Boast.

395 *rutter*] A dashing fellow, a gallant (Dyce, *Poetical Works*, 2:245–246); one so fashionable as to speak much in foreign languages (James Orchard Halliwell, *A Dictionary of Archaic and Provincial Words, Obsolete Phrases, Proverbs, and Ancient Customs from the Fourteenth Century*, 7th ed. 2 vols. [London, 1872], 2:699).

396 *Hys latin*] The following lines parody Doctour Doubble Ale's bad Latin. Translation by Seymour House and John King, *English Reformation Literature: The Tudor Origins of the Protestant Tradition* (Princeton: Princeton University Press, 1982), 264–265.

398–399 *tu non possum / Loquere latinum*] You are not able to speak Latin.

400–401 *This alum finum / Is bonus then vinum*] This excellent ale is better than wine.

402–404 *Ego volo quare / Cum tu drinkare / Pro tuum caput*] Therefore I wish to drink with you for your health/life.

405–406 *Quia apud / Te propiciacio*] Do I make myself favourable to you?

407–408 *Tu non potes facio / Tot quam ego*] You cannot do as much as I can. With the connotation that you cannot consecrate bread and wine into the body and blood of Christ.

409 *Quam librum tu lego*] Whatever book you read.

410 *Caue de me*] Watch out for me.

411 *Apponere te*] Put yourself [in the right place].

412 *Iuro per deum*] I swear by God.

413 *Hoc est lifum meum*] This is my life. A pun on the words of consecration of the host during the mass: "Hoc est enim corpus meum," "For this is my body."

414 *Quia drinkum stalum*] Therefore, to drink stale [ale].

415 *Non facere malum*] [Is] to do nothing bad. Doctour Doubble Ale could be saying that he will settle for drinking ale—being a drunkard—which according to him is not a bad thing to do, rather than carrying out his priestly duties of saying mass.

416 *dominus dodkin*] Parson Worthless; *dominus*] Master or parson. *dodkin*] A small coin of little value. See also note to l. 282.

417 *ita vera bodkin*] Such a true little body. The exact reference is unclear, although it seems to be a pun on the communion host. "God's bodkin," meaning "God's dear body!" is a contemporary oath.

418–424 The narrator comments that the alewife makes a tidy profit from the curate's drinking habits and suggests how much more profitable it would be if the curate provided food and drink for the local itinerant population as well. It is also an ironic reminder that the curate should be looking after those souls in his charge instead of spending his day drinking in taverns.

425 *beddle*] Beadle, overseer.

428 *keping*] Preservation; *cure*] Care of souls or spiritual charge of parishioners.

433–434 *Sed perlagus ista, / Si velis Papista*] But read this if you like, papist.

435 *adewe*] Adieu, farewell. Possibly an intended pun as well, because "adieu" literally means "I commend you to God" and the narrator has just explained that even ransacking hell could not yield a more dissolute curate than Doctour Doubble Ale.

436–437 *whirlary whewe*] Circling, whirling, whistling sound. *tirlary typpe*] Flighty, whirling. Skelton uses a similar kind of expression, "tyrly-tyrlowe," in *Elynour Rummynge* and *Collyn Clout*. Following Kinsman, an earlier editor, Scattergood suggests that it is perhaps the refrain of a song (Skelton, *Complete English Poems*, 451, n.292; 477, n.949).

438 *Beware of the whyppe*] A reference to the scourge of God and also a topical allusion to the Six Articles. Shepherd is addressing the papists here, linking them with the enemies of the chosen people and warning them. In the book of Isaiah, the people of Israel are assured by God that their enemies will eventually be destroyed: "For in a very little while my indignation will be directed to an end, and my anger will be directed to their destruction. The Lord of hosts will wield a whip against them" (Isa. 10:25–26). Finally, however, the rod of God's anger will be destroyed by the shoot from the tree of Jesse, who is Christ (Isa. 11:1). The warning in the line is ironic as the Six Articles were sometimes referred to as the "whyp of correction" (*A short treatyse of certayne thinges abvsed in the popysh church, longe vsed* [1548?], A iiiᵛ). The Act of Repeal of 2 December 1547 formally abolished the Six Articles and left the way clear for the introduction of more radical liturgical reforms.

"PRACTICAL DIVINITY"

RICHARD GREENHAM'S MINISTRY
IN ELIZABETHAN ENGLAND[1]

Eric Josef Carlson

STANDING ON WHAT MUST BE ONE OF LONDON'S BUSIEST CORNERS, head filled with the noise of jackhammers and internal combustion engines, one finds it almost impossible to imagine the appearance of the nave of Christ Church, Newgate, in April of 1594. The church which Elizabethan Londoners knew was destroyed by fire in 1666 and rebuilt by Christopher Wren, but Wren's church was gutted by German bombs in 1940 and has not been rebuilt. Parts of the external walls of the nave remain, and within them a rose garden has been planted. Benches, thoughtfully distributed with tasteful symmetry along the perimeter of the garden to bear the burden of weary office workers seeking a few moments of prandial peace, provide a poignant reminder of the pews which once crowded the space. The smoke of cigarettes has replaced the smoke of candles on the guttering in the drafty church. The mundane ritual of eating sandwiches and crisps, washed down with the contents of little boxes of fruit juice, has replaced the sublime ritual of the eucharistic meal of bread and wine.

In this space, on 25 April 1594, a simple burial service was held—such as was fitting for the interment of one of the leading nonconformists of the time in one of the paramount radical parishes of London—and the body of Richard Greenham was laid to rest somewhere under the floor of the church. The death of Richard Greenham, "our late preacher and a man of worthy memory,"[2] brought to a close an extraordinary career in ministry and was (in the words of his disciple Henry Holland) "no small wrack to

[1]I am grateful to Professor Margaret Spufford and Mr. Michael Sekulla for their close readings of an earlier draft of this essay and for many suggestions which have vastly improved it. I am grateful most of all to Dr. Kenneth L. Parker, who first introduced me to Greenham in 1984 and, since then, has been a generous and indulgent collaborator. My debt to him is beyond measure.
[2]G[uildhall] L[ibrary, London], MS 9163, fol. 320v.

the Church and people of God."[3] After a survey of Greenham's historical reputation, this essay will describe his life and ministry with the intention of making clear why contemporaries believed that "for practicall divinity... he was inferiour to few or none in his time."[4] To understand the Elizabethan church today, historians must restore Richard Greenham to the position of eminence accorded him by his peers and contemporaries.

∾

Within a century after his death, Greenham was being honored as the Puritan equivalent of a saint. The edifice of his posthumous reputation was erected on two sturdy pillars: his writings and his raft of disciples. The latter included, most notably, Henry Smith and Arthur Hildersham. Smith was perhaps the most famous preacher of his day, and his sermons are still easily accessible and frequently cited by historians.[5] Hildersham, recognized by his peers as one of the political leaders of the radical nonconformist clergy, actively promoted the Millenary Petition. Thanks to influential supporters, his long preaching career extended into the reign of Charles I in spite of his refusal to subscribe.[6] These were but two of many young men who studied under Greenham in the rectory seminary he established in his Cambridgeshire parish[7] and whose ministries were strongly influenced by him. Some of these devotees took notes of Greenham's sermons and pastoral advice with them for a more concrete remembrance of their teacher.

[3] *The Works of the Reverend and Faithfvll Servant of Iesus Christ M. Richard Greenham, Minister and Preacher of the word of God*, ed. H[enry] H[olland] (London, 1599), A2v.

[4] The words are those of the eminent London nonconformist Stephen Egerton in the dedicatory letter which precedes the fourth part of the fourth edition of Greenham's posthumous collected works: *The Workes of the Reverend and Faithfull Servant of Iesus Christ M. Richard Greenham, Minister and Preacher of the Word of God, collected into one volume: Revised, Corrected and Published for the further building of all such as love the trueth, and desire to know the power of godlinesse* (London, 1605), 724.

[5] See R. B. Jenkins, *Henry Smith: England's Silver-Tongued Preacher* (Macon, Ga.: Macon University Press, 1983).

[6] In 1583, Archbishop Whitgift required all clergy to sign a statement accepting royal supremacy in temporal and spiritual matters, and affirming that the Prayer Book, the political structure of the church, and the Articles of Religion were in conformity with Scripture. Those who refused were to be suspended from performing any clerical functions. Whitgift's Three Articles were essentially incorporated into the Canons of 1604 as Canon XXXVI. For the text, see E. Cardwell, *Synodalia*, 2 vols. (Oxford, 1842), 1:267–269. On the controversy over subscription and its effect on Hildersham, see Kenneth Fincham, *Prelate as Pastor: The Episcopate of James I* (Oxford: Clarendon Press, 1990), esp. chap. 7. For some other aspects of Hildersham's role as a Puritan leader, see Patrick Collinson, *The Elizabethan Puritan Movement* (London: Jonathan Cape, 1967). Although he was arguably more important in his own time than Henry Smith, Hildersham has not attracted a modern biographer.

[7] See below, 180–181.

Such manuscript notes were especially important because almost nothing penned by Greenham was published during his lifetime.[8] Thomas Crook, a leading London nonconformist, undertook the task of putting together an omnibus posthumous volume of Greenham's works. When Crook died in 1598, Henry Holland completed his labors and produced a volume in 1599.[9] This was followed by ever-thicker volumes in subsequent years. Holland died in 1603 before completing the fourth edition. Although his widow, Elizabeth, wrote the dedicatory letter to King James I, fulfilling what she stated was her husband's dying wish, it was the prominent London preacher and nonconformist Stephen Egerton who took over editorial duties. In 1612, Egerton produced a fifth and final edition of Greenham's works in which the contents were "digested after a more methodicall manner then heretofore." There was little new material but the whole composition, which had grown rather haphazardly as Holland received new manuscripts, was thoroughly reorganized and given a comprehensive (and remarkably good) index.[10]

---

[8]In 1584, a fairly pedestrian contribution to the genre which has come to be known as domestic conduct literature was published: *A godly Exhortatation [sic], and fruitfull admonition to vertuous parents and modest Matrons: Describing the holie use, and blessed insitution of that most honorable state of Matrimonie, and the encrease of godly and happy children, in trayning them up in godly education, and household discipline* (London, 1584). The only other work from his pen which saw print before his death is a piece which he addressed to Richard Cox, bishop of Ely, in 1573, published abroad shortly before his death in an anthology of significant works in the development of English nonconformity: "The Apologie or aunswere of Maister Grenham, Minister of Dreaton, unto the Bishop of Ely, being commaunded to subscribe, and to use the Romish habite, with allowance of the com. booke," in *A parte of a register, contayninge sundrie memorable matters written by divers godly and learned in our time, which stande for and desire the reformation of our Church, in discipline and ceremonies, according to the pure worde of God, and the lawe of our lande* (Middleburg, 1593), 86–93. For discussion of context of "The Apologie," see below, 166–167. I have used the passive voice deliberately in discussing this matter. Whether Greenham consented to or was in any way involved in the publication of either is unknown and, in my own view, highly unlikely.

[9]On Crook's role, see *Works* (1599), A6r. The 1599 edition was not actually the first time since his death that Greenham's works had appeared in print. A handful of brief treatises and collections of miscellaneous sayings appeared in 1595 and 1598. Holland noted grumpily in the 1599 preface that "some respecting gaine, and not regarding godlinesse, attempted [after Greenham's death] to publish some fragments of his workes, to the griefe…of many louing friends, which haue long desired and expected this impression of all his workes together" (A6r). A complete listing of all of Greenham's published works can be found in the *Short Title Catalogue*.

[10]Elizabeth Holland's letter: *Works* (1605), *3r–*3v. The title of the fifth edition retains the same wording as that of the fourth, including the attribution of editorship to Holland, but concludes with the following new phrasing: *The Fifth and Last Edition: In Which Matters Dispersed Before Through the whole booke are methodically drawne to their severall places, and the hundred and nineteenth Psalme perfected: with a more exact Table annexed.* (London, 1612).

Greenham had written and left his editors very little which could have been intended for publication. His major treatise on the sabbath is an exception but, although he made many personal corrections to his original text, when he died he had not completed revising it to his satisfaction. Meditations on some passages from Scripture and a catechism were among his literary remains, but it is unclear whether they were intended for the public. The imperfect state of these works is entirely what one would expect from a man who, as we will see, was tirelessly devoted to pastoral ministry and can have had little time for the (in his mind) indulgence of writing for the marketplace. As his posthumous works' editor noted, "such were his travels in his life time in preaching and comforting the afflicted, that hee could not possibly leave these works as he desired."[11]

The hefty volumes of his collected works would not have been possible had it not been for the manuscript material which followers sent to Crook and Holland from all over England. A number of people, especially women, sent personal letters of spiritual advice which they had received and obviously maintained and treasured for many years; letters from Richard Greenham were not ephemera. Devout Elizabethans made a habit, while attending church, of taking careful notes of sermons for later study and discussion. Greenham's editors benefited from this custom and published reconstructed versions of a number of his sermons on the basis of such notes.

The first and subsequent editions of Greenham's works also contained extensive (and ever-growing) sections of aphorisms and godly advice similar in form and content to Martin Luther's *Tischreden*.[12] The tale of how these sections came to be provides an important indicator of the widespread reverence accorded to Greenham. The 1599 edition began with a section entitled "Grave Counsels, and Godlie Observations; Serving Generallie to direct all men in the waies of true godlines, but principally applyed to instruct and comfort all afflicted consciences." In his preface, Holland expressed his anxiety that readers might think Greenham guilty of "pride or singularitie" for having produced pages of his own wise counsel. Instead, he reported, "such observations...were collected and taken by others, and not set downe by himselfe." The particular set of sayings in the

[11] *Works* (1599), A6v.

[12] Martin Luther, *Table Talk*, ed. and trans. Theodore G. Tappert, vol. 54 of *Luther's Works*, ed. Jaroslav Pelikan and Helmut T. Lehmann, 55 vols. (St. Louis: Concordia Publishing House and Philadelphia: Fortress Press, 1955–86).

first edition was supplied, according to Holland, by someone identified only as "Hopkins."[13] For a second volume, which appeared in 1600, Holland described more fully his editorial efforts. When the first edition met with a positive reception "of many, both learned and truely religious," Holland was "incouraged to seeke out the rest [of Greenham's sayings] carried about in written copies from hand to hand, and dispersed into divers parts of this land." This he did, collecting "all the copies I could heare of, and come by; I have set these Meditations in this forme of common places, reducing all to speciall chapters and arguments, whereunto they might seeme to have most relation." Holland also left out what he "thought less pertinent, or not so suitable to the rest" of the *Works*. He compared this to the way Peter Martyr's *Commonplaces*—one of the set books for study by the English clergy—were collected "to the great good of the Church."[14]

In 1601, Holland published an additional 113 "grave counsels" which had recently been sent to him "from a godly preacher" identified marginally as John Brodley, the vicar of Sowerby in the West Riding of Yorkshire. Brodley had been a student at St. John's College, Cambridge; he matriculated in 1578, and graduated B.A. in 1582 and M.A. in 1585. This would place him in Cambridge during the precise years in which Greenham's seminary was in operation five miles away at Dry Drayton and makes it highly likely that Brodley was there taking notes at the feet of the master.[15] Such student notebooks then circulated, as Holland described it, "hand to hand" and were copied by others.

One of these copies has survived, and is in the John Rylands Library in Manchester. Patrick Collinson was the first modern scholar to call public attention to this valuable source, identifying it as the record of Arthur

---

[13]John Hopkins must be Holland's source. *ΠΑΡΑΜΥΘΙΟΝ: Two Treatises of the comforting of an afflicted conscience, written by M. Richard Greenham, with certaine Epistles of the same argument: Hereunto are added two Sermons, with certaine grave and wise counsells and answeres of the same Author and argument* (London, 1598), contains "A great number of grave and wise counsels and answers, gathered by Master John Hopkins and others that attended him for that purpose" (A4r). Although there are some minor textual differences, and the order is rather different, these are clearly the same as the "Grave counsels" printed in the 1599 *Works*.

[14]*Works* (1599), A6v; quotations from the 1600 additions taken from *The Workes of the Reverend and Faithfull Servant of Iesus Christ M. Richard Greenham, Minister and Preacher of the Word of God, collected into one volume: Revised, Corrected, and Published, for the Further Building of All Such as love the trueth, and desire to know the power of godlinesse: By H. H. The Third Edition* (London, 1601), 251, 254.

[15]*Works* (1601), 463. Brodley was vicar of Sowerby, 1591–1625. This makes almost irresistible my desire to associate the Cambridge University Library copy of the 1612 edition of the *Works* with

Hildersham.[16] The manuscript is far too neat and carefully written to be the sort of notes taken down while Greenham was speaking, and many of the entries are too long and elaborate to be later recollections of the day's spiritual bons mots. This probably is a fair copy, made for personal use, of someone else's notebook. There are, in fact, enough similarities to suggest some connection to that of John Hopkins, though much work remains to be done before it will be possible to propose any hypothesis about the relationship between the Rylands manuscript and printed sets of "grave counsels."[17]

As editorial remarks in the printed editions make clear, then, even before his death there was widespread interest in Greenham's counsel and guidance and he enjoyed, thanks in no small part to his dispersed former students, what can fairly be described as a national reputation. The five editions of his *Works*, as well as the occasional inclusion of individual sermons or other pieces in collections with works of Richard Rogers, William Perkins, John Dod, and Robert Cleaver, testify to the substantial market for something more complete and durable than notebooks and letters carefully copied and handed about. Moreover, Greenham appears to have been one of the most read authors of his day.[18]

Thomas Carew, Jacobean rector of Bildeston in Suffolk, was familiar enough with Greenham's work to plagiarize it: his published sermon on the text "Teach us to number our days" (Ps. 90:12), entitled *The houre-glasse of*

Brodley. On the last page of the index of that copy is written: "This I give to my kinsman Beniamen Crabtre." Although I have not been able to identify a Benjamin Crabtree, there were Crabtrees in Sowerby and nearby with the right sorts of interests to make them likely recipients of this book: Elias Crabtree, the rector of Dickelburgh (Norf.) from 1643 until his ejection in 1660, was from Halifax, and Henry Crabtree, curate of Todmorden sometime after the Restoration, was born in Sowerby c. 1642; both were students at Christ's College, Cambridge. See J. Venn and J. A. Venn, eds., *Alumni Cantabrigienses, Part I: From the earliest times to 1751*, 4 vols. (Cambridge: Cambridge University Press, 1922–27).

[16]Rylands MS 524; Collinson, *Elizabethan Puritan Movement*, 494–495 n.10; idem, "'A Magazine of Religious Patterns': An Erasmian Topic Transposed in English Protestantism," in his *Godly People: Essays on English Protestantism and Puritanism* (London: The Hambledon Press, 1983), 508 n.36. The manuscript is made up of 72 folios. The first 68 are fair copies of notes of Greenham's sayings, kept in their original chronological order. The first entry is dated 28 July 1581; the last probably dates from 1584. The final folios are given over to a copy of one of Greenham's most well known pieces, "A letter against hardnes of hart."

[17]Dr. Parker and I are undertaking that work and will publish an edition of Rylands MS 524 as part of a larger volume on Greenham.

[18]It would be naive to assume that owning a book is proof that the book is read; my own shelves give ample testimony to the fallacy of that assumption. However, I do believe that in a period of time

a mans life, is (to put it charitably) indebted to Greenham's treatment of the same theme.[19] Corporate libraries considered Greenham's *Works* to be worthy acquisitions. Editions could be found, for example, in the More parish library (Salop) and in the Ipswich town library, established in 1599 to serve the town preachers.[20] Private individuals, mostly clergymen and academics, also owned copies. The Bodleian Library's copy of the 1601 edition of the *Works* was the property of Richard Burton, author of *The Anatomy of Melancholy.* Dr. Philip Bisse, the Puritan parson of Batcombe (Somerset) who died in 1612, had four books which he deemed worthy of mention in his will: an herbal, a Hebrew Bible, and the *Works* of both Perkins and Greenham. Heady company indeed! Philip Kettle, Fellow of Cambridge's St. John's College who died in 1606, owned a copy of the *Works* (edition unknown) which was considered significant enough to be the second—after William Perkins' *Works*—of thirteen books listed by name in his postmortem inventory.[21]

Linking Greenham with Perkins, the most important English Calvinist theologian of his day, was not unusual. As noted above, fragments of their works were anthologized together. Charles Richardson, a London minister and author, in describing the duties of a godly minister, recommended reading four authors: Greenham, Perkins, Dod, and Andrew Willett.[22]

---

in which books were far less taken for granted and buying a volume such as Greenham's *Works* was a significant allocation of resources, the likelihood of reading what was purchased was quite high.

[19]See Carew, *Certaine godly and necessarie sermons* (1603). I am indebted to Margaret Spufford for this reference, which she received from Patrick Collinson.

[20]Conal Condren, "More Parish Library, Salop," *Library History* 7 (1987), 114; John Blatchly, *The Town Library of Ipswich, Provided for the use of the Town Preachers in 1599: A History and Catalogue* (Wolfeboro, N.H.: Boydell & Brewer, 1989), 114–115, 178. I am grateful to Paul Griffiths for the first reference.

[21]A. L. Rowse, *The England of Elizabeth: The Structure of Society* (New York: Macmillan, 1951), 480 n.1; Margaret Steig, *Laud's Laboratory: The Diocese of Bath and Wells in the Early Seventeenth Century* (Lewisburg, Penn.: Bucknell University Press, 1983), 353; E. S. Leedham-Green, *Books in Cambridge Inventories: Book-Lists from Vice-Chancellor's Court Probate Inventories in the Tudor and Stuart Periods,* 2 vols. (Cambridge: Cambridge University Press, 1986), 554–555. Kettle's inventory also included a dozen unnamed books and a final entry for "all the rest of his books." This was not unusual. Only the largest and most obviously valuable books were likely to be inventoried by name. Testators like Bisse might own many more books but named in their wills only those books for which they wanted to make special provision, especially if they would not be able to give the book to the chosen beneficiary personally before death.

[22]Charles Richardson, *A Workeman, That Needeth Not to be Ashamed: Or The faithfull Steward of Gods house: A sermon describing the duety of a godly minister, both in his Doctrine and in his Life* (London, 1616), 29–30. I am grateful to Neal Enssle for this reference.

Enemies of Puritanism also twinned Greenham and Perkins as its most significant patriarchs. The poet-bishop Richard Corbett, in his satirical poem "The Distracted Puritane," places the names of only two writers in the mouth of his speaker: Greenham and Perkins (in that order). In Perkins' writing, according to Corbett's caricature, the Puritan "observ'd the black Lines of Damnation" and feared for the fate of his soul; although "in dispaire Fiue times a yeare," he was "cur'd by reading Greenham."[23]

Lay people also owned copies of Greenham's writings and, in fact, our most explicit evidence for the reading of Greenham comes from the lives of upper-class lay people. The earliest reference is from the last Sunday of December in 1599, when Lady Margaret Hoby, wife of Sir Thomas Posthumous Hoby, recorded in her diary that she and Sir Thomas returned home following the afternoon sermon and "reed of Grenhame." In what seems like an eternity and a world away from the Hobys' peaceful, godly household Greenham could still be found. In 1642, as the political crisis deepened and his own personal anxiety intensified, Edward, Lord Montagu, turned to Greenham's writings for solace. He copied out several pieces of advice, including that men must first "seeke the councell of God in his word, then to give ourselves to fervent prayer and after to use the meanes wch God hath appointed."[24] While the evidence I have used here is anecdotal, it nonetheless gives the impression that Greenham's printed works kept his name and reputation strong among the godly lay and clerical readers in the century after his death. There was ample reason to agree with the sentiments of one post-Restoration owner of the first edition of his *Works*, who wrote in his copy: "Greenham altho he is Dead/His works on Earth shall always spread."[25]

Greenham's popular fame was, ultimately, built on more than his published works and the devotion of his dispersed followers. As Patrick Collinson noted some time ago, "Throughout the Elizabethan period and its immediate sequel the only steps taken to perpetuate the memory of a

[23] *The Poems of Richard Corbett*, ed. J. A. W. Bennett and H. R. Trevor-Roper (Oxford: Clarendon Press, 1955), 58.

[24] *Diary of Lady Margaret Hoby 1599–1605*, ed. Dorothy M. Meads (London: George Routledge & Sons, Ltd., 1930), 93; Esther S. Cope, *The Life of a Public Man: Edward, First Baron Montagu of Boughton, 1562–1644* (Philadelphia: The American Philosophical Society, 1981), 190–191. I am grateful to Professor Cope for the reference to Montagu.

[25] Folger Library copy of *Works* (1599), A6r. The owner of this copy, in 1713, was Shadrash Alderson.

deceased divine of note, and that somewhat rarely, was to promote the posthumous publication of his writings."[26] This is certainly the case with Greenham. Aside from a few brief, rather generic remarks in Holland's preface to the *Works*, the details of Greenham's life were not presented in print until the latter half of the seventeenth century. Joseph Hall, a Caroline bishop and author of two laudatory epigrams printed at the beginning of every edition of Greenham's *Works*, was the first (in 1606) to canonize Greenham, "that saint of ours," in print.[27] It was in that form, through the efforts of Thomas Fuller and Samuel Clarke, that future generations were to see him—not through his writings so much as through the filter of godly hagiography.

Fuller devoted less than two pages of his monumental study of British church history to Greenham, but what he wrote is significant because it was the first explicitly biographical approach to the subject. He covers briefly Greenham's parochial ministry, his preaching at Great St. Mary's church in Cambridge, and his removal to London late in life. The tone of this compact vita is eulogistic throughout. Greenham was the selfless and sedulous pastor who "often watered [the parish] with [his] tears, and oftner with his prayers and preaching, moistened the rich with his counsel, [and] the poor with his charity" but "the generality of the Parish remained ignorant, and obstinate...." Though noted for his preaching, "his master-piece was in comforting wounded consciences" and in that way he was "an instrument of good to many, who came to him with weeping eyes, and went from him with cheerful souls."[28] A good deal of Fuller's material apparently came from his father, who knew Richard Warfield, Greenham's successor as rector of Dry Drayton. Warfield is reported to have told Fuller père stories of his illustrious predecessor.[29] The balance he might have gleaned from reading Greenham's *Works*.

---

[26]Patrick Collinson, "Magazine of Religious Patterns," 506. Collinson's references are to Thomas Becon, Thomas Wilcox, Greenham, and Perkins.

[27]*Works* (1599), A8v, reprinted in *The Collected Poems of Joseph Hall, Bishop of Exeter and Norwich*, ed. A. Davenport (Liverpool: Liverpool University Press, 1949), 102–103; Joseph Hall, *Heaven vpon earth, Or Of true Peace, and Tranquillitie of Minde* (London, 1606), §9.

[28]Thomas Fuller, *The Church History of Britain from the Birth of Jesus Christ until the Year M.DC.XLVIII.* (London, 1655), 219–220.

[29]Untitled note by C. F. S. Warren, *Notes and Queries*, 6th ser., 7 (12 May 1883): 366.

The great Puritan biographer/hagiographer Samuel Clarke published a substantial study of Greenham in 1677.[30] Although not always very linear in its arrangement, Clarke's "Life of Master Richard Greenham" is a significant advance over Fuller's brief account. Clarke provides details about Greenham's physical appearance, health, and education, as well as providing a far more elaborate description of his ministry in Dry Drayton, including such things as his daily and weekly schedule. As did Fuller, Clarke emphasizes Greenham's "excellent Faculty to relieve and comfort distressed Consciences." Unlike Fuller who gave it only the briefest notice, he spends roughly a third of the "Life" discussing Greenham's charity to the poor in detail. For Clarke, Greenham is clearly an heroic figure and every aspect of his life and work—his learning and study, his preaching and catechizing, his charity to bodies and souls, his love of the queen and abhorrence of schism—is set out in the most heroic terms. His nobility extended even to his times of ill health, when "he would suffer no body to sit up and Watch with him, that so he might more freely converse with God." Unsurprisingly, when this paragon "resigned up his Spirit unto God," the cause was his exhaustion in the service of the Lord.

This account of Greenham's death highlights how independent is Clarke's account from that of Fuller. Not only do the two authors give different years (both inaccurate), but Fuller has Greenham die rather more prosaically of the plague. Clarke clearly made as thorough a study of available sources as one could expect at the time. He used Greenham's printed efforts, including his 1573 "Apologie" to Bishop Cox, as well as some unprinted sources. Clarke presumably wrote this piece after the Great Fire destroyed most of the London churches and, with them, their records. Thus, his omission of what relevant London sources survive even to our own time may be due to an honest belief that none existed. Although Clarke occasionally plagiarized from the *Works* in a manner so blatant that it would make most modern undergraduates blush, his is the account which has provided even historians of our own century with most of what they have claimed to know about Master Greenham.

[30]Samuel Clarke, *The Lives of Thirty-Two English Divines*, 3d ed. (London, 1677), 12–15. An annotated edition may be found below. On Samuel Clarke, see: Collinson, "Magazine of Religious Patterns"; Jacqueline Eales, "Samuel Clarke and the 'Lives' of Godly Women in Seventeenth-Century England," in *Women in the Church*, ed. W. J. Sheils and Diana Wood, *Studies in Church History* 27 (Oxford: Blackwell, 1990): 365–376; and Jessica Martin, *Recollected Dust: Izaak Walton and the Beginning of Literary Biography* (Woodbridge: Boydell, forthcoming), a revision of her superb 1993 Cambridge Ph.D. dissertation, "Izaak Walton and His Precursors: A Literary Study of the Emergence of the Ecclesiastical Life."

Given the reputation he enjoyed in his own lifetime, the popular appetite for and reception of his posthumously published oeuvre, and the hagiographical treatment rendered by his biographers, speakers at a service commemorating the centennial of Greenham's death (had such a service taken place) would have predicted with understandable confidence that in 1994 as much as in 1694 Greenham would be remembered as one of a handful of preeminent Elizabethan divines. Yet in 1994, it was Richard Hooker's *Laws of Ecclesiastical Polity* that was celebrated, and about Greenham, the English church and its students were almost silent. Indeed, Greenham has suffered from severe neglect in this century and has been relegated to the role of what can only be described as a secondary—if not minor—figure in the Elizabethan church.

This would not have been predictable before World War II. In 1927, Marshall Knappen completed a doctoral dissertation entitled "Richard Greenham and the Practical Puritans under Elizabeth."[31] His biography of Greenham is dependent on Clarke. Where Knappen's work is so significant is in his identification of a group of clerics who were part of the tradition which emerged from Hugh Latimer (via Thomas Bilney) which subordinated structural and theological issues to "praxis." Like Latimer, these were men who were essentially not theologians but "practical religious leader[s] of the people" whose sermons were about "practical righteousness" such as the necessity of living in justice and peace with one's neighbors. "The general object of this school of Reformers," according to Knappen, "was to concentrate on supplying the religious needs of the average man."[32] Although Knappen's thesis is about far more than Greenham, Greenham's spirit hovers over virtually every page of the text and it is Greenham whom Knappen, through his title, clearly considers to be the unofficial leader and most important of all the men he discusses—a judgment entirely congruent with that of Elizabethans themselves.[33]

---

[31]Ph.D. dissertation, Cornell University, 1927.

[32]Ibid., 13, 20–28.

[33]In a very limited sense, Knappen (in his *Tudor Puritanism: A Chapter in the History of Idealism* [Chicago: University of Chicago Press, 1939], 383 n.8) can be said to have deflated Greenham's reputation among modern scholars. James Jackson Higginson (*Spenser's Shepherd's Calendar in Relation to Contemporary Affairs* [New York: Columbia University Press, 1912]) had, based on what he perceived to be similarities between their biographies, identified the September eclogue's Diggon Davie as Greenham. Higginson, in making this case, believed that Greenham had been suspended. He was misled by some incompetent plagiarism in Daniel Neal's work, *The History of the Puritans* (3 vols. [London, 1837], 1:229). Neal documented his claim of Greenham's suspension by citing James Peirce

William Haller ascribed to Greenham the role of patriarch of what Haller called (quoting Richard Baxter) "the affectionate practical English writers." He presents a solid and relatively lengthy, if entirely derivative, biography and does convey to the reader something of Greenham's importance in his own time.[34] After Haller, however, later historians of Puritanism and of the Elizabethan church have not uniformly done so.

Names of sixteenth-century divines are not expected to come dancing off the tongues of modern undergraduates, but even from those at higher levels one cannot escape the impression that Greenham is seen as a decidedly secondary figure, especially in comparison to such men as Edward Dering or Laurence Chaderton. In all of Patrick Collinson's definitive works on Elizabethan Puritanism, there are so few references to Greenham that it is impossible to derive from them an image of the patriarchal figure described above. In a 1964 article, Professor Collinson does quote Fuller's hyperbolic estimation that "no book in that age made greater impression on people's practice" than Greenham's treatise on the sabbath. As we have seen, Greenham's treatise was first published in 1599, but the basic draft which Greenham was still revising when he died had probably been complete for a decade or more. Nicholas Bownd wrote the earliest published English sabbatarian treatise, but since Bownd was Greenham's stepson, he must have read and been influenced by Greenham's manuscript. "Perhaps Greenham was the original source of the doctrine of the Christian Sabbath in [England]; his famous household at Dry Drayton was certainly a nursery of English Reformed casuistry," Collinson concludes.[35] While by no means ignoring Greenham in his later work, however, he does not build

---

(*Vindication of the Dissenters* [London, 1717], 97) who, in fact, says only that Greenham experienced "troubles." This is an astounding lapse, given that Neal otherwise copies Pierce verbatim. If Greenham is not a direct influence on Spenser, however, he might be an indirect one. Both were Pembroke Hall men, and Spenser would have been aware of Greenham's departure for parish work. His praise of the practical ministry of such as Diggon Davie suggests that Greenham is one of Spenser's inspirations.

[34] William Haller, *The Rise of Puritanism* (New York: Columbia University Press, 1938; paperback ed., Philadelphia: University of Pennsylvania Press, 1972), 25–29. By "practical" Baxter meant one who taught people how to believe and act; by "affectionate" he meant one who appealed to the emotions.

[35] Bownd's treatise was published in 1595. Patrick Collinson, "The Beginnings of English Sabbatarianism," in *Godly People*, 439. In his fine monograph on the subject, Kenneth Parker (now my collaborator in editing Rylands MS 524) makes a dozen references to Greenham, but does not attribute as much importance to him in the development of sabbatarian writing as does Collinson: *The English Sabbath: A Study of Doctrine and Discipline from the Reformation to the Civil War* (Cambridge: Cambridge University Press, 1988).

on this assertion and readers will not emerge from reading it with a sense of Greenham's contemporary importance.[36]

Most other authors are no better. In one of his books, Christopher Hill describes Greenham as "one of the most influential Puritans of his generation," but in a dozen further references gives only brief quotes from his *Works* or mentions his name in passing.[37] R. T. Kendall echoes Haller in calling Greenham "a patriarchal figure," but then assigns him the role of one of William Perkins' precursors. But rather than regard Greenham as John the Baptist to Perkins' Messiah, contemporaries, as we have seen, saw them as equals.[38]

Some of what has happened is understandable. In his own day, Greenham's reputation was built not on his writings but on his parish ministry, from which most of his writings emerged but which is not well captured by them. Historians relying entirely on those published pieces have perhaps had difficulties in distinguishing Greenham from other writer-divines of his generation and conjuring up the saintly figure described by Clarke. His *Works* are not, in fact, very distinguished—which is unsurprising given the way in which they were assembled. To reclaim an appreciation of Greenham's contemporary importance, it is essential to return to Greenham at the parish level, remembering that it was for his excellence in "practical divinity" and not academic theology that he was praised in his day.

In his 1958 monograph on the Reformation in Cambridge, H. C. Porter pointed the way back to Dry Drayton. While relying on Clarke and Fuller for biographical details, Porter both fully appreciated Greenham's relative importance and emphasized his standing as the epitome of the godly pastor. In a work about Cambridge University, Dr. Porter understandably stressed, however, not Greenham's work with his parishioners

---

[36]In addition to works cited above, see also Patrick Collinson, *The Religion of Protestants: The Church in English Society 1559–1625* (Oxford: Clarendon Press, 1982).

[37]Christopher Hill, *Society and Puritanism in Pre-Revolutionary England* (New York: Schocken Books, 1964), 170.

[38]R. T. Kendall, *Calvin and English Calvinism to 1649* (Oxford: Oxford University Press, 1979), 45–47. A complete survey of scholarship on Puritanism and the Elizabethan church is beyond the scope of this note; readers are referred to the most influential and significant recent books not previously noted which could or should give Greenham far more prominence than they do: Peter Lake, *Moderate Puritans and the Elizabethan Church* (Cambridge: Cambridge University Press, 1982); Paul Seaver, *The Puritan Lectureships: The Politics of Religious Dissent, 1560–1662* (Stanford: Stanford University Press, 1970). See also John Morgan, *Godly Learning: Puritan Attitudes toward Reason, Learning, and Education, 1560–1640* (Cambridge: Cambridge University Press, 1986).

but his training of ministers in a "Puritan Academe, with a touch of Little Gidding."[39] It was Margaret Spufford who went down the muddy road, to which Porter had pointed, to Dry Drayton and undertook the first archival research on Greenham since that of Samuel Clarke. Working with the wills and ecclesiastical court records in the Ely diocesan archives, Professor Spufford began to piece together a picture of Greenham with his parishioners. In her work, Greenham, who established what she labels "the first model Puritan parish in the country," was nonetheless a failure if success is measured by the revealed attitudes of one's parishioners.[40] Spufford's Greenham is recognizably closer to the man whose death was such a blow to the godly, but a mystery remains. Why would such a pastoral failure have been so revered? In spinning out in the next section as complete a biography of Greenham as sources permit, that is the question which I will address.

∾

"I Can yet learn nothing Concerning the Contrey, Parentage, orfirst [sic] Education [of] Mr. Richard Greenham," wrote Samuel Clarke in 1677. He was probably born around 1540.[41] That his family was of modest means may be inferred from his status as a sizar at Cambridge University, since he would be dependent on what we now call financial aid, but nothing else is known about the family. Greenham first appears in documentary evidence when he matriculated from Pembroke Hall on 27 May 1559. In due time he proceeded to earn his B.A., took his master's degree, and became a fellow of Pembroke in 1567. Pembroke's influence can be seen throughout his later ministry and published writing.

Shortly before his execution, the Edwardian Master of Pembroke Hall, Nicholas Ridley, wrote of the college: "Thou wast ever named since I knew thee...to be studious, well learned, and a great setter-forth of Christ's gospel, and of God's true word."[42] George Stafford, who became a fellow in

---

[39]H. C. Porter, *Reformation and Reaction in Tudor Cambridge* (Cambridge: Cambridge University Press, 1958), 216–217, 243, 267.

[40]Margaret Spufford, *Contrasting Communities: English Villagers in the Sixteenth and Seventeenth Centuries* (Cambridge: Cambridge University Press, 1974), 327–328.

[41]Greenham described himself as a "child" during the reign of Mary I: Rylands MS 524, fol. 16v. Earlier estimates of his age seem to be based on Clarke's assumption that he was around sixty when he died in 1591.

[42]Patrick Collinson, *Archbishop Grindal 1519–1583: The Struggle for a Reformed Church* (Berkeley and Los Angeles: University of California Press, 1979), 38.

1513, was famous for his "exposition of the pure word of God." No less a figure than Thomas Becon vividly remembered Stafford's lectures on the Bible in the 1520s and their impact on him. Also students at Pembroke in the 1520s, formed by their encounters with teachers such as Stafford, were John Rogers, who worked with Coverdale and Tyndale and was one of the human casualties of Mary's reign, and the polymath William Turner, who was one of Stephen Gardiner's most determined and outspoken critics and enjoys the distinction of having been an exile during the reigns of both Henry VIII and Mary I.[43] Indeed, for a small house, Pembroke fledged more than its share of Marian exiles and "martyrs," including its quondam Master Nicholas Ridley.[44]

Although it was religiously divided when Greenham arrived in 1559, Pembroke Hall's dominant influence was Edmund Grindal. For most of Edward VI's reign, Grindal had been effectively in charge of the college because of Ridley's absences; in 1559, he accepted election as Master in his own right, though he surrendered the office in 1562.[45] The spirit brooding over the waters of Master Grindal's ecclesiology was Martin Bucer and, if Greenham's later words and actions are any evidence, the young scholar not only drank deeply from but also washed often and thoroughly in those waters.

Bucer's impact on Grindal's vision of ministry was profound. For Bucer, according to Patrick Collinson, "pastoral ministry was…a matter of extreme importance, a theme to which his preaching and writings constantly returned.…" Notoriously hostile to "extreme scrupulosity" over externals such as ceremonies and institutions, Bucer subjected all matters which were adiaphora to the test of their impact on ministry. Bucer's response to the crisis which emerged in 1550 over John Hooper's refusal to undergo consecration as bishop of Gloucester wearing the (in his view) "popish" vestments required by the Ordinal is telling. Bucer would not "support a pastor whose principles had landed him in the Fleet prison rather than in the neglected diocese where his talents were so much needed." It was precisely those priorities which were Grindal's—and the

---

[43]Porter, *Reformation and Reaction*, 42, 47, 80–81. On Turner, see Whitney R. D. Jones, *William Turner: Tudor Naturalist, Physician and Divine* (London: Routledge, Chapman & Hall, 1988); Eric Josef Carlson, "The Marriage of William Turner," *Historical Research* 65 (1992): 336–339, and references therein.

[44]See Porter, *Reformation and Reaction*, chap. 4.

[45]Collinson, *Archbishop Grindal*, 37–40.

words in which Collinson reports that could quite easily, as we will see, be applied to Greenham as well: "Where there were valid pastoral reasons for nonconformity, and for the toleration of it, [Grindal] was indulgent. But where a rigid puritan scrupulosity seemed to threaten both the progress of the Gospel and the unity of the Church the puritans had no more resolute opponent."[46]

Grindal was the "decisive voice" in choosing Matthew Hutton as his successor in 1562. Hutton kept the Bucerian spirit alive at Pembroke during his tenure. In November 1565, for instance, he demonstrated his support for moderation in the service of the church's peace and unity when he signed a letter to William Cecil asking him, as chancellor, to moderate enforcement of regulations concerning vestments.[47] John Whitgift, holder in succession of the two most prestigious chairs in divinity and very briefly Hutton's successor as Master, also signed this letter. In the mid-1560s, Whitgift was widely regarded as entirely in the tradition of Ridley and Grindal, and suspected by some of favoring "precisians."[48] Although Whitgift would part company with the kindred spirits of his Pembroke Hall days, it was the younger Whitgift, along with Grindal and Hutton, who were direct influences as teachers and Masters on Richard Greenham in the 1560s, and it was the air of Pembroke Hall redolent with its rich history of evangelical godliness and the aroma of Bucer's ideal of ministry which he breathed every day for over a decade.

Shortly before he left both Pembroke Hall and Cambridge in late 1570, Greenham joined other Cantabrigians in signing two letters to William Cecil in support of Thomas Cartwright. In the spring of 1570, Cartwright had given a controversial series of lectures on the Acts of the Apostles for which he was ultimately removed from his position as Lady Margaret professor of divinity.[49] Greenham did not long remain among Cartwright's supporters, however. When the controversy spilled outside the university and threatened the stability of the church, Greenham (true to the spirit of Bucer, Grindal, and Pembroke Hall) lent his talents to a different cause. He was remembered by students at the time for preaching to them from the

---

[46]Ibid., 49–56.

[47]Ibid., 37; Peter Lake, "Matthew Hutton—A Puritan Bishop?" *History* 64 (1979), 183–184.

[48]Patrick Collinson, "The 'Nott Conformytye' of the Young John Whitgift," in *Godly People*, 325–333.

[49]A. F. Scott Pearson, *Thomas Cartwright and Elizabethan Puritanism, 1535–1603* (Cambridge: Cambridge University Press, 1925), 422–424, 426–427; Collinson, *Elizabethan Puritan Movement*, 112–113.

pulpit of Great St. Mary's, reproving them for being drawn into bootless, unedifying debates rather than attending to the studies which would prepare them for the real work of preaching and teaching.[50]

By the time Greenham preached against Cartwright in Great St. Mary's, he was no longer a resident of Cambridge town. Moved perhaps by the recollection of Bucer's criticism of Hooper, or other words in that vein, Greenham accepted that he was most needed and his education would be best employed in a rural parish. Later in his life, he stated clearly to his young followers the principle that, if perhaps not yet fully formed, must have been behind this move. The minister, said Greenham, must not always stay in his study "filling himselfe with knowledge, till he becomes as a tunne that will not sound when one knocketh upon it: but hee must come out of his closet and preach the word of God and deliver forth holsome doctrine...." Learning which did not lead to someone else's salvation was without purpose. Indeed, it was even sinful.

> The Minister therefore of Gods word must not onely bee learned but must teach also: for how can hee bee a minister of doctrine, but in this respect that he teacheth executing ye office of his ministry? And this teaching is none other thing, but to preach the word of God sincerely, and purely with a care of the glory of God, and a desire of the salvation of our breathern: & secondly a reverent administration of the sacraments, according to the order and institution of our Saviour Jesus Christ. Whosoever therfore shall not thus labour is not the minister of the Lord, but a robber and spoiler of the people of God which thrust themselves into the ministerie to fill their belly onely with the sweate of other mens browes.[51]

In Dry Drayton, five miles from Cambridge, there was a parish with an advowson in the hands of a local gentleman of zealous inclinations which was very much in need of such godly ministry.

Dry Drayton was an average-sized (2,389 acres) Cambridgeshire village. Its southern portion lies in the county's western plateau, an area of boulder clay better suited for grazing than cereal crops. The village was

---

[50]George Downame, *Two sermons, the one commending the ministrie in general: The other defending the office of bishops in particular* (London, 1608), dedicatory epistle. See also Charles Henry Cooper and Thompson Cooper, *Athenae Cantabrigiensis*, 2 vols. (Cambridge, 1858–61), 2:143–144.

[51]*Works* (1605), 781–782. See Collinson, "Magazine of Religious Patterns," for a superb discussion of the view, traced to Erasmus, that "Life is more than learning."

built at the spring line (c. 200 ft.), as were most villages along the plateau. Spreading out below the village was an area of river valley which was part chalk and part alluvium. Barley was the village's main crop. Although its soil was heavy and damp, Dry Drayton was spared many of the drainage problems of villages on the southern edges of the plateau, hemmed in by Bourn Brook and the River Rhee.

For a village of its size, Dry Drayton was relatively underpopulated for much of the sixteenth century. In 1524, as English population was recovering from its postplague lows, Dry Drayton had fewer than thirty-five households and in 1563 only thirty-one households—roughly half the density measured in 1377. Dramatic growth soon followed. The surplus of baptisms over burials in the 1570s and 1580s implies a staggering population increase, though outmigration might have kept the population from overwhelming the village's limited resources.[52]

For much of its history, lordship in Dry Drayton had been monastic.[53] In 1543, Henry VIII granted the dissolved Crowland Abbey's manor and

---

[52]*A History of the County of Cambridge and the Isle of Ely*, ed C. R. Elrington et al., 9 vols. to date (London and Oxford: various publishers, 1938–) [hereafter *VCH, Cambs.*], 9:71, 77–81; 1524–5 subsidy from P[ublic] R[ecord] O[ffice], E179/81/126, /130, /161, /163; 1563 survey from BL, Harl MS 594, fols. 198r–200v; baptisms and burials from original registers in C[ambridgeshire] R[ecord] O[ffice]. On using these sources, Roger Schofield, "Parliamentary Lay Taxation, 1485–1547"(Ph.D. thesis, Cambridge University, 1963); D. M. Palliser and L. J. Jones, "The Diocesan Population Returns for 1563 and 1603," *Local Population Studies* 30 (1983): 55–58; Michael Zell, "Families and Households in Staplehurst, 1563–64," *Local Population Studies* 33 (1984): 54–57; and Alan Dyer, "The Bishops' Census of 1563: Its Significance and Accuracy," *Local Population Studies* 49 (1992): 19–37. Julian Cornwall ("English Population in the Early Sixteenth Century," *Economic History Review*, 2d ser., 33 [1970]: 32–44) believes subsidies included the better-off but only enough others to make the assessment look realistic; by comparing subsidies to the 1522 Muster Returns, Bruce M. S. Campbell ("The Population of Early Tudor England: a Reevaluation of the 1522 Muster Returns and 1524 and 1525 Lay Subsidies," *Journal of Historical Geography* 7 [1981]: 145–154) shows that they give a fairly accurate count of adult males. To convert from assessments to total population, mean household size is taken to be 4.75 (J. Krause, "The Medieval Household: Large or Small?" *Economic History Review*, 2nd ser., 9 [1957]: 420–432; Peter Laslett, "Mean Household Size in England since the Sixteenth Century," and Richard Wall, "Mean Household Size in England from Printed Sources," both in their *Household and Family in Past Time* [Cambridge: Cambridge University Press, 1972], 125–158, 159–203). While many wage earners did not head independent households, and some who did were poor enough to be omitted entirely, I believe Cornwall exaggerated the need to adjust the base figure and multiplier. I am happy to acknowledge a disagreement with Michael Sekulla on the subject of outmigration. On the basis of his family reconstitutions, Sekulla believes that Dry Drayton families controlled and limited marriages, but he does not find evidence for significant outmigration. His sample is small enough and my own evidence suggestive enough for me simply to agree to disagree with him. I am, however, very grateful, for a stimulating exchange on this subject.

[53]D. and S. Lysons, *Magna Britannia* (Cambridge, 1808), 2[1], 179; *VCH, Cambs.*, 9:74–77; Frances M. Page, *The Estates of Crowland Abbey: A Study in Manorial Organization* (Cambridge: Cambridge University Press, 1934), 19–28.

advowson of Dry Drayton to Thomas Hutton.[54] He never exercised his right of presentation, because John Clever had been made rector in 1541 and remained in that office until 1567, by which time Thomas Hutton was dead. Clever was a nonresident pluralist, known to have been living with a woman (apparently not his wife) in Leicestershire in the 1560s.[55] In 1567, William Fairclough became rector, presumably upon presentation by Thomas Hutton's son and heir John, but much of his time in the parish was troubled. In December 1568, he was before the diocesan court, charged with adultery with Agnes Lakers. Although Fairclough admitted the charge, he refused to perform his penance and was excommunicated. After several months, he submitted and his penance was commuted in exchange for £6 given to support two poor scholars at Jesus College.[56] The charges had been brought by the churchwardens, which argues that matters had gotten very bad indeed. Churchwardens worked hard to resolve matters internally, and only handed cases over to the ecclesiastical courts as a last resort.[57]

Fairclough was a bad choice for John Hutton, who was to become well known for his nonconformity, to have made.[58] When Fairclough died in July 1570,[59] Hutton had a second chance and he turned to Richard Greenham. Hutton was apparently related to Matthew Hutton, who knew Greenham at Pembroke Hall and perhaps sensed that he would be more at home in a parish than by continuing at the university. It is very likely that it was from Matthew that John learned of Greenham. The living was offered and the offer was attractive. Dry Drayton was close enough to Cambridge for Greenham to maintain his contacts there and to continue preaching at Great St. Mary's and—as was to be important later—for people to come to him with little inconvenience. Moreover, for Greenham, unmarried at the time, there were no financial reasons to hesitate. Although it lacked glebe lands, Dry Drayton was still one of the more

[54]*Letters and Papers, Foreign and Domestic, of the Reign of Henry VIII*, ed. J. S. Brewer et al., 21 vols. (London, 1862–1920), 18[2]: #107(9).

[55][Cambridge University Library] E[ly] D[iocesan] R[ecords], B/2/3, fols. 93, 130.

[56]EDR, B/2/6, 32, 74; D/2/8, fols. 9v, 11v, 20r, 27r.

[57]Eric Josef Carlson, *Marriage and the English Reformation* (Oxford: Blackwell, 1994), chap. 7, esp. 142–156.

[58]On John Hutton, see P. W. Hasler, *The House of Commons 1558–1603*, 3 vols. (London: HMSO, 1981), 2:359–360.

[59]He was buried on 6 July: CRO, Dry Drayton parish register.

lucrative livings in the diocese.[60] Greenham accepted and resigned his fellowship.

He soon had reason to question the wisdom of his move. Fairclough's death had been one of the first in a nasty localized mortality crisis which continued until February 1571, so Greenham was forced to get to know his parishioners by burying their dead. Once the epidemic abated, a mortal threat to Greenham's life in ministry appeared. In 1571, all ministers in the diocese were commanded to sign a statement to the effect that Prayer Book was "such as conteynethe nothing in yt repugnynge or contrarie to the word of God," that the required apparel (referring especially to the surplice and square cap) was "not wicked but tollerable and to be used obediently for order and comeliness only," and that the Articles of Religion contained "most godlye and holsome doctryne agreeable unto Gods holye worde." Greenham could not and did not subscribe.[61]

For some time, Greenham was not troubled by the authorities. In 1573, probably as part of the triennial visitation, Greenham's nonsubscription caught up with him and he was faced with suspension. It was on that occasion that he wrote his famous "Apologie." While making clear that he would not wear the apparel "nor subscribe vnto it, or the communion booke," Greenham refused to say why "vnlesse [he] be forced thereto." In what reads oddly like an early plea for a policy of "don't ask, don't tell," Greenham begged Cox simply to leave him alone. He assured the bishop that he dissented out of conscience and not perversity but would voluntarily say no more. Over and over, he repeated that he would not explain himself further unless forced to do so and he begged his bishop not to ask questions. He claimed (rather disingenuously) to be a simple country lad unable to match wits with Cox or the "godly learned" who debated these issues; rather, he "occupied [him]selfe daylie...in preaching Christ crucified vnto [him]selfe and Country people" and did not stir them up with debates over ceremonies or surplices. Instead, at all times and in all places, he would "by all meanes seeke peace and pursue it...." Greenham saw in these divisions over externals the work of the Devil: "I doe not doubt but

---

[60]The value in 1535 was £21 14d.: *Valor Ecclesiasticus*, 6 vols. (London, 1817), 3:502. Note that there is a double error in *VCH Cambs.* 9:85; both the value and page reference are incorrectly given. I have checked this very carefully. Inflation is notoriously difficult to figure during this period; however, it would be reasonable to estimate a doubling in the monetary value of the living by 1570: see R. B. Outhwaite, *Inflation in Tudor and Early Stuart England* (2d ed. London and Basingstoke: Macmillan, 1982). Glebe terrier: EDR, H/1/3.

[61]EDR, B/2/6, 198.

that the common aduersarie hath shrouded in on both parties, wolues in sheepes cloathing, to cause the children of God, more egarlie to fight togither, so that the common worke of the Lorde beinge hindered, he might the more preuayle." To carry out this common work had to be deemed more important than differences over externals; to remove from his parish a man who was loyal to the queen and the church, who was no schismatic or papist, served no interests except those of Satan, the common adversary.[62]

While his impatience with "preciseness" had been growing with every passing day, Cox chose to take no action against Greenham. Cox was known to be pragmatic, not dogmatic, and in the case of the Peterhouse fellows in 1565, he demonstrated a willingness to make allowances for individual consciences.[63] Moreover, given Cox's priorities and his circumstances, he could not afford to lose Greenham. Cox's first priority was to place a minister in every parish who was well educated in the Bible and would reside in his parish to teach his flock. In 1560, he had found the diocese in a miserable state. Many parishes lacked incumbents and, even if he could persuade patrons to fill vacancies, the shortage of suitable candidates was acute. Far too many of those parishes which had incumbents (including Dry Drayton) had them in name only, since they were permanently nonresident. At first, Cox was so eager to fill vacancies that the screening process was scarcely more than a formality and, although a few were rejected, he ordained almost anyone with testicles and a pulse. As the 1560s progressed he became steadily stricter. Higher standards led to more rejections of unfit candidates. More than one-third of the candidates for ordination failed in 1568, for example. At the same time, Cox began depriving nonresidents.[64] Greenham was exactly the sort of well-educated cleric whose services Cox craved and sorely needed. He could ill afford to lose him, especially since the qualified replacements could barely fill the vacancies that would occur from other causes.

---

[62]See also Margo Todd, "'An act of discretion': Evangelical Conformity and the Puritan Dons," *Albion* 18 (1986): 581–599.

[63]Felicity Margaret Heal, "The Bishops of Ely and Their Diocese during the Reformation Period: ca.1515–1600" (Ph.D. dissertation, Cambridge University, 1972), 120–121.

[64]BL, Add. MS 5813, fols. 63ff.; EDR, A/5/1; Heal, "Bishops of Ely," 106–131; Dorothy Owen, "The Enforcement of the Reformation in the Diocese of Ely," in *Miscellanea Historiae Ecclesiasticae, III, Colloque de Cambridge, 24–28 Septembre 1968,* ed. Derek Baker (Louvain: Publications Universitaires de Louvain, 1970), 172–174.

Cox was also obsessed with a fear of Catholicism. His letters to William Cecil regularly warned "about the dangers of a Catholic crusade, and of the odious conspiracies which were being fomented by the fifth column within the country."[65] His zeal over parochial staffing was very much related to this concern, for an educated catechizing and preaching ministry was essential if superstition was to be wiped out in the countryside and the menace of popery defeated. Because of this, Cox did not resist lay patronage of nonconformists in the diocese, and he personally placed them in livings in the Isle of Ely, "remote and ignorant" as it was. The urgent need for teaching the word of God, in Cox's view, overrode any differences over adiaphora, at least if those with whom he differed were willing to preach Christ crucified and restrict their sentiments about abuses in the church to their consciences and keep them out of pulpits.[66] Greenham's own references in his "Apologie" to his single-minded efforts to preach Christ crucified and to the "common aduersarie" would have spoken directly to this episcopal concern. Cox clearly saw Greenham as an ally in the anti-Catholic struggle.

Finally, Greenham was allowed to continue because the effects of his nonconformity were moderated by the high value he placed on preserving peace in the church. One of his followers would later record his statement that in "a mere outward thing" he "would not break the peace of the church," and in "the lesser adjuncts of religion…he would not withstand or condemn any but leave them to their own reason, seeing very good men do so disagree in them or change their opinion in them."[67] Throughout his ministry he continued to justify Cox's confidence in his irenic disposition. For example, a "godly minister" who sought Greenham's sympathy when his parishioners became outraged over his pulling down "certain painted glasse windowes" received a stinging rebuke instead. Greenham told him that the minister's first duty was not to destroy but to teach, and that he should first have taught his parishioners and obtained their consent to remove the windows and replace them with "new white glass."[68] He advised another "to preach faith and repentance from sin: and when god shal have

---

[65]Heal, "Bishops of Ely," 134.

[66]Ibid., 129.

[67]Rylands MS 524, fols. 54v–55r. In another place, he said "wee may yeeld just obedience, so it bee in things meerly outward….Let us do as much as wee can with the peace of the church lest wee make the remedy of the evil wors then the evil it self": ibid., fol. 10v.

[68]Ibid., fols. 36v–37r.

given you some power, and credit in ther consciences," then to take up denouncing abuses.[69]

Greenham was never troubled over his nonconformity after 1573. It was not raised in the surviving visitation records, which are quite complete. Nor was Greenham among the eleven Cambridgeshire ministers who were threatened with suspension by Archbishop Whitgift in 1584.[70] Instead, Cox employed him in sensitive conferences with recusants and members of the Family of Love. We know, for example, that in 1580 Mary Johnson, a recusant from Tadlow (Cambs.), was ordered by Cox to confer with Greenham.[71] He also played a central role in the diocesan campaign against the heretical Family of Love in the same year, devising the articles to which suspects would subscribe and, through personal conversation, bringing some of the more tractable back to "orthodoxy." He met with Mrs. Margaret Colevyll, a widowed gentlewoman, and he "gently and lovingly confuted her errors by the scriptures, and…she by degrees yielded and in the end freely gave up her book [of Familist writings], acknowledg[ing] her errors with many tears before sufficient witnesses."[72]

The Family of Love, which was quite active in Cambridgeshire, was able as little else to rouse Greenham to extreme language. He described the sect as "pestilent" and "that phreneticall fansie."[73] Their hypocrisy was a recurring theme.[74] The juxtaposition of Catholics and Familists in Cox's assignments to Greenham is not surprising. Greenham had no truck with any who would disrupt the unity of the church. Catholic and Familist were cut from the same cloth, and its weaver was Satan. Followers recorded many different occasions when he linked the two. For example, he told the tale of a man who was in turn a Papist, a Familist, and an atheist; because of his loss of faith, he became a thief who, though he was executed, was

---

[69]Ibid., fols. 39v–40r.

[70]A. Peel, ed. *The Seconde Parte of a Register; being a calendar of manuscripts under that title intended for publication by the Puritans about 1593, and now in Dr William's library, London*, 2 vols. (Cambridge: Cambridge University Press, 1915), 1:227–228. John Hutton was one of the seven local gentlemen who wrote to Whitgift on their behalf, making it likely that Greenham would have been mentioned if he were under threat.

[71]EDR, D/2/10, fols. 195v–196r.

[72]*Tudor Royal Proclamations*, ed. Paul L. Hughes and James F. Larkin, 3 vols. (New Haven: Yale University Press, 1964–69), #652; Gonville and Caius College, Cambridge, MS 53/30, fols. 126v–129r; Christopher W. Marsh, *The Family of Love in English Society, 1550–1630* (Cambridge: Cambridge University Press, 1993).

[73]*Works* (1605), 803, 853.

[74]For example, *Works* (1601), 273, 472, 490; *Works* (1605), 803.

brought to repentance by conferring with a godly minister.[75] Typically, there is a real sense of urgency about his comments on these two enemies of the church:

> Look but to the Papists and Familie of love, how painfull and cunning they are to goe, to runne, to ride, to make one like of their heresies; see, how they will looke for you at markets, how they will entertaine you, what meekness, what mildnes they will use to salute you. This ought to shame us, this ought to make us labour more for knowledge, that when temptations invade us, when Satan accuseth us, when heresie shall assault us, we may stand stedfast and unremoveable, we may edifie one another, and in persecution not be dismaied, but resist constantly unto blood.[76]

In a sense, he believed that the church had itself to blame for these heresies. Common people were drawn to them because their parish churches failed to offer the sort of teaching and preaching necessary to meet their spiritual needs. This was also the key to crushing both Papists and Familists, for what linked the two most notably was their confidence in the works and words of men rather than of God: "If we take away...the Fathers traditions from the Papist, or the eight man his revelations from the Familist, and urge them with the word, they are gone: so that it is onely word of God, maugre the head of the divell, that unblindfoldeth all their errors, and is able to move them, and convert so many to truth as God will have saved."[77] This was, for example, his experience with Margaret Colevyll.

It is worth noting that there is a common thread woven through his known activities outside of his parish: conferring with Mary Johnson and with the Familists, and preaching in Cambridge against Thomas Cartwright and Martin Marprelate. In each case, Greenham acted to preserve the peace and unity of the church. A nonconformist Greenham might be, but could Cox hope to do any better? By the mid-1570s, John Hutton was part of Lord North's political circle, which was in a full-blown power struggle with Cox.[78] Cox had no reason to be sanguine about the prospects

---

[75]Rylands MS 524, fols. 56v–57r.

[76]*Works* (1605), 854–855.

[77]Ibid., 843. The reference to "the eight man his revelations" is to the writings of H.N.: see Marsh, *The Family of Love.*

[78]Eugene J. Bourgeois II, "The Queen, a Bishop, and a Peer: A Clash for Power in Mid-Elizabethan Cambridgeshire," *Sixteenth Century Journal* 26 (1995): 3–15. Bourgeois has argued in a private communication that Greenham was protected from Cox by Hutton and his powerful political allies. I

for a more conformable incumbent for Dry Drayton if he forced Greenham out and created a vacancy, nor could he expect anyone who would lend his efforts so effectively to the causes which agitated the aging bishop.

Yet it was not this work, but what he did in Dry Drayton itself that formed the basis for Greenham's reputation. As noted above, once having left his study, Greenham defined the primary duty of a minister to be teaching people what he had learned: "And this teaching is none other thing, but to preach the word of God sincerely, and purely with a care of the glory of God, and a desire of the salvation of our breathern: & secondly a reverent administration of the sacraments, according to the order and institution of our Saviour Jesus Christ."[79]

As William Massie said in a sermon published in 1586, "where preaching faileth there the people perisheth."[80] Preaching was the first priority of any conscientious minister, and many, including Greenham, argued that it was essential for salvation.[81] Greenham invested a great deal of time and effort in preparing for his sermons, rising every day at four in the morning to study,[82] a regimen he must have felt was essential since the other demands on his time left him little privacy during the day. He preached twice on Sunday and once every weekday (except Thursday). His weekday sermons began as soon as there was light enough to see so that his parishioners could "attend upon his Ministry" before beginning their work. He preached with such energy "that his shirt would usually be as wet with sweating, as if it had been drenched in water...."[83] Some (the notetaker did not say who) tried to persuade Greenham to preach with more

---

believe that the reasons I have given above show that Greenham was not in need of protection. Moreover, such an argument cannot explain why Cox trusted Greenham with sensitive work dealing with recusants and heretics.

[79]*Works* (1605), 781–782.

[80]William Massie, *A Sermon Preached at Trafford* (1586), quoted in Christopher Haigh, "Puritan Evangelism in the Reign of Elizabeth I," *English Historical Review* 92 (1977), 31.

[81]*Works* (1605), 779. Greenham's editor, Stephen Egerton, also made this argument: *The Boreing of the Eare* (1623). It was a common theme.

[82]Greenham noted that sometimes this backfired. When "hee studied painfully, and laboured exquisitely for a sermon" he would often become thoroughly confused, and he could preach better without any study but with some time to pray for assistance: Rylands MS 524, fol. 24v; Clarke, "Life of Master Richard Greenham," 12.

[83]Ibid., 12. Clarke also records that he used to grill his servants about the daily sermons. On this sort of enthusiastic, dramatic preaching by Puritans, see Francis Bremer and Ellen Rydell, "Puritans in the Pulpit," *History Today* (September 1995): 50–54.

restraint but he predictably refused. He had every reason to believe that his technique was appropriate, citing the malevolent energy expended by Satan to stop his mouth. This manifested itself as "very sharp and trembling fears in the flesh" which he experienced before preaching.[84]

And his method appeared to be effective as well. Once, while he preached, "a woman burst out into desperate crying, that shee was a damned soule," and Greenham left the pulpit to console her, saying, "Woman, didst thou not come into this place to hear of thy sins and of the forgivenes of them in Christ: bee of good comfort, and as thou seest thy sins so shalt thou hear pardon of thy sins."[85] He urged his students not to expect such events, however, and urged them to be patient and to persist in their preaching; he compared the preacher to a farmer who "would long after hee had sowen looke for the increas, not measuring the fruit of his labor by the time present but by the tyme to come...."[86]

Preaching was not, however, something which occurred only in the pulpit for Greenham. Indeed, he considered such preaching wholly inadequate. In speaking of the duties of a minister, he once said:

> [I]t is not sufficient that hee preach the word of God openly in the pulpet, but hee must goe to every mans house, and there diligently instruct both him and his house in the feare of God: and not as the manner of some is to goe to folkes houses to tell them a tale, and flatter them with faire words and glozing speech, to the end they might fill their bellies at another mans table, or get some other benefit which hee hunteth after. These bee hirelings and time-servers which thrust themselves into the Ministerie for lucres sake, and because they would live idly and take no paines for their living....[87]

Greenham did take pains for his living and preached from more prosaic pulpits than those in churches. After his morning sermon, he would change into dry clothes and "walk out into the Fields, and ...confer with his Neighbours as they were at Plough."[88] One can only imagine what impression that must have made upon the village's preoccupied barley farmers.

---

[84]Rylands MS 524, fols. 5v–6r, 43v.
[85]Ibid., fols. 67v–68r.
[86]Ibid., fol. 7v.
[87]*Works* (1605), 782.
[88]Clarke, "Life of Master Richard Greenham," 15.

But for Greenham, drenching another shirt in perspiration in the service of truth while his feet were immobilized in Dry Drayton's damp clay was a duty to God, to his flock, and to those who learned of ministry from him.

The private instructions which he espoused acted as a sort of bridge between preaching and formal catechizing. Recent work by Philippa Tudor and Ian Green[89] has pointed out the importance of catechizing in the Elizabethan church. Catechizing was a virtual obsession of Bishop Cox; it dominates his injunctions to the diocesan clergy in 1573,[90] and ministers came to realize that their sermons could do no good without the catechism as a base on which to build. The catechism was "such a means of knowledge as without it all preaching is to little purpose."[91] Ministers needed a variety of catechetical works. The 1549 Prayer Book included a short catechism still in use under Elizabeth. With the approval of convocation, Alexander Nowell composed a more advanced catechism, and Greenham was one of many other divines who followed with his own volume developed in response to his own situation and needs.[92]

Catechizing, claims Christopher Haigh, was the most neglected clerical task.[93] Not so in Dry Drayton. Greenham was a zealous catechizer. He introduced midweek catechism sessions (on Thursdays, in place of his sermon), which were rare at that time,[94] in addition to his regular Sunday efforts. Greenham was not above a little blackmail in the interests of catechizing: once when a man "being negligent to bee taught" brought his infant to Greenham to be baptized, Greenham would do so only after the man confessed his error and promised to reform his life and present himself for instruction.[95]

With the loss of auricular confession as part of the Reformation, ministers lost what had been an important educational tool on many levels. Yet

---

[89]Philippa Tudor, "Religious Instruction for Children and Adolescents in the Early English Reformation," *Journal of Ecclesiastical History* 35 (1984): 391–413; Ian Green, "'For Children in Yeeres and Children in Understanding': The Emergence of the English Catechism under Elizabeth and the Early Stuarts," ibid. 37 (1986): 397–425; idem, *The Christian's ABC: Catechisms and Catechizing in England c. 1530–1740* (Oxford: Clarendon Press, 1996).

[90]W. H. Frere and W. P. Kennedy, eds., *Visitation Articles and Injunctions of the Period of the Reformation*, 3 vols., Alcuin Club Collections xiv–xvi (London: Alcuin Club, 1910), 3:296–297.

[91]William Crashaw, quoted by Green, "For Children in Yeeres," 417. See also Richard Bernard, *Two Twinnes* (London, 1613), 1–29.

[92]*A Short Forme of Catechising* in *Works* (1599) and all subsequent editions.

[93]Haigh, "Puritan Evangelism," 35.

[94]Clarke, "Life of Master Richard Greenham," 12; Green, "For Children in Yeeres," 419.

[95]Rylands MS 524, fol. 65v.

ministers still had the duty of "reprehension"—of rebuking their parishioners for their sins and calling them to repentance. In place of confession, was a largely voluntary form usually called "conferring." Greenham once observed that "hee thought it good if men would confer more with ther Pastors saying, Even in earthly things when men cannot try gold themselves, they know to go to the goldsmith." While he felt that before the church was reformed, "men were too far gone with Auricular confession, now men come too short of Christian conferring."[96]

Every minister was, according to Greenham, held accountable by God for every soul entrusted to him which perished. There was no more pressing burden on the minister, therefore, than "to watch over the souls of his people, to be so careful over them, as that he will not suffer one through his negligence to perish."[97] The first step in saving the souls of his people was bringing them to an awareness of their sinfulness: "It is necessarie that the Minister of God, doe very sharply rebuke the people for their sinnes, and that he lay before them Gods grievous judgements against sinners."[98]

Although Clarke described Greenham as a "promoter of peace and concord amongst his neighbours,"[99] this did not mean that he neglected his role as prophet warning the people of their wickedness.[100] He could be quite severe, especially with his friends and followers,[101] though he preferred "private and gentle admonitions." Confronting an individual within the parish required great sensitivity. "Hee observed as a general law that soemuch as with a good conscience might bee, hee would use private warnings before publique dealings, and gentle and curteous speaches before vehement and sharp speaches and threatnings." Next, he recommended seeing if someone other than the minister might be better fit to the task. Whoever approached the sinner was to "put on the person of the offendor, that as you spare not his sin beecaus of zeale of gods glory, so you pres it not too far beecaus of compassion of a brother."[102]

---

[96]Ibid., fol. 40r. Professor Collinson has noted the similarity of the role of the confessor and the post-Reformation counselor in "The Role of Women in the English Reformation Illustrated by the Life and Friendships of Anne Locke," in *Godly People*, 275.

[97]*Works* (1612), 342, 358.

[98]*Works* (1605), 392.

[99]Clarke, "Life of Master Richard Greenham," 13.

[100]This model of the godly minister is explicit in Nehemiah Wallington's letter to his nephew Nathaniel Church: Paul Seaver, *Wallington's World: A Puritan Artisan in Seventeenth Century London* (Stanford: Stanford University Press, 1985), 107.

[101]Rylands MS 524, fols. 10v, 19v–20r.

[102]Ibid., fols. 10v–11r, 12v.

Bringing the sinner to an awareness of sin—creating an afflicted conscience —was the but the first step of Greenham's "Christian conferring." Once consciences were afflicted, he would then assure penitents of their election, if their repentance and resolution to live a godly life were sincere.[103] This was, in his view, the minister's highest calling—higher even than preaching: "It is a greater thing in a Pastor to deal wisely and comfortably with an afflicted conscience... then to preach publickly and learnedly."[104] It was this, more than anything else, on which Greenham's posthumous reputation was founded. In the words of Thomas Fuller, his "masterpiece was comforting wounded consciences."[105] He quite demonstrably did a great deal of it, and he did it well.

The woman whose emotional cloudburst during Greenham's sermon has been described above is only one of many examples which appear in the observations of Greenham's disciples. Frequently he had to offer consolation to people "extreamly througn down" by the burden of their sins.[106] His standard response to them was a reminder that "men must not think that god beholdeth them as they are in one particular defect, and at one present instant, but as they are in general purpose...."[107] According to Greenham, it was "a pollicy of sathan" to delude people into thinking that they would be condemned for particular sins. God judged the person's overall disposition and would not condemn someone for an individual sin, but for wallowing in sin: "for the particular sin bringeth not wrath, but the lying in that sin, and not repenting of it bringeth wrath which drawing in other sins withal draweth in also gods displeasure."[108]

Satan was very real and very threatening to many of those who turned to Greenham, and part of his role as pastoral counselor was to replace the medieval exorcist.[109] Claims of demonic possession occur with some regularity in his followers' notes. Greenham appears to have been concerned that people were too easily drawn into a belief that the devil owned them

---

[103]Kendall, *Calvin and English Calvinism*, 47.

[104]Rylands MS 524, fol. 61r. Professor Spufford has called attention to the need for a study of the large number of conscience and commonplace books from the period which record this sort of pastoral counsel: *The World of Rural Dissenters, 1520–1725* (Cambridge: Cambridge University Press, 1995), 79–80.

[105]Fuller, *Church History*, 219.

[106]Rylands MS 524, fol. 14r.

[107]Ibid., fol. 24r.

[108]Ibid., fol. 3v.

[109]See, for example, ibid., fol. 8r.

and that they were, therefore, beyond salvation. This was a mere delusion conjured up by Satan in an attempt to keep the sinner from turning to God for mercy. To a woman who claimed to be with child by the devil, Greenham calmly suggested that this was the imagining of a troubled conscience and told her she "must not dout of pardon by repentance.... [D]eal rather with the lord then with the devil in your affliction as did Job, who knowing the devil to bee but a vassal, goeth to the principal that is to god, as if one being ready to bee executed. It is not good to deal with the hangman who doth nothing but by authority, but it is good to go to the judge, who hath power to condemn and acquit, so it is safer to go to the lord by praier then to the devil who doth nothing but as the lord permitteth."[110] To another person who claimed to have been possessed, Greenham responded that it was true "that in as much as lyeth in you, you have given over your self to the devil, but it is not in your power to give your self unto him, neither is it in his jurisdiction to possess you."[111] When a woman having seizures which were attributed to possession was brought to him, "hee charged the person afflicted in the name of the lord Jesus Christ, that when the agony came, shee should not willingly yeeld to it, but in the lord resist, beecause experience teacheth that the overmuch fearing the temptation before it commeth, mightily incourageth sathan: and also the holy ghost biddeth us resist the devil and hee wil fly from us, and draw more unto god and hee wil draw near unto us." The woman reportedly was never troubled by fits thereafter.[112]

People from many different places brought their sorrows to Greenham. "[A] godly man that had his child and onely son drowned and therfore [was] in much anxiety of mynd" sought him out and was told that somewhere in the event was the correction of sin "as the Shunanite had her child taken away by death." Possibly, Greenham advised, God was challenging his sense of security, or punishing an immoderate love of his son or unthankfulness to God for him, or "hee might prevent some worldlines which the father might have fallen into, or some sin which the son might have falne into, which would have been a souer trouble then his death...."[113]

---

[110]Ibid., fol. 31r.
[111]Ibid., fol. 10v.
[112]Ibid., fol. 15v; see also fol. 47r.
[113]Ibid., fol. 41r.

Most of Greenham's counseling seems to have been face-to-face, but he did spend some time writing letters as well.[114] A "Godly learned man" wrote to ask him if it was permissible to use the services of a popish physician, for example.[115] Printed texts of several of his more pastoral letters were published in the 1599 edition of his Works. These include "A Letter Against hardnesse of heart," "An other comfortable Letter by Master R. G. to Master M.," and "A Letter Consolatorie, written to a friend afflicted in conscience for sinne."[116]

Greenham took "a reverent administration of the sacraments, according to the order and institution of our Saviour Jesus Christ" very seriously as well, although it was clearly secondary to teaching in its many guises: "The neglect of Gods Sacraments doth provoke him against us, as it did against Moses, for the neglect of the Circumcision of his sonne. The Lord met Moses with some such affliction; as that hee was readie to die according to the threatening."[117] At the same time, however, the sacraments and other services of the church occupied relatively little of his time. The numbers themselves tell much of the story. During all of Greenham's tenure as rector of Dry Drayton, the parish register records 203 baptisms, twenty-five marriages, and sixty-three burials.[118]

He would have performed an average of ten baptisms a year. In practice, the number ranged from a low of three in one year to four years in which there were seventeen or eighteen. In his busiest year, he would have had an average of one baptism every three weeks. He did not consider baptism essential for salvation, and he would not baptize children without investigating the faith of those who presented the child.[119] There is no

---

[114]On written spiritual direction, see Patrick Collinson, "A Mirror of Elizabethan Puritanism: The Life and Letters of 'Godly Master Dering,'" in *Godly People*, 316; A. Daniel Frankforter, "Elizabeth Bowes and John Knox: A Woman and Reformation Theology," *Church History* 56 (1987): 333–347; *Cartwrightiana*, ed. Albert Peel and Leland H. Carlson (London: George Allen & Unwin, 1951), 105–108; Seaver, *Wallington's World*, 105.

[115]Rylands MS 524, fol. 1r.

[116]*Works* (1599), 443–476. Greenham's *Works* also contain "A Profitable Treatise containing a Direction for the reading and vnderstanding of the holy Scriptures: by Master G.," which advises people to consult with ministers about their reading of the Bible, but there is no evidence that Greenham spent any time in this kind of consultation.

[117]*Works*, 2d ed. (1599), 358.

[118]Figures based on the original parish register deposited in the CRO. My count of the number of burials might be inflated; the exact date of Greenham's arrival in the parish is not known, so it is not certain that he was present for all of the burials which I have included.

[119]*Works* (1601), 267–268; (1605), 784.

indication that this inquiry was very formal or lengthy, so this ministerial function was not a time-consuming one.[120]

In several years, there were no marriages at all in Dry Drayton. This is not entirely surprising, since there may have been pressure on young people to move out of the parish in order to control population growth. When there were marriages, however, Greenham was active in preparing the couple and he would not marry them until he had done so.[121] In part this was because Greenham had a rather negative view of marriage and encouraged people to think of it only as a last resort to avoid fornication. He had himself married somewhat late. His marriage to the widow Katherine Bownd, who was his patron's sister-in-law, took place when he was over thirty years old and almost three years after he had moved to Dry Drayton,[122] allowing the cynical to speculate that he married most of all for domestic convenience. His wife is such a cipher in his *Works*, that it is difficult to imagine that this was a relationship which was emotionally central to his life.[123]

Before contracting he encouraged people to follow a long regimen of prayer, fasting, hard work, and self-control in order to discern whether they could stay chaste without marriage.[124] Once a couple was betrothed, he would not publish the banns without questioning them on several topics. First he ensured that they were not related to one another in a degree which would make the union illegal. Then he asked whether they were then or had ever been contracted to anyone else (which would bar any valid marriage), whether they had their parents' consent, and "whether

---

[120]Greenham turned away people from other parishes who came to him to baptize their children. Their reasons smack of latter-day Donatism, and Greenham would have none of that: Rylands MS 524, fol. 10r.

[121]It is possible that the burden of Greenham's marriage preparation program simply drove couples to marry elsewhere. Legally, unless licensed to do otherwise, couples had to marry in the parish in which one of them resided. Given the likelihood of exogamy at the time, most couples had at least two parishes in which they could marry without a license. See Carlson, *Marriage and the English Reformation*. I am grateful to Michael Sekulla for suggesting to me the importance of this factor in curtailing the number of marriages in Dry Drayton.

[122]August, 1573: CRO, parish register of Dry Drayton. Katherine Bownd was the sister of Sibill Hutton, who married James Hutton (brother of John) around 1564. It seems likely that she moved to Dry Drayton after her husband's death in order to be with her family, to which she remained close until her death, and met Greenham as a result. See her will, PRO, PROB 11/119; Prerogative Court of Canterbury, 41 Fenne. I am very grateful to Michael Sekulla for providing me with a copy of this important source.

[123]Eric Josef Carlson, "Clerical Marriage and the English Reformation," *Journal of British Studies* 31 (1992): 1–31.

[124]Ibid., fols. 16v, 21v–22r, 25r.

---

they did purpose to continue this action publickly and with the prayers of the church to solemnize ther meeting according to the word." After this, he would "use some exhortation for the general duties both of men and wemen," and pray with them.[125] Marriage preparation could thus be time-consuming for Greenham, but given the infrequency of registered marriages in Dry Drayton, it could not have been much of a burden.

Twenty-one of the sixty-three burials registered took place during the parish mortality crisis of late 1570. In other years, Greenham buried an average of two people. There was great disagreement at the time about the acceptability of the Prayer Book burial service and the proper role of the minister in burial. Greenham's view was characteristically moderate:

> hee said that whatsoever was not either flatly commanded, or plainly forbidden in the word, might sometimes bee used for the maintaining of love and some times bee left undone for the avoiding of superstition. And for the burial of the dead, beecaus wee read no prescript order of it. I thinck wee must follow the general rule, that is that al things bee done decently, so that ther bee neither on the one side a prophain casting of the body, nor on the other side any superstition used in the same...[and if] it is not inconvenient, to read the word and to leav out the praying, which duties distinguish between the necessary duty of the minister in the sacraments, and his function in other les actions....[126]

Greenham was only required to administer the Lord's Supper three times a year[127] and he may not have exceeded that. He did believe that when a minister was new in a parish he should "stay a good while, after his coming to his people from administering the sacrament, until after a continual publique teaching by some convenient tyme and some requisite trials of the people hee may minister both some comforts, lest doing it before, hee administer to most unworthy receivers."[128] He devoted at least

---

[125]Ibid., fol. 43r. Parental consent was extremely important, and he cooked up a scheme (which never was employed in Dry Drayton) by which a father dying before the marriage of any of his children would appoint a proxy father in his will who would give the father's consent for him: fols. 49v–50r. Greenham also wrote a betrothal service for the church which was published in his *Works* (1599), 288–299, but there is also no evidence to suggest it was ever used.

[126]Rylands MS 524, fol. 66v.

[127]Jeremy P. Boulton, "The Limits of Formal Religion: The Administration of Holy Communion in Late Elizabethan and Early Stuart London," *London Journal* 10 (1984): 135–154.

[128]Rylands MS 524, fol. 2r.

a week before the administration of the sacrament "in calling his people to private conference" and he would give over his morning preaching to the subject for two or three days, exhorting the unprepared not to come forward.[129] According to the law, the minister was responsible for excluding the unprepared and evil-livers from the Lord's Supper, and he stated that the minister "must not admit all men that come rashly to eate the flesh and drinke the bloud of Christ, for it is no small matter: but first they must eate it by faith out of the word of God, and when he hath so done, the Minister shall administer to him the outward seales of bread and wine, to confirm and strengthen his faith."[130] In practice, he was reluctant to exclude the "indifferently instructed" from the sacrament if they "lay in noe sin."[131]

Finally, there were two duties which fall outside the typical parochial duties of preaching and sacramental ministry which Greenham considered central to his vocation. He was well known for his charity and, according to Clarke, during times of scarcity Greenham personally subsidized barley sales to the poor. He also made significant personal contributions to the town granary which was maintained for poor relief. As a result of his generosity his finances were in constant disarray.[132] Greenham also refused to accept fees for marriages, baptisms, and burials and had those turned over directly to the poor of the parish.[133]

That we know so much of Greenham's parish ministry is due almost entirely to the informal seminary which sprouted in Dry Drayton. Whether its germination was or was not intentional (which is unknown), Greenham did say that one of the godly pastor's duties was to "traine up some young scholler" in imitation of Paul's training of Timothy.[134] He certainly trained more than his share, and he established a precedent which was followed by a number of Puritans in the next century.[135] As his protégés were dispersed into the rectories and vicarages of England, Greenham's example in Dry

---

[129]Ibid., fols. 38v, 39v.

[130]*Works* (1605), 784; see also "Of Examination before and after the Lords Supper," ibid., 498–505.

[131]Ibid., fols. 32v–33r. In other places, preparation seems largely to have been self-directed and introspective: John E. Booty, "Preparation for the Lord's Supper in Elizabethan England," *Anglican Theological Review* 49 (1967): 131–148.

[132]Clarke, "Life of Master Richard Greenham," 12–13.

[133]Rylands MS 524, fol. 35v. For the significance of charity, see Felicity Heal, "The Idea of Hospitality in Early Modern England," *Past and Present* 102 (1984), 80–86.

[134]*Works* (1605), 400.

[135]An excellent discussion of Puritan seminaries, to the best of my knowledge not published anywhere, is in Kenneth Shipp, "Lay Patronage of East Anglian Puritan Clerics in Pre-Revolutionary England" (Ph.D. dissertation, Yale University, 1971), App. II.

Drayton went with them and, presumably, helped to define the shape of their own ministries. Literally thousands of English lay people were, by the 1620s, in some sense the flock of Richard Greenham.

∾

In 1591, Greenham left Dry Drayton for London. He had been "often laboured" to leave it since at least 1581. One observer recorded that

> hee was altogether unwilling unto it howbeit at length hee seemed to offer these conditions. First if they would remoove him his stipend should not bee one penny more then in his present place 2ly hee requested to have the choice of the pastor 3ly hee required such a place as might not bee far from his charge present, beecause hee would stil use his fatherly care to his people as to his natural childeren in the preaching of the gospel.[136]

A decade later, Greenham can be said to have met one, and possibly two, of his conditions. He does seem to have been influential in the choice of Richard Warfield as his successor. What his stipend was in London will never be known, but there is no reason to believe that he would have used the move to improve himself financially.[137] It is the third condition which he so blatantly did not meet; London was rather far from Dry Drayton for regular visits. But by 1591, he might have been less inclined to maintain close ties with the village.

There is cause to believe that Greenham had become discouraged after two decades there. Fuller's father told the historian of a conversation in 1616 which he had with Warfield in which Greenham's successor reported receiving these final words: "Mr. Warfield (saith hee) God blesse you, and send you more fruit of yor labours then I have had: ffor I perceive now good wrought by ministerie on any but one familie."[138] Clarke later reported

---

[136]Rylands MS 524, fol. 2r. Fuller (*Church History*, 220) reported that Greenham's friends called Dry Drayton a "bushel basket" and urged him to leave it.

[137]Patrick Collinson describes Greenham's move as to "a more lucrative and comfortable post," but he gives no evidence and I am aware of none: "Shepherd, Sheepdogs, and Hirelings: The Pastoral Ministry in Post-Reformation England," *The Ministry: Clerical and Lay*, ed. W. J. Sheils and Diana Wood, *Studies in Church History* 26 (Oxford: Blackwell, 1989), 200.

[138]Warren, *Notes and Queries*, 366.

that his leaving was caused by "the untractableness and unteachableness of that people among whom he had taken such exceeding great pains."[139]

If Greenham's ministry had had a positive impact on Dry Drayton, one might hope to see an increase in fervent, personal professions of faith in will dedicatory clauses. However, after examining wills from Cambridgeshire parishes with far less praiseworthy ministers, Margaret Spufford writes that there is "less feeling of convinced Protestantism in the wills of Dry Drayton than any other parish I have examined."[140] Although the sample is small (seven wills) and there are dangers in building too much on the foundation of dedicatory clauses, as Dr. Marsh's essay in this volume shows, Professor Spufford's bleak evaluation of these wills is justified. Two of the Dry Drayton wills from 1570 to 1591 use the simplest form of commendation: "I bequeath my soul to Almighty God."[141] Roger Boyden's will, which bequeathed body and soul to

> the hands of my alone and omnisufficient savior Jesus Christ who as he hath alonely redeemed me, so do I firmly believe that I shall be saved only by the fruit and mercy of his passion and suffering for my sins, confessing that for my sins I am unworthy of the least of his mercies, yet for Christ's sake that I shall by faith possess and enjoy the kingdom of heaven prepared for all the children of God whereof I am one,

was drawn up by Greenham himself and may say more about the scribe's sentiments than the testator's.[142] Two wills begin with very brief, though undeniably Protestant, expressions. John Muns left his soul "to God almighty trusting by the death and passion of his son Jesus Christ my only savior to receive at the general judgement everlasting life." James Hutton (Katherine Greenham's sister's husband) left his soul "to Christ Jesus in whom only and wholly I by faith do repose my whole salvation." Since this clause is unique, it may be an expression of personal faith, but given the

---

[139]Clarke, "Life of Master Richard Greenham," 15; Fuller, *Church History*, 219.

[140]Spufford, *Contrasting Communities*, 328. For wills as evidence of piety, see essays by Christopher Marsh and Caroline Litzenberger, below, 201–207; Spufford, *Contrasting Communities*, 320–344; and Eric Josef Carlson, "The Historical Value of the Ely Consistory Probate Records," in *Index of the Probate Records of the Consistory Court of Ely 1449–1858*, ed. Elisabeth Leedham-Green and Rosemary Rodd, 3 vols. (London: British Record Society, 1994–96), 1: xxxvi–xlvii.

[141][Cambridgeshire Record Office,] E[ly] P[robate] R[ecords], C[onsistory] W[ill]1573 (Barbour); CW1585 (Wrattam).

[142]EPR, CW1571. Dry Drayton schoolmaster William Helsbie used an identical clause when acting as scribe for a later will: EPR, CW1580 (Ivatt).

godly proclivities in the Hutton family it is likely that Hutton's strong piety was due more to familial than ministerial influences.[143]

Eleven wills from the dozen years after Greenham's removal to London use a simple dedicatory formula. However, Thomas Gifford left his soul "into the hands of Almighty God my father who created me, second to God the son who redeemed me; thirdly to God the Holy Ghost who sanctified me, and I do believe and confess that these three persons in Trinity do make one god coequal, coeternal, in unity of person." He left his body to be buried in the churchyard "to sleep till the last day when the last trumpet shall blow and the dead in Christ shall arise first and then this my corruptible shall be made like to his glorious body and so shall ever remain with him in his glorious kingdom."[144]

Shortly after Greenham's arrival, Dry Drayton's children began increasingly to receive biblical baptismal names. Of the ten children baptized in 1575, for example, only one received a traditional parish name (Thomas). Instead, there were Peter, Appia, Daniel, Ursula, Nathaniel, Samuel, Josiah, and two Sarahs. They were soon joined by several Deborahs and Rebeccas, along with Jehosabeths and Hananiahs, Gemimah, Solomon, Manasses, Moses, Joshua, Eunice, and even Lot and Bathsheba. When Greenham left, the traditional names (William, Henry, John, Elizabeth, Alice, and Margaret were the most common in Dry Drayton) returned and biblical names were soon no longer chosen.[145]

Biblical names were clustered primarily in seven families, and this suggests Greenham's influence might have been more extensive. Since some families retained traditional naming patterns, Greenham was not simply changing outward demonstrations of piety through some sort of vulgar blackmail over the font; some individual choice must have been involved.[146] However, parents virtually ceased biblical naming as soon as

---

[143]EPR, CW1588 (Muns); CW1582 (Hutton). James and Sibill Hutton demonstrated their piety by giving their children biblical names. The seventh will has no dedicatory clause: EPR, CW1570 (Bennett).

[144]EPR, CW 1597.

[145]The baptismal register is in the CRO. The fashion for naming children with pious ejaculations, used by Dudley Fenner in Cranbrook, did not penetrate much beyond East Sussex and the Kentish weald, but the Hebraicization demonstrated in Dry Drayton's register was found elsewhere beginning in the 1560s. See Nicholas Tyacke, "Popular Puritan Mentality in Late Elizabethan England," in *The English Commonwealth*, ed. Peter Clark (Leicester: Leicester University Press, 1974): 77–92.

[146]I am deeply indebted to Michael Sekulla for providing this information and convincing me to revise my earlier views on this subject.

Greenham was no longer hovering nearby when they named their babies. What it signifies and why it ceased remains something of a mystery, but even if the practice of giving children biblical names suggests that Greenham worked some sort of conversion in several families, the change was not deep enough to withstand the pressure of custom without Greenham present. His successor was not the sort to be antipathetic to the practice, but perhaps he did not care enough to encourage it, and so people returned to customary ways.

While Greenham might have felt a sense of failure when measured against his own expectations, it is unlikely that the villagers judged him so harshly. His widow's will suggests that he was respected and valued by his neighbors. Katherine Bownd Greenham married a third time. Her last husband was a man named Wood, about whom nothing is certainly known. At some point she returned to Dry Drayton, which is where she died and was buried in 1612. Her Hutton relations must have been an attraction, but would she have returned there if her earlier time there had been so unfulfilling that her husband would have shaken (if the soil ever dried out enough to produce some) the dust from his boots? A minister's wife certainly might build a life of her own in his parish, but her circumstances and her relationships must inevitably have been influenced by her husband's role as well. In her will, Katherine Wood names five godchildren: one the son of Greenham's successor Richard Warfield, but the other four members of established village families, including a Gifford. Katherine's connection to the Huttons is too tenuous to explain this. Her role as godmother to children born during her husband's ministry is a comment on the village's view of him. While a person of credit and character in her own right, it is unlikely that villagers would have invited her to join their families in this way if they were displeased with her husband who also became, through her, part of their kin network.[147]

Indeed, in their minds Greenham had been what they sought in a minister: he had resided among them, he had performed the services which

---

[147]PRO, PROB 11/119; PCC, 41 Fenne. Katherine Wood was a fairly wealthy woman when she died. Since her copyhold passed to her daughter Anne (wife of the Puritan divine John Dod), it must have come to her either from her own family (which is unknown) or from Bownd, her first husband and Anne's father. The source of the bequests she left to nephews and nieces, godchildren and grandchildren—almost £100 spread among twenty named individuals plus forty shillings to the Dry Drayton poor—is not known. While it is possible that Dry Drayton families tried to link themselves with Katherine because of her material resources, I find that doubtful in this case, and her testamentary wealth might have come from her last husband.

marked the transitions in their lives, he had been generous with hospitality and charity. He may also have unintentionally improved the village's economy by attracting visitors who might need victuals and beds. Most importantly, he respected the customs and culture of the village. The villagers in Dry Drayton had a tradition of self-government fused with an entrenched parish oligarchy, dominated by Giffords and Boydens, with a choke hold over local government. Absentee monastic landlords created the opportunity for leet juries to undertake virtually all of the business of government, such as adopting and enforcing bylaws which regulated village farming and grazing. The leet jury also controlled village residence, and although new families appear without having married into those already resident, most movement in Dry Drayton was probably out of the parish.

Perhaps the most important function of village government was conflict resolution.[148] A well-governed village solved its own problems, and use of church courts was not only as a last recourse but was also a visible sign of the villagers' failure to maintain order in their own affairs. Some clergymen based their ministry on the text that Christ came not to bring peace but a sword, and they made careers out of disrupting peaceful communities with their preaching and efforts to discipline the godless. The nonconformist author and minister George Gifford (who was, coincidentally, born and raised in Dry Drayton) believed that one indication of true godly preaching was contention, because if the word of God were truly set out, wicked men "would storm and fret against [the preachers]."[149] In southeastern Cambridgeshire, for example, Simon Hacksuppe, rector of Weston Colville (1583–1605) tore his parish apart with his finger-wagging denunciations of sinners from the pulpit. He named names; he named sins. A flood of court cases and bitter divisions in the village were the result.[150]

In the decades before and after Greenham's tenure, Dry Drayton was responsible for remarkably little litigation in the church courts. During his tenure that did not change. The two instance cases were both suits brought against people from other parishes, cases in which Greenham could have

---

[148]Collinson, *Religion of Protestants*, 100–114.

[149]George Gifford, *A briefe discourse of certaine points of the religion, which is among the common sort of Christians, which may bee termed the Countrie Divinitie. With a manifest confutation of the same, after the order of a Dialogue* (London, 1582), fols. 47v–48r. I am grateful to Michael Sekulla for information on Gifford's lineage. The son of Boniface Gifford, he was born around 1550 and had left the parish before Greenham arrived.

[150]Carlson, *Marriage and the English Reformation*, 173–174.

little impact as a settler of conflict. Defamation cases, which were common among neighbors, did not occur at all. Since it is unlikely that Greenham succeeded in miraculously curbing the tongues of his parishioners, this suggests that tempers were cooled and disputes settled without going to court. Notably absent is tithe litigation, the most common type of suit in the church courts. This is striking because Dry Drayton apparently had no glebe land, which made Greenham unusually dependent on tithes,[151] and his heroic charity left the household perpetually short of money.[152]

Ex officio cases tell an interesting tale as well. Greenham seemingly succeeded not only in establishing harmonious relations with the leaders of the community, but also in moving the community to maintain the church while they overlooked his nonconformity in apparel. Only shortly after he left did the wardens report that they had no surplice. Perhaps Greenham had turned it over to his hard-pressed wife to be made into something more practical and all concerned had looked the other way for twenty years.[153] For those same twenty years, presentments against villagers were almost unknown.[154]

Parochial tranquility benefited from a minister like Greenham. Greenham's vision of ministry dovetailed nicely with the social vision of his parishioners. He was a gentle man, committed heart and soul to healing, and repelled by division and conflict. It is unsurprising that during his ministry the only presentments from within the parish were against one incorrigible who had put himself outside of the community by refusing to respect its order and two people who had fled the parish and removed themselves from the possibility of peaceful resolution. The others were all the result of problems which occurred outside of Dry Drayton before the parties became denizens. The pattern of internal conflict resolution and regulation of behavior which led to infrequent cases in the church courts was not entirely of the minister's creating, but Greenham was able to embrace and baptize so much of the vision and ideal of the community in which he worked that he was able to assist it in maintaining its independence. If Greenham had not succeeded in building a shining city on the

---

[151]EDR, H/1/3; *VCH, Cambs.*, 9:85. Clarke ("Life of Master Richard Greenham," 13), however, says that Mrs. Greenham was forced to borrow money "to get in his harvest," but that could refer to rented lands.

[152]Clarke, "Life of Master Richard Greenham," 12–13.

[153]EDR, B/2/11, fol. 89v.

[154]EDR, D/2/8, fols. 117r, 131v; D/2/10, fols. 57r, 132v; D/2/14, fol. 44r.; D/2/16, 35, 101–103; D/2/17a, fol. 1r.

clay, a harmonious godly commonwealth in Dry Drayton, he nonetheless succeeded in the eyes of his parishioners in what mattered to them.

His own disappointment might have prepared the way for his departure, but I do not believe it was a sufficient cause, because abandoning a mission given to him by God does not seem in character for Greenham. In fact, I would argue that Greenham left because Thomas Fanshawe and others persuaded him that there was even greater need in London. By 1591, the church was increasingly well supplied with educated ordinands, and a suitable replacement for Greenham could easily be found. But the needs in London were such, so he would have been told, that only he could meet them. His removal to London could not have been presented to him as, nor could he have believed it to be, a comfortable option.

London lectureships in the early 1580s had been a safe haven for nonconformists. By 1590, however, Whitgift and Aylmer had brought them under strict episcopal supervision and, although not eliminated entirely, the number of nonconformists in lectureships had decreased. Those who remained were well aware of hot episcopal breath on their unsurpliced backs. Professor Paul Seaver, moreover, has pointed out that "what appears to have saved the London community of Puritan radicals from impotent silence during [the 1590s] was the steady influx of mature nonconformists from the provinces."[155] Greenham was part of that influx and, I would argue, it was because of his towering stature among nonseparating nonconformists that he was recruited to help save their cause in London. He agreed to give up his rural parish because a far greater need for one of his singular status existed.

In February 1591/2, Greenham was granted a license to preach in the diocese of London. This was done in spite of Greenham's nonsubscription. The official registration of his license includes the following: "Mr Thomas Fanshawe armiger de verbo suo promisit ut domini Greenham nullas innovaciones aut contentiones de rebus suscitet vel spargat."[156] While other preachers were simply licensed "as long as (dummodo)" they did not stir up trouble, Greenham's reputation as a nonconformist patriarch required something more; Bishop John Aylmer licensed him only with the personal assurances of his good conduct from a powerful third party.

---

[155]Seaver, *Puritan Lectureships*, 211–220.

[156]G[reater] L[ondon] R[ecord] O[ffice], DL/C/335 (Liber Vicarii Generalis, 1590–95), fol. 60v.

Whether Aylmer granted the preaching license only under pressure from Fanshawe, who was Remembrancer of the Exchequer and one of the most prominent supporters of London nonconformists,[157] is not clear. Aylmer, who became bishop of London in 1576, was certainly no friend to nonconformists and he enthusiastically supported Whitgift's subscription campaigns in 1584. But there is evidence to suggest that he was similar in important ways to Greenham's previous bishop, Cox of Ely.[158] Like Cox, Aylmer had been an exile in Mary's reign and was a fierce enemy of Rome; like Cox, he desired to staff his parishes with educated clergy who could teach and preach.[159] He seemed willing, for a good cause, to make compromises with quite radical men. He constructed a naive scheme to send William Charke, Edmund Chapman, John Field, and Thomas Wilcox to Lancashire, Staffordshire, "and such other like barbarous countries, to draw people from Papism and gross ignorance."[160] George Gifford, suspended in 1584, was restored without subscribing; Gifford was respected for his work in bringing his Essex parish "to more sobreity and knowledge of true religion" and he emerged as a ferocious opponent of the separatist Henry Barrow.[161] In other words, Aylmer seems to have been willing to bend a bit, as Cox had been, in order to serve the larger needs of the church, as long as the object of his concessions was committed to the unity of the church and the defeat of its enemies.

There are even hints of the form which Aylmer's license for Greenham would take in the 1582 compromise over Robert Wright. Wright, whose patron was Lord Rich, preached without a license and was known to conduct private services not conforming to the Prayer Book. He was imprisoned but eventually released after he agreed to limited subscription and his "friends" put up a "good round sum" as insurance that his future preaching would not be disruptive of church unity.[162] Like Wright, Greenham had a powerful patron who could be called upon to stand surety for him. Perhaps Aylmer remembered the 1582 precedent when faced with a request to

---

[157]On Fanshawe, see Hasler, *House of Commons*, 2: 105–106; *DNB*, s.v. Fanshawe, Thomas (d. 1601).

[158]See above, 167–168.

[159]John Strype, *Historical Collections of the Life and Acts of the Right Reverend Father in God, John Aylmer, Lord Bp. of London in the Reign of Queen Elizabeth* (new ed., Oxford, 1821), 16–17, 21–23.

[160]Ibid., 36. On these men, see Collinson, *Elizabethan Puritan Movement*.

[161]Strype, *Aylmer*, 71–73.

[162]Ibid., 54–57. On Wright, see Seaver, *Puritan Lectureships*, 94–95, 111–112.

license a known nonconformist whose past history in Cambridgeshire showed he would serve the bishop well in defeating common enemies.

Although he had manors in Essex and Hertfordshire, Thomas Fanshawe's London residence—necessary for when he attended to Exchequer business and served in Parliament—was in Warwick Lane, and he was active and influential in the affairs of his parish.[163] Although the license does not specify which parish Greenham would preach in, Fanshawe's activities—probably as recruiter and obviously as sponsor—make clear that it would be Christ Church, Newgate Street. It was one of the six largest parishes within London's walls, which bounded it on the north and west; to the south St. Paul's Cathedral was no more than five minutes' walk from virtually any point in the parish. It was, in Greenham's day, one of London's newest parishes, having been founded in December 1546 as part of a scheme to reconstruct the dissolved foundation of St. Bartholomew's Hospital.[164] The Hospital itself, which was in the extramural West Smithfield parish of St. Bartholomew the Less, was reestablished by the City authorities as a hospital for the sick. The dissolved Franciscan, or Grey Friars, house by Newgate was converted into an orphanage (later known as Christ's Hospital) while the Grey Friars' church became the new parish church of Christ Church. This entire area was under the authority of the governors of St. Bartholomew's Hospital.[165]

From its earliest days, the parish was known for its connection with advanced reformers and prominent London religious radicals.[166] Thomas Becon was its first vicar, nominated by Robert Dudley, and later vicars included Thomas Gataker. Already in 1560, the parish had established a lectureship, which was then held by Richard Allen, one of the most extreme of London's radical preachers in the 1560s. The parochial appetite for

---

[163]He has been identified as a spokesman for the parish in its dealings; for example, with the board of governors of St. Bartholomew's Hospital, which had authority over the parish: H. Gareth Owen, "Tradition and Reform: Ecclesiastical Controversy in an Elizabethan London Parish," *Guildhall Miscellany* 2 (1961): 63–70.

[164]For what follows, see Owen, "Tradition and Reform." I am grateful to Dr. Ian Archer for discussing this parish with me and for making many constructive suggestions concerning archival resources for this essay.

[165]Rosemary Weinstein, *Tudor London* (London: HMSO, 1994), 13. The parish was created by pulling down the churches of St. Nicholas Shambles and St. Ewen, Warwick Lane, and uniting those parishes with some of St. Sepulchre within Newgate.

[166]This association continued into the seventeenth century: Tai Liu, *Puritan London: A Study of Religion and Society in the City Parishes* (Newark, Del.: University of Delaware Press, 1986).

preaching increased with feeding, for by 1590 the number of lecturers had risen to four.

When the parish was established, part of the pre-Dissolution resources had been used to endow five assistant clerks or "singing priests." These conservative fixtures, whose role hearkened back to the more "popish" church services of Henry VIII's reign, were peas under the mattresses of the religiously progressive lay folk who dominated the parish and, in 1580, they succeeded in getting the Hospital governors to remove them. The assistant clerks were replaced by a curate and four lecturers, all paid out of the endowment, which allowed the parish to stop paying for its lecturer from parochial funds.

Greenham was not intended to be one of these four lecturers, probably because his status and reputation seemed to demand a position of more prestige and a higher stipend. Instead, Thomas Fanshawe pressed a scheme on the Hospital governors to combine the positions and salaries of the four lecturers into one, which would be offered to Greenham. Although it was seriously considered, it was never adopted[167] and Greenham was presumably paid from parish funds or from the contributions of patrons like Fanshawe, who could well afford it.

Very few specific details are known about Greenham's ministry in London. His pattern of conferring with those who placed themselves outside of the church in order to win them back continued, as Aylmer must have hoped and expected. In April of 1593, Greenham joined two other divines in visiting John Penry. Since Penry reported to his wife that the ministers had "authority on their sides," this may have been a commission much like those Greenham carried out for Cox. They found Penry unwilling to accept "private intermeddling in so public an action" and instead he went to trial for "having…feloniously devised and written certain words with intent to excite rebellion and insurrection" and was executed on 29 May 1593.[168]

Penry's trial and execution took place while London was in the final stages of the third deadliest Elizabethan visitation of the plague.[169] By 2 September 1592, the plague had broken out in the area around the parish

---

[167]St. Bart[holomew]'s Hosp[ital, Archives Department], Ha 1/3, fols. 86r, 109v.

[168]John Waddington, *John Penry, the Pilgrim Martyr, 1559–1593* (London, 1852), 123; *DNB*, sub Penry, John.

[169]Paul Slack, *The Impact of Plague in Tudor and Stuart England* (London: Routledge & Kegan Paul, 1985), 151. The mortality rate in London was 14.5%.

and the Hospital governors ordered their clerk to obtain the Lord Mayor's decrees and ordinances "for the avoiding of the same sickness."[170] The church had its own response to the plague: prayer, penance, and listening to sermons. As bishop of London, Grindal had written a service to be used in all churches on Wednesdays and Fridays during time of plague. It was a lengthy service consisting of seven sermons from the Book of Homilies plus one on "the justice of God in punishing impenitent sinners" composed specially by Alexander Nowell. Bishop Aylmer revised it in 1593, severely reducing its length by cutting all but Nowell's and one other homily. The service would then be not more than an hour long, to discourage both prolonged exposure to infected people and religious "faction." Both concerns were raised by Grindal's lengthy program.[171] Greenham, as a licensed preacher, would not read from the Book of Homilies. Instead, he preached a series of fast sermons. An account book recording the receipts from these sermons shows that he was quite successful.[172]

Although he exposed himself to danger by remaining in London and carrying out his ministerial functions, it was not the plague which claimed Greenham's life. He died late in April 1594 of unknown causes and was buried in Christ Church, though no details of his funeral survive.[173] He left no will; his widow was granted the administration of his goods on 30 April.[174]

---

[170]St. Bart's Hosp, Ha 1/3, fol. 107r.

[171]Slack, *Impact of Plague*, 229.

[172]GL, MS 9163, fols. 305r–305v. According to Ian Archer, the numbers recorded are extremely high. I am grateful to Dr. Archer for his evaluation.

[173]GL, MS 9163, fol. 320v, is a list of receipts for burials. It includes a note of eight shillings received "for the buriall of Mr Richarde Grenhame oure lat preacher a man of worthie memorie who was buried the 25 Apriell 1594." Roughly two-thirds of all burials in mid-seventeenth century London took place within two days of death: Stephen Porter, "From Death to Burial in Seventeenth-Century England," *The Local Historian* 23 (1993): 199–204. For London funerals: David Cressy, "Death and the Social Order: The Funerary Preferences of Elizabethan Gentlemen," *Continuity and Change* 5 (1989): 99–119; Clare Gittings, "Urban Funerals in Late Medieval and Reformation England," in Steven Bassett, ed., *Death in Towns. Urban Responses to the Dying and the Dead, 100–1600* (Leicester: Leicester University Press, 1992): 170–183; and David E. Stannard, *The Puritan Way of Death: A Study in Religion, Culture, and Social Change* (New York: Oxford University Press, 1977), 100–104. Because of the inaccurate information in Fuller and Clarke (see *DNB*), the year of Greenham's death had been much debated. While my discovery of the burial receipt is conclusive, it should be noted that over a century ago Edward Solly (*Notes and Queries*, 6th ser., 8 [21 July 1883]: 55) argued for April 1594 because of Greenham's attendance on Penry and his comments on the Lopez case as recorded in Holland's preface to the 1599 edition of *Works*.

[174]GLRO, DL/C/335, fol. 174.

୦ଓ

Not long thereafter, Joseph Hall wrote to William Bedell, then a fellow of Emmanuel College, lamenting the death of several divines. Of Richard Greenham, Hall wrote that he "excelled in experimental divinity; and knew well how to stay a weak conscience, how to raise a fallen, how to strike a remorseless...."[175] A more apt epitaph could scarcely be imagined, for it has about it the economy of words and directness with which Greenham taught that God's word was to be preached. While he would no doubt have been horrified at the development of anything like what we might call a "cult of personality" around him, and would reject with embarrassment the attention paid to him in death as belonging only to God, Greenham might have allowed himself a small smile of relief—if not satisfaction— that what he had spent his life doing was duly noted and appreciated after his death. Hall's judgment of Greenham reflected Greenham's own sense of his vocation. Can there be anything more satisfying than to be acknowledged in death for having met one's priorities in life?

Joseph Hall became an important figure in the church. He ultimately became a bishop, first of Exeter and later of Norwich. He was one of the lonely moderate Calvinist bishops during the ascendancy of Laud, Harsnett, and Neile. As the 1630s advanced, Greenham must have become for him an even more meaningful figure than he had been in the 1590s, for Greenham had found a way to live in relative harmony as a nonconformist in the Elizabethan church. Such peaceful coexistence, based as it was on a common sense of purpose and—perhaps more importantly—on common adversaries, became almost impossible in the 1630s. While Greenham would hardly have described the climate of his life in the land between conformity and separation as temperate, four decades after his death it seemed that his ministerial life was a summer idyll scarcely to be hoped for in the Laudian winter.

Thus, it is unsurprising that when Fuller and, especially, Clarke composed their histories of the church and its "saints" Greenham occupied such a place of preeminence. Even without the "Caroline captivity of the church"[176] his pastoral activities would have merited him that place,

---

[175] *The Works of the Right Reverend Joseph Hall, D. D.*, ed. Philip Wynter, 10 vols. (Oxford, 1863), 6:150. On Bedell, see Todd, "An act of discretion."

[176] I take the phrase from the title of Dr. Julian Davies' book: *The Caroline Captivity of the Church: Charles I and the Remoulding of Anglicanism* (Oxford: Clarendon Press, 1992).

however. We live in an age less comfortable with heroes and saints, but even when the hyperbole of the hagiographer and the wistful looker-back are stripped from his life story, it is clear that Richard Greenham deserved those labels from his contemporaries; he deserves, because of that, much more recognition from us today.

APPENDIX

SAMUEL CLARKE, "*THE LIFE OF MASTER* RICHARD GREENHAM, *WHO DYED ABOUT THE YEAR*, 1591," FROM *THE LIVES OF THIRTY-TWO ENGLISH DIVINES*, 3D ED. (LONDON, 1677), 12–15.[177]

I Can yet learn nothing Concerning the Countrey, Parentage, orfirst Education Mr. *Richard Greenham*. The first place, where I find him, was in *Pembrook*-Hall in *Cambridge*, where he followed his Studies so hard, and was so eminent for his proficiency in learning, that he was chosen Fellow in that Society, and after a while he was called to a Pastoral charge at *Dry-Drayton*, not far from *Cambridge*, and like a faithfull Minister of *Jesus Christ*, he spared no paines amongst his people, whereby he might advance the good of their souls.

His constant course was to preach twice on the *Lords day*, and before the evening Sermon to Catechize the young people of the Parish. His manner also was to preach on *Mondayes, Tuesdayes*, and *Wednesdayes*, and on *Thursdayes* to catechize the youth, and again on Frydayes to preach to his people; and that on these week dayes, the people might have the better opportunity to attend upon his Ministry, his course was to be in the Pulpit in the morning so soon as he could well see. He was so earnest, and took such extraordinary pains in his preaching, that his shirt would usually be as wet with sweating, as if it had been drenched in water, so that he was forced, so soon as he came out of the Pulpit, to shift himself, and this wonderfull and excessive paines he took all his time. Twice a day he prayed in his Family, and after Sermon he used to call his servants together, and examined them of what they heard, and what they remembred. And besides all these his publike labours, he studied very hard, rising every day both Winter and Summer, at four of the clock in the morning.

He was very eminent for his charity to the Poor; whereof we have this notable Example: In a time of scarcity, when Barley was at ten groats the Bushell, (which in those daies was an extraordinary price)[178] he by his Prudence brought it to pass, that the poor had it sold to them for four groats the Bushell of every Husband-man in the Town; and thus he effected it.

There were about twenty Plough-holders in the Town,[179] all which he by his holy perswasions drew to an agreement amongst themselves, to hire a common Granary, and

[177]Explanatory notes have been provided only for those matters not directly addressed in the essay above.

[178]One groat = 4d. Barley at 3s4d per bushel (=26s8d per quarter) suggests that Clarke is referring to 1586–87. Although the barley prices recorded in Thorold Rogers' price tables do not come close to that figure, the evidence on barley for 1586–87 is extremely thin. Wheat prices were "far beyond any previous experience." The indexed figures for barley given by Thirsk also suggest that 1586 is the year in question. A reader in Clarke's day would not find this price "extraordinary," though still somewhat above average. For prices, see James Edwin Thorold Rogers, *A History of Agriculture and Prices in England*, 7 vols. (Oxford: Clarendon Press, 1866–1902), 4:290, 5:175, 268, 272; Joan Thirsk, ed., *The Agrarian History of England and Wales, vol. IV, 1500–1640* (Cambridge: Cambridge University Press, 1967), 819. According to Margaret Spufford (*Contrasting Communities*, 96–97), barley was the most important crop in Cambridgeshire, especially in the heavy clay villages; oats were second in importance.

[179]In 1563, there were 31 households in Dry Drayton. The mortality crisis (probably due to a localized epidemic) in 1570 did not reduce the number of *households*. The figure of "twenty Plough-holders" seems low, but Michael Sekulla has demonstrated that roughly one-third of the households were headed by laborers and artisans (private communication). On the 1563 survey, see Alan Dyer, "The Bishops' Census of 1563: Its Significance and Accuracy," *Local Population Studies* 49 (1992): 19–37.

therein to lay up Corn for the poor, some more, some lesse, every man accordingly to his ability; so that some laid up one Coom, some a quarter, some three Cooms, and Master *Greenham* himself laid in five Cooms, all which was delivered out to the poor at a groat a peck.[180] There was one day in the week appointed for all the poor to come and be served, at which time every one received according to their charge; where there were but two in a Family, they received one peck a week, and so more according to that proportion; only no one Family had above three pecks a week.

He kept but two Beasts himself, that the poor might have his straw, and when other men fold their straw for two Shillings the dayes thresh, he sold his for ten pence: So that in that dear time all the poor in the Parish had been well neer famished, had it not been for his prudence, and liberality which he also continued, till the price of Corn abated, which was suddainly, and extraordinarily; For that Corn which was sold for a noble the Bushell, was within one moneth after sold for fourteen pence the Bushell.[181]

But during the fore-mentioned dearth, by publike Order, the Bushels were cut and made lesse;[182] This Master *Greenham* Preached much against, and Publikely reproved wheresoever he came, and withall gave his man a charge; that if the *Clerk of the Market* sent for his Bushell to cut it, he should not carry it in, which was done accordingly, for which he came into some trouble, but the Lord delivered him out of the same. Also at this time though his Bushell was bigger then other mens, yet he would often charge his man not to strike off all the Corn. He used not to trouble himself with reckonings and accounts, but would sometimes ask his man when he came from the Market, how he sold Corn? and if it was dear, he would say, *I pray God bring down the price of it;* and if it was Cheap, he would heartily blesse God for it. Yea, his Charity was not onely extended to the poor of his own Parish, but to others also; for if at any time he had seen a poor body at a distance from him as he rode abroad, he would send his man with money to him; and when at any time he rode by the Castle at *Cambridge*, the Prisoners would never ask him for any thing, nor any one that was with him, for if he had any money in his Purse, they were sure to have part of it. By reason of his great Liberality, though his living was worth a hundred pound *per Annum*,[183] yet he usually wanted Money to get in his Harvest, so that his Wife (formerly Doctor *Bounds* Widow) was forced to borrow money to supply that want: Yet was he so well content with his present Condition that though he had proffers of livings worth three of that which he had, yet would he by no meanes be perswaded to accept of them.

He was a great Friend to, and promoter of Peace and Concord amongst his Neighbours and Acquaintance, insomuch that if any had come to him who were at Variance, he would

[180]The grain measures are as follows: 4 pecks = 1 bushel; 4 bushels = 1 coomb; 2 coombs = 1 quarter. The price being charged was 16d per bushel, fully 2s less than market price.

[181]One noble = 6s8d. Thirsk's indexed price of barley dropped from 697 in 1586 to 361 in 1587. The drop described by Clarke is far more dramatic, but that can be easily explained by taking into account that the index uses the average over the entire year and does not reflect local variations. Figures: Thirsk, ed., *Agrarian History*, 819.

[182]*Orders Devised by the Special Commandment of the Queen's Majesty for the Relief and Ease of the Present Dearth of Grain within the Realm* (1586). See also *Tudor Royal Proclamations*, #686 (2 January 1586/7). A statute of 2 Henry VII had standardized bushels at eight gallons, but in some places a larger bushel was in use creating a hardship for merchants. The royal orders sought to restore the eight gallon standard.

[183]According to the *Valor Ecclesiasticus* (3: 502), the living was worth just over £21 in 1535. The figure of £100 would have been accurate for Clarke's time (*VCH, Cambs.*, 9: 85) but not for the 1570s and 1580s.

either have made them friends himself, or if he could not prevail, he would have made use of other Friends to reconcile them together, thereby to prevent their going to Law.

When *Martin Mar Prelate* came first out,[184] Master *Greenham* being to preach at *St. Maries* in *Cambridge*, spake freely against that Book, manifesting his dislike of the same: For (said he) the tendency of this Book is to make sin ridiculous, whereas it ought to be made odious.

On a time the Bishop of *Ely* sent for him, to appear about his Nonconformity: At which time the Bishop told him that there was a great Schisme in the Church, asking him where the blame was to be laid, whether upon the Conformists, or Non-conformists? To which he readily answered, that it might lie on either side, or on neither side: For (said he) if they loved one another as they ought, and would do all good Offices each for other, thereby maintaining Love and Concord, it lay on neither side: otherwise, which party soever makes the Rent, the Schism lies upon their score. The Bishop was so pleased with this answer, that he dismissed him in Peace.

He was much troubled with a bad Concoction, whereby he had frequent sick Nights, which kept him much waking; but then his manner was (as much as possibly he could) to spend the time in Meditation and Prayer.

We have before heard of his great Charity to mens Bodies: His Charity to Souls was not less exemplary. For having great Experience, and an excellent Faculty to relieve and comfort distressed Consciences, he was sought to, far and near, by such as groaned under spiritual Afflictions and Temptations: all whom he entertained friendly and familiarly, without respecting the person of the rich more than of the poor.

Yea the fame of this spiritual *Physician* so spread abroad, that he was sent for to very many, and the Lord was pleased so farre to blesse his labours, that by his knowledge and experience many were restored to joy and comfort, out of unspeakable and insupportable terrours and torments of conscience.[185] If the Lord had not so soon translated him out of this sinfull and miserable world, there was none more fit, nor willing to have prescribed Rules, and a Method to be observed in this so little a known Art. Of his good will herein, let his own words testifie the forward desires of his heart: For upon a special occasion he thus speaketh of himself; I have had (saith he) for a long time a settled resolution, (which I hope is from God) to study the cases of Conscience, that thereby I may be the better able to succour the tempted and perplexed in spirit.

He was filled with bowels of compassion towards the afflicted, sympathizing, as if he had been afflicted with them.

Many godly and learned friends of his, perceiving his abilities and inclinations thereto, did labour much to excite and incourage him in those studies, upon these and the like grounds. First, that he might hereby the better train up some young men in the like studies, communicating his knowledge and experiences to them therein. Secondly, that he might leave to posterity a Commentary of such particular Maladies as God had made him instrumental in the cure of, together with the meanes by him used for effecting of the same. And because Precepts are wanting, Rules of direction might be framed, partly by his own observation, partly by conference with other learned and experienced persons, whereby in that, and the age following, that Art might be brought into some form and method, to the publick good and benefit of many, not only for the fruitfull curing, but also for the healthfull preventing of manifold mischief.

---

[184]1589.

[185]This is almost a direct quote from *Works* (1599), A5r.

Appendix: "The Life of Master Richard Greenham"

To such as complained to him that they were troubled with blasphemous thoughts, his counsell was, that they should not fear them, but abhorre them. And when some Poor Christians were miserably afflicted with feares, that they had committed that unpardonable sinne against the holy Ghost, he used to tell them, that if they would not have committed it, it was certain that they had not faln into it.

The graces of Gods Spirit did all abundantly shine forth in this man of God: all tempered, as with unfeigned love to *Christ*, so with bowels of love and compassion towards men; and he again was greatly beloved of all men.

In the whole course of his Ministry, he was very carefull ever to avoid (as much as was Possible) all occasions of offence, desiring in all things to approve himself as a Minister of *Christ*, and Work-man that needed not to be ashamed.[186]

He much reioyced in, and Praised God for the happy government of Queen *Elizabeth*, and for the blessed calm and peace which the Church and People of God enjoyed under the same, speaking often of it, both publickly and privately, as he had occasion, endeavouring to stirre up the hearts of all men (as much as in him lay) to Praise God with him for it, and to pray also for the continuance thereof. Yea this matter so affected him, that the day before his departure out of this world, his thoughts were much troubled, for that most men were so unthankfull for those wonderfull and happy deliverances, which the Lord of his mercy vouchsafed to that glorious Queen, from the conspiracies and dangerous practices of her *Popish* Adversaries.[187]

He was a special Instrument and meanes under God to incourage, and train up many godly and learned young men in the holy service of *Christ*, in the work of the Ministry; and to restrain, and reduce not a few from errours and *Schisme*;[188] striving by all meanes to retain them in obedience to the Lawes of the land, and to Provoke them highly to Prize, and preciously to esteem the peace of the Church, and People of God.

Having continued at *Dry-Drayton* about the space of twenty, or one and twenty years, he left it, and went from thence to *London*, about the year 1588, or 89.[189] Yet was very carefull before his remove, to get an honest and able man to succeed him in that place.[190]

---

[186]*Works* (1599), A5v.

[187]*Works* (1599), A5v. A marginal notation in *Works* makes clear that Greenham was mindful especially of the case of Roderigo Lopez. Lopez, a Portuguese Jew, had lived in England since 1559 and practiced medicine successfully in London. Queen Elizabeth I became one of his patients in 1586. In January of 1594, the earl of Essex announced his discovery of "a most dangerous and desperate treason," namely that Lopez was to be paid 30,000 crowns by the Spanish commander in the Low Countries for poisoning the queen. Essex presided over the trial which was held in the Guildhall on 28 February at which Sir Edward Coke, in the role of chief prosecutor, denounced Lopez as "a perjured and murdering villain...worse than Judas himself." Although Lopez was condemned to death at his trial, the queen did not sign the death warrant for three months and he was not executed until 7 June 1594. Clearly this trial would have been well known to Londoners such as Greenham was at the time. For details of the Lopez affair, see Wallace T. MacCaffrey, *Elizabeth I: War and Politics 1588–1603* (Princeton: Princeton University Press, 1992), 484; Lacey Baldwin Smith, *Treason in Tudor England. Politics and Paranoia* (Princeton: Princeton University Press, 1986), 209–210; *DNB*, sub Lopez, Roderigo.

[188]*Works* (1599), A5v.

[189]The correct date is 1591. See above, 187. Clarke's error in dating is inexplicable, especially in light of what follows, namely the correct reference to Greenham's having remained in Dry Drayton for 21 years. The error further complicates Clarke's calculation of Greenham's death date.

[190]Richard Warfield.

The Causes of his Removal, were, partly the untractableness and unteachableness of that people amongst whom he had taken such exceeding great paines. For besides his publick Preaching and Catechizing, his manner was to walk out into the Fields, and to confer with his Neighbours as they were at Plough: And partly he did it upon supposal that he might do far more good in a more publick place by comforting afflicted Consciences, wherein the Lord had given him such an admirable dexterity.

He wholly spent himself in the Service of God and his Church, and therefore often made use of that saying of the Prophet *David: The Zeal of thy House hath eaten me up.*[191]

He was a little Man of Stature, and usually indifferent well in Health; but when at any time he was sick, he would suffer no body to sit up and Watch with him, that so he might more freely converse with God.

He continued not in *London* above the space of two years, but being quite worn out, he comfortably and quietly resigned up his Spirit unto God, *An: Christi* 1591,[192] and about the sixtieth year of his Age.

He hath a Volume of Sermons, and Treatises of Divinity in Print.

[191]Ps. 69:9.
[192]The correct year is 1594; see above, 147.

PART 4

WILLS *and* PIETY

"DEPARTING WELL AND CHRISTIANLY"

WILL-MAKING AND POPULAR RELIGION IN EARLY MODERN ENGLAND[1]

Christopher Marsh

To MODIFY A WELL-KNOWN PROVERB, "Where there's a will, there's a group of historians arguing over what it tells them about popular religion." Wills remain one of the principal sources available to those working in this field, but in recent years their status as authentic testaments of individual faith has been called increasingly into doubt.[2] Few today would agree with W. K. Jordan's description of wills, penned in 1959, as "completely honest documents" and "mirrors of mens' souls." "Almost every will," he wrote, "begins with a carefully considered and eloquently elaborated confession of faith, in which the testator earnestly strives to set out the nature of his beliefs, to confess his own inadequacies, to confirm his confidence in the mercy of God, and to prepare himself for a death which he believes to be imminent."[3] Subsequent scholarship has rendered such wishful thinking untenable, and a majority of historians now feel rather closer to the position of Rosemary O'Day, expressed in 1986: "Far from revealing the religious beliefs of the average testator, wills and their preambles hide them from the historian's gaze."[4]

---

[1]This revised version of the author's essay, "In the Name of God? Will-making and Faith in Early Modern England," which appeared in *The Records of the Nation*, ed. G. H. Martin and Peter Spufford (Woodbridge, Suffolk: Boydell, 1990), appears by permission.
[2]See, for example, Claire Cross, "Wills as evidence of popular piety in the Reformation period. Leeds and Hull, 1540–1640," in *The End of Strife*, ed. David Loades (Edinburgh: T. & T. Clark, 1984), 44–51; J. D. Alsop, "Religious Preambles in Early Modern English Wills as Formulae," *Journal of Ecclesiastical History* 40 (1989): 40–50; Eamon Duffy, *The Stripping of the Altars: Traditional Religion in England 1400–1580* (New Haven: Yale University Press, 1992), ch. 15.
[3]W. K. Jordan, *Philanthropy in England, 1480–1640: A Study of the Changing Pattern of English Social Aspirations* (London: George Allen and Unwin, 1959), 16.
[4]Rosemary O'Day, *The Debate on the English Reformation* (London and New York: Methuen and Co., 1986), 157.

The use of wills was pioneered by historians investigating the early spread of Reformation doctrines in sixteenth-century England. From the start, however, there were difficulties. A. G. Dickens, aware that wills were perhaps not all that they seemed, cautioned historians against analyzing them "in any spirit of statistical pedantry." Margaret Spufford amplified the warning, and changed the nature of the debate by discussing the actual mechanics of will-making, and by emphasizing the importance of considering the broader local context in which any particular will was written.[5] Still the problems remained. Testators whose deep faith is known from independent sources sometimes made wills with short, unexpressive preambles, even when they were well enough to sign their names and when their particular brand of faith was in harmony with that established by law. Individual historians have also been frustrated when, after discovering a long, expressive preamble and classifying it as a deeply personal account of beliefs, their attention has been drawn to an identical preamble written a hundred miles away. Were some, or many, testators simply transcribing their preambles from printed formularies?[6]

Most recently, the techniques and interpretations used by historians in studying sixteenth-century wills have been roundly criticized by Eamon Duffy. He has argued, convincingly in the main, that insufficient account has been taken of the external pressures on testators. In Dr. Duffy's view, shifts in the wording of preambles tell us more about official religious changes and the common-sense obedience of the majority of people than about any genuine transformation of popular faith. He has argued, furthermore, that dedicatory clauses normally classified as Protestant or reformist were not necessarily anything of the sort. The orthodox traditional religion of most contemporary believers was just as Christocentric as that of their radical opponents. Midcentury preambles that declared reliance upon faith in Christ and omitted mention of the Blessed Virgin Mary were just as likely to come from traditionalists as from reformers. There are certainly some weak points in Dr. Duffy's argument, which never

---

[5]A. G. Dickens, *Lollards and Protestants in the Diocese of York, 1509–1558* (repr., London: Hambledon Press, 1982), 171; Margaret Spufford, *Contrasting Communities: English Villagers in the Sixteenth and Seventeenth Centuries* (Cambridge: Cambridge University Press, 1974), 333–334.

[6]For perspectives on this issue see John Craig and Caroline Litzenberger, "Wills as Religious Propaganda: The Testament of William Tracy," *Journal of Ecclesiastical History* 44 (1993): 415–31; Eric Josef Carlson, "The Historical Value of the Ely Consistory Probate Records," in *Index of the Probate Records of the Consistory Court of Ely 1449–1858*, ed. Elisabeth Leedham-Green and Rosemary Rodd, 3 vols. (London: The British Record Society, 1994–96), I:xxxvi–xlvi.

quite establishes that testators hoping for salvation only—rather than primarily—through faith in Christ were as frequently Catholic as Protestant; but the central point, that historians have used wills with a far higher degree of confidence than seems warranted, is certainly a forceful one.[7]

Not surprisingly, in view of this warning, it has also been noted that the wills of particular communities are not necessarily reliable in the way they reflect the ecclesiastical history of those communities.[8] Moreover, it has generally proved impossible to establish the authorship of individual preambles. Did testators generally compose or select the expressions themselves, or did the scribes they employed simply write down their own set formulae before taking advice on the temporal bequests? We need to know, in short, whether early modern testators viewed their wills as spiritual documents and testaments of faith, or whether the majority—including some of exceptional piety—were really only concerned with the disposal of worldly possessions. It may, of course, be inappropriate to distinguish so clearly between the two attitudes.

The lay people of England themselves were apparently becoming increasingly interested in the idea of making wills as the sixteenth century progressed. Across many dioceses, the numbers of wills proved annually seems to have been rising, though the exact takeoff point probably varied. The reasons for this broad increase are unclear and, unfortunately, beyond the scope of this paper. It appears, however, that an investigation of the social and spiritual context within which wills were written may be instructive. The primary aim of this paper is therefore to explore the procedures and attitudes that accompanied will-making. This will be done by studying a variety of source materials, including contemporary literature on dying well, the records from disputed will cases, and new evidence relating to the use of printed formularies. Attention will focus particularly on the composition and importance of the religious preambles that opened most wills. The sources under view may also permit some fresh insights into the nature of popular religion during the transformation still known by some as the English Reformation. Finally, suggestions will be made concerning the manner in which historians of religion can best make use of wills in the future. Optimistically, it will be suggested that where there is a will, there is indeed a way.

---

[7]Duffy, *Stripping of the Altars*, ch. 15.
[8]Spufford, *Contrasting Communities*, 335.

∾

The Reformation transformed many things, but it made little impact on the preoccupation of contemporaries with death and mortality. Literature in what may broadly be called the *ars moriendi* tradition was still written, as Helen White and others have shown.[9] This provides an early indication of what may become one of the main themes of sixteenth-century religious history in the next decade: the role of strong continuities with the medieval past in making the Reformation manageable and comprehensible for those who lived through it. There may, of course, have been important differences in attitude between godly Protestant writers and the will-making laity at large; men like Thomas Becon were presumably more likely than most Elizabethans to set a high importance on the spiritual context of will-making, and on the religious expressions contained in preambles. Nevertheless, the treatises they wrote provide a suitable starting point for this investigation of attitudes to will-making.

Becon's *The Sicke Mans Salve* first appeared in the late 1550s and enjoyed a popularity which necessitated almost thirty reprints to 1632.[10] *The Sicke Mans Salve*, though punctuated with aggressive anti-Catholic digressions, owed a considerable debt to works of the older genre. It is written in the form of a conversation between the ailing Epaphroditus and four of his trusted neighbors: Philemon, Eusebius, Theophilus, and Christopher. Epaphroditus, aware of his worsening sickness, decides to dispose of his worldly goods, "that after my departure there be no dissention nor strife for them, among such as I most wishe to be linked together with perpetual amitie and continuall friendship." He adds: "It shall also I trust, be a great quietnes unto my mind."[11]

The would-be testator accepts graciously a gentle admonition from Philemon for having delayed the matter so long, and concedes "that no man is certaine of his life until to morrowe: therefore ought we all to watch, and to provide that we be not founde unreadie when the Lord commeth." He then turns to "neighbour Theophilus" and says "I praie you bring hither pen, inke, & paper, with all expedition, and let my will be written." While

---

[9]Helen White, *English Devotional Literature 1600–1640* (Madison: University of Wisconsin Press, 1931); Sister Mary Catharine O'Connor, *The Art of Dying Well: The Development of the Ars Moriendi* (New York: Columbia University Press, 1942).

[10]Thomas Becon, *The Sicke Mans Salve* (London, c. 1558–59). The STC notes 28 reprints. My references are to the 1594 imprint.

[11]Ibid., 89–90.

Theophilus runs his errand, Epaphroditus treats his other friends to a self-congratulatory speech on the godly manner in which he has ever viewed his goods: "I have alwaies made them to serve me, and I never served them, but at al times could be contented to depart from them whensoever the glorie of God, and the commodity of my Neighbour did require." Suitably impressed, Christopher comments, "Then did you use your goods aright."[12]

The slowly-dying testator proceeds to dictate the preamble to an exceptionally pious will. His words are worth quoting at length:

> I Epaphroditus, the unprofitable servant of God, weak in bodie, and notwithstanding, strong in mind; doo willingly and with a free heart, render and give again into the hands of the Lord my God, my spirit which he of his fatherly goodnesse gave unto me, when hee fashioned this my body in my mothers wombe, by this meanes making me a living creature, nothing doubting but that this my Lord God for his mercies sake, set forth in the pretious blood of his deerely beloved son, Christ Jesu our alone saviour and redeemer wil receive my soule into his glorie, and place it in the companie of the heavenlie angels and blessed saintes.

Without pausing for breath, the testator goes on to make a similarly long and expressive statement on the future of his body:

> nothing doubting, but that according to the article of our faith, at the great day of the generall resurrection, when wee shall al appeare before the judgement seate of Christ, I shall receive it againe by the mighty power of God, wherwith he is able to subdue all thinges to himselfe, not a corruptible, mortall, weake and vile bodie, as it is now, but an uncorruptible, immortal strong, perfect [body], and in al points like unto the glorious body of my Lord and saviour Christ Jesus.[13]

Epaphroditus then asks his scribe if these expressions have been accurately recorded. Philemon's reply may sound a little impatient to the modern ear: "Yea forsooth sir. But what is your mind now concerning your worldly possessions?" It must be assumed that Becon's tongue was some way from his cheek, though the remark does serve to remind us that many

---

[12]Ibid., 90–91.
[13]Ibid., 92–93.

genuinely dying Elizabethans probably did not have the time to record their beliefs in such detail.

Epaphroditus continues to dictate, beginning with a personal pronouncement on "the blessed state of honourable Wedlocke," in which he refers to his wife, "with whome I coupled my selfe in the feare of God, and refusing all other women."[14] Not surprisingly, every bequest and statement is underpinned by some religious conviction, eloquently articulated by a testator whose periodic expressions of physical torment ("O Lord how sicke am I?") soon begin to lose their pathos. It is his duty before God to provide for his offspring, and to contribute to numerous pious causes. Epaphroditus forgives all his debtors "unto the uttermost farthing even as I would God the father should forgive me all my debts for Christ's sake." He remembers the struggling scholars at Oxford and Cambridge, and directs his overseers to his counting house where, in four bags each labeled "Money for the poore," they will find hundreds of pounds for the immediate relief of more commonplace poverty. In addition, the testator leaves money for highway repairs and provides for the delivery of eighty sermons following his departure from this "vale of myserie."[15]

Such obvious strength of faith notwithstanding, the will-making forms no more than a short section in a lengthy work. When read in context it does not seem such a fully integral part of the testator's final preparations for death. Certainly, it is the Christian's essential duty to settle his estate, on loan from God, in a manner which demonstrates gratitude and faith, and serves to signal—but not cause—his salvation. This settlement should not, however, have been left until the last sickness set in; there is a clear sense in which the will-making is viewed as a necessary but undesirable distraction, something to be completed in order that the testator can focus on more important matters in the immediate approach to death.

Having made his will, Epaphroditus is free to deliver exhortations to his wife, his children, and his servants. There are numerous prayers and a personal confession of faith which far exceeds that seen in the will preamble.[16] The will had been signed and sealed by page 120 (in the 1594 edition); the testator eventually "gave up the ghost" on page 353. Moreover, the participants in this overpoweringly godly conversation placed no direct

---

[14]Ibid., 93.
[15]Ibid., 93–104.
[16]Ibid., 155–77, 178–81, 183–92.

emphasis on the dedicatory clause, a significant omission since they are at continual pains to highlight specifically all points of importance. Epaphroditus was an individual of deep faith and therefore felt moved to include in his will a long and pious preamble, but it was rendered almost superfluous by the subsequent oral declarations of belief. An expressive preamble was not, so far as we can tell, a crucial part of his Christian responsibility. The real duty a testator performed in making a will was to dispose of his or her wealth in a godly fashion.

The same preoccupations emerge from similar works by William Perkins (1595), William Perneby (1599), and Christopher Sutton (1600).[17] All see the rendering of the soul to God as an essential part of the sick person's duty, but none places any emphasis on doing this in a will. For Perneby, the dying man, by making a will, "dothe...procure himself the more quiet in mind, the greater libertie to attend upon God and his pleasure; the best opportunity that may be to frame himselfe to another world." Perkins was explicit in regarding the will-making as an unwelcome interruption; he decided somewhat reluctantly to discuss it, even "though the making of wills belong to another place and profession."[18] Again, the implication is that modern historians, faced with little option, have focused on will preambles much more intensely than did contemporaries, including those contemporaries who wrote books teaching men and women to die in faith. When William Perkins made his own will in 1602/3 he further reinforced the point; his dedicatory clause ran: "I commend my soul into the hands of God, in Christ hoping assuredly to dye in that faith w[hi]ch I have professed & preached."[19] For a full expression of "that faith," we are to look elsewhere. Amongst these Elizabethan writers, Thomas Becon was in fact unusual in even implying by example that a pious preamble was of any significance.

For authors who stressed the sufficiency of Scripture as a guide in all situations, this lack of emphasis on the desirability of long and expressive will preambles was not, in fact, surprising. Several of them referred to biblical examples when they instructed people to bequeath their souls to God

[17]William Perkins, *A salve for a sicke man* (Cambridge, 1595); William Perneby, *A direction to death* (London, 1599); Christopher Sutton, *Disce Mori: Learne to die* (London, 1600).

[18]Perneby, *A direction*, 237; Perkins, *A salve*, 84.

[19]C[ambridge] U[niversity] L[ibrary], Wills proved in the Vice Chancellor's Court, January 1602–3. I am grateful to Dr. Ian Archer for bringing the existence of this will to my attention and to Dr. Peter Spufford for discovering in which court, and when, the will was proved.

as death approached. When Stephen was stoned to death, Perkins reminded his readers, he said "Lord Jesus receive my spirit." David had been similarly concise. There was little indication that lengthy expression was considered necessary. Such expression was not, of course, undesirable, but the godly person could perform his or her duty merely by following the examples of David and Stephen. It is a curious fact that if the words of Christ on the cross were to be included in the historian's dedicatory clause classification system, they would be judged neutral. There may then be a fault in our registering surprise that persons of known piety sometimes left neutral will preambles. Becon and Perkins had been dead for many years before one solitary writer made a direct plea for expressive preambles.[20]

The disposal of goods—whether in a will or not—was, however, a task with powerful spiritual overtones. The writers all agreed upon the necessity of promoting peace amongst one's friends and relatives. A will, said the worldly wise Perkins, "cuttes off much hatred and contention in families and it staies many suits in law." The man who neglected to settle his estate had failed in his responsibility to God. Perneby pursued the same line and warned that neighbors would say of such a shirker that "It is a great pitie that he did not set all things at a stay. You will not beleeve what ado heere is thereupon in the countrie. No peace among his children, no love betweene his friends, no quiet to any of his neighbours." The man "whom God hath indued with grace" was unlikely to leave such turmoil behind him.[21]

The testator, by consensus, had additional related responsibilities. Perkins placed particular emphasis upon an individual's duty before God to provide adequately for his children, and quoted St. Paul to reinforce the point. Perneby was especially keen on the notion that, by a godly disposal of goods, the testator was working to the glory of his Maker: "For a man making his will well and wisely doth thereby provoke others to glorifie God for giving him…wisedome so to dispose of the things of this life, and to imitate him in the like."[22] Each writer further stressed that the sick man was to restore ill-gotten goods to their rightful owners, and that he had a responsibility to make charitable bequests.

[20]See below, 210.
[21]Perkins, *A salve*, 83; Perneby, *A direction*, 237–238.
[22]Perkins, *A salve*, 85; Perneby, *A direction*, 237.

The authors also passed comment on the foolish tendency of people to neglect making wills. Perkins identified as common reasons a desire to conceal wealth and a fear that will-making was somehow tempting to death. Perneby, again following suspiciously hot in Perkins' footsteps, assured the reader that "though…he makes a thousand wills (if it were possible for one man to make so many) yet shall he die never the sooner." Having scorned such superstitious nonsense, Perneby proceeded to warn, a little inconsistently, that the evil inherent in ill-gotten goods would cleave to them still, bringing nothing but harm to the receiver.[23]

The extent to which most of these words of wisdom represented a direct continuation of advice given out by pre-Reformation moralists is striking. The matters emphasized by Becon and company had also characterized *ars moriendi* literature of the fifteenth century: the unpredictability of death and the importance of careful preparation; the need to promote Christian peace and charity; the communal nature of Christian responsibility in the face of death; the testator's need to procure spiritual peace of mind before approaching death; and the duty of glorifying God through one's worldly bequests and exemplary conduct on the deathbed. Perhaps it was the existence of continuous threads such as these, linking the Catholic past with the Protestant future, that made the English Reformation such a complex and unusual creature. Certainly, they must have made it seem considerably more familiar and understandable in the eyes of the majority of ordinary people. It is arguable that, for complicated and controversial reasons, historians of the period have tended to exaggerate the enormity and violence of the shock, particularly at the village level.

Nevertheless, the early modern period was of course one of marked and significant transition in a wide variety of spheres. Under Elizabeth I, writers like Perneby were already sharing space on the bookshelf with legal experts on will-making. In 1590, Henry Swinburne wrote *A briefe treatise of testaments and last willes* and made no mention of faith. Perneby referred specifically to the work, which he said was "common in everie Stationers open shop, or in each Civilian's private studie." The seventeenth century saw an equally dry contribution from John Godolphin. In practice too, as several modern commentators have observed, the situation was changing as clergymen steadily lost their traditional role at will-makings, and testamentary

---

[23]Perneby, *A direction*, 240, 251.

causes appeared increasingly in the Court of Chancery, rather than in the church courts.[24]

As the seventeenth century drew to a close, William Assheton, rector of a Kent parish, set his back against what he admitted was a changing fashion, and made one last appeal on behalf of religiously grounded wills. Assheton was clearly a divine on the defensive, and he felt the need to justify his purpose in a way that would have surprised a medieval priest: "And though it must be granted, That to Discourse of Wills and Testaments is chiefly the lawyer's Province; yet, I hope, it will be thought no unsuitable theme for a Divine.... For though your lawyer can best direct you to draw your will Legally and in Form; yet a Divine may be allowed to instruct you how to make it Charitably, and I may add Prudently, and consequently to your Comfort."[25]

Assheton recited some of the motivations described by the Elizabethan writers, and criticized many of the still-common failings. Confusedly, he pleaded with his readers to make their wills "in the time of health" but persistently described a will-making as the last, the concluding act of a person's life. He also sought to imbue England's testators with a sense of their personal place in history, urging them to "Remember your Will stands upon Record for Publick perusal; and therefore to be idle and extravagant in this last Act of your life, is to be hiss'd off the Stage, and to proclaim your folly to all succeeding ages."[26]

Assheton differed significantly from his Elizabethan predecessors in his statements concerning the will preamble. He told his readers to "let your Will be so composed, so framed and worded in the commendatory Part, as to declare your self a Christian." Too many wills, he lamented, broke off abruptly following a depressingly short dedicatory clause. He insisted that testators should "give...a reason of the hope that is in you," and suggested his own lengthy formula for a preamble.[27]

It seems unlikely that by the very late seventeenth century, Assheton could have expected much success in having his elaborate clause adopted. Within decades, the whole notion of a religiously worded preamble was under threat and the way was clear for the modern-style, faith-free solicitors'

[24]Ibid., 242; John Godolphin, *The orphan's legacy: or, A testamentary abridgement* (London, 1674); Anthony J. Camp, *Wills and Their Whereabouts* (London: the author, 1974), xxiv.
[25]William Assheton, *A theological discourse of last wills and testaments* (London, 1696), 2–3.
[26]Ibid., 20.
[27]Ibid., 18–19.

testament, written "in the time of health," and so lacking in color that few but the testator's relatives are tempted to study it. Assheton's personally and probably doomed attempt to reverse the process in fact looks like a spirited death rattle, performed on behalf of the traditional will.

∾

Becon's Epaphroditus was unusual. Very few testators expressed themselves at such length on questions of faith. Even the *ars moriendi* authors, with the exception of Assheton, did not encourage them to change their ways. It is tempting to speculate on the circumstances and motivation of the rare testators who did expound their beliefs at length. The state of an individual's health was an obvious factor, since detailed expression was unlikely from a testator who lacked both time and energy. The depth of an individual's faith must also have been influential, though not as clearly so as one might expect. It may not have been so much the strength of belief that set unusually expressive testators apart, as the fact that they felt self-consciously pious as they composed their preambles. Epaphroditus, though only the figment of a godly imagination, was a perfect example. The self-styled "unprofitable servant of God" was so strikingly aware of his own piety that the description is hard to accept. Fortunately, there were occasionally others who proved similarly expressive.

In December 1571, Thomas Merburie, a student at Christ's College, Cambridge, made a will which he headed "I believe in God the father, god the sone, and god the holie ghost, three persons, but one eternall and ever lyvyng god, and I do fullie looke to be saved by thys my beleiff."[28] Merburie drew attention to the uncertainty of life, and recalled "we are admonished in the 24 of matthew contynuallie to watche for that we knowe not what howr our master wyll come." Owing to this uncertainty, Merburie had decided to make a will "wherebye god wyllnge yt shalbe evident to all that during my lieffe I held the profession & belief of a trew Christian man, and goddes grace so assistynge me wyll firmlie & stedfastlye die in the same."

An extraordinarily full confession of faith followed. The testator stated his belief in salvation through Christ's death, passion, resurrection, and ascension, "whitowt all vayne opinion of any mans merites, which I do utterly rejecte, detest & abhore as marvelous Injurious to the bludd of my saviour Jesus." Merburie, amongst a great many things, also expressed an

---

[28]CUL, Wills proved in the Vice Chancellor's Court 1558–1602, fol. 62.

unshakeable belief in his own election: "I feele inwardlye in my selfe and in my conscience that before all worldes I am predestinate to eternall liefe." He asked for a modest burial, shorn of hideous papist trappings, and ended with an affirmation of his belief in the certainty of his own resurrection, "when I shall heare that joyfull voyce, come ye blessed of my father inherite yee the kyngedome prepared for yow before the begynynge of the world."

There can be no doubt whatsoever that the faith expressed in this will was Merburie's own, and tiny numbers of similarly impressive preambles exist in most archives. We must be grateful that Merburie chose to record the details of his faith in such an expansive manner, though we should also recall that his attitude towards self-expression in a will was certainly not shared by all men of faith. The counterexamples, though less exciting, are more numerous. The will of William Perkins has already been cited. The case of Bishop Cooper of Winchester was similar. His will, written in 1594, opened with a conventional statement on mortality and bequeathed his soul "into the handes of my Redeemer," with no further comment.[29] It seems reasonable to assume that the bishop, author of a printed homily on the "right use of the Lord's Supper,"[30] could have discoursed upon his faith at rather greater length, had he felt that the moment was right.

Equally instructive was the will of Thomas Adam, an innholder from Saffron Walden, dated in December 1572.[31] Adam made his will, "considring the manyfold myseries, Calamities, maladies & perills of death emynate in my mortall body & howe sodenly in these dayes the mortalitye of lyfe of man is extinct to the ensample that other may learne to be redy.…When god shall call them." This is the most conscious attempt so far found on the part of a testator to influence his neighbors for the better. The phrases were not, apparently, used in other wills written in the same area at this time; they would, then, seem to reflect the personal feelings of the innholder or, less probably, of his scribe.

Adam recorded further reasons for making his will: "And as I am sure to dye so am I unsure & uncertaine when & howe shortlye therfor to the intent I wyll avoyd worldly trobles & vayne affections in the panges & agonye of death the wch at that tyme might perhappes withdrawe my

---

[29] *Lincoln Episcopal Records in the Time of Thomas Cooper*, ed. C. W. Foster, Lincoln Record Society, 2 (Lincoln, 1912), 339.

[30] Thomas Cooper, *A briefe homily, wherein the most comfortable and right use of the Lord's Supper is very plainly opened and delivered* (London, 1580).

[31] Essex C[ounty] R[ecord] O[ffice], 336 CR 6.

mynde & godlye zeale to depart well and Chrystyanlye And furtermore to establish a direct order in the distribucion of such worldly goodes and riches as God hath lent me for the better quietness of my posteritie & succession."

Despite such expressiveness, the dedicatory clause, when it eventually came, was brief in the extreme. The testator was clearly a man whose faith meant a great deal to him, but he wrote merely "I bequeath my soul to Almighty God." Adam agreed with the godly authors that the will-making was an unwelcome distraction in the approach to death. He made his will in order that he would be able "to depart well and Chrystyanlye" when the moment arrived. His commendatory clause was neutral by any standards, because he did not regard his will as the appropriate place for a full-blown confession of faith. He may well have made such a confession at another time.

As in the pre-Reformation period, it was the subsequent worldly bequests that really reflected the strength of a testator's faith. In 1586, a yeoman named William Rushbrigg from Emneth in Norfolk made a will which displayed a short and wholly unexceptional dedicatory clause.[32] Rushbrigg demonstrated his piety instead with bequests to his church, his vicar, and the poor of his village. If his son died, the will continued, Rushbrigg's entire estate was to be used for the benefit of the poor and the community, despite the implied existence (in the form of a cousin) of more distant kin. The testator left money for the erection of an almshouse, the construction of a gate at the church stile, the repairing of the church way, the diking of the river, and the building of a bridge, "for people safely to passe." Additionally, he requested a burial sermon, four further sermons, and made extensive extra gifts to the poor.

If the legatee William Hall was truly the testator's cousin, he may—depending on his temperament and beliefs—have felt a little aggrieved to see such wealth pass out of the family. Hall received bequests that were small in comparison, though they perhaps enabled him to understand better his cousin's motives: "one pair of spectacles, one service book, and another booke callyd the Sick mans salve." Rushbrigg was obviously familiar with his Christian duty as described by Becon, and a couple of his phrases remind one of the great writer, yet he ignored completely the

---

[32]Camb[ridgeshire] C[ounty] R[ecord] O[ffice], E[ly] P[robate] R[ecords], C[onsistory Court] W[ill] 1586. I am grateful to Professor Eric Carlson for bringing this will to my attention.

implied message that a preamble, like that of Epaphroditus (the not so unprofitable servant of God), should be long and expressive. The Emneth testator was evidently thinking clearly when he made his will—so detailed was it in other respects—but he appears to have seen the full expression of his faith in the preamble as something superfluous and unnecessary. His charitable bequests spoke for themselves.

There appears, then, to have been a common body of motives uniting godly writers and godly testators. Interestingly, this unity can also be extended back in time, to encompass many of the medieval *ars moriendi* authors. None of the Elizabethan writers would have acknowledged this, focusing instead on the differences between them and their predecessors. Nevertheless, considerable areas of overlap are clear. Godly Elizabethans generally wrote wills because it was their Christian duty before God to settle their estates, of which they had been but stewards, in such a way as to promote peace, "stay disputes," and glorify God. The social nature of this duty deserves prominent emphasis, since historians have sometimes drawn connections between Protestantism, individualism, and the breakup of the traditional community. In fulfilling their responsibilities, godly testators also hoped to reach a state of spiritual tranquility, essential if they were to die "Christianly." There was also an element, sometimes at least, in which testators saw it as their responsibility to set an example to others, to lead their neighbors into similarly godly practice. Within this framework of spiritual motives and choices, a pious and eloquently elaborated preamble can perhaps be classified as "a thing indifferent."

◦⌣◦

Most of the evidence discussed so far relates to persons who had taken Protestantism to heart, who had been particularly receptive to reformed teachings. For the will-making population at large, conclusions are harder to reach. It was possible, then as now, to decide to make a will on grounds that had little to do with faith: complicated personal affairs, the desire to remember close and not necessarily godly friends, or a vain urge to influence events after one's death. All such concerns could be discussed without reference to God, even in an age when religion in English society was far more pervasive than it is today.

A small but significant minority of wills became the subjects of litigation, most frequently in the ecclesiastical courts. It is to the records of such causes that we must look in an attempt to carry this examination of testamentary motives out of godly circles and into society as a whole. The following discussion is based upon over forty disputed will cases in the dioceses of Ely, London, Exeter, Durham, and Winchester.[33]

Testamentary cause records sometimes yield to the historian a quantity of vivid detail which cannot be guessed at from the wills themselves. They are essential sources for students of death, and frequently reveal striking pictures of deathbed scenes and attitudes, including the bonds of kinship and neighborliness in the face of sickness and death and, particularly, the circumstances of will-making, and the spiritual motivation, if any, that lay behind it. There are obviously certain questions of reliability to be considered when interpreting these records. Incidents of deception are likely, especially when dealing with men like John Lawson of Darwen (Durham), described by one neighbor as "but a runner and a slave, that will say as any man will have him for a peic of bread."[34] Similarly, it can be argued that court records, by definition, describe those cases which fell outside the accepted framework of things. In countering this criticism, it is customary to observe that, even so, such records cast their own perverse light upon the norms of behavior and the expectations of local societies. Furthermore, in many of the cases, different witnesses presented their own recollections of what were clearly the same events. It does seem possible to establish a factual core; this is, after all, exactly what the courts were seeking to do.

Evidence relating to the physical circumstances of testators at the time of will-making reveals, not surprisingly, a number of common characteristics. Most were sick, though by no means all were in the final throes of disease. The "darts of death" were perceived to be on their way, but impact was not always imminent. The vicar of Sutton (Ely) arrived at the house of William Bateman, "wheare in a kytecyen...he found the sayd testator sitting by the fyr side." A widow from Little Shelford (Ely) was "lyinge uppon hir bed in a redd kertle haveing a quilte lyinge uppon hir." A clerical testator from Swavesey (Ely) was sick "in his chamber where he used always to lye hanged with paynted clothes wherein was iii beds."[35] There were many similar examples.

---

[33]I have used manuscript court records for the dioceses of Ely, London, Exeter, and Winchester. The Durham cases are taken from *Depositions and other Ecclesiastical Proceedings from the Courts of Durham*, ed. James Raine, Surtees Society, 21 (1845).

[34]*Depositions*, 265–276.

[35]CUL, E[ly] D[iocesan] R[ecords], D/2/6, fol. 22; D/2/11, fol.109; D/2/7, fol. 256.

The procedures employed in making wills also display common features. The basic pattern—calling witnesses, making the will, hearing it read, and ratifying it—was followed in numerous cases. When the details are examined further, however, there is found to be a surprisingly wide variety of practices, not all of which will be comforting to historians who count wills among their chief sources.

The Sutton (Ely) testator, William Bateman, went one better than Epaphroditus by deciding to make his will "in his good health." The will had in fact been "conceyved in writing" sometime before Bateman chose to finalize it in the presence of witnesses. Still healthy, the testator summoned several villagers to his home, including his scribe—a layman called Daniel Morton—and the local vicar, Simon Nappe. Morton then read the will to the testator, who acknowledged it as his own. The document was not dated at its original writing but at the point when Bateman ratified it for the last time.

Ironically, the testator's commendable foresight was to backfire on the night of his death. It seems that, because of changed circumstances, Bateman had wished to revise his will shortly before his decease. He had, however, been unable to have it set in writing because, as Robert Claybell informed the court, "one Danyell who should have bene the writer was in Bedd and felt himself not then well and sayd in the morning he would helpe them as earlye as they would." When Daniel Morton arrived the next day, he may have experienced feelings of guilt at finding the testator no longer "sitting by the fyr side" but "dead in a chamber." Bateman's widow then produced the first will, written by Morton, but another participant in the unfolding drama exclaimed "whye it skills no matter for that will, For the said William Bateman made another will [by word of mouth] this night and gave his wife all his house goodes lands and Cattells therein."[36]

The case cautions strongly against assuming, even in the early part of Elizabeth's reign, that a clerical witness was also the scribe. It is also of note that the dating of the written will did not coincide with its composition. In this instance, "it skills no matter" because the testator lived for two further years, but it is easy to conceive of a will, written months from death, when sickness was not extreme, but then finalized and dated when death loomed larger. The exceptionally pious will of Thomas Merburie, already quoted, is a case in point. The model student wrote or dictated his will, "being in

[36]CUL, EDR, D/2/6, fols. 22–27.

health at this present time both of bodie and mynde," but the document was dated just a few days before probate was granted and therefore very close to the time of the testator's death. This may have happened frequently enough to threaten the validity of comparing the date written on a will with that of burial or probate and concluding that most wills were composed very shortly before death. Indeed, on the face of things, Elizabethan testators do appear to have had an uncanny knack of knowing which particular bout of sickness was the final one. The common clause "revoking all former wills by me made" should also be remembered. Not all testators left their wills until the final hours.

Standard practice becomes harder to identify as more cases are studied. The right-first-time will-making, though fairly common, was far from universal. The preparation of a will was no easy matter, especially if the testator's affairs were complex, and many scribes must have found it difficult to set the will down in perfect form at the first attempt. Consequently, it appears to have been common for a scribe to carry the first draft away with him, for periods ranging from a few days to several months, in order to make a fair copy. Sometimes, scribes still managed to make crucial mistakes, as in the will of John Salmon of Willingham (Ely).[37] The testator had bequeathed to his wife "all that she brought" with her at their marriage. The scribe took the original will home with him, and absentmindedly added the words "household stuff" to the clause, when he wrote the will neatly. The resultant dispute centered on a heifer ("now grown to a good Cowe") which had been part of the bride's dowry, and which defied classification as "household stuff."

In this case, the surviving original is in fact the faulty fair copy which was never read before the testator. It bears the witnesses' names all written in the same hand, that of the incompetent scribe. Such examples have been seen as evidence that the true originals were handed back to the executors and only office copies kept by the court. It is clear, however, that the court never saw the genuine original of John Salmon's will. The scribe added further to the local historian's confusion by omitting his own name from the list of witnesses. He perhaps had good reason for wishing to remain anonymous. Salmon's dedicatory clause was strongly Protestant, but the man who may have been responsible for it is known of only through the court dispute. It sounds highly irregular, but the vicar of Meldreth displayed the

---

[37]Camb. CRO, EPR CW 1560. For records of the court case, see CUL, EDR, D/2/4, fols. 118–123.

same frustrating modesty when he wrote Robert Thurgood's will in 1594.[38] The fact that this omission of the scribe's name occurred in two out of only ten cases where the records of litigation have been compared to the original wills is alarming.

On other occasions, the procedure was not of such dubious reliability. More often, the fair copy was prepared following discussion between scribe and testator. It was then this copy that was read and witnessed. At Lent in 1570, the vicar of Swavesey (Ely) assisted "Father Stacy" in the final preparations of his will.[39] The document was then read aloud to the testator. The vicar, according to his own evidence, then "toke it whom [home] wth him to wryte it fayre, & brought it to him aboute Julye following & red it to him in the presence of John Graves." There were very similar cases in each of the five dioceses under view here.

There were also occasional cases in which the will was written up in its first form by a scribe working at home, unaccompanied by the testator. John Prowse of Brixham (Exeter) decided to summon the vicar, "for that he...felt him self sick and therefore entended to make his will."[40] The vicar duly arrived, and

> having passed somme talk about the making of the will the sayd vicare then knowing his minde and what he should doe at that tyme went from him And within a day or two or iii after as he remembreth the sayd vicare came agayne to the sayd John Prowse lyeng sick in his bedd and brought the sayd...testament reddy written with him.

We cannot tell at which point the preamble was composed, but the implication is scarcely reassuring. In this case, as in a number of others, it was not the making of the will that was witnessed, but a subsequent reading.

Some of the most striking cases are those which demonstrate that the preparation of a will could be a process of evolution through changing times, a fact which is frequently hidden in the once-for-all document with which the courts usually dealt. Sometimes, the situation changed sufficiently that a clean break was made and a wholly new will written. Richard Tickner of Wonersh (Winchester) made a will shortly before his death in

[38]CUL, EDR, D/2/9, fols. 40–43.
[39]CUL, EDR, D/2/7, fols. 155–158.
[40]Devon C[ounty] R[ecord] O[ffice], Chanter 860, fols. 141–144.

1596.[41] When it had been amended and sealed, the testator "did teare in peaces another writing w[hi]ch he…termed to be his old will. And he bid his wife to burne the pieces thereof. And he toke his said last will to his wefe & bid her lay it up."

In other cases, the necessary revisions were not quite severe enough to warrant a fresh start. The last will of a man from nearby Albury (Winchester) was extremely untidy, almost illegible in places, because of extensive amendments made in the late stages. The document was written in three different hands. The Swavesey fair copy to which reference has already been made was just the final stage in a lengthy process.[42] In September 1569, Father Stacy called on Robert Loder "to beare wytnes of his will makinge." Stacy was sick in bed, attended by his daughter and one Lawrence Milford. Stacy then made his will, which was "wrytten and drawen" by Milford. The scribe then went on his way, leaving the will with Stacy's wife.

The following Lent, six months on, Stacy again summoned Loder. Present this time was the vicar, "Syr Curtys," to whom the testator or his wife delivered the will. Stacy then ordered several alterations. An additional witness was called, and Curtis read the will to the testator, who acknowledged it gratefully as "the last will that ever he wold make."

At this point, the vicar took the will away to make the fair copy, returning four months later, when he said to the testator "I have brought your will.…[W]ill you have it redd?" Stacy agreed and, finally, a process which had lasted the best part of a year was concluded—in a document which bore one date and looked for all the world like a straightforward composition. Sadly, there is no trace of the will in the records today, so it is impossible to answer procedural questions about the dating of the document and the fullness of the witness list.

One of the implications of cases like this is that godly advice to people, that they make their wills while in health, could be impractical. Circumstances could change rapidly and radically so that old wills became outdated. A widow from Little Shelford made her will at harvest time in 1575, bequeathing a quantity of corn to certain of her relatives.[43] She then lived longer than had evidently been anticipated and was forced to make

---

[41]Hamps[hire] C[ounty] R[ecord] O[ffice], Winchester wills, B68/1–5 (1596).
[42]Hamps CRO, Winchester wills, B81/1–8 (1591); CUL, EDR, D/2/7, fols. 155–158.
[43]CUL, EDR, D/2/11, fols. 109–112.

amendments hardly less distracting than the original will-making. Harvest had been and gone, and the testator, when asked about the corn bequest, observed testily "they can not have yt nowe, it is not to be had." Later still, she made further alterations and, as the vicar recalled with surprise, "sett hir marcke unto the sayd wyll even blotted, rased, corrected & amended as it was." The vicar then made a fair copy at home, dating the will at this point. This copy, as in the Willingham case, is the so-called original, available for inspection today. It carries no trace of the widow's mark, known to have been placed on the real original. There appears to have been considerable scope for the tightening of probate procedures.

The preparation of a will could, then, be a complicated process, and testators needed to be in firm control of their mental faculties. Cases in which advantage was taken of a deranged or witless testator were rare, though the last week of Thomas Hopper of Medomsley (Durham) was a troubled time indeed.[44] Numerous deponents gave evidence that the testator had been raving during his final days. John Hunter told the court that, a week before the testator died, he "was neither of good memory nor reason, but all distracte, singinge hey roiffe songs." Similar tales abounded, as the testator came to sound increasingly like King Lear at a comparable point in his life cycle. One female deponent described the occasion when Thomas had "cauld for his dagger, and said...that if he had his dagger he would sley the fellow that had his goods." Humphrey Hopper, either the villain of the piece or a caring and protective father, had turned all visitors out of the room with the words "Away, thou troublest him." Perhaps displaying reason in madness, the testator later told his father "thou art the black devell of Edeedsbrig" and exclaimed to onlookers "Tak this man...I chardge you in the Quene's name and my Lord of Durham, for he hath stolne all my goodes and caried it to Lyddisdaill."

This case, though compelling, was highly unusual. The majority of testators were, despite sickness, firmly in control of proceedings. William Bateman was "in good and perfight mind and memorye for he talked well and ratefyed...is testament when the same was read byfour him." The description was typical. Johane Haryson easily held her own in a quarrel with her grandson over the future of a white curtain. In several cases, witnesses gave shining testimony to the testators' sanity. The scribe in a Devon case said of his testator that he "did here him talk as wiselye as ever he did

---

[44]*Depositions*, 265–276.

heare him talk in his life even almost at his last hour." Ellen Searle of Kirton (Exeter) had been equally eloquent.[45]

Most of these testators were sick when they made their wills, but they were certainly not putty in the hands of grasping relatives. In a number of instances, it seems likely that they had actually become, through age and sickness, more short-tempered and confrontational than they had been "in the time of health." Manipulation was not rife and few testators had lost either the will or the power to control events. Robert Thurgood was mentally, if not physically, agile as his will reached its final form.[46] He altered the document, after careful thought, to remove his wife as executor. He then faced the unenviable task of keeping his decision secret from her, and almost found it beyond him:

> after the said testator had confirmed the said will, he...did laye it in the corner of the windowe to drie and Joyce Thurgood his wyef comenge up takeinge it in her hand & goeinge away with it, he the said testator perceivinge it called her, desyred her to let hym have it, w[hi]ch she dyd, & soe he delivered [it] to this deponent.

It appears that the description "weak in body though sound of mind" had an accuracy which one does not necessarily associate with stereotypical phraseology.

There remained, however, an important role to be played by the friends, neighbors, and relatives of the testator. The bonds of kinship and neighborliness meant different things to different individuals, and for some deponents the motives for advising or speaking with a testator were unashamedly cynical. Urias Spicer of Chesterton (Ely) went out drinking with the testator, Thomas Willowes, and another man; and "being merrilie disposed said to...the testator you and this man are Cosens and he and I are Cosens and why may not you and I...be Cosins?" He added, as neighborly goodwill gave way to shallow greed, "I would gladly be your Cosin for that you are a wealthy fellowe and have no children that I might have some of your goodes."[47]

Court officials were always anxious to establish whether a deponent had any particular interest in the case. It appears that, cynical worldliness aside, men and women with little to gain were frequently forthcoming with

---

[45]CUL, EDR, D/2/6, fol. 22; D/2/11, fol. 110; Devon CRO, Chanter 860, fols. 142, 381–385.
[46]CUL, EDR, D/2/9, fols. 40–43.
[47]CUL, EDR, D/2/9, fols. 190–208.

words of advice and comfort. Deponents across the land dropped in on ailing neighbors to make friendly inquiries about the state of body and spirit. As Gilbert Atwell passed the gate of Ellen Serle, the Devonshire widow, he met his own brother Nicholas; "and understanding...of the sicknes of the widow Searle, lighted from his horse and went into her house to se howe she did." He continued, "after some talke betwene them he this deponent [advised] her to make her will and to distribute somewhat to the poore...and she aunswered she had made her will already and it was in George Trowbridges handes."[48] Six or more assorted friends and relatives were also present during the exchange. Deathbed gatherings of this sort must have been important social occasions, at which reputations for neighborliness could be made and lost.

In extreme circumstances, neighborly duty could be deliberately flouted in order to make a point. John Pottes of Cambridge decided not to visit his former friend, Thomas Willowes, when he fell ill in 1593.[49] Willowes later recovered and confronted Pottes, saying "that he marveiled that he came not to visite him in the time of his sicknes." To this Pottes responded "the cause is for that it is reported by manie and beleeved of some that you have given yor kinsman of horningseye all your goodes except twenty nobles and the lease of the painters house." The precise reason for Pottes' anger was his feeling that the testator was undervaluing his wife by bequeathing much of his estate to a mere cousin. He further informed Willowes that, if the rumors were true, "you will goe to the divell for...if she had ben yor servant as she is yor wyffe she had ben worthye of xx shillings a yeare and she hathe ben yor wiffe these xx yeares." Pottes clearly felt that the testator had neglected his duty, and that he, "the said deponent," was therefore absolved of his own.

Perkins had lamented the fact that many people were far from skilled at talking profitably to their sick neighbors. Later, Assheton alleged that, in too many instances, people were afraid of suggesting to their afflicted friends that a will should be made.[50] Such anxiety to avoid offense was not always evident in the court depositions. William Goodman of Chesterton (Ely), for example, displayed brutal honesty when, on meeting a neighbor

---

[48]Devon CRO, Chanter 860, fol. 381.
[49]CUL, EDR, D/2/9, fols. 190–208.
[50]Perkins, *A salve*, 60; Assheton, *A theological discourse*, 11.

in the street, he said "you have ben sicke you looke not well and you wax old I would wish you…to set things at a staye."[51]

Neighbors at a sick person's bedside could be required to ensure that tempers did not become overheated. When the Shelford widow clashed with her grandson concerning a white curtain, it was only "uppon the intrety of the cumpanye then present" that real fury was forestalled.[52] Interestingly, it was the aged widow, rather than her grandson, who was urged to moderate her conduct. Friends and neighbors played an important role in the preparation of a will, and in the broader atmosphere that surrounded it.

Naturally, therefore, testators generally selected their witnesses quite deliberately, basing their choices upon personal friendship and social respect. The testator who was conscious of the need to make his or her will "as sure as may be" would also have been aware of the need to call credible witnesses. In particular communities, therefore, the same individuals tended to appear repeatedly at local will-makings.

In most depositions, the precise reasons for a particular choice are not articulated, but at the time of will-making, the testators' servants, wives, and children were frequently sent out to request the presence of particular individuals. An Essex man was summoned, "being the nere neighbor & well willer of the testator." A witness in another case was told by the testator, "after much familiar and comfortable speeches had betwen them," that "he had sent for him…as his speciall frind that he would have his will made." Occasionally, witnesses were present for less touching reasons: Roger Hopper happened to walk past a testator's house at the right moment, "being in the way to se the yought [youth] of Kirkly play at fott ball."[53] In the majority of cases, however, witnesses—like executors—were chosen quite deliberately.

A reliable scribe could be of crucial significance. The testator needed above all a man who could be trusted to prepare a legally acceptable document. Beyond this basic criterion, factors such as personal friendship, social or moral standing, and religious affiliation may have come into play. The testator's choice was further influenced, of course, by the local availability

---

[51]CUL, EDR, D/2/9, fol. 93.
[52]CUL, EDR, D/2/11, fols. 109–112.
[53]Essex CRO, D/ACD 1, fol. 1; D/AED 1, fol. 48; *Depositions*, 79.

of scribes, and presumably by the amount of money he or she was prepared to pay in order to employ a good one.

The later sixteenth and seventeenth centuries were part of a very broad period of transition. In medieval villages, the local priest had been the almost inevitable choice as will scribe, through his superior literacy and his extensive experience in what was perceived as a traditional role. By the eighteenth and nineteenth centuries, professional legal experts had come to enjoy a similar dominance. Elizabethan England presents evidence of both types, and of a third transitional breed of will scribe—the capable local layman, who wrote wills either as a neighborly service, or on a semi-professional basis.

There is very little to indicate that "public notaries" were widely operative in rural England during the reign of Elizabeth. Will-writing in the towns may have been slightly different. In the corporate town of Wisbech (Ely), just one will from some 150 made between 1570 and 1600 was written by a self-proclaimed notary; no similar examples have been found in the wills written in villages like Balsham, Shudy Camps, and Horningsea.[54]

The clergy were, nevertheless, already declining in importance as will scribes. It has been argued that, by the middle years of Elizabeth's reign, the number of literate yeomen had increased significantly, so that the pool of potential scribes was wider and deeper than ever before.[55] When Leonard Woolward of Balsham (Ely) made his will in 1578, for example, he could have chosen from a wide range of scribes among his "friends or acquaintances." Instead, he eventually asked his barber-surgeon, literate though poor, to perform the task. The fact that they then borrowed writing implements from another neighbor seems to strengthen the case further.[56] Literacy was spreading and a growing number of villagers were skillful enough to draft a will.

Not all the evidence points the same way. Nuncupative wills remained fairly common, indicating that some testators did not share Woolward's perception of a wide selection of possible scribes. William Bateman's last will went unwritten on the night of his death, because the scribe was himself temporarily sick. For some reason, Bateman and his wife failed to find

---

[54]Camb CRO, EPR, CW 1597 (will of John Robinson).
[55]Spufford, *Contrasting Communities*, 182.
[56]CUL, EDR, D/2/11, fols. 259–261.

another. Literacy levels were undoubtedly rising, but signing one's name was considerably more straightforward than writing a will upon which much could depend. In 1595, the Wonersh yeoman Richard Tickner made his will, but "doubted that it was not set downe sufficiently...because it was written but by a young scholler." Consequently, but unusually, he sent it to a Guildford expert for checking.[57]

This need for security, combined with improving lay literacy, led to the development—in some parts of the country at least—of a body of highly literate individuals who established reputations as will-writers. Such lay specialists could be extremely desirable. Lawrence Milford, scribe of the first draft of Father Stacy's will in Swavesey (Ely), clearly enjoyed a sound local reputation. Milford, a schoolmaster and farmer, was himself resident in nearby Willingham, where he wrote a series of fifty wills between 1570 and 1602.[58] Would-be testators must frequently have waited until Milford could attend them. He did not miraculously appear at sickbeds with the aid of some sixth sense; he was summoned by the testators or their relatives, and successfully cornered the local market.

The Milford monopoly was perhaps an extreme case. Not every community had such a dominant semiprofessional lay specialist, chosen primarily for the proven legality of the documents he produced. In villages like Balsham, although watertight wills were equally important, the choice of scribe may have been affected to a greater extent by personal friendship and trust. The task of drafting late Elizabethan wills seems to have been shared in Balsham by at least half a dozen local yeomen.[59] None of the wills they wrote was called into doubt at the consistory court; the service these literate villagers provided was apparently considered satisfactory.

England's clergymen had not, however, been completely eclipsed from proceedings. Lawrence Milford may have written the first draft of Father Stacy's will, but the final version was in the hand of the minister, Edmund Curtis. In some communities, the vicar continued to write most of the wills. In villages where a range of lay scribes was also available, it can perhaps be argued that a decision to involve the vicar carried with it a significance that had not been there when he was the only literate man in the community. Robert Thurgood of Meldreth (Ely) made a spoken will in

[57]CUL, EDR, D/2/6, fols. 22–27; Hamps CRO, Winchester wills, B68/1–5.
[58]Spufford, *Contrasting Communities*, 328.
[59]For discussion of the situation in Balsham, see Christopher Marsh, *The Family of Love in English Society, 1550–1630* (Cambridge: Cambridge University Press, 1994).

1594, and said "it should serve untill he could have it written." It was several days before this was done, despite the fact that the testator's brother and his barber-surgeon were both sufficiently literate to sign the eventual will. Rather than entrust the task to either of these men, Thurgood awaited the arrival of John Gosling, the local vicar. A generous bequest to the poor strengthens the impression that the testator was a particularly religious man. Interestingly, the vicar omitted his own name from the final copy of the will, even though he wrote it "at home at his owne house."[60]

The will of William Bateman of Sutton (Ely) was similar, though in this instance the vicar was merely a witness, not the scribe. The testator's elaborate bequests to the poor were set in writing before Simon Nappe, "clericus," appeared on the scene; without the benefit of court depositions it would have been tempting to see the vicar's hand in such charity. When Mr. Nappe arrived at Bateman's house, however, he noticed—without surprise—that Daniel Morton was already present, "haveing the same [will] in his hand for that he was the writer thereof."[61] The vicar's presence was desired on grounds that had nothing to do with his literacy.

In a couple of cases, there is evidence that the old reliance on the priest as will scribe retained some of its hold. In 1586, Lancelot Morgan of Walsingham (Durham) summoned several of his friends and declared "Neighbors, here is neither minister nor clerk at home, and I would make my will, and I pray you to beare witness how I dispose my goods." With no cleric available, it was felt that the will could not be set in writing. John Hind, a Cambridgeshire husbandman, arrived at a testator's house to find the will already completed; he surmised that it was "wrytten...by William Bylducke [vicar of Little Shelford] for that there was no other clercke then & there present."[62]

The pastoral involvement of local clergymen can occasionally be traced in some detail. The enthusiasm displayed by an individual vicar in the performance of his duty could obviously have affected the degree to which testators felt conscious of the spiritual importance of a will-making. The vicar of Sandon in Essex proudly told the court that, "according to his duetye," he had visited a sick member of his flock:

[60]CUL, EDR, D/2/7, fols. 155–158; D/2/9, fols. 40–43.
[61]CUL, EDR, D/2/6, fols. 22–27.
[62]*Depositions*, 320–321; CUL, EDR, D/2/11, fols. 109–112.

and after he this deponent had godlye enstructed him and perceived him to be readie to die, he this deponent lykewise perswaded him to sett downe order for the desposinge of his goodes
and to make his will and the same testator was verie well content
therwithall confessinge that it was his onelye desier.[63]

At Merrington (Durham) the vicar was still more precise in performing his Prayer Book responsibilities, though his expressions hardly
suggest a committed Protestantism. William Melmerbye visited the sick
man, asked of his welfare, gently encouraged the making of a will and
inquired whether a bequest to the poor was intended. The testator, who
knew his own mind, replied "I gyve dayly to the poore, as other neighbours
doith, and therefore I will nothing to the poore man box." He apparently
felt that his own duties were increasingly fulfilled through more formal
contributions to traditional good causes. A pang of sickness later struck the
testator and the will-making was delayed. The vicar, fearing that the testator's time was short, said "Let us goo to the communion, and lett my
hoost advyse hym what he wold say or doo afterwarde." He perhaps felt
that, since his own attempts to encourage charity had failed, something a
little more persuasive was required. The vicar eventually wrote the will up
at home, and returned it to his dogmatic parishioner.[64]

The clergy at Norton and Shotley (both Durham) were similarly active.
Robert Blaxton, clerk of Norton, delivered his "goostly counsaill" and
administered the communion to a testator, before writing her will. William
Strothers, curate of Shotley, also administered the final communion and
wrote a testator's will.[65] Although the evidence may be distorted, it seems
that northern clergymen—more so than their counterparts in the southern
province—were consistently regarded as essential participants at a will-
making. The reason may well have lain partly in the continuing scribal
superiority of the clergy in a region where literacy was not advancing so
steadily. As at least one of these cases suggests, however, it may also have
reflected the ongoing strength of Dr. Duffy's traditional religion in the
northern parts of England.

The influence of the clergy brings us back to the point from which we
embarked: the role of religion in motivating laypeople to write their wills,

[63]Essex CRO, D/AED 1, fol. 59.
[64]*Depositions*, 212–215.
[65]Ibid., 232–233, 265–276.

and the importance of dedicatory clauses. There clearly were those occasions when the presence of a dutiful vicar, with his "ghostly counsel" and pastoral advice, must have ensured that a testator was conscious of the spiritual reasons for writing a will; but how prominent a place did these reasons occupy in the minds of the majority?

There is little suggestion in any of these cases that, for the majority of testators, the composition of the dedicatory clause was viewed as a matter of any great significance. Unfortunately, none of the testators studied here displayed exceptional puritan zeal as they approached death and will-making. This is in itself significant, but it should be remembered that such individuals did exist, and that details surrounding the making of some of their wills might be found to modify the picture. As we have seen, a handful of testators certainly did put heart and soul into the composition of their preambles. They were, however, unusual.

Deponents were almost invariably required to express an opinion on the testator's sanity at the time of will-making. It is striking that recollections concerning the composition of the preamble were not presented as evidence in any of the cases studied. Deponents spoke of the testators' ability to remember the names of their more obscure acquaintances, or the details of debts, and to express themselves forcefully when faced with difficulties. If the precise wording of preambles was a live issue at the average English will-making, the fact would surely have emerged in evidence of this type.

On the other hand, a great many testators would probably have expressed concern if their scribes had simply omitted the dedicatory clause altogether. Wills which displayed no religious content whatsoever were still extremely rare, and were to remain so for many decades.[66] Such wills were, however, accepted by the probate courts. The religious preamble would surely have had a much shorter life than it did if England's testators had no desire at all for its continuing existence. They may not have agonized unduly over the exact phraseology employed, but they probably desired their wills to be couched in the broadly traditional religious terms. To call the will preamble a matter of form is, in one sense, to argue that intense concentration by historians on the precise wording of individual wills may

---

[66]The wills written in Banbury retained religious expressions at least until the 1730s. See R. T. Vann, "Wills and the Family in an English Town: Banbury 1550–1800," *Journal of Family History* 4 (1979), 360.

be a misguided approach; in another sense, it is to say that the religious pre-amble, in whatever form, was one of the few ingredients of a will that could be assumed as desirable by virtually all testators. The relationship between fashion, form, and individual preference is obviously a complex one, but it seems probable that most testators in Elizabethan England wished their wills to reflect their basic faith, even if they rarely expressed much concern over the precise form of the reflection.

In most cases, the fundamental religious format could safely be assumed by testators, and there need have been no detailed discussion. When the vicar of Merrington (Durham) arrived at William Kirkus's house, he asked "Will ye make a will?" and "What will ye give to the poore man box?" but he did not, apparently, ask for direction on the wording of the religious preamble.[67] The testator probably felt that the vicar could be relied upon to reflect the essential nature of his belief.

The attitude of the courts is also worth discussing. A great deal of time was spent in transcribing will preambles, word for word, into court regis-ters. The precise religious nature of the documents would then appear to have been of some importance to the authorities. It is normal, at this point in the argument, to refer to the case of William Tracy, the Gloucestershire man who was exhumed in the 1530s for writing a radically Protestant will preamble. It can then be added, in the words of Dr. O'Day, that "even con-temporaries employed the preambles of wills as evidence of mens' religious beliefs."[68] It was, indeed, an important case, but the fact that it seems to be the only one of its kind ever referred to is also revealing. The authorities were not, in general, quite so quick to pounce on such irregularities. Cases where testators made Protestant wills under Henry and Mary, or Catholic wills under Elizabeth, and suffered no posthumous punishment, are far more numerous. Ten years into Elizabeth's reign, the Catholic will of Thomas Barnard of Horningsea (Ely) was registered by the consistory court officials; fourteen years later, when the executors came of age, it was registered again.[69]

It is hard to explain such cases except by arguing that, in general, the ecclesiastical authorities agreed with the godly writers in seeing wills as primarily concerned with the disposition of worldly estate according to

---

[67] *Depositions*, 212–215.
[68] O'Day, *The Debate on the English Reformation*, 155. On Tracy's will, see Craig and Litzenberger, "Wills as Religious Propaganda."
[69] Camb. CRO, EPR CW 1568, 1582.

Christian obligations. Only in extraordinary cases was the smooth passage of property considered worth disrupting on the basis of heretical faith as revealed in will preambles.

Testators were similarly reluctant to rock the boat. The risk involved in writing a preamble which expressed prohibited beliefs was smaller than is often assumed, but it was still not a risk worth taking. In the early years of the Reformation there were surely more Protestant testators than there were Protestant wills. This may have reflected a fear of punishment or an unwillingness to disobey the governors outwardly, but it may also have reflected a perception that the will preamble was not a sufficiently important expression of faith to merit taking even a small risk. This was clearly not true in all cases, as demonstrated by the strikingly radical early Protestant wills discussed by A. G. Dickens and others. Derek Plumb has argued that such wills present indisputable evidence of the existence of deeply committed individuals. Nevertheless, it should not escape notice that nearly half of the Lollard wills he traced opened with conservative preambles. The natural, but misleading, tendency is to concentrate on the 14 percent of Lollards who left radical wills.[70] Wills were testaments of faith, since individuals were performing a spiritual duty and the way in which they did so reflected their religiosity; but pious actions spoke louder than pious words, and the exact expressions used in a will's preamble were generally of only secondary importance.

From the disputed will cases under discussion here, there is just one which reflects on this question directly. The Devon widow, Ellen Serle, used no fewer than three scribes in the preparation of her will. The second of these, George Trowbridge, told the court that around Candlemas in 1580 "he this deponent was requested by Elene Searle to write her testament." He agreed, so the widow "delivered him a peece of paper which hadd a forme of the beginninge of her testament bearing date the xxix daye of december last past and writen as he nowe remembreth to those words, First I give and bequeath my soule to Almightie god so farre being written by the handes of one John Hollacomb." No further details were forthcoming, but it seems that, as Mistress Serle began to feel that a will was in order, she obtained from a man with a local name—whether a friend, a notary, or a vicar we

[70]Dickens, *Lollards and Protestants*; Derek Plumb, "John Foxe and the Later Lollards of the Thames Valley" (Ph.D. thesis, Cambridge University, 1987), 60.

cannot tell—a stereotyped will "forme." It was then two months before she proceeded to fill in the main body of the document.[71]

An Ely original will, made in the 1590s, implies a similar procedure: the preamble and the main text were written in different hands.[72] There was clearly some demand for will forms, though it is not possible to assess its strength with any confidence. It would be fascinating to know how exactly John Hollacomb operated; at present, it seems most likely that will forms, if desired, were obtained from friends and not from those working more commercially.

There is, however, nothing here to invalidate the original view that an exceptionally expressive and pious preamble does reflect profound and personal faith. Scribes were perfectly well aware for whom they were writing, and by whom they were directed. There is no reason found in these cases to suggest that scribes deemed it fitting to impose long and idiosyncratic clauses upon those who had not asked for them. It may well have seemed a waste of time to do so. When John Gosling, vicar of Meldreth, wrote the will of Robert Thurgood, he had not, so far as we can tell, been asked for any particular form of preamble. He wrote, "First I doe bequeath my soul unto Almighty God." When the vicar came to make his own will some years later (adding a fluent signature and perhaps writing the document himself) he expanded considerably upon his earlier format: "First I doe bequeath my soule unto Allmightie god my most mercifull creator & unto Jesus Christ his deare son my onely redeemer & unto the holy gost & blessed spirit proceding from them both my sanctifier & sanctifier of all the elect people of God."[73] Without detailed knowledge of local practice, it is unwise to dwell too long on the implications of this one example. It seems likely, however, that this scribe, at least, reserved his most thoughtful preamble for those, like himself, who desired (and deserved?) it.

Having said this, will-making appears to have been characterized by a surprising degree of variety, and deviant cases are always a strong possibility. It can no longer be considered appropriate to form any but the most timid judgments from individual wills viewed in isolation; the importance of studying the wills of a community in detail, for evidence of custom,

---

[71]Devon CRO, Chanter 860, fols. 366, 381–385.

[72]I am indebted to Professor Eric Carlson for this information.

[73]Camb. CRO, EPR CW 1594 (Robert Thurgood), 1616 (John Gosling).

stereotypical formulae, and striking individuality, can hardly be empha-sized strongly enough.[74]

Not surprisingly, religion played a lesser role in the average will-making than it did for Becon's Epaphroditus. The attitudes expressed or reported in court depositions could, on occasion, be downright ungodly. The case of Thomas Willowes of Cambridge was an object lesson in the trouble that could follow if a man failed to make a will and "set all things at a stay."[75] Several deponents reprimanded the sick man for planning to leave a high proportion of his estate to a cousin, at the expense of his own wife, who had "toiled and moiled" at his side for many years. On one occasion, however, the testator (as he was called, for want of a more precise descrip-tion) was swift to scotch the rumor: "my Cozen Willowes of Horningsey shall have a turde he shall have none of my goodes nor thou neither.... I will live and spend the goodes my selfe." Epaphroditus would have turned in his "simple not sumptuous" grave.[76]

Other cases, however, show that several of the motivations com-mended by Becon, Perkins, Perneby, and Sutton did play an important part in the popular consciousness. As John Prowse of Brixham (Exeter) approached death in 1579, he clearly had thoughts of posthumous har-mony on his mind.[77] On the day the will was witnessed, he made a touching speech before those present: "I praye you agree togither and love one an other when I am gonne and let there be no strife among you that menne maye not saye these goods were ill-gotten." Perneby later made a similar association in print. Prowse was also aware, however, that making a will was not an answer in itself. He therefore made an extra bequest to his daughter, "because thou maiest be a meane of quietnes betwene the exequi-tors." The testator's fears that all would not run smoothly were apparently realized. The same desire for peace was expressed by others: Alison Cham-bers of Blackwell (Durham) told her witnesses "I feele myself not right....I pray you all...to beare witnes of my will, that there be no comber betwixt my brethren."[78]

On several occasions, the desire to prevent "comber" was overridden by other concerns, which themselves had the effect of making conflict more

---

[74]See Spufford, *Contrasting Communities*, 333–334.
[75]CUL, EDR, D/2/9, fols. 190–208.
[76]Becon, *The sicke mans salve*, 119.
[77]Devon CRO, Chanter 860, fols. 141–144.
[78]*Depositions*, 328.

likely. The Kerton (Exeter) widow Ellen Serle made her will partly at least to ward off the advances of a grasping relative, who she felt had already received more than his fair share. The testator was fully aware that trouble might follow, and she would perhaps have laughed wryly at Perneby's rhetorical question "for when every one knowes his part and portion, how shal they not accord and agree?" For widow Serle, the interests of her sons ranked above any wish to promote peace.[79]

The spiritual motivations for will-making also ran in opposite directions in the case surrounding Robert Thurgood of Meldreth (Ely).[80] One witness told her questioners that the testator, sick in bed just two days before his death, "did take this deponent by the hand sayeinge I am a don man, I shall never escape this sicknes I shall never see my children brought up, but I trust the Lord will send them frendes when I am gon, I have made a Newe will, & I knowe there wilbe some stirre aboute it when I ame gon, I shall not heare it, but I hoape it wilbe the better for my children that I have made a newe will & put oute my wyef from beinge myne executor & made Michaell Newlinge myn executor." He was indeed on dangerous ground; as the case of Thomas Willowes has shown, the perceived neglect of a widow-to-be could unleash a storm of community censure. Robert Thurgood was evidently thinking rationally, though the deponent did add that nobody else had heard the exchange, except for the testator's wife "whoe was sleepinge in the said chamber." She may not have been as soundly slumberous as he imagined.

The testator's peace of mind, recommended by Becon as a valuable consequence of will-making, had been almost destroyed in this case. In others, enhanced spiritual tranquility was specifically identified as a reason for making one's will. A Newcastle glover visited his former master in 1568 and, "according to his dewtie and good will, moved hym, for the quietnes of his mynde, to make his will and dispose his goods, which wold be a greate occasion of such quietnes in his hart, that thereby, by the grace of God, he should recover health the better."[81] The deponent was mindful of his Christian "dewtie," but where Perneby saw the peace of mind acquired as necessary for the testator to die properly, this northern glover, aware that even terminal illness could be stress-related, saw it as a possible route to

[79]Devon CRO, Chanter 860, fols. 381–385; Perneby, *A direction*, 233.
[80]CUL, EDR, D/2/9, fols. 40–43.
[81]*Depositions*, 85.

bodily recovery (with the aid of God). Here, in a nutshell, was the difference between will-making as perceived by those of extraordinary piety, and will-making as viewed by less exceptional Christians. Ordinary people may have tended to think more in worldly terms, but many of them knew their duties and operated, expressed themselves, within a committedly Christian framework.

There are also indications that many of the common failings and misplaced motives criticized by the godly writers did indeed enjoy some popularity. Wills were generally delayed until sickness, although, when seen in practical terms, this was often quite sensible. Some people may even have viewed the making of a will—which carried an unwanted feeling of finality—as more trouble than it was worth. When, in 1569, visitors arrived at the home of William Kirkus of Merrington, this master of the pithy comment told them dryly "Heere is Mr Vicar, which wuld have me make a will with great circumstanc; and many maks a will that he repentith all the daies of his life."[82] Perhaps the minister had been emphasizing the spiritual importance of will-making; if so, his dying parishioner had been unimpressed.

There were also those, as alleged by Perkins, Perneby, and Assheton, who deferred the making of their wills because they hoped to live longer, and perhaps felt that a will, once written, gave death the taste of victory. Thomas Wilkinson of Newcastle was, in 1568, "sore syke and in great danger of deathe, by thestimacion of many discreit men and women that had ben to se as he dyed." Despite the advice of such people, the sick man would "in no wyse...be moved and persuadyd...to make his testament, havinge ever such an hope in his owne amendment." Similarly, Thomas Willowes of Cambridge told an advice-giving neighbor, "if I mend not within these two or thre daies I will make a will in writenge." He failed to do so and later became so "grievouslie tormented with pain" that the will was still unwritten when Willowes died; and all manner of strife broke out.[83]

The criticisms and commendations of the godly writers were, then, both reflected in practice. A significant number of testators clearly did approach will-making with the right reasons in mind; others were equally devoted to the wrong reasons. Not surprisingly, it often appears that even

[82]Ibid., 213.
[83]Ibid., 85; CUL, EDR, D/2/9, fols. 190–208.

the highest principles were implemented in practice with something of a worldly emphasis, or that they clashed with one another and could not therefore be implemented in their purest form. The overriding function of the will was to dispose of worldly estate for worldly peace. This function had important spiritual overtones, but a detailed and explicit confession of faith was rarely a primary concern. A basic religious framework for a will was assumed and probably desired, but it was through the bequests that testators performed their Christian duty. Once again, it is tempting to draw attention to the continuities of impulse and understanding that existed with the medieval past. There were, of course, very marked changes in the official theology and ceremony of death, but these snapshots of ordinary people dealing with mortality in their own homes imply that the brand of social Christianity lying close to their hearts also placed them firmly in touch with their ancestors.

∾

As John Hollacomb, the mysterious Devonshire scribe, demonstrated with his "forme of the beginninge of a testament," there was scope for the distribution of stereotyped skeletal wills for use by the testators of England. One of the debates concerning early modern wills has centered on the use of printed legal formularies in the preparation of English testaments. In 1984, Dr. Claire Cross wrote an important article on the wills written in Leeds and Hull between 1540 and 1640.[84] She quoted the long and seemingly personal preamble of a Leeds chapman, written in 1566, but noted the existence of two almost identical examples in wills of the early seventeenth century, one from each town. Dr. Cross traced the source of these later versions to William West's *Symbolaeographia*, published in 1590. The earlier version, she surmised, must have been taken from a similar legal handbook. West would then have borrowed the formula for his own book. Dr. Cross concluded, her faith in wills fading: "The wide circulation of these Tudor legal formularies would suggest that lawyers and scriveners were in England exercising considerably more influence upon the composition of wills than has hitherto been recognized."[85] It was a perfectly reasonable argument; West's book was bulky and expensive, containing draft

---

[84]Claire Cross, "Wills as Evidence."
[85]Ibid., 48.

documents of many types. It was unlikely to have been owned by the less formal lay scribes discussed above.

Other historians had discovered isolated versions of the same formula and concluded that they were looking at evidence of exceptional personal piety.[86] Dr. Cross's discoveries appeared seriously to undermine their position. The common assumption underlying this growing pessimism may, however, be open to question. Is it appropriate to reason that a preamble (or any apparently personal statement for that matter) loses much of its value as evidence of individual belief if it occurs in the exact same form somewhere else? The logic seems based upon what may be a distinctly modern view of the relationship between expressiveness and originality. The latter is all-important to many twentieth-century western minds, but the same attitude may not be entirely applicable to early modern society. It was certainly important to a small number of testators that their will preambles were full and expressive, but did it necessarily detract from the worth of their pious pronouncements if those pronouncements were not original?

In 1697, Assheton lamented the brevity of many preambles, calling it "scandal to the Christian Religion." He urged the use of more detailed (and, we assume, more personal) phrases; but Assheton proceeded to recommend a lengthy set formula of his own composition, presumably with the intention that it be employed by others.[87] The value of a will preamble, for Assheton, was to be measured primarily by its expressiveness, not by its originality. Perhaps we should adopt a similar attitude; if will preambles were, as suggested here, generally seen as matters of indifference, then the testator or scribe who used an unusually expressive format, even if it was not original, may well have done so because of strong personal religious conviction.[88]

Whatever the merits of this argument, the fact that West's book was a legal formulary does certainly appear to diminish the significance of will preambles as testaments of faith. It should be noted, however, that the long format presented by West was just one of four versions available.[89] The preamble differed in each one, implying that public demand may have

---

[86]See, for example, Spufford, *Contrasting Communities*, 341–342; Hartley Thwaite, letter printed in *Local Population Studies* 8 (spring, 1972), 64–67.

[87]Assheton, *A theological discourse*, 18–19.

[88]See Craig and Litzenberger, "Wills as Religious Propaganda."

[89]William West, *Symbolaeographia* (London, 1590), sections 404–405.

required a choice, ranging from the very short preamble to the very long. If testators were offered all four alternatives, did not their decision to adopt the longest and most expressive clause say something of their faith?

There remains the problem that several writers have discovered versions of the long clause, later adopted by West, at dates which make the use of his formulary impossible. The preamble was, for example, used by a testator from Milton in Cambridgeshire in January 1569. He wrote:

> I Geffrye Homes, the unprofitable servant of God, weake in bodye & yet stronge in mynde do with a free hart, render & geve agayne into the handes of the lord my god, my spirite, which he of his fatherly goodnes gave unto me, by this means making me a living creature....[90]

And so it went on. With minor exceptions, Homes' preamble was identical to that used by Epaphroditus in Becon's *The Sicke Mans Salve*. William West did not, therefore, lift his model preamble from a legal formulary, but from an immensely popular godly work by one of the English Reformation's foremost writers. Testators who used the "unprofitable servant of God" preamble, before 1590 at least, did so not because they employed professional scribes who owned legal formularies, but because they possessed or had access to a work of which the exclusive purpose was to teach men and women to face death in a godly fashion. A decision to use Epaphroditus' preamble implied that the book had been read and appreciated by one at least of the testator and scribe, and almost certainly reflects unusually strong religious convictions.

Modern computer technology has made it possible to trace all the testators in the Ely diocese (excluding those whose wills were proved in the Prerogative Court of Canterbury) who described themselves as "unprofitable servants of God."[91] The results of this exercise provide the final angle from which attitudes to will-making will be examined in this paper. How, exactly, was Epaphroditus's preamble put to use?

The first example was that already quoted, dated 20 January 1569. The testator (or scribe) used Becon's formula in a very full version, though he did omit certain phrases, abbreviate several expressions, and change a number of words. Nothing new was added and the alterations were not

[90]Camb CRO, EPR CW 1568.
[91]I am extremely grateful to Dr. Elisabeth Leedham-Green for assisting me in this project, as well as to the staff of the Cambridge University Library Computing Centre.

significant. It is possible that the testator or his scribe had memorized the preamble and reproduced it without copying directly from *The Salve*. The testator used the clause about matrimony, though when referring to his wife he omitted, perhaps revealingly, the phrase "refusing all other women"!

The "unprofitable servant" label was used on a further sixty-seven occasions, the last example being in the will of a Whittlesey widow named (appropriately?) Faith King in 1693. The enthusiasm Geffery Homes had demonstrated for the full form was not, however, shared by many of the testators who followed him. Only thirteen of the wills included a reasonably complete version of the preamble, and very few testators indeed retained the clause on "the blessed state of honourable Wedlocke."

In many instances the form used by Becon and West was shortened, often drastically. A number of the wills, particularly those later in the run, suggest that the label "unprofitable servant of God" had assumed an identity of its own.[92] The most revealing cases were those in which the testator shortened the preamble substantially but was still clearly using one or other of the two sources. Fifteen testators fell into this category, and the significance of their behavior seems likely to lie in the perception, already discussed, that a long and expressive preamble was somewhat excessive and unnecessary. By the same token, it can perhaps be argued that an unusually full use of the preamble implied genuine conviction.

The chronology of the sixty-eight wills is also informative, though in the numerous instances where only the original label was retained, it is possible that neither of the two works was in use. There were only five Elizabethan usages, despite the popularity of *The Salve*. There were probably many more testators, like William Russbrigg of Emneth, who owned or had read the book, but who chose not to employ such an expressive preamble.

West's *Symbolaeographia* appeared in 1590, but there was a surprising twenty-five-year gap before the formula was used again in the diocese. In 1615, John Thompson of Ely, a gentleman, used a full form of the preamble. He clearly took it from West, whose version differed very slightly from that of Becon. Thompson also bequeathed to a relative "all my lawe-bookes, latine bookes, french bookes and storie bookes whersoever they be

---

[92]The label is biblical. See, for example, Matt. 25:30, Luke 17:10. If it had found a place in the godly household vocabulary of the day, I suspect that the credit lay more with Becon than with West. *The sicke mans salve* enjoyed a wide popularity that had nothing to do with its incidental role as an occasional formulary. The same can hardly be said of *Symbolaeographia*.

in England." His will began a series of testaments using the formulary, from a wide range of parishes, and the wordings by this date are all closer to West's than to Becon's. The sudden increase in the numbers of testators using the preamble from 1615 is not easy to explain. It seems possible that it had been published in a more readily available form, possibly as a broadsheet.[93]

When Edmund Neave, a tailor from Chesterton, made his will in 1618, he retained the "unprofitable servant" label, but rather than recite the long preamble, he switched to West's second alternative version. The preamble was still committedly Protestant, though much shorter. Again, there is an implication that the longer form was seen as superfluous.

It is also possible to trace the involvement of individual scribes and to examine the way in which they used the formulary. A number of men adopted a version of the preamble and used it in wills by no means all of which were written in their own villages. Roger Amye acted as scribe in Ickleton, Duxford, and Hinxton. Toby Clifford was active in Landbeach and Milton. For sheer numbers of wills written, however, Richard Field was unsurpassed; between 1626 and 1651 he labeled seventeen Ely testators as "unprofitable servants of God." He clearly had West's formulary, or a copy of the relevant section, at his disposal, but only in the very first will of the series did he use a relatively full version of the preamble. Thereafter, he perhaps decided that such length of expression was unnecessary.

In one group of wills, the use of the preamble can be traced, in a gradually evolving version, through three generations of scribes from several connected families. In 1618, Roger Amye wrote the will of an Ickleton shepherd and included a very full version of West's formula, omitting only the clause on marriage. Four years later, Amye reappeared in Duxford, a neighboring village, to write the will of John Willows. He used a shortened, but still quite full, version of the Becon/West preamble, but now added a clause of his own, referring to the goods "wherwith it hath pleased Almighty God to endue me with all & to make me steward of heare in this world & vale of miserie." The phrase "vale of misery" had also issued from Epaphroditus' lips, but it may well have been taken here from the *Book of Common Prayer*. In 1625, Amye wrote a will in Hinxton, returning to a more complete version of the formula.

---

[93]I am grateful to Ms. Helen Weinstein for discussing this possibility with me.

This was the end of Roger Amye's visible involvement, but in 1639 a widow named Mary Amye made her will in nearby Great Abington. Her witnesses were Thomas and Henry Amye. In this will, the unprofitable servant label survived, but the Becon/West preamble was replaced by new and completely different expressions. The resultant preamble was still lengthy and committedly Protestant. Interestingly, the clause referring to the stewardship of worldly goods "here in this life and vale of misery," not supplied by either Becon or West, was retained. It seems likely that one of the younger Amyes inherited their father's role as a local will scribe, but decided to keep only certain elements of his formula. The unprofitable servant label is the only link with the original Becon preamble but it is clear that, through William West, Roger Amye and one of his sons, the new format had evolved out of the old. Thomas Amye, used the new preamble for two more wills, written in Duxford in 1647 and Babraham in 1648.

Even this is not the full picture. The new preamble clearly took on its own identity in the Hinxton area, and was adopted by scribes from the North and Swann families during the 1640s and 1650s. Following the Restoration, the preamble underwent yet another transition with the phrase "vale of misery" dropped and some new expressions added. Still the unprofitable servant designation was retained, together with several phrases from the "vale of misery" format. A scribe named William Howsden had also taken up the formula and used it in Ickleton and West Wratting. It was employed for the last time in 1670, when William Swann—one of the earlier scribes—included it in his own will. Possibly, the "unprofitable servant" was then finally dismissed and the evolution went on.[94]

This fascinating process suggests a far greater fluidity in the way preambles were used than can be detected in the bare fact that some scribes did make use of formularies. In this subset of the unprofitable servant wills, phrases were dropped and added, new expressions were developed, and gradually evolving formulae were passed around—either in manuscript or by memory—amongst neighbors who also served as local scribes. It seems clear that the expressions used must have been the subject of local discussion, though the fact that the apparently stock preamble was such a lengthy form may suggest that we are focusing here on an unusual group of scribes and testators. In a similar series of wills from the parishes of Balsham and

[94]All the wills cited above are in the Camb. CRO, EPR Will Register.

Bottisham, written between 1609 and 1619, it is known from other sources that the scribes using another elaborate formula were men of exceptional piety. Perhaps the same was true of the Amye scribe group. Most locally recurrent formulae were considerably shorter.

Without detailed local research, the discussion cannot be carried much further. It is noticeable that the total number of unprofitable servant wills written by each individual scribe was not large. If they wrote no other wills, then the testators they served were a select group (and possibly an elect group). These scribes were not in the semiprofessional league of the Willingham schoolmaster, Lawrence Milford. It is also possible, however, that each scribe had more than one formula in his repertoire, and offered the testator a choice. Either way, the decision to use a particularly expressive formula at a will-making probably reflects an unusual depth of feeling on the part of one at least of the individuals involved.

Some people were, then, concerned about the precise nature of religious expression in will preambles, and must have discussed the matter. It still seems unlikely, however, that they were typical. It is also improbable that a large number of scribes were using printed formularies. Even if all sixty-eight of the unprofitable servant preambles had simply been transcribed from West, which they certainly were not, they would represent a very small proportion of the total number of wills written in the diocese. Admittedly, there may have been other printed formularies—particularly in the second half of the seventeenth century—but the much more common process seems to have involved locally composed preambles passed around among acquainted scribes.[95]

∾

The material presented in this paper can hardly be reassuring to those historians who have classified and counted dedicatory clauses in order to chart the shifts in popular religion during the sixteenth century. The exact expressions used in the religious preambles to wills appear to have had little importance in the minds of most English testators, even those of proven piety. The theological nuances historians have analyzed in order to distinguish between traditional, neutral, reformist, and radical wills do not seem to have been on the agenda at the average will-making. Most testators

---

[95]For evidence of other seventeenth-century will formularies, see Bernard Capp, "Will Formularies," *Local Population Studies* 14 (spring, 1975), 49.

probably knew and felt the need to commend their souls to God at the opening of a will, but the inclusion of a detailed, personal, and expressive preamble was not generally perceived as an important part of the duty they were performing. It becomes easier to understand why a man like John Bourne of Wisbech, whose deep faith can be established from other sources, bequeathed his soul "into the hands of god etc." in 1593/4. Bourne was well enough to sign his name at the time of will-making, but neither he nor his scribe put much thought into the wording of the preamble.[96] Unfortunately for us, the same was probably true of most will-makings.

The exceptions to this rule are few and far between, but they are of immense significance. Expansive and personal preambles, in which testators did articulate their faith in great depth, can legitimately be interpreted as evidence of genuine piety. This may even be true of preambles that were lengthy but formulaic, since these too represented a decision to go well beyond the norm.

The majority of testators, then, paid scant attention to the wordings of their preambles, but it would be utterly misguided to infer that will-making was not perceived as a spiritual event or process. The longevity of the religious preamble implies a widespread consensus about the spiritual importance of the document, even if the precise wordings were not discussed in detail by testators and their companions. On those occasions when we can eavesdrop on conversations held around the sickbed, we can frequently hear hints that participants were aware of the religious duties they were fulfilling. Testators were undoubtedly interested in looking after their own, but most of them probably knew that this impulse had a spiritual dimension. By disposing their estates in a responsible fashion, they were promoting peace within the Christian community and paying their respects to God as they prepared to meet Him. Edward Leach of Milton (Ely) voiced a widespread feeling in 1644, making his will "because there should be no controversy after my death for my goods and possessions and for the maintenance of love and peace in the world."[97] Testators, scribes, witnesses, executors, and legatees all had a responsibility to play their parts in the realization of this ambition. The court cases studied above demonstrate that not all of them did so, but we should remember that the vast majority did.

---

[96]Camb CRO, EPR CW 1593.
[97]Cited in Spufford, *Contrasting Communities*, 343.

The centrality of the social dimension of popular Christianity as revealed in the evidence examined here is striking. Certainly, there were individuals at all social levels who took a profound interest in theological questions, but for the majority it seems that matters of godly social conduct and communal cohesion were closer to the core of their faith. This partially explains why most of the people gathered around early modern sickbeds did not indulge in heated discussions over the expressions included in the dedicatory clauses of wills. Their religiosity was warm, positive, and robustly Christian, even if it often fell far short of the standards demanded by England's more zealous ministers. It also had a considerable amount in common with the religiosity of those who had gathered around the beds of testators in the late medieval period. Arguably, the elements of continuity within this social Christianity, existing beneath the level of radical religious change, were a vital factor in the gradual, flexible, and paradoxical process that was the English Reformation. As Tessa Watt has argued in her analysis of cheap religious literature, this was as much a period of unspectacular spiritual adjustment, in which old and new were blended, as it was one of violent and radical transformation.[98]

Wills remain an extremely valuable source for historians of early modern faith, but the ways in which they are put to use may need to change. The statistical analysis of categorized preambles is beginning to look like a somewhat limited exercise. The general trends that emerge will tend to mirror official policy rather than genuine shifts in the nature of popular religion, though individual wills or groups of wills that run counter to the predominant developments are clearly not to be dismissed lightly. Most individuals, as we have seen, did not regard the preamble as in any way the defining feature of a will, and they did not use it as an opportunity to present their theological leanings in a personal fashion. Furthermore, each will conceals a wealth of unarticulated motives and unknowable influences that make statistical analysis unreliable.

The most valuable treatments of wills will undoubtedly be those that adopt a microscopic approach to the local context in which these documents were created. This may be an unwelcome lesson, but it is also an unavoidable one. Historians cannot reliably dip into wills for swift and easy results. Only by developing a feel for the many factors that influenced the

[98]Tessa Watt, *Cheap Print and Popular Piety, 1550–1640* (Cambridge: Cambridge University Press, 1991).

contents of a will—the scribe's identity, other testaments written by the same scribe, phrases used in other wills from the area, the religious disposition of those present at the sickbed, and so on—can the spiritual meaning of an individual document be understood. It is equally important to draw the patterns of giving, both secular and religious, into any analysis. It was, after all, through the bequests that most testators expressed their sense of Christian responsibility and performed their godly duties. Once again, the local context will be all-important, for a solid grounding within it will enable the historian to locate the boundary between the conventional and the exceptional in a way that would not otherwise be possible.

The socioreligious importance of will-making also suggests that one extremely valuable interpretative technique might be to focus, again within a local context, on the interpersonal networks of contact and sympathy that can be reconstructed more fully from wills than from any other source. Testators chose their executors, witnesses, and legatees with great care, and the patterns of affinity that emerge from a study of large collections of wills written in a particular community can potentially tell us a great deal about spiritual interconnection within that community. Ideally, these networks would be analyzed against the background of complementary evidence from other sources that sheds light on individual religious affiliations. This technique has recently been used in an attempt to explore the social and religious history of the Family of Love, one of the most mysterious of early modern spiritual fellowships.[99] In essence, this approach requires historians to shift their gaze from the openings of wills, with their religious preambles, to the concluding lines, with their lists of witnesses and executors. Put thus, it sounds like a minor adjustment, yet it is one that could carry our understanding of wills and of popular religion more generally into fresh and invigorating areas.

[99]Marsh, *The Family of Love.*

LOCAL RESPONSES *to* RELIGIOUS CHANGES

EVIDENCE FROM GLOUCESTERSHIRE WILLS[1]

Caroline Litzenberger

IN HER WILL, written in February 1551, Elizabeth Lane, widow of Sandhurst, bequeathed her soul "to Almyghty God to our Lady and to all the hoole Company of Heaven." One of her witnesses was Robert Hogges, her vicar or ghostly father, and she included a bequest of four pence to the "Mother Church."[2] Although bequests to the Mother Church (i.e., the cathedral) and references to "my ghostly father" continued through the remainder of Edward's reign, this may have been the last Edwardian will in Gloucestershire to include that most traditional of all soul bequests. Perhaps this was due to the energetic administration of the new bishop of Gloucester, the radical Protestant, John Hooper. Consecrated on 8 March 1551, Bishop Hooper immediately set about reforming the slack religious practices he found in his diocese.[3] Chief among his actions was the promulgation of a set of visitation articles, injunctions, and interrogatories issued in the summer of 1551. Article forty-six of the interrogatories asked "whether any of [the clergy] make or write any mans testament with this stile, I commend my soule unto God, to our blessed Lady and the Saints of heaven, which is injurious to God, and perilous as well for the salvation of the dead, as dangerous unto the maker."[4]

---

[1]Portions of this essay were published as "Local Responses to Changes in Religious Policy Based on Evidence from Gloucestershire Wills (1540–1580)," in *Continuity and Change* 8 (1993): 417–439. Copyright of that article is held jointly by the author and Cambridge University Press, and it is reprinted here with the permission of Cambridge University Press.

[2]G[loucestershire] R[ecord] O[ffice], Gloucestershire Wills, 1551/16.

[3]Lambeth Register, Cranmer, fols. 105, 332–333.

[4]"Bishop Hooper's Visitation Booke," Dr. Williams' Library, Morice MS 31.L, Item 3, 16. This was the last will in Edward's reign to contain the standard traditional preamble, based on a reading of over 3,000 Gloucestershire wills for the period from 1541 to 1580.

A few months later, in September 1551, the opening paragraph of the will of Joan Davis of Nimpsfield read:

> I commytt me unto God and to hys mercye trustynge without eny dowett or mysstrust in his grace and the meryttes of Jhesus Chryst and bye the virtue off hys passyon and off hys resurrexyon off boddye and soll: For I belev thatt my redemer lyevyth and yn the last daye I shall ryse owett off the yearth and yn my flesshe shall see my savyowre thys my hope ys laid up yn my bosom.[5]

This was an exact copy of the opening paragraph from the will of William Tracy, which was written in 1531 and had been printed in four editions (in 1535 and 1546, and twice in 1548) after it had been declared heretical by convocation.[6] Thus, Joan Davis's use of this statement is a clear indication of Protestantism.

However, it would be extremely misleading to stop here, and perhaps leave the impression that Gloucestershire had turned abruptly and overwhelmingly to Protestantism by the autumn of 1551. Nothing could be farther from the truth. In general, the people of that county seem to have been rather slow to embrace the new religion.[7]

The English Reformation, particularly between 1540 and 1580, was marked by dramatic swings in official religious policy between varying degrees of Protestantism and traditional religion, before stabilizing during the first half of Elizabeth's reign with the implementation of the Protestant Elizabethan Settlement. Recent historiographic debate about the nature of those changes has been intense and has centered on the speed and catalysts of reform. In other words, did England embrace Protestantism quickly or

---

[5]GRO, Gloucestershire Wills, 1551/62.

[6]*The Testament of Master Wylliam Tracie esquier / expounded both by William Tyndale and Jhon Frith* (Antwerp, 1535); "The testament of W. Tracie expounded by W. Tindall," in *Wyclyffes wycket: Whyche he made in kyng Rycards days the second in the yere of our lorde God M.CCC.XLV.* (London, 1546); also printed in "The Testament of Master William Tracy, Esquire, expounded by William Tyndale," in *Tyndale's Answer to Sir Thomas More's Dialogue etc.*, ed. H. Walter (Cambridge, 1850), 271–283; "The testament of W. Tracie expounded by W. Tindall," in *Uvicklieffes wicket: Faythfully ouerseene and corrected*, ed. M. Coverdale (London, 1548?); *The Union of the two noble and illustrate famelies of Lancastre and Yorke* (London, 1548), fols. 211–11v. See also John Craig and Caroline Litzenberger, "Wills as Religious Propaganda: The Testament of William Tracy," *Journal of Ecclesiastical History* 44 (1994): 415–431.

[7]In this article the terms, "the old religion," and from Mary's reign on, "Catholicism," will be used synonymously with "traditional religion" to describe the standard pre-Reformation religion, and its subsequent forms. The terms "Protestantism" and "the new religion" will be used interchangeably to describe the forms of religion introduced by the Reformation.

was the progress of reform slow? Further, did the impetus for change come from above or below?[8] Much of the argument in support of a fast Reformation is based on the idea that the laity turned from traditional religion to Protestantism quite promptly, and that England was predominantly Protestant by the end of the reign of Edward VI.[9] Meanwhile, others declare that the Reformation was slow to take effect in the localities, seeing the decade of the 1570s as the time when Protestantism became the principal religion.[10]

This essay enters the fast/slow debate at the local level by examining the nature of lay piety as expressed in wills written and proved in Gloucestershire in the west of England. It is based on an analysis of over 3,000 of the 8,000-plus extant wills written by testators in Gloucestershire between the creation of the diocese (1541) and 1580.[11] Table 1 shows that the number includes all extant women's wills (which number 1,325) and a systematic

TABLE 1[A]
NUMBER OF WILLS BY GENDER AND REIGN

Reign	Women	Men	Totals
Henry	148	245	393
Edward	138	142	280
Mary	263	251	514
Elizabeth (1559–69)	362	310	672
Elizabeth (1570–80)	414	337	751
Totals	1,325	1,285	2,610

    a. Source: GRO, Gloucestershire Wills 1541–1580.

[8]Christopher Haigh, "The Recent Historiography of the English Reformation," *Historical Journal* 25 (1982): 995–1007; A. G. Dickens, "The Early Expansion of Protestantism in England, 1520–1558," *Archiv für Reformationgeschichte* 78 (1987): 187–222.

[9]G. R. Elton, *Reform and Reformation: England, 1509–1558* (Cambridge, Mass.: Harvard University Press, 1977), 371. See also A. G. Dickens, *The English Reformation*, 2d ed. (London: B. T. Batsford, Ltd., 1989).

[10]Christopher Haigh, *Reformation and Resistance in Tudor Lancashire* (Cambridge: Cambridge University Press, 1975); J. J. Scarisbrick, *The Reformation and the English People* (Oxford: Basil Blackwell, 1984).

[11]While the terms "will" and "testament" legally refer to two different instruments, they are used synonymously in this article. For a discussion of the distinctions between the terms see F. Pollock and F. W. Maitland, *The History of English Law before the Time of Edward I*, 2 vols., 2d ed. (1898; reprint, Cambridge: Cambridge University Press, 1968), 2:314–56; Stephen Coppel, "Wills and the Community of Tudor Grantham," in *Probate Records and the Local Community*, ed. Philip Riden (Gloucester: Alan Sutton, 1985), 72–74. For further discussion of wills, probate, and testamentary cases in the consistory court, see Ralph A. Houlbrooke, *Church Courts and the People during the English Reformation, 1520–1570* (Oxford: Oxford University Press, 1979), 89–116.

sample of 1,285 laymen's wills drawn from the 6,000 extant male wills from the period proved in the Gloucester consistory court.[12] In addition, all the surviving wills from the parishes of Tewkesbury and Cirencester have been examined to gain further insight into local scribes' roles in determining the content of these documents.

Much has been written about the selection of religious preambles or soul bequests in early modern English wills, and yet, more remains to be said.[13] Margaret Spufford demonstrated that local scribes played a key role

[12]Approximately 8,000 Gloucestershire wills proved in the diocesan consistory court survive in the archives of the GRO for the period of this study. In addition to all extant wills of female testators, 20 percent of the wills of lay men were included. Since the wills were filed alphabetically by first name within probate year, it was possible to select the sample of male wills by identifying the first man's will in each year based on a random number (modular 5), and then reading every fifth man's will through the rest of that year. The resulting sample includes approximately equal numbers of women's and men's wills. In this case, assuming the highest possible variability of the sample from the population, the results of the analysis of the sample will be within 0.97 percent of that for the entire population at a confidence level of 95 percent. Further, chi-square tests, which measure the strength of relationships and the importance of differences, have been used to identify important patterns in groups of wills, at a significance level of 0.001. R. S. Schofield, "Sampling in Historical Research," in *Nineteenth-Century Society: Essays in the Use of Quantitative Methods for the Study of Social Data*, ed. E. A. Wrigley (Cambridge: Cambridge University Press, 1972), 146–84; H. M. Blalock, *Social Statistics*, rev. ed. (London: McGraw-Hill, 1981), 183–86; R. Floud, *An Introduction to Quantitative Methods for Historians*, 2d ed. (1973; reprint, London and New York: Methuen, 1986), 136.

[13]Margaret Spufford, "The Scribes of Villagers' Wills in the Sixteenth and Seventeenth Centuries and Their Influence," *Local Population Studies* 7 (1972): 28–43; Matlock Population Studies Group,"Wills and Their Scribes," ibid., 8 (1972): 55–57; R. C. Richardson, "Wills and Will-Makers in the Sixteenth and Seventeenth Centuries: Some Lancashire Evidence," ibid., 9 (1972): 33–42; Bernard Capp, "Will Formularies," ibid., 14 (1975): 49; Michael L. Zell, "The Use of Religious Preambles as a Measure of Religious Belief in the Sixteenth Century," *Bulletin of the Institute of Historical Research* 50 (1977): 246–249; R. T. Vann, "Wills and the Family in an English Town: Banbury, 1550–1800," *Journal of Family History* 4 (1979): 346–367; Lorraine C. Attreed, "Preparation for Death in Sixteenth-Century Northern England," *Sixteenth Century Journal* 13 (1982): 37–66; G. J. Mayhew, "The Progress of the Reformation in East Sussex 1530–1559: The Evidence from Wills," *Southern History* 5 (1983): 38–67; Robert Whiting, "'For the health of my soul': Prayers for the Dead in the Tudor South-West," *Southern History* 5 (1983): 68–94; Claire Cross, "Wills as Evidence of Popular Piety in the Reformation Period: Leeds and Hull, 1540–1640," in *The End of Strife*, ed. David Loades (Edinburgh: T & T Clark, 1984): 44–51; Nesta Evans, "Inheritance, Women, Religion and Education in Early Modern Society as Revealed by Wills," in *Probate Records*, ed. Riden, 53–70; Stephen Coppel, "Wills and the Community," in ibid., 71–90; David Cressy, "Kinship and Kin Interaction in Early Modern England," *Past & Present* 113 (1986): 38–69; Claire Cross, "Northern Women in the Early Modern Period: The Female Testators of Hull and Leeds 1520–1650," *Yorkshire Archaeological Journal* 59 (1987): 83–94; J. D. Alsop, "Religious Preambles in Early Modern English Wills as Formulae," *Journal of Ecclesiastical History* 40 (1989): 19–27; Clive Burgess, "Late Medieval Wills and Pious Convention: Testamentary Evidence Reconsidered,"in *Profit, Piety and the Professions in Later Medieval England*, ed. M. A. Hicks (Gloucester: Alan Sutton, 1990): 14–33; Christopher Marsh, "In the Name of God? Will-Making and Faith in Early Modern England," in *The Records of the Nation*, ed. G. H. Martin and Peter Spufford (Woodbridge: Boydell Press, 1990): 215–249; Motoyasu Takahashi, "The Number of Wills Proved in the Sixteenth and Seventeenth Centuries: Graphs, with Tables and Commentary," ibid., 187–213; Mary Prior, "Wives and

in the will-making process, and asserted that unless the testator "had strong religious convictions, the clause bequeathing the soul may well have reflected the opinion of the scribe or the formulary book the latter was using," rather than that of the testator. Claire Cross and others have pointed out that most such statements of faith were, in fact, formulaic.[14]

With these observations in mind, we must ask a number of questions about the evidence. How much variety do we see in such will preambles and what were the sources for the formulas? Furthermore, who made the preamble selection: the scribe, the will-maker, or the two working in tandem? Did the testator exercise any control at all? Finally, can the religious preamble be used in determining the testator's beliefs? In this essay I propose to address these and related questions for the period from approximately 1530 to 1580, looking primarily at the diocese of Gloucester. I will begin by discussing the will-making process in early modern England. Then, using the Gloucester wills, as well as selected wills from other dioceses, I will identify a number of typical formulas used in religious preambles and trace their origins. More generally, I will explore the degree to which the testator controlled the selection of the form to be used, and therefore the expression of religious beliefs, in his or her will. Finally, I will discuss changes in lay piety based on the evidence from those wills.

The testamentary depositions contained in English diocesan records provide glimpses of the actual will-writing process. In June 1579, Margaret Grodie was sick with the plague and, wanting to make her last will and testament, she employed an ingenious means of accomplishing the task without exposing her scribe to that dreaded disease:

> She cawsed [her neighbor] Thomas Key to be called for and in the windoe of his owne howse the saide Key stoode, and she being in her awne chamber did make her will and Thomas Key did wryte yt and at any tyme when he dowted... [the] word she spoke he wold

---

Wills, 1558–1700," in *English Rural Society, 1500–1800*, ed. John Chartres and David Hey (Cambridge: Cambridge University Press, 1990): 201–225; Marjorie Keniston McIntosh, *A Community Transformed: The Manor of Havering, 1500–1620* (Cambridge: Cambridge University Press, 1992), 85–91, 188–94; Eamon Duffy, *The Stripping of the Altars: Traditional Religion in England, c. 1400–c. 1580* (New Haven: Yale University Press, 1992), 504–523; Craig and Litzenberger, "Wills as Religious Propaganda"; and the essay by Dr. Marsh in this volume.

[14]Spufford, "Scribes of Villagers' Wills," 28–43; Cross, "Wills as Evidence of Popular Piety," 44–51.

aske the women that were [caring for her]…and they wold tell him in her heeringe.[15]

This may have been an unusual case, but it provides a glimpse of a portion of the will-writing process, albeit under extenuating circumstances.

In most cases, the will was originally drafted in the presence of the testator and scribe alone. Only later was it read before witnesses and dated. This public reading of the will was followed by the subscription of witnesses' names. This seems to have been a normal part of the preparation for death in sixteenth-century England. John Bubbe of King's Norton was typical when, in the late 1540s, he sent for Edmund Robyns of the same town and Richard Shot of nearby Barnwood to come to his house to hear his will read. The day before he died, he "cawsed one to goe for his ghostly father [that is, his priest] and to cawse him to bryng the testament withe hym to thintent that…[his witnesses] might here it redde."[16] In these and many other instances will-writing was a three-step process which included writing, reading, and signing. Some wills, however, had a more convoluted provenance. The will of Alice Lynet of Charlton Kings, written in 1550, is a case in point. William Hall, her curate, said in a deposition that her servant, Jane Fynche, was sent to summon him to her house. "In the hall at the chimney before the fyre and about x of the clock aforenoen…, [with the] deponent sittyng at the high table fowre yardes or there aboutes distant from the said chimney," he wrote her will, but it was not read to her at that time. A month later Alice sent for Hall and he read the will to her, "noon other bodie beyng [present]." She then took it to show to her children. Later, a lodger in her house asked if she had heard her will read since she had taken it from the priest, and when she said no, he urged her to hear it. She agreed and he went to find his son, John, who could read. "And than she rose from the fyre and went to a cupbord in a table bord and fetched out thense a white boxe wherein was the testament," and heard it read in the presence of the boarder and his son. She died eight days later.[17] Even in this instance the testator followed the basic pattern. She sent for the scribe after becoming ill and dictated her will, but only later did she have it read before witnesses.

---

[15]GRO, G[loucester] D[iocesan] R[ecords], vol. 45, fol. 138v. Unless otherwise noted, this and all other examples cited are from Gloucestershire parishes.

[16]GRO, GDR, vol. 3, 65–67. This is similar to the process described by Dr. Marsh above.

[17]GRO, GDR, vol. 8, 87–91.

The acts of writing and reading the will are but two aspects of the will-making process; the creation or selection of the religious preamble is another. Christopher Marsh has identified numerous wills which begin by declaring "I...the unprofitable servant of God...geve agayne into the handes of my lord my god, my spirite, which he of his fatherly goodnes gave unto me." He has traced this preamble formula back to the character Epaphroditus, in Thomas Becon's book *The Sicke Mans Salve*, who gives advice on dying well. Other similar publications also appeared in the late sixteenth and early seventeenth centuries, and were similarly mined for will preamble formulas.[18]

However, the genre was not new; printed guides instructing the laity in the art of living and dying well had been available from the late fifteenth century onward. These primers, as they were known, contained collections of prayers, psalms, and readings from Scripture, intended primarily for use in the private devotions of lay people.[19] However, they typically included sections entitled "The Dirge" and "Paradise of the Soul," and these proved to be a rich source of statements suitable for use in will preambles. In 1538, for example, in the Cotswold parish of Stow-in-the-Wold the wills of Thomas Benett and nine of his neighbors used a common preamble which included the following passage: "I comytt my solle to Almythy God to be saved by the merytes and passyon of hys sone Jhesus which Jhesus onely hath redemed me and pasyfyed the wrathe of his father for my fawtes."[20] This was in all likelihood based on a passage from William Marshall's very Protestant *Prymer in Englyshe*, which had been printed in London three years earlier, in 1535. The passage reads: "The power of fayth is to justefye us: that is, to dispoyle us from all our vices and laye them to Christes back which hathe pacefyed the Fathers wrathe towardes us."[21]

Eight years later, in 1546, William Hugeford's will included the request that God "receyve my soule comynge to them whiche in this lyfe is an outlawe and pylgrym."[22] He or his scribe had probably used Bishop Hilsey's *Manual of Prayers* as a guide for his preamble. Published in 1539, it included the following prayer: "In the last houre of my departynge from

[18]See Marsh, "In the Name of God?"; Cross, "Wills as Evidence of Popular Piety," 47–48.
[19]For the use of primers see Duffy, *Stripping of the Altars*, 209–265.
[20]H[ereford and] W[orcestershire] R[ecord] O[ffice], Diocese of Worcester Wills, 1538/263.
[21]*A Prymer in Englishe, with certayn prayers & godly meditations, very necessary for all people that vnderstonde not the Latyne tongue*, ed. W. Marshall (London, 1534), STC 15986.
[22]GRO, Gloucestershire Wills, 1546/238.

this world receyve my soule, commyng to the[e], which in this lyfe is an outlawe, and a pylgryme."[23]

Other testators seem to have derived their religious will statements from particularly distinctive preambles used in the earlier wills of others. The first known example is the rather notorious "Testament of Master William Tracie, esquier," which was the source of preamble language used in a number of wills proved in diocesan courts all over England between 1537 and 1640, including that of Joan Davis, cited earlier.[24] William Tracy was a prominent member of the Gloucestershire gentry, who had known and probably discussed theology with William Tyndale. Tracy's will was refused probate in the Prerogative Court of Canterbury in 1531, and the contents prompted an official of Tracy's diocese to exhume and burn his body. The first of the four paragraphs which comprise Tracy's will reads:

> First and before all other thyng, I commit me unto God, and to his mercy, trustyng without any doubt or mistrust, that by his grace and the merites of Jesus Christ, and by the vertue of his passion and of his resurrection, I have and shal have remission of my sinnes and resurrection of body and soule, accordyng as it is written Job xix. I believe that me redemer lyveth, and that in the last day I shal rise out of the earth, and in my flesh shall see my Saviour, this my hope is layd up in my bosome.

This will was being passed among Protestants in manuscript form as early as 1531, the year of Tracy's death.[25] The printed editions with commentaries by William Tyndale and John Frith followed, beginning in 1535, and its use then began to spread rapidly. Over the next one hundred years testators all over England took all or part of the Tracy will and modified it slightly to make it their own. Joan Davis had used only a portion of the first paragraph. Joan Tymmes of Sutton-under-Brailes used more, declaring,

> *I commytt me unto God and to hys mercy trustynge wythowt doubt or mystrust that by hys grace and by the merytes of Jesu Chryst and by vertue off hys passyon and resurectyon I have and shall have remyssyon off my synnes and resurrectyon off body and soule accordingly as ytt ys written. Job xix I beleve that my sawyoure lyveth and*

[23]John Hilsey, *Manual of prayers; or the prymer in Englysh and Laten* (London, 1539), Sig. Rii.

[24]See Craig and Litzenberger, "Wills as Religious Propaganda."

[25]John Foxe, *Acts and Monuments of John Foxe*, ed. George Townsend, 8 vols. (London, 1846), 5:29–30, 38.

that in the last day I shall ryse owte of the earth and in my fleshe shall se my savyoure: this my hope ys layed up in my bosome and thys my *faythe rehersed ys suffycyent* I trust *wythout any* merytes or *workes* eyther off me or any other wherfore *wyll I bestowe no parte off my goods* eyther abowte the buryenge off my body wych I commend unto the earth as earth to earth and ashes to ashes neyther to any purpose to *that intent that any man shuld* pray *or do* any thyng for my soules health when I am departed thys miserable worlde yett notwythstandyng as frutes off my fayth I wyll that all my goods…shalbe bestowed after such sorte and manner as here doth folowe.[26]

The individuals whose wills included "Tracy preambles" appear to have selected their own religious statements. More often, of course, the choice of a preamble was probably made, at least initially, by a will scribe. However, this apparently independent scribal action does not invalidate sixteenth-century English wills as statements of the testators' religious beliefs. As God's steward on earth it was the Christian's duty to use the last will and testament as a means of promoting and supporting God's work in the world. Testators did view will-making as an important devotional act, and at least probably approved the preamble, even if it was initially supplied by a scribe. The selection or approval of a suitable formula, may well have been a genuine expression of the testator's true beliefs; creativity was not required.

In fact, an analysis of the wills from two Gloucestershire parishes, Tewkesbury and Cirencester, indicates that testators may indeed have had a good deal of preamble choice if they wanted to exercise it.[27] The 188 wills from Tewkesbury employed a total of twenty-seven different preambles. Of those 188, nearly three-quarters used either the standard traditional preamble in which they bequeathed their souls to "Almighty God, the Blessed Virgin Mary and the whole company of heaven," or the most common ambiguous preamble, leaving their souls simply to Almighty God. The remaining one-quarter, however, give evidence of the variety of soul bequests available in Tewkesbury. This one-quarter, the wills of fifty-two testators, is divided between twenty-three additional preambles. Similarly in Cirencester, a number of preambles were employed. The soul bequests

---

[26]GRO, Gloucestershire Wills, 1552/43. (Italics indicate those portions of the preamble which match Tracy's.)

[27]Based on Gloucestershire wills held in the GRO.

of the 106 wills are divided among twenty-six separate preamble forms. Unlike Tewkesbury, however, only half used one of the two standard formulas. The other half (51 wills) are divided among the remaining twenty-four preambles. A wide spectrum of choice is implied by the number of distinctive preambles used.

At this point this analysis is purely impressionistic. However, it appears that the testators of both Cirencester and Tewkesbury could, if they so chose, select from a number of different and varied soul bequests; but how did the process work? Quite possibly the answer lies in the number of scriveners functioning within each town, and the number of different preambles each used. In Gloucestershire during this period will scribes seldom explicitly identified themselves as such. However, by examining handwriting, spelling, and the use of particular phrases, and then combining that analysis with the witnesses listed for each will, it is possible to make informed judgments as to the identity of scribes.[28]

Eleven Tewkesbury scribes have been identified for this period. From this group three emerge as the town's primary will-writers: John Cole, Nicholas Crondale, and John Gase. The rest accounted for only a few wills each. John Cole was the longest functioning of the three, active from 1546 to at least 1586. He was the parish clerk, and responsible for making the leather baldrics for the church bells, as well as writing wills. As a scribe he wrote forty-four wills and employed eleven different preambles. Cole used the standard ambiguous form for his preambles during the last years of Henry VIII's reign. He continued to use the ambiguous form through the reigns of both Edward VI and Mary; however, during Mary's reign he added the standard traditional soul bequest. He continued then to use these two forms in Elizabeth's reign, but also added a more expansive but still ambiguous preamble. Finally, he replaced the standard ambiguous formula with his own variation: "I bequethe my solle into the handys off Allmighty God the father of our Lorde Jhesus Chryste."[29] As religious policy changed over the forty years of his scribal activity, John Cole's preamble repertoire grew.

Meanwhile in 1553, Tewkesbury's curate, Nicholas Crondale, began writing wills. He wrote at least twenty-nine between 1553 and 1572,

---

[28]This is similar to the methodology employed by Marjorie McIntosh in identifying will scribes, although her approach differs somewhat due to differences in the information available for analysis: McIntosh, *A Community Transformed*, 88.

[29]GRO, Gloucestershire Wills, 1559/216.

usually employing one of the most popular ambiguous formulas, which bequeathed the soul "to Almighty God my maker and redeemer." Still more choice was added for Tewkesbury testators in 1556 when John Gase appeared as another scribe. During the ten years of his activity he wrote eighteen wills, all of which were either traditional or ambiguous. Additionally, those seeking a Protestant preamble could summon one of three other scribes. Thus, in Tewkesbury during the period from 1540 to 1580 a growing number of preamble formulas were available for use as the number of scribes, as well as their individual repertoires, increased.

In Cirencester, as in Tewkesbury, the variety of preambles is evidence of the availability of options for testators there. In contrast to Tewkesbury's eleven scribes, however, only four have been identified for Cirencester. Of these, only two wrote more than two wills each. Peter Gery wrote at least eleven wills between 1545 and 1557. He used either the standard traditional form or his own distinctive but ambiguous statement, bequeathing the soul "to Almighty God, the Lord and giver of all goodness."[30]

Gery disappeared as a scribe in 1557, and Thomas Faryngton, a tucker (or cloth finisher) began to function in that capacity. He can be associated with at least twenty-two Cirencester wills between 1557 and 1578, as well as one in Tewkesbury in 1573. His first wills in Cirencester used the standard preambles, either traditional or ambiguous. However, only a year later, in the will of Thomas Turner, weaver, Faryngton used a new, albeit traditional, form, bequeathing the soul "unto Almyghty God the Father, to Jesu Chryst his onlye sonne our redemer, and to the Holye Goost the Comforter and to all the blessyd company of hevyn."[31] For the following fourteen years Faryngton relied upon his own variant of a traditional soul bequest. Then in 1571 he began to modify it. In the will of Alice Adys, he changed his preamble by replacing the reference to the company of heaven with an "etc." as she bequeathed her soul "to Allmightye God the Father, to Jhesus Christ my onely salvyor and to the Holy Ghost the comforter etc."[32] Technically, Thomas Faryngton's new preamble was no longer traditional, but rather ambiguous, since only the testator and scribe could have been sure of the exact meaning of "etc." He continued to use his original formula, but also employed the newer ambiguous version of 1571, and more

---

[30]GRO, Gloucestershire Wills, 1555/29.
[31]GRO, Gloucestershire Wills, 1558/223.
[32]GRO, Gloucestershire Wills, 1571/18.

changes would follow. By 1573 it appeared to be nothing more than the most standard ambiguous form of a soul bequest. Significantly, however, he retained the "etc." so that it read, "I bequeath my soule to Almighti God etc."[33] Not only did Faryngton provide a variety of traditional and ambiguous preambles; he modified his own traditional formula in such a manner as to offer a welcome solution to Elizabethan followers of the old religion who were anxious to appear conformist but did not want to misrepresent their true faith, even in their wills. As the evolution of Thomas Faryngton's preamble demonstrates, the well-placed use of an "etc." could conceal whole theological systems in a seemingly ambiguous soul bequest. Clearly those Tewkesbury and Cirencester testators wishing a degree of control over the nature of their soul bequest had the means at their disposal, and the fact that individual scribes employed a variety of forms supports the supposition that at least a portion of the populace did give attention to their preambles.

Looking more broadly at all 3,000-plus Gloucestershire wills, roughly 20 percent used a preamble that was solely their own or was used at most by only nine other people. This accounts for 325 of the 350 different preamble formulas used in the county between 1540 and 1580. It thus appears that a significant proportion of Gloucestershire testators exercised some control over the religious content of their wills. Thus, though religious preambles included in early modern English wills were often formulaic, in 20 to 25 percent of such wills the testator appears to have exercised some control over the content of their soul bequests. They may have made the choices themselves or chosen from among the formulas preselected by their scribes. The form may have originated in a primer, an advice book, or the *Book of Common Prayer*. It may even have been based on someone else's will. Hence, early modern English wills may still be a valuable source of information on popular piety.

However, wills, and especially will preambles, must still be used carefully and cautiously. Both Professor Spufford and Professor Dickens warned of the need to "avoid statistical pedantry when attempting to derive doctrinal impressions from testamentary records."[34] However, the real problem stems not from the use of statistics, in general, but from the particular methods employed. Ignoring the complexity and variety contained

---

[33]GRO, Gloucestershire Wills 1575/124, 1577/80.

[34]A. G. Dickens, *Lollards and Protestants in the Diocese of York* (1959; reprint, London: Hambledon Press, 1982), 221.

in will preambles, codifying them too early in the analytical process, or relying on an inadequate sample can lead to inaccurate and distorted conclusions. A more detailed analysis is required.

This study uses a very precise set of soul bequest categories, as well as selected charitable bequests, to perform such an analysis. Through textual content analysis to classify and codify the individual soul bequests found in the wills, it is possible to study the changing usage of key phrases in preambles over time and gain some knowledge of responses to changes in official religious policies.[35] By such means seventeen categories of religious will preambles have been identified describing a spectrum of beliefs ranging from very traditional to distinctly Protestant.

However, labeling them further is quite problematic. In order to gain a view of the forest rather than just a few trees further combination is necessary, but the process of categorization requires careful thought. For purposes of this analysis I have identified five categories as traditional, five as Protestant, and the remaining seven as ambiguous (see table 2). All the

TABLE 2[A]
WILL PREAMBLE CATEGORIES DIVIDED INTO THREE GENERAL GROUPS

Traditional:
- References to the blessed Virgin Mary and/or the holy company of heaven
- Use of "only" with references to the blessed Virgin Mary and/or the holy company of heaven
- References to being associated with the blessed Virgin Mary and/or the holy company of heaven (or the word "elect" used in place of a reference to the saints)
- Otherwise traditional bequests which include references to Christ's passion
- Otherwise traditional bequests which include statements of trust in salvation through Christ's death

Ambiguous:
- Bequests to the Holy Trinity
- Bequests to Almighty God and/or Jesus Christ (the most ambiguous forms)
- References to God's mercy (without mention of the blessed Virgin Mary or holy company of heaven)
- References to the merits, precious blood and/or passion of Jesus Christ or Almighty God
- Use of "only" (e.g., "my only redeemer") with bequests to Almighty God and/or Jesus Christ
- References to Christ's resurrection
- References to "reigning with the elect," or being one of the "number of the elect"

Protestant:
- References to assurance of salvation (without any doubt or mistrust)
- Testator directly addressing God
- Use of the phrase, "I have and shall have" salvation or forgiveness of sins
- Use of the phrase, "and by no other means"
- Use of the phrase, "not by any work or works of mine"

a. Source: GRO, Gloucestershire Wills 1541-1580.

[35]The wills data was collected in as much detail as possible, including *verbatim* transcriptions of the preambles. Subsequently, a set of codes was developed based in the textual content analysis to describe every distinctive soul bequest found in the wills that had been read, and the coded preambles were categorized. Then, statistical analysis was performed by examining the incidence of the various preamble categories as percentages of the whole.

categories grouped as traditional are distinguished by the inclusion of a reference to the Blessed Virgin Mary, to the company of heaven, or both. Additionally, these preambles may also describe Christ's passion as a means of their salvation, and may even refer to Christ or God as "my only saviour" or "my only creator," but the mention of the Virgin Mary or the saints is the determining factor in their classification as traditional. The most standard of these preamble formulas is of course, "I bequeath my soul to Almighty God, to our Lady and to all the whole Company of Heaven." At the other end of the spectrum all the categories labeled Protestant explicitly refute traditional means of salvation, such as the efficacy of works or prayers for the soul of the testator, express unqualified assurance of the salvation of the testator, or address God directly. Thus declarations of faith in salvation by the death and passion of Jesus Christ, "and by no other means," or "without any doubt or mistrust" have been designated as Protestant.

The remaining collection of categories has been grouped under the rubric "ambiguous" and consists of those forms which could be used in good conscience by individuals espousing a wide range of beliefs, including people leaning toward either Protestant or traditional faith. This subset comprises preambles which bequeath the soul to the Holy Trinity, as well as those which refer to God's mercy. Also classified in this group are statements which mention Christ's passion or resurrection, or describe God or Christ as "my only redeemer," all of which could be (and were) used comfortably in wills which otherwise expressed a range of beliefs. While it is true that preambles which refer to the passion or the resurrection, as well as those which use the word "only" and omit all reference to the Virgin Mary or the saints, often go on to make explicitly Protestant statements, they occasionally continue by asking St. Mary and all the saints to pray for the soul of the testator. Hence when they do neither they have been included in the ambiguous group.

Additionally, the use of the word "elect," so often associated with Protestantism, has required special attention. In some cases it is clearly used in place of a reference to all the saints, and thus that preamble is categorized as traditional. In other cases, however, it is employed more ambiguously in phrases such as "reigning with the elect" or being "one of the number of the elect" and therefore is labeled as ambiguous, albeit at the Protestant end of the spectrum of ambiguous statements. Finally, the ambiguous category includes the standard form, "I bequeath my soul to Almighty God," and its slightly more expansive offspring, "I bequeath my soul to Almighty God my maker and redeemer," which seems to have gradually superseded the shorter form in popularity by 1580. The demarcation lines in this forest of expressions of faith can indeed be quite vague and difficult to establish. They have been included here to facilitate the discussion of lay religion, a tool to help us understand the past. In the final analysis it must be remembered that we are dealing with a wide spectrum of beliefs, rather than with three clearly defined boxes into which we can place people and their wills.

Using these categories, aspects of individual lay piety are revealed by the wills. The analysis of the systematic sample of lay wills from the entire diocese of Gloucester for the period from 1541 to 1580 shows some remarkable and pronounced changes over time (see fig. 1 and table 3).[36]

FIGURE 1
ALL WILL PREAMBLES: THREE-YEAR ROLLING AVERAGE

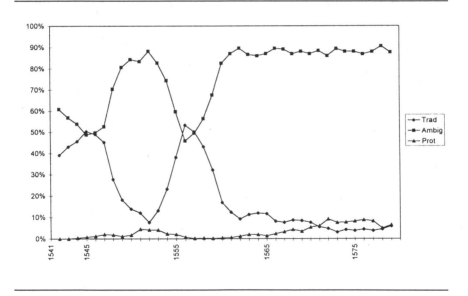

[36]See fig. 1 and table 3 with a chi-square value of 525.95 with 8 degrees of freedom, a very significant value. This value was determined by analyzing preamble counts by reign or portion of reign within the general categories (traditional, ambiguous, and Protestant) and comparing the differences in the preference for each over time with that which would have been expected based on the overall percentage of wills with preambles in each general category. The reigns or portions of reigns include the last years of the reign of Henry VIII, the complete reigns of Edward VI and Mary, and the first half of the reign of Elizabeth I, with the latter divided into two separate portions for purposes of analysis: Henry VIII (1541–46), Edward VI (1547–53), Mary (1553–58), Elizabeth I (1559–69 and 1570–80). These periods are used throughout the analysis described in this essay.

TABLE 3[A]
TOTAL PREAMBLES AND PERCENTAGES BY REIGN AND GENERAL CATEGORY

Reign	Trad.	Amb.	Prot.	Totals	Trad. (%)	Amb. (%)	Prot. (%)
Henry	182	209	2	393	46.3	53.2	0.5
Edward	47	225	8	280	16.8	80.4	2.9
Mary	241	269	4	514	46.9	52.3	0.8
Elizabeth (1559–69)	81	578	13	672	12.1	86.0	1.9
Elizabeth (1570–80)	37	659	55	751	4.9	87.8	7.3
Totals	588	1,940	82	2,610			

a. Source: GRO, Gloucestershire Wills 1541–1580.

During the last years of Henry's reign nearly half the wills written included traditional soul bequests. However, this changed dramatically during Edward's reign, as scribes and at least some individual testators eschewed traditional forms and ducked for cover behind ambiguous preambles. True, some testators (and I do think the testators were making the choices in these cases) opted for clear expressions of Protestant beliefs, as did Joan Davis and Joan Tymmes. Nevertheless, most of the diocesan-wide move away from traditional formulas was toward ambiguous soul bequests, and the standard traditional soul bequest disappears from the extant wills after February 1551. Clearly Bishop Hooper's visitation had an effect on the expressions of faith contained in Gloucestershire wills during his episcopate; however, it does not seem to have been the effect he would have desired.

The content of wills following Mary's accession seems to confirm that many of those who had clung to the old religion had chosen ambiguous preambles under Edward (and Hooper). The percentage of testators choosing traditional will preambles increased steadily under Mary to over 57 percent by 1557. Furthermore, while Protestant soul bequests vanished, the most significant difference from Edward's reign was the move away from ambiguous statements. Under Mary, individuals who had clung to the old religion were free once again to proclaim their beliefs publicly, and over half the Gloucestershire testators took advantage of that opportunity. The proportion of wills containing traditional preambles was even higher than it had been during the last years of the reign of her father, and the pronounced swing in this direction after Edward's death lends credence to the assertion that the choice of ambiguous statements when Protestantism had held sway was, in fact, a means of safely concealing one's true Catholic faith.

Some historians have asserted that the preference among Marian testators for traditional faith statements was a result of official coercion rather than genuine belief. However, while it is certainly true that such changes reflect the influence of official policy, the response in this case appears to have been to welcome the return to the old religion, especially when considered in conjunction with provisions for worship which were being made at the same time in parish churches.[37] Furthermore, pressure from the ecclesiastical hierarchy and the crown may very well have dissuaded most testators from employing explicitly Protestant formulas, but ambiguous preambles would still have been an acceptable alternative as they had been for conservatives under Edward. Such statements did in fact serve multiple purposes. In cases where the testator was too sick to express a preference, or more rarely to dictate the contents of a statement of faith, or where such a statement was not important to the testator, an ambiguous preamble would have provided the obvious solution. However, they could also be used to conceal one's true beliefs, and that, in fact, is probably what those with traditional beliefs had done during Edward's reign. With Mary's accession the wills of those who had clung to the old religion during the previous reign employed traditional soul bequests.

The renewed preference for traditional preambles did not, however, mean that Marian testators and their scribes had settled back into the same limited set of faith statements used by their Henrician predecessors. Simple soul bequests were still quite common; however, the variety of specific formulas had multiplied between 1547 and 1553, and the Marian Restoration did not change that. Preambles may have returned to expressions of traditional beliefs, but they did not necessarily return to the old traditional forms. Emphasis on the Christological aspects of faith had begun to grow in importance before the introduction of Protestantism, and that trend was continuing. There also seems to have been an increasing desire to express one's personal beliefs more fully in the preamble than had previously been the case. Both testators and scribes appear to have perceived the need for more complete and complex descriptions of salvation theology than had

---

[37]For discussion of the parish provisions in Gloucestershire for liturgical conformity to Marian Catholicism, see Caroline Litzenberger, *The English Reformation and the Laity: Gloucestershire 1540–1580* (Cambridge: Cambridge University Press, 1997).

been deemed necessary before the introduction of Protestantism. Thus, when Joan Holder, widow of Charlton Kings, wrote her will in 1556, she was expressing traditional beliefs, bequeathing her soul "vnto Almighty God my creator and redemer vnto whose mercye I commytt my selfe vnto, trusting by the merytes of hys passion to inheryt the kingdome of heavin, and also desiring owre blessed Ladye with all the whole companye off heavin to preye for me."[38] Similarly, a year later John Dyston of Winchcombe committed his soul "to Almighty God and to Jhesus Christ his only son and to all the hole blessyd company of heaven most steadfastly beleving that the thing that is commyttyd to their charge can not perysshe but be preservyd and in beter wyse restoryd at the latter day."[39] This mixture of explicitly articulated faith in salvation through Christ's death and passion, combined with either requests for intercessions on behalf of the testator by the Blessed Virgin Mary and all the saints, or invocations to the saints was a common feature of Marian wills.

The complexity and variety of soul bequests continued to grow within all categories of wills through the first half of Elizabeth's reign. The proportion of wills using ambiguous preambles stabilized at 85 percent, while those using traditional soul bequests declined steadily and those expressing Protestant beliefs began to increase very slowly. Clearly, traditional expressions of faith were falling from favor, but Protestant statements had not yet become the preferred alternative. There appears to have been some change in beliefs; however, the predominance of ambiguous forms indicates that both established scribes and followers of the old religion were increasing their reliance on those forms.

Not all groups of Gloucestershire testators, nevertheless, followed the general pattern described above. Table 4 sets out the use of Protestant, ambiguous, and traditional forms of preambles. The wills of slightly more women than men included Protestant preambles in Edward's reign. However, the greatest discrepancy was in their uses of ambiguous forms as compared to their continued reliance on traditional statements.[40] By 1580

---

[38]GRO, Gloucestershire Wills, 1556/64.

[39]GRO, Gloucestershire Wills, 1557/224.

[40]In comparing the use of ambiguous preambles by men and women there is a chi-square value of 26.70 with 4 degrees of freedom. The chi-square value for ambiguous preambles was determined by tabulating those particular preambles by gender and by reign or portion of reign. Then the actual preferences for ambiguous statements in women's and men's wills over time were compared to determine if there was a significant difference by gender. The test for Protestant wills is probably not statistically significant due to the small numbers of wills involved.

TABLE 4[a]

TRADITIONAL, AMBIGUOUS, AND PROTESTANT PREAMBLES BY REIGN AND
SEX OF TESTATOR

Reign	Women				Men			
	Trad. %	Amb. %	Prot. %	Total (n)	Trad. (%)	Amb. (%)	Prot. (%)	Total (n)
Henry	47.3	52.0	0.7	148	45.7	53.9	0.4	245
Edward	15.2	80.4	4.4	138	18.3	80.3	1.4	142
Mary	48.7	50.2	1.1	263	45.0	54.6	0.4	251
Eliz. (1559–69)	11.6	86.5	1.9	362	12.6	85.5	1.9	310
Eliz. (1570–80)	3.4	89.6	7.0	414	6.8	85.5	7.7	337
Totals				1325				1285

a. Source: GRO, Gloucestershire Wills 1541–1580.

traditional soul bequests were almost nonexistent in women's wills.
Women and their scribes seem to have opted for ambiguity in place of the
traditional declarations used earlier, as the popularity of ambiguous forms
increased steadily through the 1570s. On the other hand, during the same
period ambiguous statements maintained their earlier level of appeal
among male testators and their scribes, and traditional forms did not
decline as markedly as they did among women. In men's wills the popularity of traditional forms was roughly equal to that of Protestant preambles. The differences are slight and it is important not to overstate them,
but perhaps women with traditional beliefs were choosing to conceal them
behind ambiguous statements, while their male counterparts were not. Or
perhaps scribes were treating women differently than they were treating
men, seeking to protect them.

Even less significant than the gender differences in will preambles are
those between men from different levels of society. The testator's status was
seldom included in wills written before the accession of Elizabeth; however, nearly half of the Gloucestershire men writing wills during the first
half of Elizabeth's reign did include either status or occupation.[41] Unfortunately, the total number is still quite small; however, it remains possible to
gain an impression of the religious preferences of men from different levels

[41]Two hundred seventy-five of the 647 Elizabethan men (42.5 percent) who left wills included
either their status or occupation. It is not possible to analyze Elizabethan women's wills in this way,
because most merely gave their status as "widow" without further elaboration, and their wills seldom
included material evidence of their social position or wealth.

of society. Among the leaders, few of whose wills are included in the sample, one-third (three) chose traditional preambles, one man chose a Protestant statement, and the remaining five employed ambiguous forms. Meanwhile, approximately 14 percent of the 200 husbandmen, yeomen, and artisans leaving wills included a traditional soul bequest, while none of the dozen mercers or merchants and very few textile workers (18 of whom are included in this study) made similar choices. Instead, the latter opted primarily for ambiguous statements. Artisans and merchants were the only groups to turn in any numbers to Protestantism, with just over 13 percent (5 of 36) choosing such statements. Nonetheless, the clearest conclusion to be drawn from this set of wills is that preference for ambiguous preambles was not distinguished by social position. While a small minority may have differed in their choice of traditional or Protestant statements, approximately 80 percent of the testators in every group selected ambiguous soul bequests.[42]

Regional preferences in the 1560s and 1570s were more distinctive than those based on either gender or social status.[43] The diocese of Gloucester is long and narrow; in it the Vale of the Severn extends from north to south, flanked on the west by the Forest of Dean and on the east by the Cotswolds. Table 5 sets out preferences for preamble type by region. In the northern Severn Valley and the Forest of Dean after 1570 there was a substantial preference for ambiguous preambles combined with a sharp decline of traditional soul bequests. Protestant preambles increased only very slightly there during that time. Once again, there is evidence that people turned from traditional to ambiguous preambles, suggesting the use of ambiguity to hide personal theology. In fact, only in the Cotswolds and in the city of Gloucester can we find notable signs of acceptance of Protestantism. In the 1570s 14 percent (5 of 36) of Gloucester testators and 11 percent (29 of 256) of those in the Cotswolds used distinctly Protestant preambles.

While changes in the popularity of different categories of will preambles shed light on alterations in lay religious beliefs, so too do evolving preferences for different charitable bequests, both large and small. These

---

[42]Fewer of the aldermen and gentry chose ambiguous statements, but with only nine wills in that segment of the sample, their preferences cannot be considered representative.

[43]Chi-square value = 46.05 with 16 degrees of freedom. This value was determined by comparing the preferences for ambiguous wills over time in each region, having accumulated the will counts by reign or portion of reign.

TABLE 5ᴬ
TRADITIONAL, AMBIGUOUS, AND PROTESTANT PREAMBLES BY REIGN AND
REGION

Region & type	Henry	Edward	Mary	Eliz. (1559–69)	Eliz. (1570–80)
Cotswolds					
Traditional (%)	51.9	16.1	54.7	18.3	8.2
Ambiguous (%)	48.1	77.8	44.2	77.4	80.5
Protestant (%)	0.0	6.1	1.1	4.3	11.3
N =	131.0	99.0	190.0	208.0	256.0
Forest of Dean					
Traditional (%)	69.4	17.4	38.2	14.7	1.7
Ambiguous (%)	30.6	78.3	61.8	85.3	95.8
Protestant (%)	0.0	4.3	0.0	0.0	2.5
N =	49.0	46.0	55.0	102.0	118.0
Gloucester City					
Traditional (%)	51.9	17.6	33.3	6.5	0.0
Ambiguous (%)	48.1	82.4	66.7	90.3	86.1
Protestant (%)	0.0	0.0	0.0	3.2	13.9
N =	27.0	17.0	24.0	31.0	36.0
North Vale of Severn					
Traditional (%)	35.3	27.5	49.6	6.5	1.7
Ambiguous (%)	64.7	72.5	49.6	92.9	94.2
Protestant (%)	0.0	0.0	0.8	0.6	4.1
N =	102.0	40.0	133.0	154.0	121.0
South Vale of Severn					
Traditional (%)	35.7	11.5	37.5	9.1	5.5
Ambiguous (%)	61.9	88.5	61.6	89.8	88.6
Protestant (%)	2.4	0.0	0.9	1.1	5.9
N =	84.0	78.0	112.0	177.0	220.0

a. Source: GRO, Gloucestershire Wills 1541–1580.

included bequests to parishes, municipalities, and the poor, as well as provisions for prayers for the souls of the departed. Clearly, changes in religious policies and practices had a major impact on parish bequests, and gifts to parishes dropped off substantially following the accession of Edward and the introduction of the first set of Edwardian changes in 1548 (see fig. 2 and table 6). Most parish bequests were ritualistic; simple legacies of a few pence or a little grain. Some were for lights or the high altar, traditional use and traditional language, while others were just given to the

FIGURE 2
PERCENT PARISH BEQUESTS: THREE-YEAR ROLLING AVERAGE

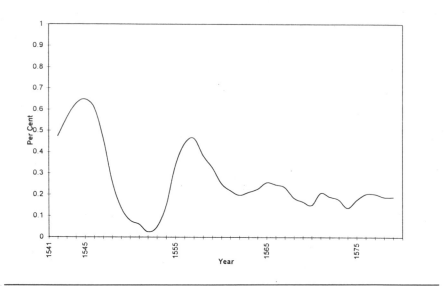

TABLE 6[A]
BEQUESTS TO PARISHES BY GENDER OF TESTATOR AND REIGN

Reign	Women			Men		
	Bequests	All wills	%	Bequests	All wills	%
Henry	91	148	61.5	146	245	59.6
Edward	22	138	15.9	17	142	12.0
Mary	92	263	35.0	100	251	39.8
Elizabeth (1559–69)	79	362	21.8	77	310	24.8
Elizabeth (1570–80)	66	414	15.9	69	337	20.5
Totals	350	1,325		409	1,285	

a. Source: GRO, Gloucestershire Wills 1541–1580.

parish with no further stipulation or were not explicitly connected with traditional practices. During the last years of Henry's reign over 60 percent of all testators made such bequests, with most specifying traditional uses. However, the popularity of ritualistic gifts to parishes lessened substantially under Edward and never returned to its earlier level, in spite of some renewed interest during the Marian Restoration. After Elizabeth's accession the decline continued through the 1560s before stabilizing somewhat in the 1570s. Interestingly, the decline in bequests is similar for both men and women. Municipal bequests suffered somewhat, as well, although the decrease was less pronounced. Approximately 8 percent of the late Henrician testators gave something for public works, usually for bridge repair, but then under Edward the percentage declined slightly. The annual proportion of wills including such gifts had, however, been quite erratic since at least 1541 and continued in like manner through the late 1550s and 1560s, before settling down to an average of only 2 percent in the 1570s. Ritualistic bequests to the poor were another matter. The popularity of these provisions increased substantially between 1541 and 1580 (see fig. 3). During the last years of Henry's reign approximately 8 percent of all testators made small bequests of money, bread, or drink to the poor.

FIGURE 3
PERCENT BEQUESTS TO THE POOR: THREE-YEAR ROLLING AVERAGE

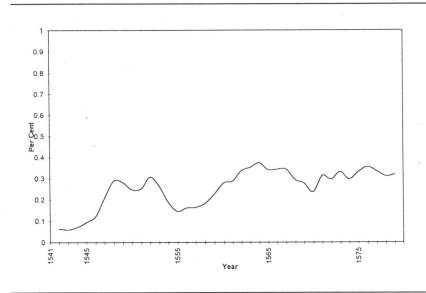

The percentage jumped substantially under Edward, and after dropping back to almost the late Henrician level of popularity under Mary, rebounded immediately and achieved a new high of nearly 30 percent by the mid-1560s, a level that was then maintained at least until the late 1570s. Once again the trend holds for both men and women (see table 7). This increase may have been due, at least initially, to the introduction of the statutory poor box in every parish. However, references to the box disappear from wills early in Elizabeth's reign, and the bequests are to be distributed by the executrix (or executor) or by the overseers of the will, instead of being dispensed through the parish.

TABLE 7[a]
BEQUESTS TO POOR BY GENDER OF TESTATOR AND REIGN

Reign	Women			Men		
	Bequests	All wills	%	Bequests	All wills	%
Henry	13	148	8.8	19	245	7.8
Edward	42	138	30.4	35	142	24.6
Mary	37	263	14.1	41	251	16.3
Elizabeth (1559–69)	107	362	29.6	101	310	32.6
Elizabeth (1570–80)	126	414	30.4	109	337	32.3
Totals	325	1,325		305	1,285	

a. Source: GRO, Gloucestershire Wills 1541–1580.

Unlike ritualistic gifts, more generous and distinctive charitable bequests continued sporadically throughout the period of this study. Although there are not enough of these for more than an impressionistic view, the changes in religious policy do not appear to have affected the size or frequency of these gifts. In the case of parish bequests, the stipulated uses may have changed, but the gifts kept coming. Similarly, major gifts to the poor continued, albeit without the explicit quid pro quo of prayers for the benefactor which would have been a provision of such largesse before the Reformation. In 1562, Margaret Hyckes, widow of Tewkesbury, stipulated that the rents from specified lands were to be used to aid the poor.[44] A short distance to the south in the city of Gloucester a few years later, William Goldeston, his brother, Richard, and Richard's wife, Joan, all left land, tenements, or money to almshouses or (in the case of Joan) for wood and coal to be distributed to the poor annually.[45] In none of these cases were the poor asked to pray for the dead, although some testators may have hoped for that response. However, based on the religious preambles in these particular wills, it is clear that at least the Goldestons would not have wanted any such works on their behalf. They seem to have been acting out of a belief in their own responsibility for the stewardship of God's creation, combined with a sense of civic duty.

[44]The funds bequeathed by Margaret Hyckes were to be administered by the parish churchwardens. GRO, Gloucestershire Wills, 1562/71.
[45]GRO, Gloucestershire Wills, 1569/156, 1574/143, 1579/107.

The last group of bequests to be considered are those which made explicit provisions for prayers for the dead. This decidedly traditional category was reasonably popular toward the end of Henry's reign, appearing in approximately 15 percent of the wills of the period. However, within a year of Henry's death such provisions had virtually vanished from Gloucestershire wills, except for a small rally under Mary (see table 8). None appears in the sample after 1563, which may be an early indication of the effects of changing religious policy under Elizabeth.

TABLE 8[A]

WILLS CONTAINING PROVISIONS FOR PRAYERS FOR THE DEAD BY SEX OF TESTATOR AND REIGN

Reign	Women			Men		
	Requests	All wills	%	Requests	All wills	%
Henry	22	148	14.9	34	245	13.9
Edward	1	138	0.7	6	142	4.2
Mary	4	263	1.5	7	251	2.8
Elizabeth (1559–69)	1	362	0.2	3	310	1.0
Elizabeth (1570–80)	0	414	0.0	0	337	0.0
Totals	28	1,325		50	1,285	

a. Source: GRO, Gloucestershire Wills 1541–1580.

The analysis of two other terms often included in traditional wills also helps gauge the rate of change in lay piety in Gloucestershire. Both were used by Elizabeth Lane, whose will was quoted at the beginning of this essay.[46] In traditional wills, as in Widow Lane's, the parish priest is often referred to as "my ghostly father," and the cathedral is called the "mother church." Both phrases fell from favor with Edward's accession, and after remaining at a consistently low level through the 1550s, resumed their decline under Elizabeth. References to "my ghostly father" disappeared by 1570, while those to the "mother church" were appearing in just 2 percent of the wills by 1580.

How did the laity of the diocese of Gloucester respond to changes in religious policy? Wills can only provide part of the answer; however, based on this evidence it appears that the most dramatic responses came in Edward's reign when the appeal of both traditional preambles and traditional charitable bequests decreased dramatically. In this instance, the

[46]GRO, Gloucestershire Wills, 1551/16.

changes were so abrupt and so great that they almost certainly were a result of Bishop Hooper's policies and actions. These were more specific and more distinctively Protestant than those of any other Edwardian bishop, except perhaps Nicholas Ridley, bishop of Rochester and then London. These responses seem to reflect a combination of rigid conformity to Hooper's visitation articles by priests and other scribes, and a largely defensive response by many of the laity. Although it is important not to ignore individual testators like Joan Tymmes whose wills attest to their Protestantism, for the most part the laity and scribes of Edwardian Gloucestershire seem to have been reluctant to give up the old in favor of the new religion. Rather, they opted for some portion of the middle ground and used ambiguous will preambles.

The contents of Marian wills support this analysis, given the wholesale swing back to traditional wills in both statements of faith and charitable bequests. Initially, Elizabeth's accession brought a response which was quite similar to that seen in Edward's reign. Certainly, traditional soul bequests declined sharply in popularity and had nearly disappeared by 1580. However, many testators probably still clung to the old religion, concealing their faith behind ambiguous preambles. It is difficult to quantify, but clearly the use of ambiguous formulas was divided primarily between those who would have preferred a more traditional statement and those who left the decision totally in the hands of the scribe. Only in the late 1570s do we see the use of Protestant preambles increasing in popularity, and even then the incidence of such statements is widely scattered, each particular form being used in a maximum of only two or three wills. Based on the evidence from wills, the laity of Gloucestershire appear to have responded very slowly to the religious changes introduced during the period to 1580. Thus, in that county and diocese, those historically minded insomniacs to whom Professor Collinson has referred would probably still have been counting Protestants, rather than Catholics, in 1570 and beyond.[47]

---

[47] Patrick Collinson, *The Birthpangs of Protestant England: Religious and Cultural Change in the Sixteenth and Seventeenth Centuries* (Basingstoke: Macmillan, 1988), ix.

CRITICAL
AFTERWORDS

NEGOTIATING *the* REFORMATION

Norman Jones

IN THE MIDDLE OF THE SIXTEENTH CENTURY, people had to attempt to fulfill their ideals while thinking pragmatically about what to do if the law
suddenly frowned on those ideals. No matter what one's faith one had to
find a path—perhaps even a via media—through the confusion of the Reformation. The will of George Seyntpole of Northaulton in Lincoln presents
a classic case of this pragmatic idealism. Drafted in the Christmas season
of 1558 it shows a sensible awareness of the mutability of laws. Seyntpole
wished to endow a chantry priest to pray for the souls of his mother, his
father, himself, and his family. The terms of this endowment were carefully
worked out over a folio page. He named the priest, he provided for the
selection of his successor, and he concluded by directing what should be
done with the money if religion changed. All the stipulated things were to
be carried out "Provided alwayes that if any lawe hereafter be made within
this Realme by parliament or other wise that the saide gift for fynding of a
priest shall not be goode" his son John could redirect the money. As George
Seyntpole had foreseen, by the time his will was proved in late February of
1559 Parliament was moving to abolish purgatory, making the founding of
a chantry impossible.[1] George Seyntpole was afraid of purgatory. No heretical law could really abolish it. But that law could take away his money and
put it into the crown's pocket so it was incumbent upon him to protect his
property. Believing firmly in the power of the Blood of Christ he also
believed firmly in the power of Parliament over this world. And so he
planned accordingly.

The essays in this volume reflect the difficulty three generations of
English people faced as they negotiated the changes wrought by the Reformation. No matter where their religious allegiances lay they were involved

---

[1] P[ublic] R[ecord] O[ffice], PROB 11/42A, fols. 338v–341v. My thanks to Dr. Wabuda for
bringing this will to my attention.

in a spiritual battle that had very secular implications. They still had to live, no matter what the ultimate truth about heaven, purgatory, hell, works, election, or *magisterium* might be. Like most people at all times, Tudor people were not necessarily thrilled about change. Even those whose sympathies were with the reformers must have pondered the difficulties the changes imposed and mourned in some measure the disappearance of comfortable village customs. For those conservatives who did not cherish Protestant desires, reform must have been a truly miserable experience.

Recently we have been reminded of the strength of conservative beliefs and habits that resisted the Reformation until late in Elizabeth's reign. Eamon Duffy and Christopher Haigh are right in pointing out the complexity of the Reformation, and Haigh's idea of multiple "reformations" is a sound one. Nonetheless, their works provoke the question of how, then, did England come to be so Protestant by the mid-seventeenth century that a bloody civil war would be fought over what kind of Protestants to be rather than, as might have been predicted, over whether to be Catholic again? The missing equation is the actual process of reform—the ways in which people adapted to reformed ideas, new laws, and general social change. If we are to understand the way Protestantism changed England we have to ask how individuals, families, and institutions negotiated the changes.

Individuals are the most difficult to study because their private worlds leave few records, which is why the study of wills has been so enthusiastically embraced by historians of the Reformation. However, their value as documentation of religious change is a vexed question. Christopher Marsh's study of how wills were actually made is a very important contribution to this debate because he helps us understand that preambles declaring, as George Seyntpole's did, that the testator bequeathed his soul to "god omnipotent who hathe redemed the same with his most precious bloode" should not be overvalued as indicators. The scribes, the testator, the books they read, the presence or absence of the vicar, all play a part in the composition of the will and it is hard to assign an individual spiritual value to the finished product.

Caroline Litzenberger, however, argues effectively that we can still use wills as examples of how people's sentiment toward religion evolved. Combining preambles, bequests to the parish church, and requests for prayers for the dead while comparing on the basis of gender she convincingly shows that wills did respond to changing religious and legal ideas. But how they responded is fascinating. They became increasingly ambiguous rather than assertively Protestant.

Not surprisingly, the wills of Gloucestershire people show the greatest change in the middle of the century. Wills made in the 1540s were much more Catholic than those made in the 1570s. Obviously those facing death in the 1540s were still Catholic in most essentials. The younger folk who lived through the reigns of Edward and Mary wrote wills less infused with the ideals that maintained the parish life Duffy so carefully documented. As they thought about how to do their Christian duty and dispose of their property they either no longer desired to make—or cynically abandoned—bequests like those of their parents.

In the wills we can see people making value statements not about theology but about the uses of property. Their traditional concepts were being undermined from many sides. Of course just observing the behavior of Henry, Edward, Mary, and Elizabeth toward religious endowments could induce skepticism about their legal value, but educational processes were at work, too. Traditional ideas and the priests who held them were the targets of reformers all the time and of the Crown some of the time. Of course the reformers themselves were sometimes the targets of the government, providing reform with some blazing publicity.

Susan Wabuda's story of how Bishop Latimer, plucked by Cromwell from obscurity and made an instrument of both reform and the royal supremacy, used his power to send more preachers into the country to undermine the old values is instructive. The intense hostility their sermons stirred in some was not surprising. However, it is instructive to note that Latimer's victorious enemy, Archdeacon Bell, who when fortunes reversed became the next bishop of Worcester, was sure that Latimer had spread heresy throughout the diocese. He forced Latimer's preachers to submit and preach sermons against their errors. If we consider the impact of the preachers we cannot expect much in the way of instant conversion, but we can suspect that the recanted sermons attacking the church and then recanting were leaching away the limestone on which the traditional practices rested.

Lee Wandel's recent study of iconoclasm in Switzerland demonstrates that one of the motivations behind the destruction was the belief on the part of some that the church was literally misappropriating the money supplied by the believers by wasting it on statues and windows rather than helping the poor.[2] In England similar ideas were being planted, and once planted they grew even in people who remained loyal to the mass. By mid-century the nation seemed quite convinced that the seizure of church property for the good of the commonwealth was a fine thing. As both Mary and Elizabeth learned when their Parliaments took up their proposed religious changes, the Lords and Commons were willing to change faith but not give up lands that had belonged to the church.

With Erasmian and reformist criticism of the church in the air it was a hard time to be a servant of the Lord. The Catholic Reformation was already budding at Trent in the 1550s, so that priests of the old school were increasingly out of favor with both Protestants and Catholics. This meant that they were targets of opprobrium and satirical laughter. Pity Harry George, priest of St. Sepulchre-without-Newgate in London. His life was not an easy one. He began his ecclesiastical career by becoming an Augustinian monk and had presumably expected to remain one. When his community at Saint Bartholomew's Hospital was dissolved he was given a pension and he took up the trade of parish priest. When the next turn of the religious wheel introduced the English prayer book he refused to use it, continuing to say the Latin mass. And so he became the target of a scurrilous satire, "Doctour Doubble Ale."

Launched by Luke Shepherd, who understood the necessity of discrediting priests like George if reform was to become more than statute, its purpose was baldly stated. Any priest who ignored the king's new commissions and superstitiously prayed for dead folks' souls supported the pope's attempt to make himself God's peer. Such men had to be brought down. Ad hominem attacks must have been useful in the parish of St. Sepulchre and its neighbors because it made the conservative priest appear an ineffective, drunken figure of ridicule. Not all his neighbors would have laughed, however. Certainly his friend John Twyford approved of his confessor's conservative opinions, which in turn suggests the sort of tensions the Reformation introduced into parish life. Twyford, a "furious papist," was hated by his fellow parishioner Thomas Merial. Merial was forced to carry a heretic's faggot at Paul's Cross because Twyford reported his heterodoxy to the

---

[2]Lee Palmer Wandel, *Voracious Idols and Violent Hands. Iconoclasm in Reformation Zurich, Strasbourg and Basel* (Cambridge: Cambridge University Press, 1995).

authorities. Surely Merial despised Twyford and his parish priest, George, for what they had done to him (i.e., to Merial).[3]

What fractures ran through the parish church at these times depended on the personalities of the priest and his parishioners. Charged with guiding his flock a committed priest or pastor might take a firm stand in favor of a theological position or he might waffle, conforming and asking his parishioners to conform with him. Peter Marshall's recent study of the Catholic clergy suggests that there were priests who had true vocations, and those vocations were tightly bound to a role in the community.[4] The Protestants understood this, too, in both negative and positive ways. Certainly their cries for a better clergy and their attacks on the morals of the conservatives were part and parcel of the same knowledge.

As they recognized, the personality and zeal of the minister determined the religious peace of the parish. His ability to instruct was key to conversion of the parish, but he had to proceed with care. Too much radical change provoked hostility to the messengers of reform until the ideas on which their platform rested became internalized at the beginning of the seventeenth century. Or, to put it another way, the tension declined when the generation born in the 1560s and 1570s came to dominate parish politics. They in their turn would find Laudianism an ugly threat to their conceptions of proper worship and clerical behavior.

Given the time it took for new ideas to become naturalized, it was sad that Richard Greenham left Dry Drayton when he did. Had he stayed longer he might have seen the fruits of his labors. Although he became famous for his pastoral skill and preaching he believed he had little impact on his congregation, a conclusion historians seem to confirm. His stiff-necked and hard-hearted parishioners were not, in the years he preached and lived a Christian life among them, very interested in the niceties of his theology. Perhaps the younger Dry Draytoners went on to see life as their nonconforming minister wanted them to see it.

Maybe Greenham felt better about his ability to carve out his own life of conscience within the confines of the established church. Although he had firm beliefs he was willing to find common ground with conformists in their campaign to spread the gospel. Caught between the indifference of

---

[3]Susan Brigden, *London and the Reformation* (Oxford: Clarendon Press, 1989), 272, 421.

[4]Peter Marshall, *The Catholic Priesthood and the English Reformation* (Oxford: Clarendon Press, 1994).

his people and the authorities' insistence on conformity he had to live his own via media within the Elizabethan church.

Although Greenham would not wear a surplice he did catechize and use the *Book of Common Prayer* and perhaps it was this, rather than preaching, that had the most impact. Sharon Arnoult's study of Prayer Book worship makes it clear that the book was a powerful tool for creating a Protestant community. Regardless of the theological issues that surrounded the established church, the routine of congregational worship taught the English their communal religious identity. It was an identity that was hostile to clerical authoritarianism—perhaps to Greenham's chagrin—and it met the Laudian reforms with skepticism.

The most important thing about the use of the *Book of Common Prayer* was that it helped paper over the religious cracks within the community. The paper was easy to tear, but it did create a religiously neutral ground where confused people could gather as they slowly, unconsciously absorbed its rhythms and messages. The essence of the message was biblical, since the Ante-Communion, with its recitation of the Creed and Bible reading, was the service most often used. Its language, using careful doubling and other syntactical tricks to emphasize and teach, sank into people's minds and gradually affected their gut-level sense of right and wrong. As John Booty has observed, the Prayer Book was self-consciously designed by men who wished to create a sense of a Christian Commonwealth. And it worked.[5]

Tensions continued in the parishes, but Prayer Book worship helped negotiate those tensions. In other communities there were similar strains brought on by the Reformation that had to be worked out. People had to find a way to focus on their common ground and ignore their disagreements if guilds, colleges, companies, ships, and local governments were to go on working. Harry Porter reminds us that the Cambridge of John Fisher was also the Cambridge of Thomas Cranmer; that John Scory was the last Dominican to take a degree in the University as well as the first Elizabethan bishop of Hereford. In the small world of a college the Reformation was no abstraction. It meant accommodating, or expelling, or being expelled.[6]

---

[5]John E. Booty, "Communion and Commonweal: *The Book of Common Prayer*," in Booty, ed., *The Godly Kingdom of Tudor England: Great Books of the English Reformation* (Wilton, Conn.: Morehouse-Barlow Co., 1981), 205.

[6]H. C. Porter, *Reformation and Reaction in Tudor Cambridge* (Hamden, Conn.: Archon Books, 1972), 3, 12.

By the same token, local elites were in the process of switching from power networks based on kinship to networks based on religious affiliation. As Peter Bearman puts it, "traditional relations gave way to modern rhetorics as the primary building blocks of English elite social structure."[7] The effect of the institutionalization of competing religious orthodoxies was the collapse of the traditional county community as the basis of social action. For, as Holmes and Heal have observed, by late in Elizabeth's reign, religion, humanist ideals of gentlemanly education, and the lure of London and the court had combined to change the nature and outlook of the gentry and their more illustrious neighbors.[8] And yet the elites survived, changed but not gone.

The same was true of the cathedrals. In their chapter houses the changes came hard, since the property rights of the prebendaries conflicted with the theological desires of the bishops. In Canterbury, Cranmer scarcely succeeded in changing his church after the dissolution of Christ Church monastery. Many of his new foundation were old monks, and although the members of the new Chapter of Thirteen were supposed to preach quarterly they scarcely agreed on what the message should be. Deep ideological tensions split them between Protestants far to the left of Cranmer's Prayer Book and unreformed conservatives. One member of the chapter, Robert Searle, left his soul to God, "our blessed Lady His mother," and all the holy company of Heaven when he died in 1570. He even arranged Catholic obsequies for himself. Startlingly, the will was probated without problem by his colleagues on Archbishop Parker's staff. One of Searle's colleagues, Robert Pownall, gave thanks in his will for his vocation "by the voice of the Gospel from idolatry, superstition, and that false Religion...to the believing and professing of the pure Religion of God." They probated Pownall's will, too.

Pownall and Searle remind us again that although the Reformation created terrible rifts in communities, the members of those communities often found ways to survive. They may have hated one another but their inability to conduct wholesale purges forced them to cooperate on some level. Perhaps that is why Patrick Collinson has observed that the story of

---

[7]Peter S. Bearman, *Relations into Rhetorics: Local Elite Social Structure in Norfolk, England, 1540–1640* (New Brunswick, N.J.: Rutgers University Press, 1993), 175.

[8]Felicity Heal and Clive Holmes, *The Gentry in England and Wales 1500–1700* (Stanford: Stanford University Press, 1994), 381.

the Chapter of 13 in Elizabeth's reign becomes decreasingly ideological and increasingly institutional.[9]

The same is true of the trade organizations. Joe Ward's fascinating look at the Grocers' Company suggests the kind of internal tensions generated by religious change in small communities. The officers of the Company recognized the problems the membership faced in negotiating the changes and took steps to minimize them. The transmutation of their social customs and their exhortations to unity; their willingness to administer wills that contained conflicting religious values; and their use of their advowsons all suggest that by Elizabeth's reign they had separated the demands of state and religion from the Company's higher purpose, the maintenance of their trade.

Profound changes occurred in English society between 1500 and 1620 and the folk like the Grocers who lived through them adapted their lives and their institutions to compensate. For some this meant a wholesale change in lifestyle—Edmund Campion's progression from Oxford don to Jesuit missionary comes to mind—but for most it meant slow adaptations. The old faith in England was not removed by a radical operation; it died the death of a thousand cuts.

The studies in this volume provoke us to remember that the Reformation was not a *thing* or an event; it was a process of change that happened in people's lives. They experienced it on every level and they were forced to make choices accordingly. It is in these studies of communities and people that the meaning of the Reformation can be found.

---

[9]Patrick Collinson, "The Protestant Cathedral," in Patrick Collinson, Nigel Ramsay, and Margaret Sparks, eds., *A History of Canterbury Cathedral* (Oxford: Oxford University Press, 1995), 159–60, 169, 172.

THE REFORMATION *in* ITS PLACE

Robert Tittler

THE MORE ONE LEARNS about the progress of the English Reformation in specific communities the more one comes to appreciate the distinctiveness of the local experience. Much of the advent of Reform seemed to hinge on local as well as national traditions, on the role of inspired individuals in particular places, and on the circumstances of local government and politics. There is of course a danger in emphasizing this approach, for the forest must never be neglected for the trees. But there is great value as well. Such observations serve to remind us that what we know (and think we know) about historical movements such as this often reflect mere generalizations about the human experience: shorthand representations of the myriad small events and actions which come to push our perception of that broad experience in a particular direction. But however necessary the business of generalization may be, it inevitably sacrifices important nuance and detail. In the wake of such loss it is not difficult for distortions to creep in or for our understanding to be lost.

While retaining a much more traditional methodology than, for example, the Italian practitioners of "microhistory,"[1] most of the essays in this collection pay close attention to the local experience in the hope of elucidating, clarifying, and accounting for the larger picture. They each consider, some of course more successfully than others, particular aspects of that monolithic term "Reformation" in particular places, the diocese, parish, town or, figuratively speaking, the guild.

Caroline Litzenberger's study of Gloucestershire wills employs wills as evidence of religious sentiment. It marks a useful contrast to Christopher

---

[1]See for example the pages of the journal *Quaderni storici* published since 1966, and the work of such pioneers as, e.g., Guido Ruggiero, Carlo Ginzburg, and their co-workers in this productive field. The distinctions between the essays in the collection at hand and the microhistory of the Italian school are several in number, mostly having to do with the greater presence of social scientific method and theory in the latter. But the close focal range and many of the objectives of both approaches are the same.

Marsh's piece which, albeit not rooted in a study of any single area, speaks for those who remain skeptical that wills have particular value as devotional barometers. Though the results of both authors' findings have appeared elsewhere, these essays bring to the collection a useful sampling of each side of a current and important debate.

Susan Wabuda's discussion of Hugh Latimer's emphasis on preaching in his four years as bishop of Worcester could also do with a stronger contextual or historiographical framework. Yet it does both usefully address an important period in Latimer's life and demonstrate the potential for episcopal leadership at the diocesan level in moving the Reformation along the rails. Coupled with, for example, Paul Wilson's recent observations of Bishop Hooper's emphasis on preaching in the neighboring diocese of Gloucester,[2] this seems an important building block to an understanding of the role of episcopal leadership in the early stages of Reform. Wabuda at least implicitly encourages us to think that this sort of initiative amongst a committed coterie of early reformers may not at all be exclusive to Latimer in his Worcester diocese, and that his forceful encouragement of the pulpit's use may be a more central element in reformed practice than we have yet recognized.

Eric Carlson's full and leisurely discussion of the largely forgotten Richard Greenham not only resuscitates the accomplishments of a worthy man, but gives us a useful vignette into the life of a reformed cleric of the Elizabethan era. Bent more on narrative than on argument, Carlson's study affords us our own opportunity to draw conclusions about Greenham's significance in the larger picture. There is much value in this portrait of the scrupulous and devoted village cleric, one of the presumed many who gained the esteem of his parishioners by a life of selfless labor in the service of reformed religion. If this is an accurate assessment we should not be so surprised that Greenham's fame has been slow to reach us, for so much more often than not (at least before the advent of modern media) the printed word conveys much sharper memories than the spoken.

The two essays which speak most directly to the Reformation experience of a particular community are those by Joseph Ward and Muriel McClendon, and perhaps it is these which should receive closest attention under the banner unfurled at the head of these comments. Ward's Grocers'

---

[2]Robert Paul Wilson, "John Hooper and the English Reformation under Edward VI, 1547–1553," Ph.D. dissertation, Queen's University [Ontario], 1994.

Company may not have had as distinct a geographic boundary as a parish or a town, though its members did mostly dwell in London, but it was a community nonetheless, and one of a sort—a community of occupation and status—which we know least about. And in drawing upon the extremely rich, not to say now miraculously preserved, records of the city of Norwich, McClendon promises insights into one of the largest and religiously most interesting provincial centers of the era.

By beginning with the assumption of Susan Brigden and John Sommerville that religious change disrupted the traditional sense of community, Ward sets his own study in a useful and important contextual framework. He employs Grocers' Company records to argue that, because they took deliberate steps to minimize such disruptions, the Grocers were able to avoid the disunifying effects of religious change which Brigden and Sommerville have observed elsewhere. In consequence, he finds that some Company members persisted in holding quite traditional beliefs well into the seventeenth century, and that the diversity of religious views amongst its members, when carefully managed, did not necessarily undermine the essential harmony of the whole. An important part of this management was the accommodation, and thus the perpetuation, of the communal memory of the Company to changing circumstances.

Ward's study challenges common assumptions about the divisiveness of religious change in other sorts of communities, especially in the urban context, where they have been most often studied. It also challenges the assumption, held by several historians, that the Reformation necessarily disrupted the common memory, and hence the sense of local heritage and identity, of particular communities.[3] His findings raise several possibilities which bear further consideration. It may of course be that there is something about the community of a metropolitan guild like the Grocers' Company which would allow it greater flexibility and accommodation in the face of religious change than we find in most towns. It may be, too, that the apparent divergence of the Grocers' experience from what Brigden, Sommerville, and others have found in urban communities arises not so much from distinctions between two types of community as from hasty

---

[3]Charles Phythian-Adams, "Ceremony and the Citizen: The Communal Year at Coventry, 1450–1550," in Peter Clark and Paul Slack, eds., *Crisis and Order in English Towns, 1500–1700* (London: Routledge, 1972), 57–85; Eamon Duffy, *The Stripping of the Altars: Traditional Religion in England 1400–1580* (New Haven: Yale University Press, 1992), esp. 327–337; Robert Tittler, *The Reformation and the Towns in England* (in press), esp. chap. 13.

assumptions that the urban communities in which change did provoke conflict were not themselves typical.

Both possibilities must be taken seriously, but one also wonders whether it is necessarily the element of religious change as such which most provoked disunity or other, ancillary, elements of what we label "the Reformation." The rapid, widespread, and virtually dramatic changes in the control of land, resources, and political authority in urban communities following the Dissolutions of the 1530s and 1540s may have played a vivid role as well. These are of course not changes of doctrine, but they were important aspects of what might still be labeled the Henrician and Edwardian Reformations. And though these changes did affect some activities of organizations like the Grocers' Company, which lost some of its chantries and associated institutions, they probably did not do so to the same extent as in urban communities as such. These broad social and economic elements of "the Reformation" may well account at least in part for the differences between Ward's findings for a City Company and Brigden's findings for the City as a whole.

McClendon's study adds another voice to the theme of community-harmony-despite-Reformation, and she too takes up the strategy of accommodation adopted by local governing officials. By surveying the record of the Norwich city magistrates in hearing cases against clerics or concerning doctrinal infractions, she is able to show that, at least on that evidential base, magistrates preferred to dampen the possibility of public controversy rather than to enforce the strict letter of the law on doctrinal issues. She accounts for this partly by their concern for civic order, and partly by their own division of sentiment on matters doctrinal. Though her argument would have been better served by a larger number of cases to examine, it does add weight to others, like Ward, who have emphasized the adaptability of local communities faced with sweeping change. If not yet ready to take on Mahler, this is now at least a sturdy chamber choir of well-blended tone. We need to listen to it carefully.

In sum, that majority of essays in this volume which deal with the Reformation in a particular place serve several functions. Taken together, these studies suggest the full range of the uses to which case studies may usefully be put. Litzenberger employs a case study to test an extant hypothesis. Though it is by no means without value in and of itself, its greatest potential may only be attained when the same test can be applied to a variety of other counties with similar result. Given the strong body of opinion stacked against her confidence in the efficacy of wills in elucidating belief, of which Marsh's fine essay is but one example, such additional case studies seem all the more important. Until that time, any more general conclusions which it may suggest run headfirst into the problem of typicality. Something of the same virtues and limitations apply to Wabuda's offering, in which the problem of typicality applies both to a particular diocese and a particular bishop, and to Ward's, where it applies both to livery companies as a type of community and to the Grocers' Company of London as an example of that type. At present, each of these three studies presents an exception to a stated presumption (though in Wabuda's case the presumption remains implicit). Each opens the possibility that such exceptions may be found elsewhere, or even that, if found in a sufficient number of parallel studies, they may not be exceptions at all.

Carlson focuses his lens on a particular community especially to observe the fine grain of parish life at this particularly ticklish time. Though he remains slightly bashful in stating conclusions, he succeeds in elucidating some aspects of the relations of parishioners and clergy. In so doing he provides textured descriptions which should help us understand the ingredients for successful parochial service and the importance of personal relations for the progress of doctrinal change. And both McClendon and Ward again succeed in exploring the way in which secular communities managed the challenges presented by doctrinal change. Both the variety of research in this collection and the relative youth of the researchers lead us to the pleasant contemplation of a new and active generation of Reformation scholars. Who can cavil at that?

REVISIONISM REVISED

Diane Willen

ALTHOUGH HISTORIANS have a natural inclination to emphasize change, revisionism during the last two decades has inculcated new respect for the place of continuity in early modern England. Whether writing about seventeenth-century Parliaments, the Jacobean church or the English Reformation, revisionists have especially challenged perceptions and interpretations of change within a Whig conceptual framework, that is, change perceived as irreversible, progressive, and if not inevitable, at the least, rooted to deeply entrenched causes. Arguing as empiricists, often mastering an impressive variety of local sources, revisionist scholars of the Reformation discovered a strong degree of continuity in the persistence of Catholicism, resistance to Protestantism, and attachment to traditional rituals. The culmination of the revisionist approach is best seen in Christopher Haigh's survey of sixteenth-century religion, revealingly titled *English Reformations*. Arguing against the notion of successful Protestantization during the Henrician and Edwardian reigns, Haigh emphasizes instead the political, hence contingent, nature of a series of reformations, the success of the Marian counterreformation, and the minority status of evangelical Protestants even at the end of Elizabeth's reign.[1]

The easy tendency is to see revisionism in direct contrast to the scholarship and legacy of A. G. Dickens. Through his studies of Lollardy and his own masterful survey, *The English Reformation*, Dickens established a process of Protestantization which neither the Catholic Church in England, made vulnerable by its own excesses, nor later, a caesaro-papal state under Henry VIII could easily control. This interpretation emphasizes the nation at large rather than the Reformation from above and brings to center stage

---

[1]Christopher Haigh, *English Reformations. Religion, Politics, and Society under the Tudors* (Oxford: Clarendon Press, 1993). For earlier revisionist works, see Haigh, ed., *The English Reformation Revised* (Cambridge: Cambridge University Press, 1987), and J. J. Scarisbrick, *The Reformation and the English People* (Oxford: Basil Blackwell, 1984).

the influence of the vernacular Bible.[2] Interestingly, Haigh too emphasizes Protestantism as a bibliocentric religion, but for him, its dependency upon literacy impeded rather than accelerated the new religion.

The moment is now ripe within the historiographic debate to recognize the commonalities which link these competing interpretations, a direction suggested by the essays in this volume. Even authors who focus on the process of Protestantization—Wabuda and Devereux—acknowledge the strength of conservatism and its resistance to change from above. Several authors point to the continuities which survived legislative religious changes: e.g. Ward, Litzenberger, and Marsh. In their recognition of continuity, however, these essays do not deny change. Rather, in Marsh's words, they point to "the role of strong continuities with the medieval past in making the Reformation manageable and comprehensible for those who lived through it." Continuities allowed the English to become Protestant while containing some of the novelty of Protestantism, to develop religious pluralism while avoiding (at least in the sixteenth century) sustained wars of religion, and to create a distinctive religious settlement, aptly described as "the building of a Protestant Church which remained haunted by its Catholic past."[3]

One way to minimize change was to retain or adapt traditional ritual: contemporaries attached new meaning or doctrine to former practices and forms of piety. Ward demonstrates that such behavior allowed members of the Grocers' Company to retain their identity as members of a spiritual community even as religious differences developed among them. The Grocers celebrated the May feast day of St. Antonin, their patron saint, with worship and dinner, a tradition linked to their roots as a medieval fraternity and continuing through the mid-sixteenth century. During the Elizabethan period, the Grocers reinvented the ritual: they still dined together each May although now ostensibly to commemorate the origins of the company, an adaptation of ritual clearly reflected in their own rhetoric: "the feast of St Antonin alias the commemoration dinner...."

---

[2]A. G. Dickens, *The English Reformation*, 2d ed. (University Park: Pennsylvania State University Press, 1989). *The English Reformation* was originally published in 1964, but Dickens remains convinced of the essential validity of its thesis. For his most recent arguments, see his essays in Dickens, *Late Monasticism and the Reformation* (London: Hambledon Press, 1994).

[3]Diarmaid MacCulloch, *The Later Reformation in England 1547–1603* (New York: St. Martin's Press, 1990), 6.

Litzenberger and, to an even greater extent, Marsh show continuities and adaption of rituals involving death and dying. Both authors join a growing list of scholars who have both examined and evaluated wills as evidence for popular religious sentiment, a process begun by Dickens' work on the Lollards and his attempt to trace opinion outside statutory prescription.[4] Litzenberger's analysis of preambles reinforces revisionist arguments about the survival of Catholicism, albeit the retention of traditional religion was often obscured through ambiguous language. Her findings are all the more noteworthy given past claims that Gloucestershire proved receptive to the Reformation.[5]

Litzenberger is cautious in using wills as evidence; Marsh is skeptical enough to discount their value and turns his analysis instead to other aspects of will-making, to the literature of *ars moriendi,* and to the rituals associated with the deathbed. His conclusions about popular piety are compatible with Litzenberger's as he warns that historians have tended to exaggerate the shock of Protestantism, "particularly on the village level." Marsh draws attention to the social or communal responsibilities incumbent upon the individual even as he or she faced death: hence the importance of exemplary conduct on the deathbed and the disposal of worldly goods. For Marsh, the social nature of Christian duty in the face of death linked Elizabethans to their medieval predecessors and curbed the Protestant impulse toward individualism, an impulse whose influence historians are prone to exaggerate. Litzenberger agrees: testators demonstrated Christian responsibility and civic duty even as they gave up expectation of prayers for the soul.

Marsh comes to revisionist conclusions, yet rituals of dying reflected adaptation as well as continuities, individualism as well as communalism. By the seventeenth century, Puritans perfected and embraced the good death as a final opportunity for edification by and for the godly. The deathbed itself became a customary feature in funeral sermons which eulogized the deceased. The publication of such sermons established exemplars for the godly community, a Protestant device which may have satisfied the

---

[4]A. G. Dickens, *Lollards and Protestants in the Diocese of York 1509–1558,* 2d ed. (London: Hambledon Press, 1982). Dickens reaffirms the value of using the preambles of wills in his essay "The Early Expansion of Protestantism in England, 1520–58," in *Late Monasticism and the Reformation,* 125–129.

[5]Dickens, *Late Monasticism and the Reformation,* 103–104, 112, and 115–116, notes 51–52.

psychological need formerly served by prayers for the dead.[6] Strikingly, the deathbed was a ritual accessible to individuals notwithstanding restraints of class or gender. Clergy praised the example of godly women, and many females used the deathbed as a platform not only to promote communal responsibilities but also to edify and exert their personal influence as members of the elect.[7]

Except for Litzenberger's study (whose evidence does not allow firm conclusions about gender), none of these essays uses gender as a category of analysis. Here is a missed opportunity, for gender offers promising lines of inquiry to understand how religious change was both experienced and contained in early modern England. Historians have established that the prescriptive literature on gender roles reflected continuity and consistency across the religious spectrum. Throughout the sixteenth and seventeenth centuries, clerics exhorted women to embrace traditional Christian feminine virtues (chastity, obedience, humility, silence, piety) and assume a significant but subordinate role within the family. Indeed the trauma of change—political and social as well as religious—seems to have made contemporaries all the more determined to resist the most threatening of all change, that involving relationships between the sexes. Even the rhetoric of gender minimized or contained change as Catholics and Protestants alike retained traditional metaphors, castigating enemies as the whore of Babylon and praising either the church or individuals as the bride of Christ.[8]

Although such continuities suggest that gender as an analytic category supports a revisionist approach to the Reformation, gender analysis often reveals a process of Protestantization. Scholars of gender distinguish between conventional social theory and innovative practice, a distinction most obvious during acts of legal defiance (for example, acts of heresy or

[6]Ralph Houlbrooke, "Death, Church, and Family in England between the Late Fifteenth and the Early Eighteenth Centuries," in *Death, Ritual, and Bereavement*, ed. Ralph Houlbrooke (London: Routledge, 1989), 36.

[7]Diane Willen, "'Communion of the Saints': Spiritual Reciprocity and the Godly Community in Early Modern England," *Albion* 27 (1995), 28–29.

[8]For the tenacity of the ideology of gender, see Susan Amussen, *An Ordered Society: Gender and Class in England 1500–1750* (Oxford: Blackwell, 1989), and Merry Wiesner, *Women and Gender in Early Modern Europe* (Cambridge: Cambridge University Press, 1993). A rich and long bibliography exists on women and religion in the early modern period. In addition to Wiesner, see especially Patricia Crawford, *Women and Religion in England 1500–1750* (London: Routledge, 1993); Phyllis Mack, *Visionary Women. Ecstatic Prophecy in Seventeenth-Century England* (Berkeley and Los Angeles: University of California Press, 1992).

radical sectarianism) but also evident in the Protestant impulse to literacy, the companionate marriage, and the Puritan agenda of godliness, all daily activities. Gender can help us better understand many issues discussed in these essays, as for example, the appeal of Anglican spirituality, Richard Greenham's practical divinity, lay-clerical relationships, and reactions to Protestantism. Critics of the Reformation eagerly seized upon gender to discredit proponents of the new religion. What are we to make of Dr. Roger Edgeworth, the conservative cleric who not only denounced Bishop Latimer for having infected the diocese of Worcester with Protestantism (cited by Wabuda), but also criticized women of the new religion for studying, teaching, and disputing Scriptures? Edgeworth's denunciations demonstrate the fear provoked by Latimer's policies in the diocese of Worcester. The priesthood of all believers threatened both the prescribed relationship between clergy and laity and the natural relationship between men and women.[9]

The revisionist debate about the nature and success of the English Reformation in the sixteenth century has its counterpart in the scholarship on the English church in the early seventeenth century. Eschewing a model of radical, confrontational Puritanism that naturally led to revolution, historians like Patrick Collinson and Nicholas Tyacke see the English church in the late Elizabethan and Jacobean period as a stable, inclusive institution able to accommodate a variety of Protestant inclinations.[10] According to this conceptual framework, Puritans emerge as zealous but de-radicalized Protestants, practicing a style of piety rather than espousing distinctive theology, driven later to separatism or activism only by the Arminian policies of Laud and Charles. Nonetheless, even if scholars acknowledge the validity of the consensual model for the Jacobean church, their research points to the complexity of spiritual and ecclesiological issues dividing English Protestants. Peter Lake has argued that two styles of piety emerged by the Jacobean period: one, a form of spirituality that emphasized the visible church and the beauty of its ritual, the importance of public worship,

---

[9]Martha C. Skeeters, *Community and Clergy: Bristol and the Reformation c. 1530–c. 1570* (Oxford: Clarendon Press, 1993), 64–65.

[10]See Patrick Collinson, *The Religion of Protestants: The Church in English Society 1559–1625* (Oxford: Clarendon Press, 1982), and Nicholas Tyacke, *Anti-Calvinists: The Rise of English Arminianism c. 1590–1640* (Oxford: Clarendon Press, 1987). Peter Lake provides a full discussion of the historiography in "Defining Puritanism—Again?" in *Puritanism: Transatlantic Perspectives on a Seventeenth-Century Anglo-American Faith*, ed. Francis J. Bremer (Boston: Northeastern University Press for Massachusetts Historical Society, 1993): 3–29.

and most significantly, the centrality of the sacrament; the other, espoused by Puritans, a word-centered predestinarian style of piety, imposing its own program of godliness and, whatever the intent of its advocates, often divisive in practice.[11] Lake looks especially at the clergy, but studies of lay Puritans by other scholars likewise reassert the divisive, politicized implications of godliness.[12] More recently, Kenneth Fincham describes moderate Puritans as partial conformists who enjoyed an ambiguous relationship with conformist Calvinists. Fincham, moreover, rejects the notion of a stable, harmonious Jacobean church. Rather, the existence of anti-Calvinists, who advocated worship based upon strict observance of the *Book of Common Prayer* and an inclusive national church, created a Jacobean church "riven with friction and disagreement."[13]

Essays in this volume speak directly to issues in this debate. As noted, Ward and Marsh see efforts to exercise civic responsibility and maintain local unity as a significant means to contain change even as religious pluralism emerged as a new reality. In her study of Norwich magistrates, Muriel McClendon discovers similar efforts "to mute expressions of religious conflict" in the earliest stages of the Reformation. The records of the Norwich Mayoralty Court reflect a clear preference for an inclusive church that accommodated diverse opinion and communal harmony during the Henrician and Edwardian period. McClendon suggests that because Norwich magistrates were able to promote such values in the face of their own religious differences, they may have "begun to forge a distinction between the religious and secular spheres...." In fact, their acceptance of both de facto religious pluralism and the need for external religious unity reflects the Erastian and Erasmian nature of the English Reformation even more than it suggests the beginning of genuine secularism. Taken together,

[11]Peter Lake, "Lancelot Andrewes, John Buckeridge, and Avant-garde Conformity at the Court of James I," in *The Mental World of the Jacobean Court*, ed. Linda Levy Peck (Cambridge: Cambridge University Press, 1991): 113–133, building upon arguments in Lake, *Anglicans and Puritans? Presbyterianism and English Conformist Thought from Whitgift to Hooker* (London: Unwin Hyman, 1988); Lake, "Defining Puritanism—again?," esp. 22–29.

[12]For example, William Hunt, *The Puritan Moment: The Coming of Revolution in an English County* (Cambridge: Harvard University Press, 1983); Jacqueline Eales, *Puritans and Roundheads: The Harleys of Brampton Bryan and the Outbreak of the English Civil War* (Cambridge: Cambridge University Press, 1990); John Morrill, "Sir William Brereton and England's Wars of Religion," *Journal of British Studies* 24 (1985): 311–332; *The Culture of English Puritanism, 1560–1700*, ed. C. Durston and J. Eales (Basingstoke: Macmillan, 1996).

[13]Kenneth Fincham, "Introduction," in *The Early Stuart Church, 1603–1642*, ed. Kenneth Fincham (Stanford: Stanford University Press, 1993), 6–11.

however, the work of McClendon, Marsh, and Ward reaffirms the notion of a stable and comprehensive church resting upon a moderate Protestant consensus.

Eric Carlson's study of the nonconformist cleric Richard Greenham demonstrates how a program of practical divinity allowed the godly to avoid divisive liturgical issues, at least with the compliance of pragmatic bishops like Richard Cox and John Aylmer. Through analysis of Greenham's reputation at the hands of both his contemporaries and his historians, Carlson identifies the Elizabethan divine as a leading Puritan. The essay does not explicitly define Puritanism although Greenham's refusal to subscribe to the *Book of Common Prayer* as containing nothing contrary to the word of God, his concern for edification or "Christian conferring," and the high priority he placed upon preaching speak to his godliness. Greenham, however, stood within the ranks of the moderates. The premium he placed upon unity and peace within the church muffled his support of Thomas Cartwright and later led him to rebuke the iconoclasm of a zealous minister. Rather than present parishioners to the church courts, he preferred a process of edification that brought individual parishioners to awareness of their sin. Carlson cites as other examples of moderation Greenham's reluctance to exclude parishioners from the sacrament of the Lord's Supper and his reasonable approach to the burial of the dead. This combination—godliness, yet aversion to schism and unnecessary dissension—explains the admiration of Greenham's biographer Samuel Clarke even as it qualifies views of Greenham still found in current scholarship.[14]

Sharon Arnoult brings another dimension to our understanding of the English church with her focus on its practice of worship. Arnoult joins those historians who recognize a form of spirituality that was distinguishable from both Puritanism and Laudianism and that proved popular and tenacious enough to survive the midcentury civil wars. Judith Maltby has written of "Prayer Book Protestantism" and Peter Lake, coining a variety of phrases, warns of the anachronistic problems in appropriating the term "Anglican."[15] Arnoult herself speaks of "a distinctly English Protestantism."

[14]Martin Ingram, "From Reformation to Toleration: Popular Religious Cultures in England, 1540–1690," in *Popular Culture in England, c. 1500–1850,* ed. Tim Harris (New York: St. Martin's Press, 1995), 108.

[15]Judith Maltby, "'By this Book': Parishioners, the Prayer Book and the Established Church," in *The Early Stuart Church,* ed. Fincham, 115–137; Lake, "Defining Puritanism—Again?" 29, n. 41. Compare Lake's discussion of "conformist differentiation" (22) with "avant-garde conformity" in his "Lancelot Andrewes, John Buckeridge and Avant-garde Conformity."

Whatever the label, this form of piety embraced the sacraments as a promise of grace, valued corporate prayer and lay participation in the worship service, presumed the inclusive nature of the visible church, and treated devotion as "the key to sanctification." Its practitioners, as described by Arnoult, emerge as a far different breed than "the parish Anglicans" whom Christopher Haigh identifies as the greatest number within the Elizabethan population. For Haigh, parish Anglicans—in contrast to evangelical Protestants or recusant Catholics—were least affected by the Reformation. Theirs was a habitual form of Christianity. Although Arnoult agrees that the worship service in the English church did not expound on intellectual comprehension of doctrinal points, she nonetheless establishes a genuine and widespread Protestant commitment by the late Elizabethan period.

The Reformation then remains a process of Protestantization. These essays, taken as a whole, demonstrate the validity of a number of approaches and interpretations of religious change as experienced by the English people. They compel us to recognize the achievements of the Reformation, yet also its complexity and limitations, its compromises and continuities with England's Catholic past, its diverse styles of piety, and the richness of its historiographic traditions.

PRINCIPAL CONTRIBUTORS

SHARON L. ARNOULT is an instructor in history at Southwest Texas State University in San Marcos, Texas, and a recent Ph.D. recipient at the University of Texas at Austin. Her dissertation is entitled: "'A Reasonable, Holy and Lively Sacrifice': *The Book of Common Prayer* and the Development of English Religious Identity, 1559–1662." Her publications include "The Sovereignties of Body and Soul: Women's Political and Religious Actions in the English Civil War," in Louise Fradenburg, editor, *Women and Sovereignty* (Edinburgh: Edinburgh University Press, 1992).

∽

In addition to his book *Marriage and the English Reformation* (Oxford: Basil Blackwell, 1994), ERIC CARLSON has contributed to *The World of Rural Dissenters 1520–1725*, edited by Margaret Spufford (Cambridge: Cambridge University Press, 1995) and published a number of journal articles. His book on the Elizabethan divine Richard Greenham, coauthored with Kenneth L. Parker, will be published by Scolar Press in 1998. He received his Ph.D. from Harvard University in 1987 and is a Fellow of the Royal Historical Society and associate professor of history at Gustavus Adolphus College in St. Peter, Minnesota. He is currently working on the post-Reformation rural English clergy.

∽

JANICE C. DEVEREUX, a former high school English and drama teacher, has recently completed her Ph.D. at the University of Otago in New Zealand. She is currently preparing an edition of Luke Shepherd's satires for publication. Her academic interests include Tudor and Stuart history and literature, contemporary feminist writers, and creative writing.

∽

Before becoming assistant professor of history at West Virginia University, CAROLINE LITZENBERGER received her M.A. from Portland State University and her Ph.D. from the University of Cambridge. She has published a number of articles and essays, and an edition of the Tewkesbury churchwardens' accounts. Her book on the Reformation in Gloucestershire has been published by Cambridge University Press.

CHRISTOPHER MARSH is lecturer in history at The Queen's University of Belfast in Northern Ireland. He received his Ph.D. from the University of Cambridge. A revised version of his dissertation on the Family of Love was published in 1994 by Cambridge University Press. He also contributed to *The World of Rural Dissenters 1520–1725* and has produced a teaching pack with audio tapes on "Songs of the Seventeenth Century."

∾

MURIEL MCCLENDON received her Ph.D. from Stanford University in 1990. Since then, she has taught at the University of California, Los Angeles. She has published in *The Sixteenth Century Journal* and has completed a book on the impact of the Reformation on the government and governors of Norwich. It will be published in 1998 by Stanford University Press.

∾

Since receiving her doctorate from the University of Cambridge, SUSAN WABUDA has been assistant professor of history at Fordham University. She is the author of several articles and essays, and her forthcoming monograph, *Preaching during the English Reformation,* will be published by Cambridge University Press.

∾

JOSEPH P. WARD teaches at the University of Mississippi. He is the author of *Metropolitan Communities: Trade Guilds, Identity, and Change in Early Modern London,* which was published in 1997 by Stanford University Press. He is currently investigating London's influence on early modern national culture.

∾

INDEX

❧

Composed by Thomas Jefferson University Press
at Truman State University
Cover art and title page by Timothy Rolands
Manufactured by Thomson-Shore, Dexter, Mich., U.S.A.
Text and ornaments set in Minion 11/13.
Display Type is Waters Titling.

❧